王守仁 刘玉红 赵宇◎编著

英美短篇小说

British and American Short Stories

南京大学出版社

图书在版编目(CIP)数据

英美短篇小说：英文 / 王守仁，刘玉红，赵宇编
. — 南京：南京大学出版社，2012.1(2021.7重印)
ISBN 978-7-305-09551-1

Ⅰ. ①英⋯ Ⅱ. ①王⋯ ②刘⋯ ③赵⋯ Ⅲ. ①英语—高等学校—教材②短篇小说—小说评论—英国③短篇小说—小说评论—美国 Ⅳ. ①H319.4：I

中国版本图书馆CIP数据核字(2011)第281491号

出版发行　南京大学出版社
社　　址　南京市汉口路22号　　邮　编　210093
出 版 人　金鑫荣

书　　名　英美短篇小说
编　　著　王守仁　刘玉红　赵宇
责任编辑　罗思遥　董颖　　　　编辑热线　025-83596997
照　　排　南京南琳图文制作有限公司
印　　刷　南京百花彩色印刷广告制作有限责任公司
开　　本　787×1092　1/16　印张 21　字数 524 千
版　　次　2012年1月第1版　2021年7月第6次印刷
ISBN 978-7-305-09551-1
定　　价　49.00元

网址：http://www.njupco.com
官方微博：http://weibo.com/njupco
官方微信号：njupress
销售咨询热线：(025) 83594756

* 版权所有，侵权必究
* 凡购买南大版图书，如有印装质量问题，请与所购
　图书销售部门联系调换

导 言

"短篇小说"在英文中是 short story,在汉语中我们将这一文学样式也称之为"短篇故事"。短篇小说含有故事的成分,常常讲述一个故事,但这并不意味着任何故事都是短篇小说。乔叟的《坎特伯雷故事》(1386—1400)采用"英雄双韵体"(the heroic couplet)讲了 20 多个故事,但它是一部诗歌杰作。如果说现代意义上的长篇小说(the novel)兴起于 18 世纪,短篇小说迄今也有三百多年历史。伊恩·瓦特在《小说的兴起》一书中将《鲁滨逊漂流记》(1719)视为英国小说的起源,而笛福的鬼故事名篇《维尔夫人显灵记》早在 1705 年就已问世。在英美文学史上,许多长篇小说作家同时都进行短篇小说创作,如霍桑、马克·吐温、哈代、康拉德、乔伊斯、劳伦斯等。实际上,短篇小说与长篇小说只是篇幅上有差别,并不存在本质的不同。

在各种文学体裁中,小说最为大众所接受,影响面最广,而短篇小说是一种微雕艺术,在方寸中写乾坤。通过学习英美短篇小说,我们可以从以下几个方面获益:

首先,虚构的文学作品是用审美的方式来把握生活,表达真理。作为文学体裁的小说既是对现实的一种表征,也是对现实的一种认识。短篇小说往往工笔细描人类经验的某一片断,聚集于某一瞬间。许多富有社会责任感的作家直面生活,以小见大,利用短篇小说一锤激起耀眼火花的力量来反映时代,揭示生活的真相。短篇小说同时关注人类的精神世界和人性的方方面面。阅读短篇小说能够帮助我们开拓视野,洞察社会、人生和人性,使我们变得更有智慧。

第二,文学是文化的重要组成部分。英美短篇小说既有对英美国家社会生活、风土人情的细节刻画,也有对人物内心世界的细腻描写,集中体现了英美人民的认知方式、价值判断、审美取向。通过研读优秀的英美短篇小说,我们可以获得对英美国家历史、传统、社会的知识,了解英美文化中根本性的思想观点、人们经常使用的视角以及对这些思想观点和视角的批评,从而在深层次上领悟中西文化差异,增强跨文化交际意识和能力。

第三,短篇小说和长篇小说一样,是通过塑造人物、叙述故事、描写环境来反映生活,表达思想。作家在创作长篇小说和短篇小说时采用了几乎相同的技巧,因此,用来读解长篇小说的批评方法也大都可以用来读解短篇小说。而要学习小说要素,短篇小说则提供了更为理想的例子,因为它情节紧凑,人物集中,结构精巧,读者可以一口气读完整个作品,对细节进行反复咀嚼,寻微探幽。本书介绍了主题、情节、人物、视角、象征等小说要素。研究和分析短篇小说中的这些小说要素,可以帮助我们有效地掌握文学批评方法,学会欣赏英美文学。

第四,从短篇小说对于英语学习的功用看,它是提高英语水平的重要途径。文学是语言的艺术,只有英语文学作品才能充分展示英语丰富的表现力和独特的魅力。短篇小说由于受篇幅的限制,在形式、叙述手法和遣词造句方面比长篇小说更富挑战性,作家需要在语言上更加用心,铸词造境,妙笔生花。本书精选英美文学大家的精品之作,仔细阅读文本,学习他们的用词之妙,发现和体验语言之美,可以增强语感,有效提高我们的英语水平。

本书收选短篇小说共 20 篇,按小说要素分组排列,其中康拉德的《青春》篇幅稍长,也可视为中篇小说,故单列。将某个短篇小说归到特定的小说要素名下,只是为了能够更有针对性地分析、阐释文学现象,并不意味着只能运用这一小说要素去分析该文本。亨利·詹姆斯说过:"故事是有生命的,和其他的有机体一样自成一体,不断发展,平衡得当,我们会发现,在每一部分当中都有其他部分的存在。"[1]因此,我们在实际研读过程中,可以并且应该综合地运用主题、情节、人物、视角、象征等小说要素,以全面地理解和赏析文学作品。

短篇小说的特点是以小见大,凝练精致。学生在掌握了阅读短篇小说的方法之后,有必要去尝试阅读一两部英语长篇小说,以领略英美小说的风貌。建议教师采用"课内短篇,课外长篇;课内细读,课外泛读;课内指导,课外自学"的教学思路,鼓励学生课外多读英美著名作家的长篇小说,并把课内学到的文学批评方法应用到实践中。

---

[1] Henry James, *Selected Literary Criticism*. Ed. By Morris Shapira (Cambridge: Cambridge University Press, 1981), p. 58.

目 录

导言 ·· 1

1. 主题(Theme) ·· 1
    Kate Chopin: *Story of an Hour* ·· 3
    William Carlos Williams: *The Use of Force* ··························· 11
    Katherine Mansfield: *The Fly* ·· 20

2. 情节(Plot) ·· 30
    James Joyce: *Araby* ·· 32
    William Faulkner: *A Rose for Emily* ······································ 42
    John Updike: *A & P* ·· 55

3. 人物(Characters) ··· 66
    Ernest Hemingway: *Soldier's Home* ······································ 68
    Katherine Anne Porter: *The Jilting of Granny Weatherall* ······ 79
    Richard Wright: *The Man Who Was Almost a Man* ··············· 94
    Truman Capote: *Miriam* ·· 111

4. 视角(Point of View) ··· 125
    Sherwood Anderson: *I'm a Fool* ·· 127
    Flannery O'Connor: *A Good Man Is Hard to Find* ··············· 142
    Doris Lessing: *A Woman on a Roof* ···································· 161

5. 象征(Symbol) ··· 174
    Nathaniel Hawthorne: *Rappaccini's Daughter* ······················ 176
    D. H. Lawrence: *The Blind Man* ··· 204
    John Steinbeck: *The Chrysanthemums* ································ 226
    Bernard Malamud: *The Magic Barrel* ································· 241

6. 实验小说(Experimental Fiction) ……………………………… 261
    Donald Barthelme: *The School* …………………………………… 263
    Keith Fort: *The Coal Shoveller* ………………………………… 271

Joseph Conrad: *Youth* …………………………………………………… 294

Glossary of Critical Terms ……………………………………………… 326

后记 …………………………………………………………………………… 330

1. 主题(Theme)

我们读了一篇小说,常常会谈到它讲的是什么意思。这个"意思"就是主题,它是作者通过作品的内容和形式表现出来的中心思想,是对故事主旨的概括性陈述。主题是作品的轴心,情节的构建、人物的塑造、基调的确立、风格的选取都以它为导向。小说的主题是客观的,因为它所涉及的故事情节是一种客观存在;同时又是主观的,因为每个读者的经验和感受都是独一无二的,对同一故事的理解就会见仁见智,所谓"一千个读者就有一千个哈姆雷特"。小说主题的这一双重性说明读解作品没有唯一"正确的"方法,同时读者也不能武断地天马行空,把自己的思想强加给作品,只能解释作品作为一个整体所表现出的含义。

传统故事往往传递一个明确的主题思想,最典型的例子是寓言故事,例如伊索寓言表面讲的是动物的故事,在结尾处则以一句道德说教点明主旨:

狐狸和葡萄

饥饿的狐狸看见葡萄架上挂着一串串晶莹剔透的葡萄,口水直流,想要摘下来吃,但又够不着。它看了一会儿,无可奈何地走了,边走边自我安慰道:"这葡萄没有熟,肯定是酸的。"

这故事是说,有些人对自己得不到的东西,就说它不好。

在现代小说中,主题很少如此鲜明直白,许多作品和寓言故事讲的是同样的道理,但讲述的方式充满艺术性,隐晦曲折,需要读者用心去琢磨。有些作品情节看似简单,主题却会有多重读解。威廉·卡洛斯·威廉姆斯的《暴力的使用》情节简单:一个医生去给一个小女孩看病,强迫她张开嘴,以便进行检查,却遭到小女孩的激烈反抗。但它的主题思想很丰富。我们可以说,这个故事讲的是"盲目的拒绝源于恐惧和无知"。也可以说"使用暴力有时是必要的,但会产生负面影响"。也可以说"使用暴力可以打败一个人的肉体,但无法征服他的思想"。这些读解也许不是百分之百的准确,但各有道理。和《暴力的使用》相比,凯瑟琳·曼斯菲尔德的《苍蝇》情节更为单一:一个公司老板把自己关在办公室里,用墨水折磨一只苍蝇,直到它死去。由于作者特别善于以看似单薄的情节来刻画人物内心,进而反映社会现实,也因为她极少说明创作意图,因而常引起众说纷纭。有人认为这反映了常年为疾患所困的作者对生命的悲观态度。有人认为老板因儿子死于战场而无法自拔,这是对残酷的战争的批判,表现了反战主题。还有人认为这个故事体现了"人生而必死"的存在主义思想。小说本身提供了多种读解的可能性,让读者去思考、回味,而文学作品的魅力就在于多义性,在于激发人的思考。我们在陈述故事主题时,应避免简单化,努力表达其蕴含的意味。故事主旨太直白,就如一杯白开水,读来淡而无味;多义性虽然给阅读带来一定挑战性,但却能带来思考的愉悦,同时能磨砺心智,启迪思想。

我们在讨论短篇小说的主题时,尤其要关注细节。故事是具体的,主题是概括性的,是对细节的抽象总结。如此,思考主题就成了一种读解行为,我们不仅要仔细寻找有意义的细节,而且要跳出作品,进入抽象思维的境界。关注细节可以从篇名、人物姓名、重复出现的词语、有特别意义的动物或景物入手,这些都很可能是用来体现主题思想的手段。如《被抛弃的韦罗瑟尔奶奶》中"韦罗瑟尔"(Weatherall)这个名字意为"饱经沧桑",加上"抛弃"(jilting),我们可以预想这是一个关于女性生活艰辛的故事。主题作为中心思想,是连接作品各部分的纽带,作家会围绕主题选择和安排细节。读者掌握了主题,对普通平常的细节也会赋予新的意义,或在原本孤立的细节之间建立起联系。同时,主题的表述应该是适用于整个作品,而不是仅仅适用于作品的个别细节。

Kate Chopin (1850—1904)

作者简介

凯特·肖邦(Kate Chopin,1850—1904)出生在美国密苏里州圣路易斯市。父亲是一位成功的商人,母亲是当地法国人社区的积极分子。肖邦5岁时父亲死于火车事故,此后她一直生活在母亲家族的法国文化背景中,深受其影响。肖邦21岁嫁给法国后裔的商人,在新奥尔良定居,育有六个子女。1882年丈夫染病去世,留下12 000美元债务,她独自经营丈夫留下的农场和商店。1884年母亲去世,这使肖邦不但生活艰辛,而且陷入了精神崩溃状态。在家庭医生的建议下,肖邦决定以写作来增加收入,同时缓解精神压力。从此她开始了短暂但颇有成就的文学创作生涯。但是,写作并未给肖邦带来多少收入,她主要靠在路易斯安那州和圣路易斯市的投资来维持生计。1904年肖邦因脑溢血去世,享年54岁。

文学创作

肖邦一生创作了两部长篇小说:《过失》(*At Fault*,1890)和《觉醒》(*The Awakening*,1899),和大量的短篇小说,共有100多篇,收入三部集子中:《牛轭湖的人们》(*Bayou Folk*,1894)、《在阿卡迪的一夜》(*A Night In Acadie*,1897)和《职业和声音》(*A Vocation and a Voice*,1961)。因长期生活在法语文化的氛围中,肖邦大部分作品描写的都是新奥尔良和路易斯安纳州中部的风土人情,以及当地法国人后裔的生活和文化传统,这使她成为一位地方色彩小说家。

肖邦最著名的作品是《觉醒》。女主人公埃德娜不甘扮演贤妻良母的角色,大胆追求自由,在无法解决自我和道义的冲突后,她跳海自杀,以死来维护心所向往的独立与自由。《觉醒》因大胆表达女性情欲而在当时被斥为有伤风化。埃德娜的死揭示了男性社会对女性的压抑,这一人物反映出肖邦超前于时代的思想。

肖邦的短篇小说主题丰富,除了反映女性的追求与社会现实之间的冲突,还有种族问题,这方面的名篇是《德西蕾的孩子》("Désirée's Baby")。弃婴德西蕾为一富裕家庭所收养,长大后嫁给当地的有钱人阿曼德,生了个黑男孩。阿曼德怀疑妻子是黑人,将其赶出家门,德西蕾抱着儿子投河自尽。阿曼德后来意外发现有黑人血统的原来不是妻子,而是自己。反讽是这篇小说最突出的手法:丈夫以为自己是白人,非常骄傲,到头来却发现自己是黑奴的儿子。种族歧视终于导致家破人亡。

《觉醒》问世后招来始料不及的谴责声,肖邦逐渐被批评界遗忘。20世纪60年代末、70年代初,肖邦的独特性和创造性得到重新评价。现在她已经是公认的美国文学史上一位重要的妇女小说家。

作　　品

Story of an Hour

　　Knowing that Mrs. Mallard was afflicted with a heart trouble, great care was taken to break to her as gently as possible the news of her husband's death.

　　It was her sister Josephine who told her, in broken sentences, veiled hints that revealed in half concealing. Her husband's friend Richards was there, too, near her. It was he who had been in the newspaper office when intelligence of the railroad disaster was received, with Brently Mallard's name leading the list of "killed." He had only taken the time to assure himself of its truth by a second telegram, and had hastened to forestall[1] any less careful, less tender friend in bearing the sad message.

　　She did not hear the story as many women have heard the same, with a paralyzed inability to accept its significance. She wept at once, with sudden, wild abandonment, in her sister's arms. When the storm of grief had spent itself she went away to her room alone. She would have no one follow her.

　　There stood, facing the open window, a comfortable, roomy armchair. Into this she sank, pressed down by a physical exhaustion that haunted her body and seemed to reach into her soul.

　　She could see in the open square before her house the tops of trees that were all aquiver with the new spring life. The delicious breath of rain was in the air. In the street below a peddler[2] was crying his wares. The notes of a distant song which some one was

---

[1] forestall:预先阻止。
[2] peddler:沿街叫卖的小贩。

singing reached her faintly, and countless sparrows were twittering in the eaves[1].

There were patches of blue sky showing here and there through the clouds that had met and piled one above the other in the west facing her window.

She sat with her head thrown back upon the cushion of the chair, quite motionless, except when a sob came up into her throat and shook her, as a child who has cried itself to sleep continues to sob in its dreams.

She was young, with a fair, calm face, whose lines bespoke[2] repression and even a certain strength. But now there was a dull stare in her eyes, whose gaze was fixed away off yonder on one of those patches of blue sky. It was not a glance of reflection, but rather indicated a suspension of intelligent thought.

There was something coming to her and she was waiting for it, fearfully. What was it? She did not know; it was too subtle and elusive to name. But she felt it, creeping out of the sky, reaching toward her through the sounds, the scents, the color that filled the air.

Now her bosom rose and fell tumultuously[3]. She was beginning to recognize this thing that was approaching to possess her, and she was striving to beat it back with her will—as powerless as her two white slender hands would have been.

When she abandoned herself a little whispered word escaped her slightly parted lips. She said it over and over under her breath: "free, free, free!" The vacant stare and the look of terror that had followed it went from her eyes. They stayed keen and bright. Her pulses beat fast, and the coursing blood warmed and relaxed every inch of her body.

She did not stop to ask if it were or were not a monstrous joy that held her. A clear and exalted perception enabled her to dismiss the suggestion as trivial.

She knew that she would weep again when she saw the kind, tender hands folded in death; the face that had never looked save with love upon her, fixed and gray and dead. But she saw beyond that bitter moment a long procession of years to come that would belong to her absolutely. And she opened and spread her arms out to them in welcome.

There would be no one to live for during those coming years; she would live for herself. There would be no powerful will bending hers in that blind persistence with which men and women believe they have a right to impose[4] a private will upon a fellow-creature. A kind intention or a cruel intention made the act seem no less a crime as she looked upon it in that brief moment of illumination.[5]

And yet she had loved him—sometimes. Often she had not. What did it matter! What could love, the unsolved mystery, count for in face of this possession of self-

---

[1] eaves:屋檐,房檐。
[2] bespoke:显示。
[3] tumultuously:剧烈地。
[4] impose:强加。
[5] A kind intention... brief moment of illumination. 她在顿悟的那一刻明白了,无论是出于善意还是恶意,这种将个人意志强加于人的做法不亚于一种犯罪。

assertion which she suddenly recognized as the strongest impulse of her being!

"Free! Body and soul free!" she kept whispering.

Josephine was kneeling before the closed door with her lips to the keyhole, imploring for admission. "Louise, open the door! I beg, open the door—you will make yourself ill. What are you doing Louise? For heaven's sake open the door."

"Go away. I am not making myself ill." No; she was drinking in a very elixir[1] of life through that open window.

Her fancy was running riot along those days ahead of her. Spring days, and summer days, and all sorts of days that would be her own. She breathed a quick prayer that life might be long. It was only yesterday she had thought with a shudder that life might be long.

She arose at length and opened the door to her sister's importunities[2]. There was a feverish triumph in her eyes, and she carried herself unwittingly like a goddess of Victory. She clasped her sister's waist, and together they descended the stairs. Richards stood waiting for them at the bottom.

Some one was opening the front door with a latchkey. It was Brently Mallard who entered, a little travel-stained, composedly carrying his grip-sack[3] and umbrella. He had been far from the scene of accident, and did not even know there had been one.

He stood amazed at Josephine's piercing cry; at Richards' quick motion to screen him from the view of his wife.

But Richards was too late.

When the doctors came they said she had died of heart disease—of joy that kills.

1894

赏 析

《一个小时的故事》是肖邦最著名的短篇小说,作品表达的女性主义思想引起评论家的注意。一般认为,从作者当时所处的社会环境、马拉德夫人对自由的热切渴望和为之而死来看,该短篇小说批判了男权(夫权)对妇女的压迫。19世纪末的美国在法律上和经济上赋予丈夫控制妻子的权力,做贤妻良母和顺从丈夫是女人的本份。她们没有自我,只是别人的母亲、妻子、女儿、情妇。马拉德先生似乎爱妻子,夫妻关系也不错,但是马拉德夫人对丈夫的爱几乎没有什么回应,相反,她对未来没有丈夫的生活感到兴奋,因为"将不会有强大的意志在盲目的坚持中来折弯她的意志,怀有这种意志的男男女女相信,他们有权力把个人的意志强加于其他人。她在顿悟的那一刻明白了,无论是出于善意还是恶意,这种将个人意志强加于他人的做法不亚于一种犯罪。"由此可见,丈夫对妻子的爱实际上是以自己主观、武断的爱来剥夺妻子的意志,这也是一种暴力。

作者用象征、衬托、反讽等多种手法来描写马拉德夫人情感由悲到喜,由喜到崩溃的过程。

---

[1] elixir:灵丹妙药。
[2] importunities:纠缠不休地再三要求,强求。
[3] grip-sack:手提包,旅行包。

如"heart trouble"是指心脏有病,同时暗示女主人公在感情上出了问题。马拉德夫人在卧室里看到的窗外春景衬托并暗示了她自我意识的觉醒。结尾医生说她死于过度高兴,其实她是死于极度的失望。

小说的女性主义思想不但表现在情节的构筑上,而且体现在三对空间中,楼上/楼下、窗内/窗外、门里/门外。相对于楼上的卧室,楼下是个公共空间,马拉德夫人的悲伤表现符合妻子这个社会身份。一旦进到卧室这个属于自己的空间里,她就成了追求自由的独立女性。窗外的春景和盎然的生机,反衬窗内人生活的压抑,暗示未来生活的美好。相比之下,门内/门外的对比非常简略,但不失深意。门内是真正的自我,门外是以亲人为代表的外部世界,空间的隔离暗示亲人尽管关心马拉德夫人,但并不理解她内心的渴望。

《一个小时的故事》不像肖邦其他作品有明显的地方色彩,但它语言简洁,字词精挑细选,意象鲜明生动,情节层层细心铺垫,处处隐含深意,富于讽刺意味的开放性结尾读后令人回味。

相关评论

Fatal Self-Assertion[1] in Kate Chopin's "The Story of an Hour"
Lawrence L. Berkove

Kate Chopin's thousand-word short story, "The Story of an Hour," has understandably become a favorite selection for collections of short stories as well as for anthologies of American literature. Few other stories say so much in so few words. There has been, moreover, virtual critical agreement on what the story says: its heroine dies, ironically and tragically, just as she has been freed from a constricting marriage and has realized self-assertion as the deepest element of her being. Confidence in this interpretation, however, may be misplaced, for using the standard proposed for the story by Toth and Seyersted—"every detail contributes to the emotional impact"—there is evidence of a deeper level of irony in the story which does not regard Louise Mallard as a heroine but as an immature egotist[2] and a victim of her own extreme self-assertion. This self-assertion is achieved not by reflection but, on the contrary, by "a suspension of intelligent thought" masked as "illumination." As a result, a pattern of basic contradictions and abnormal attitudes emerges which gives structure to the story and forecasts its conclusion. The key to recognizing this deeper, ironic level is to carefully distinguish between the story's narrator, author, and unreliable protagonist.

Seyersted's early biography of Chopin describes the story neutrally as "an extreme example of the theme of self-assertion." More recent interpretation has largely followed a strong, and at times an extreme, feminist bent. Representative of this in both approach and language is Emily Toth's well-known characterization of the story as one of Chopin's "most radical ... an attack on marriage, on one person's dominance over another." Toth further elaborates this position in a later article in which she comments

---

[1] self-assertion:自我坚持,自我要求。
[2] egotist:自我主义者。

that "Although Louise's death is an occasion for deep irony directed at patriarchal blindness about women's thoughts, Louise dies in the world of her family where she has always sacrificed for others." Ewell similarly sees in the story's "surfaces" Louise's struggle for selfhood against "society's decree" for female "selflessness, being for others."

But in the text of this very short story there is no hard evidence whatsoever of patriarchal blindness or suppression, constant or selfless sacrifice by Louise, or an ongoing struggle for selfhood. These positions are all read into the story from non-textual assumptions. The simple truth is that this story is not about society or marriage, but about Louise Mallard. The single possible reference in the text to difficulties in her life is a sentence, which says that the lines of her face "bespoke repression and a certain strength." It is not at all clear, however, what the cause of that "repression" was; whether, for instance, it might have been external, in society or in her marriage, or whether it was internal, a recognition that it takes strength to control one's feelings or whims. Such few hints as the story supplies incline toward the latter position. While the text enables us to make certain inferences about Louise, it does not supply us with any information about the truth of her life except her perceptions, and these, as I intend to show, are unreliable and, insofar as they are taken as the statements of the story's omniscient[1] narrator, misleading and contradicted by other textual evidence.

Support for this position is spread throughout the story but the most dramatic elements appear in the following three paragraphs:

> There would be no one to live for her during those coming years; she would live for herself. There would be no powerful will bending hers in that blind persistence with which men and women believe they have a right to impose a private will upon a fellow-creature. A kind intention or a cruel intention made the act seem no less a crime as she looked upon it in that brief moment of illumination.
>
> And yet she had loved him—sometimes. Often she had not. What did it matter! What could love, the unsolved mystery, count for in face of this possession of self-assertion which she suddenly recognized as the strongest impulse of her being!
>
> "Free! Body and soul free!" she kept whispering.

In these paragraphs, the story's omniscient narrator takes us into Louise's mind. However, while the attitudes expressed are definitely Louise's there is no textual justification for also ascribing them to the narrator. Further, it would be a mistake to project them onto Chopin, for that would confuse narrator with author, a move that denies Chopin the full range of literary technique, and that would reduce this brilliant and subtle work of fiction to behind-the-scenes sermonizing.

It is significant, in the quotation's first line, that Louise wishes to "live for

---

[1] omniscient: 全知的。

herself." This has been generally understood to imply that she had hitherto[1] sacrificed herself for her husband; however, there is no evidence for this in the text. Nor is there any evidence that her husband had done her living "for her," whatever that might mean. It is an *ipse dixit*[2] comment, arbitrary, without support, one of several she makes.

In the quotation's second paragraph, Louise discounts[3] love as secondary to self-assertion. While this is undoubtedly her position, there is no textual reason to assume it is also Chopin's. Louise also recognizes self-assertion "as the strongest impulse of her being." This is a peculiar value for a married person and is indeed incompatible with marriage, where an emphasis upon shared goals and mutual commitment is the opposite of self-assertion. The unreasoning self-centeredness of Louise partly explains the first two sentences of the quotation's second paragraph, and they tell us more about her than about her husband. Of course, even married people who sincerely love each other have occasional disagreements and may not feel much love for the other at particular times. For most lovers this is not so much a contradiction as a paradox; the moments of hate occur within the larger context of love. But the warmest sentiment that Louise can express after being married to a man whose benevolence the previous paragraph explicitly affirms with its description of his "kind, tender hands" and his face "that had never looked save with love upon her" is the niggardly[4] concession that she had loved him "sometimes."

It is obvious that there is quite a discrepancy[5] between the way Louise and Brently Mallard feel about each other, but all the mystery of the difference is on Louise's side.

Whatever her original reason had been for marrying Brently, it is clear now that feeling the way she does about him she would be better off not being married. Her love for herself—"she would live only for herself"—does not leave room for anyone else. How, then, would she live?

Her justification[6] for preferring to live for herself, the second and third sentences of the quotation's first paragraph, are extravagant, unrealistic statements, each segment of which is controversial. She views her husband's constant love as a "powerful will bending hers in a blind persistence." Blind? Why is it blind? Inasmuch as[7] Louise has apparently repressed her true feelings about her husband and marriage, if his love for her is blind it is because she has blinded him. In the absence of open communication about her feelings, how would he know what she wants, or what to do or say? In that circumstance, his persistence, which clearly annoys her, may only be a natural attempt

---

[1] hitherto:迄今,到目前为止。
[2] *ipse dixit*:〈拉丁语〉武断的言词。
[3] discount:低估;怀疑地看待,不信。
[4] niggardly:极少的,不足的。
[5] discrepancy:差异,不一致。
[6] justification:理由,辩解。
[7] inasmuch as:因为,由于。

on his part to please her and to convince her of his love. The failure of Brently's persistence is due at least in part to Louise's strange view of love—and the wording of the second sentence includes her as well as her husband—as a "crime," a powerful will that "bends" the other person. This is a distorted view of love, which typically delights in pleasing and giving to the other. Believing love a "crime" cannot be considered a normal attitude, much less an emotionally healthy one.

Source: *American Literary Realism* 32.2 (Winter 2000).

问题与思考

1. What stages of emotional transformation does Mrs. Mallard experience after she receives the news of her husband's death?
2. What do you think really kills Mrs Mallard?
3. What is the function of the scene outside the bedroom window?
4. Analyze the irony in the ending of the story.

阅读链接

1. http://www.katechopin.org：凯特·肖邦国际协会，包括肖邦的生平介绍、长篇小说《觉醒》和《过失》以及短篇小说的出版情况、主要人物和参考书目等。
2. http://etext.virginia.edu/toc/modeng/public/ChoAwak.html：可下载电子版《觉醒》。
3. http://books.google.com/books?id=0E9TWXk1d6IC&dq=kate+chopin&printsec=frontcover&source=bl&ots=mHsBrCCyeG&sig=_Tsyod13jSSkIVEOT8EG46yJxAU&hl=en&ei=A0hAS7irE82OkQWH0cDyDA&sa=X&oi=book_result&ct=result&resnum=9&ved=0CC0Q6AEwCA#v=onepage&q=&f=false：可下载电子版《牛轭湖的人们》。

William Carlos Williams (1883—1963)

作者简介

威廉·卡洛斯·威廉姆斯（William Carlos Williams，1883—1963）生于美国新泽西州鲁瑟福德市，父亲是英国移民，母亲来自波多黎各。1896 年，威廉姆斯从公立学校毕业，到瑞士和法国上了两年学，后转到纽约一所学校。1902 年他进入宾夕法尼亚大学医学院，在那里结识了美国意象派领袖人物庞德、H. D. 和画家查尔斯·德穆思。友情孕育了他的才思，激发了他对写诗的热情。1906 年威廉姆斯获得医学博士学位后，又去德国莱比锡大学深造，1910 年返回故乡鲁瑟福德行医。他的医术精良，后来担任帕特森市总医院儿科主治医师。据统计，他在 1910 到 1952 年间共接生过 2 000 多个孩子。威廉姆斯在忙于工作之际，挤出时间创作了大量的散文和诗歌。1948 年他心脏病发作，此后健康状况逐渐下降。20 世纪 50 年代他停止行医，全身心投入文学创作。晚年他双目失明，疾病缠身，但仍继续文学创作。1963 年 3 月 4 日威廉姆斯在家乡去世，享年 79 岁。

文学创作

威廉姆斯虽一生行医，但常在看病的间隙记下创作灵感，且笔耕不辍，其创作面涵盖诗歌、小说、剧本和文学评论，是美国当代一位多产而卓有成就的作家。去世那年，他获得了普利策奖。威廉姆斯的诗歌意象生动、用词通俗、短小精悍、节奏明快，名作包括六卷长诗《帕特森》（Paterson，1946—1962）、意象派经典短诗《红色手推车》（The Red Wheelbarrow，1923）、诗歌集《爱之旅》（Journey to Love，1955）等。威廉姆斯坚持用美国本土语言写作，成为美国现代诗歌

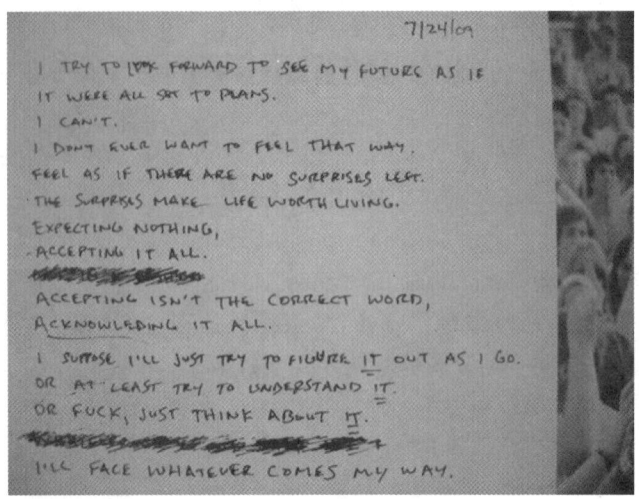

的代表,其诗风对20世纪的美国诗歌产生了重要影响。威廉姆斯的其他作品包括颇具讽拟和元小说风格的长篇小说《伟大的美国小说》(*The Great American Novel*,1923),研究美国国民性的历史著述《美国性情》(*In the American Grain*,1925),反映他敏锐的观察力和内省深度的《自传》(*The Autobiography*,1951)等。

威廉姆斯共发表了50多篇短篇小说,收在《时代之刀》(*The Knife of the Times and Other Stories*,1932)、《帕塞伊克河沿岸的生活》(*Life along the Passaic River*,1938)、《蔑视》(*Make Light of It*,1950)和《农夫的女儿》(*The Farmers' Daughters*,1961)等故事集中,著名的有《暴力的使用》("The Use of Force")、《吉恩·贝基》("Jean Beicke")和《一脸粉刺的女孩》("The Girl with a Pimply Fame")。威廉姆斯虽爱写医生的故事,但故事题材广泛,如带自传色彩的《黑姑娘》表达了他对黑人女性一贯的钟情;《吉恩·贝基》描写为一个畸形婴儿的验尸过程,揭示穷人孩子无人照看的悲惨境地;而《时代之刀》讲述的是同性之爱。威廉姆斯相信短篇小说能够使

作者"充满感情地阐明某一个观点"。他尤其擅长将哲学思考融入日常生活的某个细节中,风格则颇似他的意象派短诗,聚焦于某一速写或片断,笔法是临床医生所喜欢的客观和简洁,用词和语法明白易懂,但在这种仿佛是不经意的冷静记录背后是深刻的哲学思考和社会反思。

The Use of Force

They were new patients to me, all I had was the name, Olson[1]. Please come down as soon as you can, my daughter is very sick.

When I arrived I was met by the mother, a big startled looking woman, very clean and apologetic who merely said, Is this the doctor? and let me in. In the back, she

---

[1] Olson:斯堪的那维亚普通姓氏。

added. You must excuse us, doctor, we have her in the kitchen where it is warm. It is very damp here sometimes.

The child was fully dressed and sitting on her father's lap near the kitchen table. He tried to get up, but I motioned for him not to bother, took off my overcoat and started to look things over. I could see that they were all very nervous, eyeing me up and down distrustfully. As often, in such cases, they weren't telling me more than they had to, it was up to me to tell them; that's why they were spending three dollars on me.

The child was fairly[1] eating me up with her cold, steady eyes, and no expression to her face whatever. She did not move and seemed, inwardly, quiet; an unusually attractive little thing, and as strong as a heifer[2] in appearance. But her face was flushed, she was breathing rapidly, and I realized that she had a high fever. She had magnificent blonde hair, in profusion. One of those picture children often reproduced in advertising leaflets and the photogravure sections of the Sunday papers[3].

She's had a fever for three days, began the father and we don't know what it comes from. My wife has given her things, you know, like people do, but it don't do no good[4]. And there's been a lot of sickness around. So we tho't[5] you'd better look her over and tell us what is the matter.

As doctors often do I took a trial shot[6] at it as a point of departure. Has she had a sore throat?

Both parents answered me together, No... No, she says her throat don't hurt her.

Does your throat hurt you? added the mother to the child. But the little girl's expression didn't change nor did she move her eyes from my face.

Have you looked?

I tried to, said the mother, but I couldn't see.

As it happens we had been having a number of cases of diphtheria[7] in the school to which this child went during that month and we were all, quite apparently, thinking of that, though no one had as yet spoken of the thing.

Well, I said, suppose we take a look at the throat first. I smiled in my best professional manner and asking for the child's first name I said, come on, Mathilda, open your mouth and let's take a look at your throat.

Nothing doing.

Aw, come on, I coaxed[8], just open your mouth wide and let me take a look.

---

[1] fairly:几乎要。
[2] heifer:小母牛。
[3] the photogravure sections of the Sunday papers:星期天报纸的彩色照片版;photogravure:照相凸版印刷。
[4] it don't do no good = it hasn't done any good:没起到什么效果。
[5] tho't = thought.
[6] took a trial shot:尝试性地探问病情。
[7] diphtheria:白喉(症)。
[8] coaxed:哄,劝诱。

Look, I said, opening both hands wide, I haven't anything in my hands. Just open up and let me see.

Such a nice man, put in the mother. Look how kind he is to you. Come on, do what he tells you to. He won't hurt you.

At that I ground my teeth in disgust. If only they wouldn't use the word "hurt" I might be able to get somewhere. But I did not allow myself to be hurried or disturbed but speaking quietly and slowly I approached the child again.

As I moved my chair a little nearer suddenly with one catlike movement both her hands clawed instinctively for my eyes and she almost reached them too. In fact she knocked my glasses flying and they fell, though unbroken, several feet away from me on the kitchen floor.

Both the mother and father almost turned themselves inside out in embarrassment and apology. You bad girl, said the mother, taking her and shaking her by one arm. Look what you've done. The nice man...

For heaven's sake, I broke in. Don't call me a nice man to her. I'm here to look at her throat on the chance that she might have diphtheria and possibly die of it. But that's nothing to her. Look here, I said to the child, we're going to look at your throat. You're old enough to understand what I'm saying. Will you open it now by yourself or shall we have to open it for you?

Not a move. Even her expression hadn't changed. Her breaths however were coming faster and faster. Then the battle began. I had to do it. I had to have a throat culture[1] for her own protection. But first I told the parents that it was entirely up to them. I explained the danger but said that I would not insist on a throat examination so long as they would take the responsibility.

If you don't do what the doctor says you'll have to go to the hospital, the mother admonished her severely.

Oh yeah? I had to smile to myself. After all, I had already fallen in love with the savage brat[2], the parents were contemptible to me. In the ensuing struggle they grew more and more abject[3], crushed, exhausted while she surely rose to magnificent heights of insane fury of effort bred of her terror of me.

The father tried his best, and he was a big man but the fact that she was his daughter, his shame at her behavior and his dread of hurting her made him release her just at the critical times when I had almost achieved success, till I wanted to kill him. But his dread also that she might have diphtheria made him tell me to go on, go on though he himself was almost fainting, while the mother moved back and forth behind us raising and lowering her hands in an agony of apprehension.

---

[1] culture:试样。

[2] brat:(蔑称)小家伙。

[3] abject:难堪的,绝望无助的。

Put her in front of you on your lap, I ordered, and hold both her wrists.

But as soon as he did the child let out a scream. Don't, you're hurting me. Let go of my hands. Let them go I tell you. Then she shrieked terrifyingly, hysterically. Stop it! Stop it! You're killing me!

Do you think she can stand it, doctor! said the mother.

You get out, said the husband to his wife. Do you want her to die of diphtheria?

Come on now, hold her, I said.

Then I grasped the child's head with my left hand and tried to get the wooden tongue[1] depressor between her teeth. She fought, with clenched teeth, desperately! But now I also had grown furious—at a child. I tried to hold myself down but I couldn't. I know how to expose a throat for inspection. And I did my best. When finally I got the wooden spatula behind the last teeth and just the point of it into the mouth cavity, she opened up for an instant but before I could see anything she came down again and gripping the wooden blade between her molars[2] she reduced it to splinters before I could get it out again.

Aren't you ashamed, the mother yelled at her. Aren't you ashamed to act like that in front of the doctor?

Get me a smooth-handled spoon of some sort, I told the mother. We're going through with this. The child's mouth was already bleeding. Her tongue was cut and she was screaming in wild hysterical shrieks. Perhaps I should have desisted[3] and come back in an hour or more. No doubt it would have been better. But I have seen at least two children lying dead in bed of neglect in such cases, and feeling that I must get a diagnosis now or never I went at it again. But the worst of it was that I too had got beyond reason. I could have torn the child apart in my own fury and enjoyed it. It was a pleasure to attack her. My face was burning with it.

The damned little brat must be protected against her own idiocy, one says to one's self at such times. Others must be protected against her. It is a social necessity. And all these things are true. But a blind fury, a feeling of adult shame, bred of a longing for muscular release are the operatives[4]. One goes on to the end.

In a final unreasoning assault I overpowered the child's neck and jaws. I forced the heavy silver spoon back of her teeth and down her throat till she gagged[5]. And there it was—both tonsils covered with membrane[6]. She had fought valiantly to keep me from knowing her secret. She had been hiding that sore throat for three days at least and lying to her parents in order to escape just such an outcome as this.

---

[1] wooden tongue：压舌板。
[2] molars：臼齿。
[3] desisted：停止。
[4] operatives：指起作用的因素。
[5] gagged：使张开嘴。
[6] both tonsils covered with membrane：两个扁桃体上长有一层膜。

Now truly she was furious. She had been on the defensive before but now she attacked. Tried to get off her father's lap and fly at me while tears of defeat blinded her eyes.

1933,1938

赏　析

《暴力的使用》故事很简单。一位医生被请到家里给一个小女孩看病,他怀疑小女孩得了致命的白喉病,需要查看喉咙的情况,可小女孩抵死不张嘴。面对女儿的顽固和敌意,父母无可奈何,医生越来越生气,最后他使用汤匙撬开小病人流血的嘴,终于看到了病症,她的确患了白喉病。

小说体现了威廉姆斯擅长以小见大的才能。医生和小女孩一场意志的对抗折射出一个根本性问题:我们能够以暴力来表达善意吗?而且,如果我们对这种行为乐在其中,是不是应该感到羞耻?

小说以医生的内心独白为叙述视角,威廉姆斯的才能表现在蕴含深意的平常话语中。开篇即说"他们是第一次找我看病的病人……"平平常常的一句话却耐人寻味:看病的只是小女孩,为什么说他们都是病人呢?其实故事里的所有人物都有"病":小女孩身体有病;父亲和母亲无法胜任看护和驾驭孩子的职责,母亲只会说些帮倒忙的话,抱着女儿的父亲一到关键时刻就手软,同样帮不上忙;医生本是治病救人,却奇怪地变成暴力的实施者,救死扶伤和毁灭欲望是如此接近。故事画龙点睛之笔在于医生最后的坦白:"盛怒之下,我本可以亲手把这孩子撕成两半,我会乐在其中的,攻击她是件快乐的事情。想到这儿,我的脸热得发烫。"这时,职业道德已经让位于黑暗的本能。

医生这种非正常心态与故事的氛围相呼应,医生进门后,迎接他的一家三口"全都非常紧张,一脸怀疑地上下打量我",面无表情的小女孩更是"冷冷地紧盯着我,像是要把我吃掉"。如果说威廉姆斯想以此说明与行医有关的话题,如:医生怎样在一个陌生甚至有敌意的环境中迅速探查病情?如何行使医生的权力?那么,贯穿故事的这些话题也反映了大萧条时期(故事最初发表于1933年)美国普通民众对一切充满疑虑的心态。

相关评论

Theme and Style in "The Use of Force"
Linda Wagner-Martin

Williams makes the reader question, here, in 1933, is this the kind of doctor I'd want for my child? Why is he calling her "a savage brat"? Why all this emphasis on the conquering role of the physician? But what the writer does is intensify the drama of a simple, daily occurrence by giving vitality to the characters' actions. The erotic undercurrents add a dimension to the struggle that is inherent in all male-female interaction, even if polite society—which the Olsons represent—denies its presence. Williams charges the story with a duel[1] between the language of the Olsons and that of

---

[1] duel:决斗,抗争。

the physician: "He won't hurt you," says Mrs. Olson. Yet the reader is caught up in the dramatic irony of knowing that the physician would indeed hurt her if he had to, because his only aim is to diagnose her illness. What he has to do to accomplish that matters little. Her parents begin labeling; they advise their struggling child to let the "nice" doctor have his way, while they call her "bad." Williams' physician sides with the child, and wonders how he could appear "nice" to her when he is struggling to overpower her so that he can jam things into her mouth.

Williams' style is both explicit and swift. No word is superfluous[1]; everything that appears on the page is useful for the reader. But the spareness[2] is not a skeletal journalistic treatment that oversimplifies. Rather, Williams' fiction remains intentionally suggestive and, often, refreshingly ambivalent[3] about moral attitudes. While he is best known as a poet, having won the Pulitzer prize for poetry shortly after his death in 1963, Williams may eventually be seen as an equally important innovator in prose. "The Use of Force" remains a great American short story, precise in its delineation of character and carefully direct in its execution of narrative.

Source: *Reference Guide to Short Fiction*. Ed. Noelle Watson. Detroit: St. James Press, 1994.

The Adult Image in "The Use of Force"
Anonymous

From the outset, the doctor appears to be compassionate and keen to human behavior, characteristic of a good doctor, though he is also undeniably blunt and slightly prejudiced. Williams' choice to use interior monologue[4] as a "stream-of-consciousness" tool reflects the narrator's experience of dialogue and gives insight into the character and his appraisal[5] of the situations he encounters. He immediately assesses the mother upon seeing her as "clean and apologetic," and dedicates more time a much more thorough description for the daughter, to whom he already has taken a fancy. He portrays the parents as eager to cooperate, yet nervous and distrustful of the stranger who is only in their house by forced circumstance, and therefore he finds them obstructive[6]. In any case, his contempt for the parents (whom he barely knows) changes from implicit to overt as they are cajoling[7] the young girl after initial efforts, particularly when he grinds his teeth in disgust at being called a "nice man." Their inane[8] comments serve to

---

[1] superfluous:多余的。
[2] spareness:这里指简略,略而不说。
[3] ambivalent:含混的。
[4] interior monologue:内心独白。
[5] appraisal:评估,评价。
[6] obstructive:妨碍的。
[7] cajole:哄骗。
[8] inane:无意义的,空洞的。

do nothing but hinder the doctor's efforts to get the child to understand what he needs to do, and the placement of their comments in the speaker's own internal thoughts allow them to be felt in the same way the speaker felt them (usually as spontaneous and substanceless interjections[1]: "Do you think she can stand it, doctor! Said the mother.") The father (who receives very little characterization) provides one example of the weakness and ineptitude[2] of the parents in dealing with the situation when he is attempting to hold his daughter back and fails restrain her at each pivotal[3] moment due to his fear of hurting her. This behavior and the behavior of the family as a whole is spectacularly ironic, considering that all of their fears are preventing them from stopping what they should truly be fearing: a fatal case of diptheria.

The weakness on the parents' part and the stubbornness on the daughter's part contribute to the doctor's escalating[4] frustration, to the point where he asserts his power: with a smooth spoon, he forces the girl's mouth open. He admits that he could have taken a more rational approach and tried again in an hour, of course, but he confesses that he had become just as irrational as everyone else in the room: "I could have torn the child apart in my own fury and enjoyed it. It was a pleasure to attack her. My face was burning with it." It is evident that he had been forceful and enjoyed it, but it is not likely that he would have done it in any other case. "The damned little brat must be protected against her own idiocy, one says to one's self at such times. Others must be protected against her. It is social necessity. And all these things are true. But a blind fury, a feeling of adult shame, bred of a longing for muscular release are the operatives." Indeed, it appears that he was compelled to action more strongly by his fury than his professional duty. As a professional, he has a barrier of rationality that prevents him from doing such irrational things; however, in this case, he had a strong justification for that action due to its "social necessity," which then permitted him to act upon his primal[5] instincts without conscientious interference.

Source: http://www.associatedcontent.com/article/1572368/overview_of_william_carlos_williams.html?cat=25

问题与思考

1. Which character do you feel the most sympathy for? Why?
2. What part of the story seems exposition? At what point does the dramatic conflict become apparent? What is the climax of the story?

---

[1] interjections:插话。
[2] ineptitude:无能。
[3] pivotal:关键的。
[4] escalating:逐步升级的。
[5] primal:原始的。

3. Does the doctor act out of a sense of responsibility or "a blind fury"?
4. Since the use of force seems a necessity in preserving orderly civilization, what does the story say about civilized life in general?

阅读链接

1. http://en.wikipedia.org/wiki/William_Carlos_Williams：介绍威廉姆斯的生平、创作生涯、诗歌、散文（包括长短篇小说）和戏剧作品目录，以及相关链接。
2. http://www.english.illinois.edu/maps/poets/s_z/williams/williams.htm：介绍威廉姆斯的生平和创作，对包括《红色手推车》在内的诗歌的评论。
3. http://www.learner.org/catalog/extras/vvspot/Williams.html：威廉姆斯诗歌朗诵的视频和录音。

Katherine Mansfield (1888—1923)

作者简介

凯瑟琳·曼斯菲尔德(Katherine Mansfield,1888—1923)生于新西兰的惠灵顿,本名卡瑟琳·包姗普,父亲是富商与银行家。她13岁去伦敦王后学院求学,1906年回国,因不满英国前殖民地新西兰闭塞狭隘的生活,两年后再度返回伦敦从事文学创作。在那里,她结识了现代主义作家 D. H. 劳伦斯和弗吉尼亚·伍尔芙,并成为很好的朋友。在经历了一场短暂的不幸婚姻后,她前往欧洲寻找阳光充足的气候,在德国巴伐利亚住了一段时间。她的第一个短篇小说集便是描写了她在巴伐利亚地区所见所闻的人情世态。1912年她邂逅编辑兼批评家约翰·米德尔顿,并嫁给了他。第二次婚姻给她带来了幸福,但她因罹患肺结核再也无法返回故乡新西兰。1923年1月9日,曼斯菲尔德逝世,年仅35岁。

文学创作

凯瑟琳·曼斯菲尔德在短暂的一生中以短篇小说著称文坛。去世时,她已经出版了多部故事集,是现代英语文学中一位杰出的短篇小说作家。曼斯菲尔德的大部分作品收入《幸福集》(*Bliss and Other Stories*,1920)、《园会集》(*The Garden Party and Other Stories*,1922)和《鸽巢集》(*The Doves' Nest and Other Stories*,1923)等短篇小说集。对曼斯菲尔德创作影响最大的是俄罗斯作家契诃夫,有评论家指出,曼斯菲尔德"已经达到了这样的境界,她不是围绕一个情节而是围绕一个场景来构筑故事,有时她走得更远,她不是围绕一个场景而是围绕两个主题来构筑故事,她更像在创作一部乐曲"。曼斯菲尔德的短篇小说很少追求结构的严密,故事的时间变换较大,谋篇布局常有扑朔迷离之感,以对一个有意义的瞬间的洞察为高潮。文字力求简化,描写精确,廖廖数语即能准确展现出生活的全貌。此外,她还大量使用象征手法,在象征中除传统意义之外还赋予了自己特殊的主观感情和寓意。曼斯菲尔德的独创性表明,20世纪初短篇小说脱离了故事加说教的旧传统,进入了通过刻画人物内心来揭示外部世界的时代。在现当代小说家中,最受曼斯菲尔德影响的要数英国作家 D. H. 劳伦斯和中国现代作家徐志摩。徐志摩在她去世半年前去拜访过她,在她去世后写下深情的《哀曼殊斐儿》哀悼她,又译过她的多篇作品在国内出版。

作 品

The Fly

"Y'are very snug[1] in here," piped[2] old Mr. Woodifield, and peered out of the great, green-leather armchair by his friend the boss's desk as a baby peers out of its pram[3]. His talk was over; it was time for him to be off. But he did not want to go. Since he had retired, since his... stroke, the wife and the girls kept him boxed up[4] in the house every day of the week except Tuesday. On Tuesday he was dressed and brushed and allowed to cut back to the City[5] for the day. Though what he did there the wife and girls couldn't imagine. Made a nuisance of himself to his friends, they supposed... Well, perhaps so. All the same, we cling to our last pleasures as the tree clings to its last leaves. So there sat old Woodifield, smoking a cigar and staring almost greedily at the boss, who rolled in his office chair, stout, rosy, five years older than he, and still going strong, still at the helm[6]. It did one good to see him.

Wistfully, admiringly, the old voice added, "It's snug in here, upon my word!"

"Yes, it's comfortable enough," agreed the boss, and he flipped the *Financial Times* with a paper-knife. As a matter of fact he was proud of his room; he liked to have it admired, especially by old Woodifield. It gave him a feeling of deep, solid satisfaction to be planted there in the midst of it in full view of that frail old figure in the muffler.

"I've had it done up[7] lately," he explained, as he had explained for the past —how many! —weeks. "New carpet," and he pointed to the bright red carpet with a pattern of large white rings. "New furniture," and he nodded towards the massive bookcase and the table with legs like twisted treacle[8]. "Electric heating!" He waved almost exultantly towards the five transparent, pearly sausages glowing so softly in the

---

[1] snug:温暖舒适的。
[2] piped:尖声说话。
[3] pram:(英口)婴儿车,perambulator 的缩写。
[4] boxed up:限制,束缚。
[5] cut back to the City:去伦敦重温退休前的生活。Cut back:(电影术语)倒叙;the City:指伦敦城(the City of London),伦敦金融中心,英国主要银行总部、证券交易所所在地。
[6] at the helm:掌舵,控制(公司)。
[7] done up:重新装修。
[8] with legs like twisted treacle:桌腿像是呈螺旋形的糖浆。

tilted copper pan.

But he did not draw old Woodifield's attention to the photograph over the table of a grave-looking boy in uniform standing in one of those spectral photographers' parks[1] with photographers' storm-clouds behind him. It was not new. It had been there for over six years.

"There was something I wanted to tell you," said old Woodifield, and his eyes grew dim remembering. "Now what was it? I had it in my mind when I started out this morning." His hands began to tremble, and patches of red showed above his beard.

Poor old chap, he's on his last pins[2], thought the boss. And, feeling kindly, he winked at the old man, and said jokingly, "I tell you what. I've got a little drop of something here that'll do you good before you go out into the cold again. It's beautiful stuff. It wouldn't hurt a child." He took a key off his watch-chain, unlocked a cupboard below his desk, and drew forth a dark, squat bottle. "That's the medicine," said he. "And the man from whom I got it told me on the strict Q.T.[3] it came from the cellars at Windsor Castle[4]."

Old Woodifield's mouth fell open at the sight. He couldn't have looked more surprised if the boss had produced a rabbit. "It's whisky, ain't it?" he piped feebly.

The boss turned the bottle and lovingly showed him the label. Whisky it was.

"D'you know," said he, peering up at the boss wonderingly, "they won't let me touch it at home." And he looked as though he was going to cry.

"Ah, that's where we know a bit more than the ladies," cried the boss, swooping across for two tumblers that stood on the table with the water-bottle, and pouring a generous finger[5] into each. "Drink it down. It'll do you good. And don't put any water with it. It's sacrilege[6] to tamper with stuff like this. Ah!" He tossed off his, pulled out his handkerchief, hastily wiped his moustaches, and cocked an eye at old Woodifield, who was rolling his in his chaps[7].

The old man swallowed, was silent a moment, and then said faintly, "It's nutty!"

But it warmed him; it crept into his chill old brain—he remembered.

"That was it," he said, heaving himself out of his chair. "I thought you'd like to know. The girls were in Belgium last week having a look at poor Reggie's grave[8], and they happened to come across your boy's. They're quite near each other, it seems."

Old Woodifield paused, but the boss made no reply. Only a quiver in his eyelids

---

[1] photographers' parks:照相馆的布景室。
[2] on his last pins:快不行了。源于成语 on one's pins:活着,健康。
[3] on the strict Q.T.:绝对秘密地。Q.T.:(俚)quiet 的缩写。
[4] Windsor Castle:温莎城堡,英国王室成员居住地,在伦敦以西。
[5] a generous finger:一手指宽度的量。
[6] sacrilege:亵渎神圣。
[7] chaps:嘴或颌。
[8] grave:这里指第一次世界大战期间英军阵亡将士在比利时的墓地。

showed that he heard.

"The girls were delighted with the way the place is kept," piped the old voice. "Beautifully looked after. Couldn't be better if they were at home. You've not been across, have yer?"

"No, no!" For various reasons the boss had not been across.

"There's miles of it," quavered old Woodifield, "and it's all as neat as a garden. Flowers growing on all the graves. Nice broad paths." It was plain from his voice how much he liked a nice broad path.

The pause came again. Then the old man brightened wonderfully.

"D'you know what the hotel made the girls pay for a pot of jam?" he piped. "Ten francs! Robbery, I call it. It was a little pot, so Gertrude says, no bigger than a half-crown[1]. And she hadn't taken more than a spoonful when they charged her ten francs. Gertrude brought the pot away with her to teach 'em a lesson. Quite right, too; it's trading on our feelings. They think because we're over there having a look round we're ready to pay anything. That's what it is." And he turned towards the door.

"Quite right, quite right!" cried the boss, though what was quite right he hadn't the least idea. He came round by his desk, followed the shuffling footsteps to the door, and saw the old fellow out. Woodifield was gone.

For a long moment the boss stayed, staring at nothing, while the grey-haired office messenger, watching him, dodged in and out of his cubbyhole[2] like a dog that expects to be taken for a run. Then: "I'll see nobody for half an hour, Macey," said the boss. "Understand! Nobody at all."

"Very good, sir."

The door shut, the firm heavy steps recrossed the bright carpet, the fat body plumped down in the spring chair, and leaning forward, the boss covered his face with his hands. He wanted, he intended, he had arranged to weep. ...

It had been a terrible shock to him when old Woodifield sprang that remark upon him about the boy's grave. It was exactly as though the earth had opened and he had seen the boy lying there with Woodifield's girls staring down at him. For it was strange. Although over six years had passed away, the boss never thought of the boy except as lying unchanged, unblemished in his uniform, asleep for ever. "My son!" groaned the boss. But no tears came yet. In the past, in the first months and even years after the boy's death, he had only to say those words to be overcome by such grief that nothing short of a violent fit of weeping could relieve him. Time, he had declared then, he had told everybody, could make no difference. Other men perhaps might recover, might live their loss down, but not he. How was it possible! His boy was an only son. Ever since his birth the boss had worked at building up this business for him; it had no other

---

[1] crown:英国旧制 5 先令硬币。
[2] cubbyhole:舒适的小房间。

meaning if it was not for the boy. Life itself had come to have no other meaning. How on earth could he have slaved, denied himself, kept going all those years without the promise for ever before him of the boy's stepping into his shoes[1] and carrying on where he left off?

And that promise had been so near being fulfilled. The boy had been in the office learning the ropes[2] for a year before the war. Every morning they had started off together; they had come back by the same train. And what congratulations he had received as the boy's father! No wonder he had taken to it marvellously. As to his popularity with the staff, every man jack[3] of them down to old Macey couldn't make enough of the boy. And he wasn't in the least spoilt. No, he was just his bright natural self, with the right word for everybody, with that boyish look and his habit of saying, "Simply splendid!"

But all that was over and done with[4] as though it never had been. The day had come when Macey had handed him the telegram that brought the whole place crashing about his head. "Deeply regret to inform you ..." And he had left the office a broken man, with his life in ruins.

Six years ago, six years ... How quickly time passed! It might have happened yesterday. The boss took his hands from his face; he was puzzled. Something seemed to be wrong with him. He wasn't feeling as he wanted to feel. He decided to get up and have a look at the boy's photograph. But it wasn't a favourite photograph of his; the expression was unnatural. It was cold, even stern-looking. The boy had never looked like that.

At that moment the boss noticed that a fly had fallen into his broad inkpot, and was trying feebly but desperately to clamber out again. Help! Help! said those struggling legs. But the sides of the inkpot were wet and slippery; it fell back again and began to swim. The boss took up a pen, picked the fly out of the ink, and shook it on to a piece of blotting-paper. For a fraction of a second it lay still on the dark patch that oozed round it. Then the front legs waved, took hold, and, pulling its small, sodden body up, it began the immense task of cleaning the ink from its wings. Over and under, over and under, went a leg along a wing as the stone goes over and under the scythe[5]. Then there was a pause, while the fly, seeming to stand on the tips of its toes, tried to expand first one wing and then the other. It succeeded at last, and, sitting down, it began, like a minute cat, to clean its face. Now one could imagine that the little front legs rubbed against each other lightly, joyfully. The horrible danger was over; it had escaped; it was ready for life again.

---

[1] stepping into his shoes:接他的班。
[2] learning the ropes:熟悉公司的业务。
[3] every man jack:人人。
[4] done with:完毕。
[5] scythe:割草的大镰刀。

But just then the boss had an idea. He plunged his pen back into the ink, leaned his thick wrist on the blotting-paper, and as the fly tried its wings down came a great heavy blot. What would it make of that! What indeed! The little beggar seemed absolutely cowed, stunned, and afraid to move because of what would happen next. But then, as if painfully, it dragged itself forward. The front legs waved, caught hold, and, more slowly this time, the task began from the beginning.

He's a plucky[1] little devil, thought the boss, and he felt a real admiration for the fly's courage. That was the way to tackle things; that was the right spirit. Never say die; it was only a question of... But the fly had again finished its laborious task, and the boss had just time to refill his pen, to shake fair and square[2] on the new-cleaned body yet another dark drop. What about it this time? A painful moment of suspense followed. But behold, the front legs were again waving; the boss felt a rush of relief. He leaned over the fly and said to it tenderly, "You artful little b..." And he actually had the brilliant notion of breathing on it to help the drying process. All the same, there was something timid and weak about its efforts now, and the boss decided that this time should be the last, as he dipped the pen deep into the inkpot.

It was. The last blot fell on the soaked blotting-paper, and the draggled fly lay in it and did not stir. The back legs were stuck to the body; the front legs were not to be seen.

"Come on," said the boss. "Look sharp![3]" And he stirred it with his pen—in vain. Nothing happened or was likely to happen. The fly was dead.

The boss lifted the corpse on the end of the paper-knife and flung it into the waste-paper basket. But such a grinding feeling of wretchedness seized him that he felt positively frightened. He started forward and pressed the bell for Macey.

"Bring me some fresh blotting-paper," he said sternly, "and look sharp about it." And while the old dog padded away he fell to wondering what it was he had been thinking about before. What was it? It was... He took out his handkerchief and passed it inside his collar. For the life of him he could not remember.

1922

赏 析

《苍蝇》是曼斯菲尔德去世前不久创作的。身体羸弱的退休雇员来看望主人公,一家公司的老板。来客一句不经意的话搅起老板的丧子之痛。送客后,他把自己关在新装修的办公室里,把一只在墨水瓶里挣扎的苍蝇救出后,又一再折磨它,直到苍蝇死去。故事背景非常具体,专注于人物的内心活动,但作者从未清楚地说明这篇小说的用意,于是众说纷纭。人们常视之为批

---

[1] plucky:(尤指成功的希望渺茫时仍)勇敢的,坚决的。
[2] fair and square:不偏不倚。
[3] Look sharp:(军事用语)赶快。

判第一次世界大战的残酷,以及随之而来的绝望。有研究者注意到故事的自传成分:两个老人的儿子战死沙场的时间设定在1915年,就在这一年,曼斯菲尔德的弟弟也死在战场上。在战争中葬送性命的人犹如故事中的那只苍蝇,被自己无法控制的力量杀戮。在曼斯菲尔德的笔记、书信和故事中常出现苍蝇这一形象,用来形容一个婴儿、穿黑衣的小男孩或她的疾病。她曾说,她感到自己像只苍蝇"掉到牛奶罐里,又给捞出来"。苍蝇隐喻无名力量的牺牲品。创作这篇小说时她重病缠身,虚弱无力,对战争感到失望,被放射性治疗弄得疲惫不堪。她就是这只苍蝇,为生存拼命挣扎,最后被命运之轮碾碎。也有评论家认为小说的意义要广泛得多,它展现了人之必死这一不容回避的存在现实,以及人不愿接受这一事实的心理,如两位老人的儿子英年早逝,伍迪菲尔德"虚弱苍老",行将就木,老板的仆人麦西像一只"老狗"。苍蝇的求生失败分别代表了人之生死的几种形态,而老板"对于他自己的生活,他想不起来了"反映出他不愿去想自己终将衰老、必将死亡的逃避心理。曼斯菲尔德虽然并未接触过存在主义,但她的作品已经表达了生存之荒诞的存在主义思想。所以有人说,《苍蝇》是曼斯菲尔德小说中最阴郁的一篇。

  故事体现曼斯菲尔德语言简洁,微言大义的一贯特点。它采用第三人称视角描写人物的心理,更具客观性。人物细微的表情、动作和言语都暗示出心理的变化,如老板送客时他不知所云地应和道:"好啊,好啊。"这暗示他心绪纷乱。背景(老板的办公室)显得非常真实,一下把读者吸引到故事中。另外,多层次的象征也是故事的另一特色,如作为多种隐喻的苍蝇和象征无可逃避的生存环境的墨水瓶。

相关评论

The Use of Symbolism in Katherine Mansfield's "The Fly"
Kai Jansson

  "The Fly," by Katherine Mansfield, is a short story which can be understood best as social criticism. It has long been a staple of literature for authors to veil social criticism with allegory and symbolism in subtle ways, thus forcing the reader to determine for himself what a story may actually mean. For example, the act of the boss dropping ink onto the fly repeatedly to see what it will do makes little sense if taken at face value, but the scene begins to make sense once it is acknowledged that the boss and the fly, as well as the situation itself, are symbols best understood in the context of World War One. In fact, it can be demonstrated that the use of symbolism and allegory is carefully employed in "The Fly" in order to criticise the British military leaders and the elder generation of the early twentieth century who supported the first World War out of unthinking patriotism and a childish desire to win at all costs, themselves remaining willfully ignorant of the horrors of modern warfare into which they sent their nation's sons.

  The fly, first and foremost, is a symbol of the young men who went to war not knowing what horrors awaited them. We are given a glimpse into the fly's point of view in the line which reads, "The horrible danger was over; it had escaped; it was ready for life again." Likewise, no young men who are sent off to war believe that they are going to die. Just as the fly escapes one close scrape with death only to find itself doused with one blot of ink, then another, and another, many of the young soldiers in World War

One were thrust forward into battle again and again until they, like the fly, were killed. As the fly is the boss' plaything, able to live or die based on the latter's whim, the soldiers were little more than pawns in a game waged by old men who knew nothing of what the war was truly like on the frontline.

The boss can be seen as a symbol of the elder class of British who blindly supported the war for the sake of war regardless of the fate of their sons and grandsons. This question must first be asked: Does the boss truly grieve for his son? It may be inferred from the following references that his attempt to mourn is done in order to prove to himself and everyone else that he is very patriotic and has more reason to grieve than anyone. In fact, the boss seems to have set himself up as chief mourner, as indicated in the text: "Other men perhaps might recover, might live their loss down, but not he." After all, "his boy was an only son" who died in the service of the British Empire. The line which reads, "'I'll see nobody for half an hour, Macey,' said the boss. 'Understand? Nobody at all,'" is a strong indication that Macey and the rest of the office staff know full well that the boss has "arranged to weep", indicating that the boss's grief is all for show and that he is trying to fool himself and everyone else that he remains in mourning for his son. His attitude concerning the death of his son seems very emotional on the face of it, but he seems to mourn in a very calculated way, as evidenced in the line which goes, "He wanted, he intended, he had arranged to weep." However, the fact that, after the episode with the fly, he has completely forgotten that he had "arranged to weep" for his son is strong evidence that his surface emotions are not genuine.

The boss also keeps a photographic portrait of his son dressed in his army uniform in his office, despite the fact that he does not particularly like it. "The boss took his hands from his face; he was puzzled. Something seemed to be wrong with him. He wasn't feeling as he wanted to feel. He decided to get up and have a look at the boy's photograph. But it wasn't a favourite photograph of his; the expression was unnatural. It was cold, even stern-looking. The boy had never looked like that." If he wanted to remind himself of the way his son really was, then he surely could have picked a better photograph to adorn his office wall. This photograph seems to be there in order to properly motivate him to mourn when he "arranges" to do so, as well as to exhibit his patriotism. It also allows him to preserve the image of his son as a soldier unblemished by warfare. The truth of his son's wartime death, which was likely very grisly and painful, is something he refuses to acknowledge, as indicated by the passage which reads, "It was exactly as though the earth had opened and he had seen the boy lying there with Woodifield's girls staring down at him. For it was strange. Although over six years had passed away, the boss never thought of the boy except as lying unchanged, unblemished in his uniform, asleep for ever." After all, "for various reasons the boss had not been across" to visit his son's grave in Belgium. To do this would shatter the image in his mind of his son being the type of valiant soldier popularised in wartime propaganda.

The boss is thus also symbolic of the inept military leaders who never saw the war firsthand but planned the battles from well behind the front and who did not care as much about the fate of the young soldiers who fought their battles as much as winning the war. Indeed, when the boss watches the fly struggle for life after having dropped a blot of ink upon it, his thoughts read like the type of patriotic, yet hollow-sounding, slogans a British military leader at the time would try to rally his troops with: "He's a plucky little devil, thought the boss, and he felt a real admiration for the fly's courage. That was the way to tackle things; that was the right spirit. Never say die." He later adds "Look sharp!" to this list of hackneyed phrases. The act of dropping ink upon the fly after watching it struggle back to life is itself symbolic of the way the young soldiers were sent off to various battles which served no purpose but to reduce the numbers of soldiers on both sides in that war of attrition. The boss treats the fly as a plaything, just as the British military leaders treated their soldiers in the "game of war". He pushes the fly to its limit and, once he sees that the fly is beginning to recover from the last blot of ink, he drops just one more which, of course, ends up killing the fly. One may easily imagine that, if the boss is given an endless supply of flies to play within such a way, he will never grown tired of playing his game with each and every one of them, casually tossing aside their corpses when they prove to be physically and mentally unable to handle the challenges he sets before them, just as the British generals threw a seemingly endless supply of soldiers into the slaughtering grounds of World War One.

This short story is an excellent example of social criticism through symbolism and allegory. Furthermore, it holds a lesson within it which is as important today as it was when it was originally published in 1923: War is not a game. The last line of this short story which reads, "For the life of him he could not remember, must be taken as a warning to all to remember the hard-won lessons of war "lest we forget" and find ourselves in a war which is much worse. Sadly, the war-torn history of the world in the eighty-five years and more since the end of the so-called "War to End All Wars" has proven that mankind has yet to learn the ultimate folly of war.

Source: http://www.kaijansson.com/docs/thefly.pdf.

问题与思考

1. In what way is the fly a symbol? What does the fate of the fly imply?
2. What is the importance of the boss's description of his office?
3. How is the boss characterized at the beginning of the story? How does that characterization change? How does he treat Woodifield and Macey?
4. Discuss the part in which the boss toys with the fly. What is his motivation in torturing it?
5. What does the story's conclusion mean? "For the life of him he could remember."

What and why can't he remember? Who or what does the boss represent?

阅读链接

1. http：//www.readbookonline.net/readOnLine/1355：收集了曼斯菲尔德16篇短篇小说,可全文阅读并下载。
2. http：//www.katherinemansfield.net/life/briefbio1.htm：全面介绍曼斯菲尔德的创作及影响,她的部分作品文本,纪念她的活动,及相关链接。
3. http：//www.bookcouncil.org.nz/writers/mansfieldk.html：对曼斯菲尔德的评论。

2. 情节(Plot)

情节是指叙事性文学作品中由人物关系、人物行动所构成的一系列生活事件，体现人和社会、人和人、人和具体环境之间的矛盾和冲突。它一般包括开端(exposition)、冲突(conflict)、高潮(climax)、结局(denouement)四个阶段。情节是作品的基本要素之一，由场景、人物和事件构成。

情节(plot)有别于人们常说的故事(story)。故事是"按时间先后顺序安排的叙述性事件"，[1]如"国王死了，后来王后也死了。"情节是对事件进行艺术性的重排，不一定完全遵循时间顺序。例如，"王后死了，没人知道原因，后来才发现她是因国王去世过于悲痛而去世的。"这个情节包含了悬念和刻意设计的叙述形式。故事呈现的是事件的内容，而情节强调的是事件的因果关系。

作家在创作短篇小说时，会根据创作意图对构成情节的四个阶段进行灵活处理。开端一般提供故事发生的基本背景，如时间、地点、人物身份和社会历史背景。讲究开门见山的短篇小说通常会省略这些背景或一笔带过。冲突指人物的行为、意志、欲望的对抗和交锋。相对于长篇小说，冲突在短篇小说中更为集中，是整个作品的核心。冲突有明显的，如《暴力的使用》中医生要小女孩张嘴，而小女孩拼命反抗。也有不明显的，如乔伊斯的《集市》中小男孩的浪漫幻想和现实世界的冲突。高潮是冲突达到顶峰的那一刻，标志情节发生重大转折，为收尾做铺垫，高潮意味着主人公实现了或没有实现目标。紧随其后的是结尾，陈述高潮带来的后果，是对冲突的最后解决。短篇小说的精彩之处通常表现在紧密相连的高潮和结尾。优秀的短篇小说一个显著特点就是在高潮发生突转，结尾令人感到意外但又合情合理。许多短篇小说的叙述线索比较清楚，如厄普代克的《"A & P"》分为开端(商场里年轻的收银员被三个穿比基尼的姑娘所吸引)、冲突(三个姑娘与思想保守的商场经理发生冲突，被赶出商场)、高潮(收银员与经理发生冲突，辞职)和结局(辞职后痛苦的迷茫)。

为了表现主题、刻画人物或增加艺术感染力，现代短篇小说常以顿悟性(epiphany)情节来取代冲突性情节，有意打乱事件的发展顺序，一般有两种情况：一种以结尾开始，如《献给爱米丽的玫瑰》这个构思精巧的故事以爱米丽之死开头，然后以倒叙展开，在一个个悬念中刻画爱米丽这一美国旧南方"淑女"的悲剧形象；另一种从中间部分(medias res)开始，先展示令人激动或有意义的情节，然后才返回开头。如劳伦斯的《盲人》以女主人公伊莎贝尔在家里盼望丈夫回家开始，再回头评述夫妻关系。在推进事件时，闪回(flashback)和铺陈(foreshadowing)是两种有用的技巧。闪回即唤醒人物记忆中的某一情景，使与眼前最为相关的过去随时显现。如在《被抛弃的韦罗瑟尔奶奶》中，韦罗瑟尔奶奶在半清醒半昏迷的状态中不断回忆自己一生中的重大事件。铺陈则通过重要的暗示使后面发生的、看似无甚意义的事件或细节有了意义，从而激起读者的兴趣。例如在《献给爱米丽的玫瑰》中，对"臭味"的描写预示了后来人们发现荷马·巴伦的尸骨。

在顿悟性情节中，主人公相对被动，不是由他的意志来推动情节，而是事情接二连三发生在

---

[1] E. M. Forster, *Aspects of the Novel* (Penguin Books, 1984), p. 87.

他身上，结尾展现人物对真理的一种理解，对生活的一种感悟。乔伊斯的《集市》讲的是一个小男孩去赶集的故事，情节并不扣人心弦。小男孩初坠情网，却遭遇粗俗的现实，他最终意识到浪漫的爱情不过是一场幻想，在痛苦中从天真走向成熟。故事的核心当然不是赶集这一普通事件，而是主人公小男孩于平凡生活中获得的顿悟。因此一个赶集的故事就成了一个人成长的心路历程。

情节是对事件的安排，要把握故事情节，读者在阅读时需要记忆和思考并用。一方面，我们要记住读过的细节；另一方面，对于阅读过程向前推进时不断发现的新情况，我们要把它们与前面的线索联系起来进行重组，思考新出现的因果关系，从而理解整个故事的来龙去脉。

James Joyce (1882—1941)

作者简介

詹姆斯·乔伊斯(James Joyce,1882—1941)出生于爱尔兰都柏林一个境况一般的家庭,在教会学校里接受了良好的教育,成绩出众,并显示出非凡的文学才能。1898年他进入都柏林大学学习现代语言。1902年大学毕业,随后赴巴黎学医,次年4月因母亲病危回到都柏林。1904年他与在芬恩饭店工作的诺拉相识,两人一见钟情,于同年10月一起离开爱尔兰,前往瑞士苏黎世,因工作没有着落,随即转到意大利东部城市的里雅斯特。乔伊斯认为爱尔兰会压抑他的文学才华,便选择留在欧洲大陆,以教授英语和为报刊撰稿维持生计。第一次世界大战爆发后,乔伊斯于1915年7月离开的里雅斯特,来到苏黎世,在那里得到英国女权主义者和出版商哈丽叶·肖·韦弗的大力资助。在接下来的25年中她
每年接济他几千英镑,使他不再为生活所累,可以专心创作。从1920年起他定居巴黎。乔伊斯常年饱受眼疾折磨,尽管接受过多次手术,到晚年几乎完全失明。1940年6月巴黎沦陷,乔伊斯于年底携全家前往苏黎世,第二年元月因患胃溃疡致胃穿孔去世,终年59岁。

文学创作

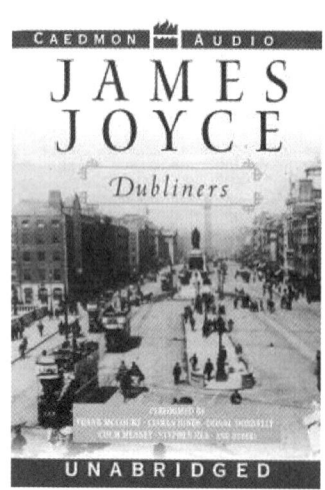  

如果要列出对20世纪西方文学影响最大的三四个作家,那么詹姆斯·乔伊斯会名列其中,他被公认为是"继莎士比亚之后英语文学史上最伟大的作家"。乔伊斯的主要作品包括短篇小说集《都柏林人》(*Dubliners*,1914)、长篇小说《青年艺术家的画像》(*A Portrait of the Artist as a Young Man*,1916)、意识流小说《尤利西斯》(*Ulysses*,1922)和《芬尼根的守灵夜》(*Finnegans*

Wake,1939)。

乔伊斯虽然长年侨居国外,但他的作品几乎都是关于故土爱尔兰的,讲述它的历史、宗教、民族独立和国民性,并使之成为全人类及其历史的缩影。1904 年他开始创作《都柏林人》,它包括 15 个主题连贯的短篇小说,意在"展示都柏林这个城市瘫痪的灵魂"。带有强烈自传色彩的《青年艺术家的画像》以主人公斯蒂芬·代德勒斯的内心意识为视角,讲述其成长历程,阐明了现代社会中艺术家与社会的矛盾关系:艺术家是负有社会使命的孤独者。他的意识流杰作《尤利西斯》展现了三个小人物一天的生活和内心活动,着重塑造了布鲁姆这个既卑俗又高尚的反英雄(anti-hero)形象。作品创造性地使用了大量的意识流手法,不同的人称视角频繁交错,片断、无标点的长篇独白、古今散文体等多种文本形式杂糅在一起,被很多评论者认为是 20 世纪最伟大的一部小说。《芬尼根的守灵夜》以都柏林近郊一家酒店老板的潜意识和梦幻为线索,充满了外国语言、人造的词汇、违规的语法,还有大量的双关语、字谜和其他文字游戏,至今大多数人依然难以读懂。

读乔伊斯的小说,人们最强烈的感受是"难",难在密集的典故,错综复杂的结构和源源不断的意识流。不过,乔伊斯对英语语言节奏的敏感,他的幽默感,他对人类行为和情感的细致观察,富于表现力的描写以及独创精神,又使得这种难的背后充满了阅读的乐趣。

作 品

Araby

North Richmond Street, being blind[1], was a quiet street except at the hour when the Christian Brothers' School set the boys free. An uninhabited house of two storeys stood at the blind end, detached from its neighbours in a square ground. The other houses of the street, conscious of decent lives within them, gazed at one another with brown imperturbable faces.

The former tenant of our house, a priest, had died in the back drawing-room. Air, musty from having been long enclosed, hung in all the rooms,[2] and the waste room behind the kitchen was littered with old useless papers. Among these I found a few paper-covered books, the pages of which were curled and damp: *The Abbot*, by Walter Scott, *The Devout Communnicant* and *The Memoirs of Vidocq*[3]. I liked the last best because its leaves were yellow. The wild garden behind the house contained a central apple-tree and a few straggling bushes under one of which I found the late tenant's rusty bicycle-pump. He had been a very charitable priest; in his will he had left all his money to institutions and the furniture of his house to his sister.

When the short days of winter came dusk fell before we had well eaten our dinners. When we met in the street the houses had grown sombre. The space of sky above us was

---

[1] being blind: being a dead-end street,一条死胡同。
[2] Air, musty from... all the rooms: 由于长期关闭,所有的房间都弥漫着一股霉湿的气味。
[3] *The Abbot*: 英国小说家 Walter Scott(1771—1832)写的传奇小说。*The Devout Communnicant*: 18 世纪英国方济各会(Franciscan)修道士 Pacificus Baker(1695—1774)写的宗教著作。*The Memoirs of Vidocq*: 法国人 Francois-Jules Vidocq(1775—1857)写的回忆录,此人曾是罪犯,后成为一名侦探。

the colour of ever-changing violet and towards it the lamps of the street lifted their feeble lanterns. The cold air stung us and we played till our bodies glowed[1]. Our shouts echoed in the silent street. The career of our play brought us through the dark muddy lanes behind the houses where we ran the gantlet of the rough tribes from the cottages[2], to the back doors of the dark dripping gardens where odours arose from the ashpits, to the dark odorous stables where a coachman smoothed and combed the horse or shook music from the buckled harness. When we returned to the street light from the kitchen windows had filled the areas. If my uncle was seen turning the corner we hid in the shadow until we had seen him safely housed. Or if Mangan's sister came out on the doorstep to call her brother in to his tea we watched her from our shadow peer up and down the street. We waited to see whether she would remain or go in and, if she remained, we left our shadow and walked up to Mangan's steps resignedly[3]. She was waiting for us, her figure defined by the light from the half-opened door. Her brother always teased her before he obeyed and I stood by the railings looking at her. Her dress swung as she moved her body and the soft rope of her hair tossed from side to side.

Every morning I lay on the floor in the front parlour watching her door. The blind[4] was pulled down to within an inch of the sash so that I could not be seen. When she came out on the doorstep my heart leaped. I ran to the hall, seized my books and followed her. I kept her brown figure always in my eye and, when we came near the point at which our ways diverged, I quickened my pace and passed her. This happened morning after morning. I had never spoken to her, except for a few casual words, and yet her name was like a summons to all my foolish blood.

Her image accompanied me even in places the most hostile to romance. On Saturday evenings when my aunt went marketing I had to go to carry some of the parcels. We walked through the flaring streets, jostled by drunken men and bargaining women, amid the curses of labourers, the shrill litanies[5] of shop-boys who stood on guard by the barrels of pigs' cheeks, the nasal chanting of street-singers, who sang a *come-all-you* about O'Donovan Rossa,[6] or a ballad about the troubles in our native land. These noises converged in a single sensation of life for me: I imagined that I bore my chalice[7] safely through a throng of foes. Her name sprang to my lips at moments in strange

---

[1] till our bodies glowed: 直到我们全身发热。
[2] we ran the gantlet... the cottages: 我们遭到住在那些小屋子里的粗人们的咒骂。run the gantlet: 古代军队里的一种刑法。受惩罚的人要从两排不断挥舞木棍的人中间走过挨打。现在这个短语意为"to proceed while under attack from both sides, as by criticism, gossip, etc."。
[3] resignedly: 顺从地。
[4] The blind: 百叶窗。
[5] litanies: (宗教仪式里的)连祷文,通常有固定的问答格式。这里指 shopboys 单调重复的叫卖声。
[6] who sang a come-... O'Donovan Rossa: 都柏林街头歌手卖唱时,往往以 Come all you gallant Irishmen/And listen to my song 为引子。O'Donovan Rossa: 指 Jeremiah O'Donovan(1831—1915)爱尔兰独立运动领导人,被人称为 Dynamite Rossa。
[7] chalice: 圣杯。

prayers and praises which I myself did not understand. My eyes were often full of tears (I could not tell why) and at times a flood from my heart seemed to pour itself out into my bosom. I thought little of the future. I did not know whether I would ever speak to her or not or, if I spoke to her, how I could tell her of my confused adoration. But my body was like a harp and her words and gestures were like fingers running upon the wires.

One evening I went into the back drawing-room in which the priest had died. It was a dark rainy evening and there was no sound in the house. Through one of the broken panes I heard the rain impinge upon the earth, the fine incessant needles of water playing in the sodden beds. Some distant lamp or lighted window gleamed below me. I was thankful that I could see so little. All my senses seemed to desire to veil themselves and, feeling that I was about to slip from them, I pressed the palms of my hands together until they trembled, murmuring: "O love! O love!" many times.

At last she spoke to me. When she addressed the first words to me I was so confused that I did not know what to answer. She asked me was I going to Araby. I forgot whether I answered yes or no. It would be a splendid bazaar, she said she would love to go.

— And why can't you? I asked.

While she spoke she turned a silver bracelet round and round her wrist. She could not go, she said, because there would be a retreat that week in her convent[1]. Her brother and two other boys were fighting for their caps and I was alone at the railings. She held one of the spikes, bowing her head towards me. The light from the lamp opposite our door caught the white curve of her neck, lit up her hair that rested there and, falling, lit up the hand upon the railing. It fell over one side of her dress and caught the white border of a petticoat, just visible as she stood at ease.

— It's well for you, she said.

— If I go, I said, I will bring you something.

What innumerable follies laid waste my waking and sleeping thoughts after that evening! I wished to annihilate the tedious intervening days. I chafed against[2] the work of school. At night in my bedroom and by day in the classroom her image came between me and the page I strove to read. The syllables of the word Araby were called to me through the silence in which my soul luxuriated and cast an Eastern enchantment over me. I asked for leave to go to the bazaar on Saturday night. My aunt was surprised and hoped it was not some Freemason[3] affair. I answered few questions in class. I

---

[1] a retreat... in her convent: 她上的教会学校里那个星期有次静修。retreat: 指在一段时间内更加严格遵守教规。convent: 修道院；这里指 Miss Mangan 上的教会学校。

[2] chafed against: 对……感到不耐烦。

[3] Freemason: 共济会。国际性秘密团体，旨在传授并执行其互助纲领，提倡仁爱、贞洁、互助精神。爱尔兰的天主教会把共济会纲领视作基督教徒反对天主教的阴谋。所以这里主人公的姨妈希望他夜访 Araby 集市与共济会的事情无关。

watched my master's face pass from amiability to sternness; he hoped I was not beginning to idle. I could not call my wandering thoughts together. I had hardly any patience with the serious work of life which, now that it stood between me and my desire, seemed to me child's play, ugly monotonous child's play.

On Saturday morning I reminded my uncle that I wished to go to the bazaar in the evening. He was fussing at the hallstand, looking for the hat-brush, and answered me curtly:

—Yes, boy, I know.

As he was in the hall I could not go into the front parlour and lie at the window. I left the house in bad humour and walked slowly towards the school. The air was pitilessly raw and already my heart misgave me.[1]

When I came home to dinner my uncle had not yet been home. Still it was early. I sat staring at the clock for some time and, when its ticking began to irritate me, I left the room. I mounted the staircase and gained the upper part of the house. The high cold empty gloomy rooms liberated me and I went from room to room singing. From the front window I saw my companions playing below in the street. Their cries reached me weakened and indistinct and, leaning my forehead against the cool glass, I looked over at the dark house where she lived. I may have stood there for an hour, seeing nothing but the brown-clad figure cast by my imagination, touched discreetly by the lamplight at the curved neck, at the hand upon the railings and at the border below the dress.

When I came downstairs again I found Mrs. Mercer sitting at the fire. She was an old garrulous woman, a pawnbroker's widow, who collected used stamps for some pious purpose. I had to endure the gossip of the tea-table. The meal was prolonged beyond an hour and still my uncle did not come. Mrs. Mercer stood up to go: she was sorry she couldn't wait any longer, but it was after eight o'clock and she did not like to be out late as the night air was bad for her. When she had gone I began to walk up and down the room, clenching my fists. My aunt said:

— I'm afraid you may put off your bazaar for this night of Our Lord[2].

At nine o'clock I heard my uncle's latchkey in the halldoor. I heard him talking to himself and heard the hallstand rocking when it had received the weight of his overcoat. I could interpret these signs. When he was midway through his dinner I asked him to give me the money to go to the bazaar. He had forgotten.

— The people are in bed and after their first sleep now, he said.

I did not smile. My aunt said to him energetically:

— Can't you give him the money and let him go? You've kept him late enough as it is.

---

[1] The air was... misgave me:空气阴冷得近乎无情,我心中已是惴惴不安。raw:又冷又湿,令人难受;misgive:使人产生怀疑、忧虑或恐惧。

[2] this night of Our Lord:这个星期六晚上。

My uncle said he was very sorry he had forgotten. He said he believed in the old saying: "All work and no play makes Jack a dull boy." He asked me where I was going and, when I had told him a second time he asked me did I know *The Arab's Farewell to his Steed*[1]. When I left the kitchen he was about to recite the opening lines of the piece to my aunt.

I held a florin tightly in my hand as I strode down Buckingham Street towards the station. The sight of the streets thronged with buyers and glaring with gas recalled to me the purpose of my journey. I took my seat in a third-class carriage of a deserted train. After an intolerable delay the train moved out of the station slowly. It crept onward among ruinous house and over the twinkling river. At Westland Row Station a crowd of people pressed to the carriage doors; but the porters moved them back, saying that it was a special train for the bazaar. I remained alone in the bare carriage. In a few minutes the train drew up beside an improvised wooden platform[2]. I passed out on to the road and saw by the lighted dial of a clock that it was ten minutes to ten. In front of me was a large building which displayed the magical name.

I could not find any sixpenny entrance and, fearing that the bazaar would be closed, I passed in quickly through a turnstile, handing a shilling to a weary-looking man. I found myself in a big hall girdled at half its height by a gallery[3]. Nearly all the stalls were closed and the greater part of the hall was in darkness. I recognised a silence like that which pervades a church after a service. I walked into the centre of the bazaar timidly. A few people were gathered about the stalls which were still open. Before a curtain, over which the words *Café Chantant*[4] were written in coloured lamps, two men were counting money on a salver[5]. I listened to the fall of the coins.

Remembering with difficulty why I had come I went over to one of the stalls and examined porcelain vases and flowered tea-sets. At the door of the stall a young lady was talking and laughing with two young gentlemen. I remarked their English accents and listened vaguely to their conversation.

— O, I never said such a thing!

— O, but you did!

— O, but I didn't!

— Didn't she say that?

— Yes. I heard her.

---

[1] *The Arab's Farewell to his Steed*:英国诗人 Caroline Norton 写的歌谣。这首诗名应为 *The Arab to His Favorite Steed*,叙述了一个阿拉伯人卖掉了心爱的马,继而伤心不已,便将卖马所得的金钱全都扔了。这里"我"的叔叔提及这首诗是因为他错将 Araby 听成了 Arab。

[2] improvised wooden platform:临时搭成的木板站台。

[3] a big hall... by a gallery:一个大厅,由一条环形长廊将其分成上下两层。

[4] *Café Chantant*:巴黎一家夜总会的名称。

[5] salver:(行圣餐礼时经常使用的)银质托盘。

—O, there's a...fib[1]!

Observing me the young lady came over and asked me did I wish to buy anything. The tone of her voice was not encouraging; she seemed to have spoken to me out of a sense of duty. I looked humbly at the great jars that stood like eastern guards at either side of the dark entrance to the stall and murmured:

—No, thank you.

The young lady changed the position of one of the vases and went back to the two young men. They began to talk of the same subject. Once or twice the young lady glanced at me over her shoulder.

I lingered before her stall, though I knew my stay was useless, to make my interest in her wares seem the more real. Then I turned away slowly and walked down the middle of the bazaar. I allowed the two pennies to fall against the sixpence in my pocket. I heard a voice call from one end of the gallery that the light was out. The upper part of the hall was now completely dark.

Gazing up into the darkness I saw myself as a creature driven and derided by vanity; and my eyes burned with anguish and anger.

1905

赏 析

《集市》是《都柏林人》中的第三篇短篇小说,讲述了一个小男孩浪漫幻想破碎的成长故事,属于乔伊斯早期的作品。

故事中的小男孩爱上了邻居家的女孩,星期六晚上去集市上为她买一样东西来表达自己的爱意。叙述者没有点明女孩的真实姓名,男孩只知道她是"曼根的姐姐"。这一细节表明:他爱上的只是一个美丽的意象,而不是真正的人。当他赶到快要散去的集市时,一个女摊主和两个年轻的英国男子的打情骂俏令他看到生活真实的一面。他走出集市,凝望黑暗,心里只剩下"炽热的痛苦和愤怒"。小男孩梦想的破灭暗示了理想与现实的冲突。无人居住的小楼、散发霉味的房间、冰冷的空气、微弱的街灯、阴暗泥泞的巷子等等,这些都暗示了这一苦涩的现实就是都柏林陈腐的氛围对人的情感的压抑。乔伊斯注重用词的视觉效果,以光影的幻动来刻画环境,烘托小男孩的浪漫情感,强调其情绪的突变。

在故事中,宗教成了一种隐喻。小男孩和婶婶去赶集,他拎着东西,穿过人群,这时,他激情满怀,把自己视为宗教英雄,"手捧圣餐杯"穿过"成群的仇敌",而女孩的名字成了伴随他的祷文和颂词。小男孩借宗教来理想化自己的情感,然而朦胧的浪漫幻想又使他的宗教情感流于表面。

《集市》放弃了传统小说"冲突-高潮"的情节结构。乔伊斯按照"顿悟"来谋篇布局。根据乔伊斯自己的定义,"顿悟"(epiphany)是"一种突然的精神显现,或者是发生在卑俗的言词或行动中,或者是发生在心灵本身一个难忘的阶段。"《集市》故事结尾时,小男孩从他理想化的追求中惊醒,意识到自己一直生活在"自负和虚荣"之中。乔伊斯把兴趣焦点投射到人物精神世界的变

---

[1] fib:(无伤大雅的)谎言。

化上面,"顿悟"的结构模式为他提供了一个有效手段,也使《集市》成为现代短篇小说的佳作。

相关评论

"Araby": Singing in the Rain
Gerald Doherty

Perhaps the most remarkable feature of the short opening paragraph is its paradoxical fusion of vision and blindness: in foregrounding the visual, it also downgrades it. The description of North Richmond street—itself a sharply edged vignette[1]—seems instantly to come under a blind, a shutdown on looking: objects face, without seeing each other. Here *blind* is the key word, whether it connotes[2] the nature of the street ("being blind"), or the spot where the uninhabited house stands ("at the blind end"), or the dazed "gaze" of the houses which register, without perceiving each other ("with brown imperturbable faces"). From the start, it seems the visual may *not* be the predestined medium to project the boy's rapturous[3] erotic release.

The paragraph that follows confirms this prognosis[4]. Moving dejectedly[5] about the silent house and garden, a jaded[6] camera-eye picks out only the dusty, "musty," and "rusty." Latching on to the privative, it splits off objects from their once burgeoning functions: the "musty" back drawing-room where the priest died, the dusty "waste room" littered with paper, the "rusty bicycle-pump" in the garden. Such dry itemizing has its corollary[7] in the obsession with listing: the titles of those "paper-covered books" (*The Abbot*, *The Devout Communicant*, *The Memoirs of Vidocq*) strewn inconsequentially around the waste room. The inventory[8] impulse exhausts itself not, it seems, for lack of further objects to list, but because the short-story rubric demands such economy.

The third paragraph seals the association between vision and deprivation: eyes are mere supplementary organs, linked to the failing or the absence of light. Because "feeble lanterns" alone light up the streets, "shouts" are the sole index of where the local boys are, as they blindly chase through the "dark muddy lanes" and the "dark dripping gardens." With uncanny proleptic[9] precision, this first evocation of wetness ("dripping") also triggers the first authentic *sound*-image—the coachman shaking

---

[1] vignette:虚光照片(或画像)。
[2] connote:隐含,意味着。
[3] rapturous:欣喜若狂。
[4] prognosis:预测。
[5] dejectedly:沮丧地,灰心地。
[6] jaded:厌倦的,腻烦的。
[7] corollary:必然的结果;推论。
[8] inventory:详细清单。
[9] proleptic:预期的,预想的。

"music from the buckled harness." Linking musical vibration with soft lubrication, it loosens up and liberates elements previously knotted and tangled together.

Source: Jelena O. Krstovic, ed. *Short Story Criticism* Vol. 118.

Blind streets and seeing houses: Araby's dim glass revisited
Margot Norris

The curious figure of the reflective darkness ("Gazing up into the darkness I saw myself") of an extinguished dream ("the light was out"), suggests that this story will be illuminated by blindness, and that the boy who finds emptiness in "Araby," the figure of romance, is in turn found empty, a personification rather than a person, by the story. This strange locution[1] at the story's end, that has the darkened gallery of "Araby" appear to "see" the boy in a way that lets him see himself, as though it were a dark mirror catching him in its eye, recapitulates[2] the strange topopoeia[3] of the story's opening, where streets are personified as "blind" and houses as "seeing." This topographia[4] frames the narration in a way that sets it up for a chiasmus[5]: the story that opens with the "real" estate of North Richmond Street closes with its antipode[6] of the "unreal" estate of "Araby"—but only after the two places have, as it were, traded places. What makes the crossing over possible is that "Araby," the name of a longing for romance displaced onto a mythologized Oriental geography, suppresses the mediation of commerce and conceals the operations by which the fantasy of an exoticized and seductive East is a commercial fabrication produced by that realm the boy finds "most hostile to romance"—the marketplace. Commerce produces not only the trinkets[7] and commodities the boy does not want, the vases and tea sets he spurns, and the parcels he bears like an irksome cross while shopping with his aunt every Saturday night. Commerce also produces fantasy and magic through language, "The syllables of the word Araby were called to me through the silence in which my soul luxuriated and cast an Eastern enchantment over me." The narration of "Araby" is presumably neither a commodity, or a charity, like the ambiguously configured bazaar in the story. But it resorts to the same power of language, the power to aestheticize and glamorize what is common and mean ("the magical name"), that the operation of advertising borrows from poetry.

Source: *Studies in Short Fiction*. 32.3 (Summer 1995): 309.

---

[1] locution:表达方式。
[2] recapitulates:扼要重述,概括。
[3] topopoeia:图像制作艺术。
[4] topographia:地形描绘。
[5] chiasmus:交错配列。
[6] antipode:恰恰相反的事物,另一个极端。
[7] trinket:小饰物,小摆设。

问题与思考

1. Often a setting can do more than tell the reader where the action is taking place and convey the atmosphere; it can express a quality of life. Read the beginning sentences carefully. What do the beginning sentences do besides describing the physical space? What does it say about Dublin?
2. At what moments in the story does the boy romanticize, or project an air of enchantment upon the ordinary life? At what other moments in the story does the boy confront reality? What does he find so bitterly disillusioning in his visit to the bazaar?
3. What is the nature of the boy's sudden realization? How does Joyce help prepare the readers for this moment of illumination?
4. "I imagined that I bore my chalice safely through a throng of foes." What does the author use the word chalice? Notice other religious images in the story. Discuss their significance with regard to theme.
5. From what point of view is the story told? What is the relation between the narrator and the boy? Are they exactly the same person?

阅读链接

1. http://www.online-literature.com/james_joyce：乔伊斯生平,收录他部分的长短篇小说、戏剧和诗歌作品。
2. http://www.creativequotations.com/one/617.htm：乔伊斯名言录。
3. http://www.jamesjoyce.ie：内容最为全面的乔伊斯网站。

William Faulkner (1897—1962)

作者简介

威廉·福克纳(William Faulkner,1897—1962)出生于密西西比州北部的纽爱尔巴尼。五岁时,全家迁至密西西比奥克斯福县,福克纳在那里生活了一辈子,很少离开。和美国的许多作家一样,福克纳没有上过大学,但他学习勤奋,阅读广泛,从《圣经》到现代的法国象征派诗歌、乔伊斯和艾略特都有涉猎。1919 年,福克纳开始写作,多为诗歌。1925 年,他和当时已经成名的作家舍伍德·安德森建立友谊。在安德森的影响下,他从诗歌转向小说,以自己的家乡奥克斯福县为蓝本,虚构了"约克纳帕塔法县",创作了一系列长篇和短篇小说,蜚声文坛。福克纳曾到欧洲旅行五个多月,游览了意大利、法国、英国等地的名胜古迹,开阔了视野,并最终成为南方旧传统的批判者。1949 年,福克纳获诺贝尔文学奖,此后他从未停止过文学创作。1962 年 7 月 6 日,福克纳在自己最后一部长篇小说《强盗们》(*The Reivers*,1962)出版一个多月后去世,终年 65 岁。

文学创作

福克纳是美国当代一位伟大的作家,南方文艺复兴最杰出的代表。他的大部分作品讲述的都是发生在他那片"邮票般大小的故土"上的故事。在他笔下,这片土地成为美国旧南方衰败的缩影:经济落后,道德沦丧,顽固抵制北方工业文明的进程。他作品中的人物大多来自南方贵族家庭,但家道中落,风光不再,他们心理扭曲,行为乖张,大都是清教主义、种族主义、父权制度和拜金主义的牺牲品。福克纳的代表作品包括《喧嚣与骚动》(*The Sound and the Fury*,1929)、《我弥留之际》(*As I Lay Dying*,1930)、《圣殿》(*Sanctuary*,1931)、《八月之光》(*Light in August*,1932)、《押沙龙,押沙龙》(*Absalom,Absalom*!,1936)等。

  长篇小说《喧嚣与骚动》是福克纳的第一部约克纳帕塔法小说,也是他最有名的作品。书名出典于莎士比亚悲剧《麦克白》第五幕第五场中主人公麦克白的著名独白。故事发生在20世纪初的约克纳帕塔法县杰斐逊镇,通过一个姓康普生的南方世家的没落,为南方传统和贵族精神谱写了一曲挽歌。《喧嚣与骚动》采用多角度叙述手法,结合意识流、蒙太奇、闪回等多种现代主义创作手法,颠覆了平铺直叙的传统叙事模式,是一部复线结构的经典之作。

  在主题和人物方面,福克纳的不少长篇小说源自短篇小说。虽然短篇小说很少使用长篇小说的意识流手法,但同样注重艺术手法,如经常用长句进行场景描写,句式愈复杂,人物的思想和心理也愈复杂,如《烧马棚》("Barn Burning")里对主人公沙地害怕父亲被杀时紧张心情的描写。场景与场景、场景与人物链接在一起,达到过去与现在的并置、人与景的合而为一,如《献给爱米丽的玫瑰》("A Rose For Emily")中爱米莉所住的老宅的外观和她的模样相互映照。环境与主题关系密切,如在《干燥的九月》("Dry September")中,炎热使人失去理智,从而暗示种族主义思想的冷酷。总之,福克纳总能依照主题选择合适的风格,他的小说创作因此独树一帜。

作　　品

A Rose for Emily

I

  When Miss Emily Grierson died, our whole town went to her funeral: the men through a sort of respectful affection for a fallen monument[1], the women mostly out of curiosity to see the inside of her house, which no one save an old manservant—a combined gardener and cook—had seen in at least ten years.

  It was a big, squarish frame house that had once been white, decorated with cupolas and spires and scrolled balconies in the heavily lightsome style[2] of the seventies, set on what had once been our most select street. But garages and cotton gins[3] had encroached and obliterated even the august names of that neighborhood; only Miss Emily's house was left, lifting its stubborn and coquettish decay[4] above the cotton

---

[1] a fallen monument:倒塌的纪念碑。这里指 Miss Emily Grierson 之死。她被视作传统观念及生活方式的象征,她的去世犹如一座纪念碑的倒塌。

[2] decorated with cupolas... lightsome style:装点着19世纪70年代风格的圆形屋顶、尖塔和涡形花纹的阳台,带着一种既沉重又轻盈的气息。

[3] cotton gins:轧棉机。

[4] coquettish decay:这是矛盾修饰法。coquettish(轻浮的、卖弄风情的)使人想到生命力的旺盛,decay 使人想到死亡。把这两个词并置,如同前句中的 heavily lightsome,给整篇作品带上了一种奇特而阴郁的色彩。

wagons and the gasoline pumps—an eyesore among eyesores. And now Miss Emily had gone to join the representatives of those august names where they lay in the cedar-bemused cemetery[1] among the ranked and anonymous graves of Union and Confederate[2] soldiers who fell at the battle of Jefferson.

Alive, Miss Emily had been a tradition, a duty, and a care; a sort of hereditary obligation upon the town, dating from that day in 1894 when Colonel Sartoris, the mayor—he who fathered the edict[3] that no Negro woman should appear on the streets without an apron—remitted her taxes, the dispensation dating from the death of her father on into perpetuity. Not that Miss Emily would have accepted charity. Colonel Sartoris invented an involved tale to the effect that[4] Miss Emily's father had loaned money to the town, which the town, as a matter of business, preferred this way of repaying. Only a man of Colonel Sartoris' generation and thought could have invented it, and only a woman could have believed it.

When the next generation, with its more modern ideas, became mayors and aldermen[5], this arrangement created some little dissatisfaction. On the first of the year they mailed her a tax notice. February came, and there was no reply. They wrote her a formal letter, asking her to call at the sheriff's office at her convenience. A week later the mayor wrote her himself, offering to call or to send his car for her, and received in reply a note on paper of an archaic shape, in a thin, flowing calligraphy[6] in faded ink, to the effect that she no longer went out at all. The tax notice was also enclosed, without comment.

They called a special meeting of the Board of Aldermen. A deputation waited upon her, knocked at the door through which no visitor had passed since she ceased giving china-painting lessons eight or ten years earlier. They were admitted by the old Negro into a dim hall from which a staircase mounted into still more shadow. It smelled of dust and disuse—a close, dank smell. The Negro led them into the parlor. It was furnished in heavy, leather-covered furniture. When the Negro opened the blinds of one window, they could see that the leather was cracked; and when they sat down, a faint dust rose sluggishly about their thighs, spinning with slow motes in the single sunray. On a tarnished gilt easel[7] before the fireplace stood a crayon portrait of Miss Emily's father.

They rose when she entered—a small, fat woman in black, with a thin gold chain descending to her waist and vanishing into her belt, leaning on an ebony cane with a

---

[1] cedar-bemused cemetery:深思的雪松环绕着墓园。bemused:沉思的。
[2] Union and Confederate:指美国内战(American Civil War, 1861—1865)中交战的双方。Union:指 the United States of America,即联邦(北方);Confederate:指 the Confederate States of America,即邦联(南方)。南部邦联由 11 个州组成,这些州曾宣布退出联邦。
[3] fathered the edict:制定了法规。
[4] to the effect that:大意是,意思是说。
[5] aldermen:市参议员。
[6] a thin, flowing calligraphy:书法流利,字迹细小。
[7] a tarnished gilt easel:失去金色光泽的镀金画架。

tarnished gold head. Her skeleton was small and spare; perhaps that was why what would have been merely plumpness in another was obesity in her[1]. She looked bloated, like a body long submerged in motionless water, and of that pallid hue. Her eyes, lost in the fatty ridges of her face, looked like two small pieces of coal pressed into a lump of dough as they moved from one face to another while the visitors stated their errand.

She did not ask them to sit. She just stood in the door and listened quietly until the spokesman came to a stumbling halt. Then they could hear the invisible watch ticking at the end of the gold chain.

Her voice was dry and cold. "I have no taxes in Jefferson. Colonel Sartoris explained it to me. Perhaps one of you can gain access to the city records and satisfy yourselves."

"But we have. We are the city authorities. Miss Emily. Didn't you get notice from the sheriff, signed by him?"

"I received a paper, yes," Miss Emily said. "Perhaps he considers he self the sheriff ... I have no taxes in Jefferson."

"But there is nothing on the books to show that, you see. We must go, by the—"

"See Colonel Sartoris. I have no taxes in Jefferson."

"But, Miss Emily—"

"See Colonel Sartoris." (Colonel Sartoris had been dead almost ten years.) I have no taxes in Jefferson. Tobe!" The Negro appeared. "Show these gentlemen out."

II

So she vanquished them, horse and foot[2], just as she had vanquished their fathers thirty years before about the smell. That was two years after her father's death and a short time after her sweetheart—the one we believe would marry her—had deserted her. After her father's death she went out very little; after her sweetheart went away, people hardly saw her at all. A few of the ladies had the temerity[3] to call, but were not received, and the only sign of life about the place was the Negro man—a young man then—going in and out with a market basket.

"Just as if a man—any man—could keep a kitchen property," the ladies said; so they were not surprised when the smell developed. It was another link between the gross, teeming world and the high and mighty Griersons.

A neighbor, a woman, complained to the mayor, Judge Stevens, eighty years old.

"But what will you have me do about it, madam?" he said.

"Why, send her word to stop it," the woman said. "Isn't there a law?"

---

[1] perhaps that was... obesity in her: 也许正因为这个缘故,在别的女人身上不过是丰满,而在她却给人以肥胖的感觉。

[2] horse and foot: 彻底地。

[3] temerity: 鲁莽,冒失。

"I'm sure that won't be necessary," Judge Stevens said. "It's probably just a snake or a rat that nigger of hers killed in the yard. I'll speak to him about it."

The next day he received two more complaints, one from a man who came in diffident deprecation. "We really must do something about it, Judge. I'd be the last one in the world to bother Miss Emily, but we've got to do something." That night the Board of Aldermen met—three graybeards[1] and one younger man, a member of the rising generation.

"It's simple enough," he said. "Send her word to have her place cleaned up. Give her a certain time to do it in, and if she don't…"

"Dammit, sir," Judge Stevens said, "will you accuse a lady to her face of smelling bad?"

So the next night, after midnight, four men crossed Miss Emily's lawn and slunk about the house like burglars, sniffing along the base of the brickwork and at the cellar openings while one of them performed a regular sowing motion with his hand out of a sack stung from his shoulder. They broke open the cellar door and sprinkled lime there, and in all the outbuildings. As they recrossed the lawn, a window that had been dark was lighted and Miss Emily sat in it, the light behind her, and her upright torso motionless as that of an idol. They crept quietly across the lawn and into the shadow of the locusts[2] that lined the street. After a week or two the smell went away.

That was when people had begun to feel really sorry for her. People in our town, remembering how old lady Wyatt, her great-aunt, had gone completely crazy at last, believed that the Griersons held themselves a little too high for what they really were. None of the young men were quite good enough for Miss Emily and such. We had long thought of them as a tableau[3]; Miss Emily a slender figure in white in the background, her father a spraddled silhouette[4] in the foreground, his back to her and clutching a horsewhip, the two of them framed by the back-flung front door[5]. So when she got to be thirty and was still single, we were not pleased exactly, but vindicated; even with insanity in the family she wouldn't have turned down all of her chances if they had really materialized[6].

When her father died, it got about that the house was all that was left to her; and in a way, people were glad. At last they could pity Miss Emily. Being left alone, and a pauper, she had become humanized. Now she too would know the old thrill and the old

---

〔1〕 graybeards: 老者。
〔2〕 locusts: 洋槐树。
〔3〕 tableau: 舞台造型。这里把 Grierson 一家人看作画中人物。
〔4〕 a spraddled silhouette: 叉开腿站立的侧影。spraddle: (方言,口语)是 spread 与 straddle 两词的合并,意为"两腿叉开很大"。
〔5〕 the two of them… back-flung front door: 一扇向后开的前门恰好定格了他俩的身影。
〔6〕 if they had really materialized: 如果机会真的出现的话。materialized: 突然出现。

despair of a penny more or less[1].

The day after his death all the ladies prepared to call at the house and offer condolence and aid, as is our custom. Miss Emily met them at the door, dressed as usual and with no trace of grief on her face. She told them that her father was not dead. She did that for three days, with the ministers calling on her, and the doctors, trying to persuade her to let them dispose of the body. Just as they were about to resort to law and force, she broke down, and they buried her father quickly.

We did not say she was crazy then. We believed she had to do that. We remembered all the young men her father had driven away, and we knew that with nothing left, she would have to cling to that which had robbed her[2], as people will.

Ⅲ

She was sick for a long time. When we saw her again, her hair was cut short, making her look like a girl, with a vague resemblance to those angels in colored church windows—sort of tragic and serene.

The town had just let the contracts for paving the sidewalks, and in the summer after her father's death they began the work. The construction company came with niggers and mules and machinery, and a foreman named Homer Barron, a Yankee—a big, dark, ready[3] man, with a big voice and eyes lighter than his face. The little boys would follow in groups to hear him cuss the niggers, and the niggers singing in time to the rise and fall of picks. Pretty soon he knew everybody in town. Whenever you heard a lot of laughing anywhere about the square, Homer Barron would be in the center of the group. Presently we began to see him and Miss Emily on Sunday afternoons driving in the yellow-wheeled buggy and the matched team of bays[4] from the livery stable.

At first we were glad that Miss Emily would have an interest, because the ladies all said, "Of course a Grierson would not think seriously of a Northerner, a day laborer." But there were still others, older people, who said that even grief could not cause a real lady to forget *noblesse oblige*[5]—without calling it *noblesse oblige*. They just said, "Poor Emily. Her kinsfolk should come to her." She had some kin in Alabama; but years ago her father had fallen out[6] with them over the estate of old lady Wyatt, the crazy woman, and there was no communication between the two families. They had not even been represented at the funeral.

And as soon as the old people said, "Poor Emily," the whispering began. "Do you

---

[1] know the old thrill and the old despair of a penny more or less: 体会到多一分钱就激动喜悦,少一分钱就痛苦失望的那种人之常情。
[2] cling to that which had robbed her: 抓住那个曾经剥夺了她一切的人。这里的 that 指她父亲。
[3] ready: (思维)敏捷的。
[4] the yellow-wheeled buggy and the matched team of bays: 黄轮轻便马车,套上一对栗色马。
[5] *noblesse oblige*: (法语)贵人举止。
[6] fallen out: 争吵。

suppose it's really so?" they said to one another. "Of course it is. What else could…" This behind their hands[1]; rustling of craned silk and satin behind jalousies[2] closed upon the sun of Sunday afternoon as the thin, swift clop-clop-clop of the matched team passed: "Poor Emily."

　　She carried her head high enough—even when we believed that she was fallen[3]. It was as if she demanded more than ever the recognition of her dignity as the last Grierson; as if it had wanted that touch of earthiness to reaffirm her imperviousness[4]. Like when she bought the rat poison, the arsenic. That was over a year after they had begun to say "Poor Emily," and while the two female cousins were visiting her.

　　"I want some poison," she said to the druggist. She was over thirty then, still a slight woman, though thinner than usual, with cold, haughty black eyes in a face the flesh of which was strained across the temples and about the eye-sockets as you imagine a lighthouse-keeper's face[5] ought to look. "I want some poison," she said.

　　"Yes, Miss Emily. What kind? For rats and such? I'd recom—"

　　"I want the best you have. I don't care what kind."

　　The druggist named several. "They'll kill anything up to an elephant. But what you want is—"

　　"Arsenic," Miss Emily said. "Is that a good one?"

　　"Is…arsenic? Yes. Ma'am. But what you want—"

　　"I want arsenic."

　　The druggist looked down at her. She looked back at him, erect, her face like a strained flag[6]. "Why, of course," the druggist said. "If that's what you want. But the law requires you to tell what you are going to use it for."

　　Miss Emily just stared at him, her head tilted back in order to look him eye for eye, until he looked away and went and got the arsenic and wrapped it up. The Negro delivery boy brought her the package; the druggist didn't come back. When she opened the package at home there was written on the box, under the skull and bones: "For rats."

IV

　　So the next day we all said, "She will kill herself"; and we said it would be the best thing. When she had first begun to be seen with Homer Barron, we had said, "She will marry him." Then we said, "She will persuade him yet," because Homer himself had remarked—he liked men, and it was known that he drank with the younger men in the Elks' Club—that he was not a marrying man. Later we said, "Poor Emily" behind the

---

[1] behind their hands: 用手捂住嘴轻轻地说。
[2] jalousies: 百叶窗。
[3] fallen: 堕落的,指女人失去贞操。
[4] it had wanted… reaffirm her imperviousness: 需要同世俗接触来重新肯定她那不受影响的性格。
[5] a lighthouse-keeper's face: 这是一个比喻,指脸上带有一种因紧张而扭曲的表情。
[6] a strained flag: 像一面拉紧了的旗子。这里指 Miss Emily 脸上那种严厉、紧张的表情。

jalousies as they passed on Sunday afternoon in the glittering buggy, Miss Emily with her head high and Homer Barron with his hat cocked and a cigar in his teeth, reins and whip in a yellow glove.

Then some of the ladies began to say that it was a disgrace to the town and a bad example to the young people. The men did not want to interfere, but at last the ladies forced the Baptist minister—Miss Emily's people were Episcopal[1]—to call upon her. He would never divulge[2] what happened during that interview, but he refused to go back again. The next Sunday they again drove about the streets, and the following day the minister's wife wrote to Miss Emily's relations in Alabama.

So she had blood-kin under her roof again and we sat back to watch developments. At first nothing happened. Then we were sure that they were to be married. We learned that Miss Emily had been to the jeweler's and ordered a man's toilet set in silver, with the letters H. B. on each piece. Two days later we learned that she had bought a complete outfit of men's clothing, including a nightshirt, and we said, "They are married." We were really glad. We were glad because the two female cousins were even more Grierson than Miss Emily had ever been.

So we were surprised when Homer Barron—the streets had been finished some time since—was gone. We were a little disappointed that there was not a public blowing-off[3], but we believed that he had gone on to prepare for Miss Emily's coming, or to give her a chance to get rid of the cousins. (By that time it was a cabal, and we were all Miss Emily's allies to help circumvent the cousins[4].) Sure enough, after another week they departed. And, as we had expected all along, within three days Homer Barron was back in town. A neighbor saw the Negro man admit him at the kitchen door at dusk one evening.

And that was the last we saw of Homer Barron. And of Miss Emily for some time. The Negro man went in and out with the market basket, but the front door remained closed. Now and then we would see her at a window for a moment, as the men did that night when they sprinkled the lime, but for almost six months she did not appear on the streets. Then we knew that this was to be expected too; as if that quality of her father which had thwarted her woman's life so many times had been too virulent and too furious to die.

When we next saw Miss Emily, she had grown fat and her hair was turning gray. During the next few years it grew grayer and grayer until it attained an even pepper-and-salt iron-gray, when it ceased turning. Up to the day of her death at seventy-four it was still that vigorous iron-gray, like the hair of an active man.

From that time on her front door remained closed, save for a period of six or seven

---

[1] Baptist minister:浸礼会牧师;Miss Emily's people:指 Miss Emily 的亲属;Episcopal:圣公会。
[2] divulge:吐露,泄露(秘密)。
[3] blowing-off:长时间的议论。
[4] By that time it... circumvent the cousins:这时已经形成了一个秘密小集团,我们都站在 Miss Emily 一边,帮她踢开这一对堂姐。circumvent:以计策胜出,智取。

years, when she was about forty, during which she gave lessons in china-painting. She fitted up a studio in one of the downstairs rooms, where the daughters and granddaughters of Colonel Sartoris' contemporaries were sent to her with the same regularity and in the same spirit that they were sent to church on Sundays with a twenty-five-cent piece for the collection plate[1]. Meanwhile her taxes had been remitted.

Then the newer generation became the backbone and the spirit of the town, and the painting pupils grew up and fell away and did not send their children to her with boxes of color and tedious brushes and pictures cut from the ladies' magazines. The front door closed upon the last one and remained closed for good. When the town got free postal delivery, Miss Emily alone refused to let them fasten the metal numbers above her door and attach a mailbox to it. She would not listen to them.

Daily, monthly, yearly we watched the Negro grow grayer and more stooped, going in and out with the market basket. Each December we sent her a tax notice, which would be returned by the post office a week later, unclaimed. Now and then we would see her in one of the downstairs windows—she had evidently shut up the top floor of the house—like the carven torso of an idol in a niche[2], looking or not looking at us, we could never tell which. Thus she passed from generation to generation—dear, inescapable, impervious, tranquil, and perverse.

And so she died. Fell in the house filled with dust and shadows, with only a doddering[3] Negro man to wait on her. We did not even know she was sick; we had long since given up trying to get any information from the Negro. He talked to no one, probably not even to her, for his voice had grown harsh and rusty, as if from disuse.

She died in one of the downstairs rooms, in a heavy walnut bed with a curtain, her gray head propped on a pillow yellow and moldy with age and lack of sunlight.

V

The Negro met the first of the ladies at the front door and let them in, with their hushed, sibilant[4] voices and their quick, curious glances, and then disappeared. He walked right through the house and out the back and was not seen again.

The two female cousins came at once. They held the funeral on the second day, with the town coming to look at Miss Emily beneath a mass of bought flowers, with the crayon face of her father musing profoundly above the bier[5] and the ladies sibilant and macabre[6]; and the very old men—some in their brushed Confederate uniforms—on the

---

[1] the collection plate:教堂里做礼拜时用于募捐的盘子。
[2] like the carven torso of an idol in a niche:像摆放在神龛中的偶像的雕塑躯干。
[3] doddering:老态龙钟。
[4] sibilant:(语音)发嘶音的。
[5] bier:棺材。
[6] macabre:恐怖的;毛骨悚然的。with the ladies sibilant and macabre:意为这些女人喋喋不休地低声谈着 Miss Emily 的死。

porch and the lawn, talking of Miss Emily as if she had been a contemporary of theirs, believing that they had danced with her and courted her perhaps, confusing time with its mathematical progression, as the old do, to whom all the past is not a diminishing road but, instead, a huge meadow which no winter ever quite touches, divided from them now by the narrow bottleneck of the most recent decade of years.

Already, we knew that there was one room in that region above stairs which no one had seen in forty years, and which would have to be forced. They waited until Miss Emily was decently in the ground before they opened it.

The violence of breaking down the door seemed to fill this room with pervading dust. A thin, acrid pall as of the tomb seemed to lie everywhere upon this room decked and furnished as for a bridal: upon the valance curtains[1] of faded rose color, upon the rose-shaded lights, upon the dressing table, upon the delicate array of crystal and the man's toilet things backed with tarnished silver, silver so tarnished that the monogram[2] was obscured. Among them lay collar and tie, as if they had just been removed, which, lifted, left upon the surface a pale crescent in the dust. Upon a chair hung the suit, carefully folded; beneath it the two mute shoes and the discarded socks.

The man himself lay in the bed.

For a long while we just stood there, looking down at the profound and fleshless grin. The body had apparently once lain in the attitude of an embrace, but now the long sleep[3] that outlasts love, that conquers even the grimace of love, had cuckolded[4] him. What was left of him, rotted beneath what was left of the nightshirt, had become inextricable from the bed in which he lay; and upon him and upon the pillow beside him lay that even coating of the patient and biding dust.

Then we noticed that in the second pillow was the indentation of a head. One of us lifted something from it, and leaving forward, that faint and invisible dust dry and acrid in the nostrils, we saw a long strand of iron-gray hair.

1931

赏　析

《献给爱米丽的玫瑰》是约克纳帕塔法小说中的一篇,自发表以来,一直是福克纳被收录入集最多的短篇小说,曾在1987年被改编为电影。

《献给爱米丽的玫瑰》是一篇美国现代南方哥特小说。作为文学体裁的哥特小说起源于1764年一部叫《奥特兰托城堡》(*The Castle of Otranto*)的小说,这类作品通常以古堡和荒郊野外为背景,气氛阴郁、恐怖,故事多与鬼魂、凶杀、死亡有关。《献给爱米丽的玫瑰》中阴森的大宅、心理扭曲的古怪人物、谋杀、与死尸同睡都具有传统哥特小说的特点。作者借哥特式的阴

---

[1] valance curtains:床沿挂帘。
[2] monogram:姓名字母图案。
[3] the long sleep:死亡。
[4] cuckolded:原指妻子与人通奸的,这里意为"使之驯服的"。

郁和恐怖揭示了女主人公爱米丽的变态心理。她在恋爱不成后，不惜杀死自己的情人，并与尸体同床共枕几十年，令人毛骨悚然。然而，福克纳并不满足于揭示一个人的非正常心理。爱米丽尽管心理变态，是个杀人犯，但福克纳认为她是旧南方的牺牲品，其悲剧命运无法避免，令人同情。同时，她敢于蔑视传统，勇于追求爱情，令人尊敬，所以要献给她一朵玫瑰。福克纳借爱米丽的所作所为，批判了旧南方认为女子必须遵守门当户对的婚姻规范和必须顺从父亲意愿的"淑女观念"。这种观念反映了旧南方无视女性精神追求的道德观和男权主义对女性情感的极度压抑。

《献给爱米丽的玫瑰》虽然是短篇小说，时间跨度却长达半个世纪，以小容大。故事采用第一人称复数，以"我们"代表小镇居民的口吻和心态，让读者感受到爱米丽与代表旧传统的居民之间的紧张关系。在叙事上打断了线性时序，从爱米丽的去世开始，回溯过去，再回到她的死亡，这种回旋式的叙述手法使读者在拼凑爱米丽的生活轨迹中深刻地理解人物和主题。

相关评论

The Atmosphere in "A Rose for Emily"
Ray B. West, Jr.

Atmosphere is defined in the *Dictionary of World Literature* as "the particular world in which the events of a story or a play occur: time, place, conditions, and the attendant mood." When, as in "A Rose for Emily," the world depicted is a confusion between the past and the present, the atmosphere is one of distortion—of unreality. This unreal world results from the suspension of a natural time order. Normality consists in a decorous[1] progression of the human being from birth, through youth, to age and finally death. Preciosity[2] in children is as monstrous as idiocy in the adult, because both are *unnatural*. Monstrosity, however, is a sentimental subject for fiction unless it is the result of human action—the result of a willful attempt to circumvent time. When such circumvention produces acts of violence, as in "A Rose for Emily," the atmosphere becomes one of horror.

Horror, however, represents only the extreme form of maladjusted nature. It is not produced in "A Rose for Emily" until the final act of violence has been disclosed. All that has gone before has prepared us by producing a general tone of mystery, foreboding[3], decay, etc., so that we may say the entire series of events that have gone before are "in key"—that is, they are depicted in a mood in which the final violence does not appear too shocking or horrible. We are inclined to say, "In such an atmosphere, anything may happen." Foreshadowing is often accomplished through atmosphere, and in this case the atmosphere prepares us for Emily's unnatural act at the end of the story. Actually, such preparation begins in the very first sentence:

---

[1] decorous: 恰当的。
[2] preciosity: 过分讲究, 过于细心。
[3] foreboding: 凶兆。

> When Miss Emily Grierson died, our whole town went to her funeral: the men through a sort of respectful affection for a fallen monument, the women mostly out of curiosity to see the inside of her house, which no one save an old manservant—a combined gardener and cook—had seen in at least ten years.

Emily is portrayed as "a fallen monument," a *monument* for reasons which we shall examine later, *fallen* because she has shown herself susceptible to death (and decay) after all. In the mention of death, we are conditioned (as the psychologist says) for the more specific concern with it later on. The second paragraph depicts the essential ugliness of the contrast: the description of Miss Emily's house "lifting its stubborn and coquettish decay above the cotton wagons and the gasoline pumps—an eyesore among eyesores." (A juxtaposition[1] of past and present.) We recognize this scene as an emblematic presentation of Miss Emily herself, suggested as it is through the words "stubborn and coquettish." The tone—and the contrast—is preserved in a description of the note which Miss Emily sent to the mayor, "a note on paper of an archaic shape, in a thin, flowing calligraphy in faded ink," and in the description of the interior of the house when the deputation from the Board of Aldermen visit her: "They were admitted by the old Negro into a dim hall from which a stairway mounted into still more shadow. It smelled of dust and disuse—a close, dank smell." In the next paragraph a description of Emily discloses her similarity to the house: "She looked bloated, like a body long submerged in motionless water, and of that pallid hue."

Emily had not always looked like this. When she was young and part of the world with which she was contemporary, she was, we are told, "a slender figure in white," as contrasted with her father, who is described as "a spraddled silhouette." In the picture of Emily and her father together, framed by the door, she is frail and apparently hungering to participate in the life of her time, we have a reversal of the contrast which has already been presented and which is to be developed later. Even after her father's death, Emily is not monstrous, but rather looked like a girl "with a vague resemblance to those angels in colored church windows—sort of tragic and serene." The suggestion is that she had already begun her entrance into that nether-world[2] (a world which is depicted later as "rose-tinted"), but that she might even yet have been saved, had Homer Barron been another kind of man.

Source: Laurie Lanzen Harris and Sheila Fitzgerald, ed. *Short Story Criticism*. Vol.1. Detroit: Gale Research, 1988.

问题与思考

1. What is the time sequence in the story, and why is it divided into five sections?

---

[1] juxtaposition:并置。
[2] nether-world:阴曹地府,冥界。

2. What foreshadowings of the discovery of Homer Barron's body does the author give us in the story? Do the foreshadowings give away the ending of the story? Do they heighten your interest?
3. Compare the character and background of Emily Grierson and Homer Barron. What general conclusions about the society that Faulkner described can be made from his portraits of the two characters and from his account of life in Jefferson?
4. Who is the narrator and what is his relationship to the story? Why does the narrator deliberately rearrange the chronology of the story's events? How does this technique heighten and reinforce the atmosphere?
5. What contrasts does the narrator draw between changing reality and Emily's refusal or inability to recognize change?
6. What do you infer is Faulkner's attitude toward Emily Grierson? Is she simply a murderous madwoman? What do you think the author called his story "A Rose for Emily"?
7. Notice the tone of the story. Is it a totally grim story or is it a story of any humor?

阅读链接

1. http://www.olemiss.edu/mwp/dir/faulkner_william：对福克纳生平和创作有详细的介绍，并配有图片。
2. http://www.mcsr.olemiss.edu/%7Eegjbp/faulkner/faulkner.html：对福克纳小说所涉及的地方、人物、年代及事件进行了较为详细的介绍。
3. http://reading-group-center.knopfdoubleday.com/2010/01/09/a-guide-to-the-works-of-william-faulkner/#sound：对福克纳的《喧嚣与骚动》等几部重要的长篇小说提出了富有启发性的讨论问题。

John Updike (1932—2009)

作者简介

约翰·厄普代克(John Updike，1932—2009)出生于美国宾夕法尼亚州的希灵顿。他的母亲曾努力成为一名作家，这影响了厄普代克，他也生发了同样的志向。1950年，厄普代克以优异成绩从中学毕业，获得哈佛大学的全额奖学金，1954年毕业于哈佛大学，随后去英国牛津大学学了一年的艺术。厄普代克回国后，全家迁至纽约，他开始向著名的杂志《纽约客》投稿诗歌和短篇小说，1955至1957年他在《纽约客》编辑部工作，并有许多作品发表在这一刊物上。20世纪50年代，厄普代克开始阅读西方现代存在主义先驱克尔凯郭尔和瑞士基督教神学家卡尔·巴特的著作，并深受影响。50年代末，厄普代克离开纽约，搬到波士顿东北部的小镇伊普斯威奇居住，专门从事写作。他曾访问过东欧、亚洲、南美和非洲多个国家。厄普代克一生获得过国家图书奖、普利策奖和欧·亨利短篇小说奖等多个重要奖项。2009年1月27日，他因肺癌去世，享年76岁。

文学创作

厄普代克是美国当代著名的现实主义作家，被誉为"社会历史变化的准确记录者"。他多才多艺，出版的长篇小说超过25部，还发表了十几部短篇小说集以及大量的散文、游记、评论和诗歌集。他的作品涉及多种题材，尤以描写美国东部小城镇白人中产阶级的生活见长，代表作"兔子"四部曲包括《兔子，跑吧》(*Rabbit, Run*, 1960)、《兔子回家》(*Rabbit Redeux*, 1971)、《兔子富了》(*Rabbit Is Rich*, 1981)和《兔子休息了》(*Rabbit at Rest*, 1990)。四部曲讲述了一个绰号叫"兔子"的普通美国人哈里的人生故事：他从事过各种工作，经历过家庭危机，成了保守而平庸的新富人,最后在无人理解的孤寂中死去。这四部长篇小说从50年代写到80年代末,全面展示了美国当代中产阶级的生活图景,勾画出"战后美国社会的道德史"。厄普代克的文学才华还表现在长篇小说《乔特鲁德与克劳迪斯》(*Gertrude and Claudius*,2000)中。作品取材于莎士比亚著名悲剧《哈姆雷特》,但主要人物不再是哈姆雷特,而是他的母亲乔特鲁德和叔叔克劳迪斯,他们也不再是有悖道德和良心的坏人,而是两个为情所困的中年人。这部作品"语言古朴优雅,充分展现了作者驾驭英语的能力"。

和长篇小说一样,厄普代克的短篇小说数量多、题材广、视野宽,主要有《鸽羽及其他故事》(*Pigeon Feathers and Other Stories*,1959)、《奥林格故事集》(*Olinger Stories*,1964)、《远则难行》(*Too Far To Go*,1979)、《父亲的眼泪》(*My Father's Tears and Other Stories*,2009)等。厄普代克擅长挖掘普通人物和普通事件的趣味性和戏剧性,擅长刻画人物所面临的心理压力和道德困境,并以独特的中产阶级口语风格见长。

作　　品

A & P [1]

In walks these three girls in nothing [2] but bathing suits. I'm in the third check-out slot [3], with my back to the door, so I don't see them until they're over by the bread [4]. The one that caught my eye first was the one in the plaid green two-piece. She was a chunky kid, with a good tan and a sweet broad soft-looking can [5] with those two crescents of white just under it, where the sun never seems to hit, at the top of the backs of her legs. I stood there with my hand on a box of HiHo crackers [6] trying to remember if I rang it up [7] or not. I ring it up again and the customer starts giving me hell. She's one of these cash-register-watchers, a witch about fifty with rouge on her cheekbones and no eyebrows, and I know it made her day to trip me up [8]. She'd been watching cash registers forty years and probably never seen a mistake before.

By the time I got her feathers smoothed [9] and her goodies into a bag—she gives me a little snort in passing, if she'd been born at the right time they would have burned her over in Salem [10]—by the time I get her on her way the girls had circled around the bread

---

[1] A & P:超级市场名。
[2] In walks... in nothing:三个只穿着游泳衣的姑娘走进了商场。这是倒装句,动词walk用了第三人称单数,表示故事里的"I"把三位姑娘视作一个整体。
[3] check-out slot:超级市场出口处顾客付款的地方。
[4] the bread:面包柜台。
[5] can:(俚)臀部。
[6] HiHo crackers:HiHo牌饼干。
[7] rang up:在收款机上记账。
[8] it made her day to trip me up:她挑出我的差错,心里十分快活。make sb's day:使某人的日子过得快活。trip up:挑剔,使失败。
[9] got her feathers smoothed:平息她的怒气。
[10] burned her over in Salem:在Salem将她烧死。Salem是美国马萨诸塞州的城市。1692年曾在此发生美国历史上著名的女巫审判案,处死了19名所谓的女巫。戏剧家阿瑟·米勒(Arthur Miller)曾以此为素材创作名剧 *The Crucible*。

and were coming back, without a pushcart, back my way along the counters, in the aisle between the check-outs and the Special bins. They didn't even have shoes on. There was this chunky one, with the two-piece—it was bright green and the seams on the bra were still sharp and her belly was still pretty pale so I guessed she just got it (the suit)—there was this one, with one of those chubby berry-faces, the lips all bunched together under her nose, this one, and a tall one, with black hair that hadn't quite frizzed[1] right, and one of these sunburns right across under the eyes, and a chin that was too long—you know, the kind of girl other girls think is very "striking" and "attractive" but never quite makes it[2], as they very well know, which is why they like her so much—and then the third one, that wasn't quite so tall. She was the queen. She kind of led them, the other two peeking around and making their shoulders round[3]. She didn't look around, not this queen, she just walked straight on slowly, on these long white prima donna[4] legs. She came down a little hard on her heels, as if she didn't walk in her bare feet that much, putting down her heels and then letting the weight move along to her toes as if she was testing the floor with every step, putting a little deliberate extra action into it. You never know for sure how girls' minds work (do you really think it's a mind in there or just a little buzz like a bee in a glass jar?) but you got the idea she had talked the other two into coming in here with her, and now she was showing them how to do it, walk slow and hold yourself straight.

She had on a kind of dirty-pink—beige maybe, I don't know—bathing suit with a little nubble all over it and, what got me, the straps were down. They were off her shoulders looped loose around the cool tops of her arms, and I guess as a result the suit had slipped a little on her, so all around the top of the cloth there was this shining rim. If it hadn't been there you wouldn't have known there could have been anything whiter than those shoulders. With the straps pushed off, there was nothing between the top of the suit and the top of her head except just *her*, this clean bare plane of the top of her chest down from the shoulder bones like a dented sheet of metal tilted in the light. I mean, it was more than pretty.

She had sort of oaky hair that the sun and salt had bleached, done up in a bun[5] that was unravelling, and a kind of prim face. Walking into the A & P with your straps down, I suppose it's the only kind of face you *can* have. She held her head so high her neck, coming up out of those white shoulders, looked kind of stretched, but I didn't mind. The longer her neck was, the more of her there was.

She must have felt in the corner of her eye me and over my shoulder Stokesie in the

---

[1] frizzed:卷曲。
[2] never quite makes it:总是不够漂亮动人。make it:成功做到。
[3] making their shoulders round:弯下身子。
[4] prima donna:歌剧的主要女演员;这个词在句中作形容词,意为"像女明星那样的"。
[5] done up in a bun:(头发)梳成一个高高的髻。

second slot watching, but she didn't tip[1]. Not this queen. She kept her eyes moving across the racks, and stopped, and turned so slow it made my stomach rub the inside of my apron, and buzzed[2] to the other two, who kind of huddled against her for relief, and they all three of them went up the cat-and-dog-food-breakfast-cereal-macaroni-rice-raisins-seasonings-spreads-spaghetti-soft-drinks-crackers-and-cookies aisle[3]. From the third slot I look straight up this aisle to the meat counter, and I watched them all the way. The fat one with the tan sort of fumbled with the cookies, but on second thought she put the packages back. The sheep[4] pushing their carts down the aisle—the girls were walking against the usual traffic[5] (not that we have one-way signs or anything)—were pretty hilarious. You could see them, when Queenie's white shoulders dawned on them, kind of jerk, or hop, or hiccup[6], but their eyes snapped back to their own baskets and on they pushed. I bet you could set off dynamite in an A & P and the people would by and large keep reaching and checking oatmeal off their lists[7] and muttering "Let me see, there was a third thing, began with A, asparagus, no, ah, yes, applesauce!" or whatever it is they do mutter. But there was no doubt, this jiggled[8] them. A few house-slaves in pin curlers even looked around after pushing their carts past to make sure what they had seen was correct.

You know, it's one thing to have a girl in a bathing suit down on the beach, where what with the glare nobody can look at each other much anyway, and another thing in the cool of the A & P, under the fluorescent lights, against all those stacked packages, with her feet paddling along naked over our checkerboard green-and-cream rubber-tile floor.

"Oh Daddy," Stokesie said beside me. "I feel so faint."

"Darling," I said. "Hold me tight." Stokesie's married, with two babies chalked up on his fuselage[9] already, but as far as I can tell that's the only difference. He's twenty-two, and I was nineteen this April.

"Is it done?" he asks, the responsible married man finding his voice. I forgot to say he thinks he's going to be manager some sunny day, maybe in 1990 when it's called the Great Alexandrov and Petrooshki Tea Company or something.

What he meant was, our town is five miles from a beach, with a big summer colony out on the Point, but we're right in the middle of town, and the women generally put on

---

[1] but she didn't tip: 可她连眼都不朝我斜一下。
[2] buzzed: 喊喊喳喳地说。
[3] the cat-and-dog-food... aisle: 指专门出售这类商品的地方，两边是货架，中间有通道供顾客选购商品时通过。
[4] sheep: 温顺的人，循规蹈矩者。这里指超级市场里的其他顾客。
[5] the girls... usual traffic: 姑娘们没有顺着大家常走的路线，而是迎着其他顾客走过去。
[6] hiccup: 打嗝。
[7] checking oatmeal off their lists: 将燕麦片从购物单上划掉。
[8] jiggled: 震动。
[9] with two babies chalked up on his fuselage: 已经有了两个孩子。chalk up: 记账；fuselage: 弹壳。chalked up on his fuselage: 原为军事用语，指士兵用粉笔在弹壳上记下他打死敌人的数目。作者用这个典故来表达一种幽默。

a shirt or shorts or something before they get out of the car into the street. And anyway these are usually women with six children and varicose[1] veins mapping their legs and nobody, including them, could care less. As I say, we're right in the middle of town, and if you stand at our front doors you can see two banks and the Congregational church and the newspaper store and three real-estate offices and about twenty-seven old freeloaders[2] tearing up Central Street because the sewer broke again. It's not as if we're on the Cape; we're north of Boston and there's people in this town haven't seen the ocean for twenty years.

The girls had reached the meat counter and were asking McMahon something. He pointed, they pointed, and they shuffled out of sight behind a pyramid of Diet Delight peaches. All that was left for us to see was old McMahon patting his mouth and looking after them sizing up their joints[3]. Poor kids, I began to feel sorry for them, they couldn't help it.

Now here comes the sad part of the story, at least my family says it's sad but I don't think it's sad myself. The store's pretty empty, it being Thursday afternoon, so there was nothing much to do except lean on the register and wait for the girls to show up again. The whole store was like a pinball machine[4] and I didn't know which tunnel[5] they'd come out of. After a while they come around out of the far aisle, around the light bulbs, records at discount of the Caribbean Six or Tony Martin Sings[6] or some such gunk[7] you wonder they waste the wax[8] on, sixpacks of candy bars, and plastic toys done up in cellophane that fall apart when a kid looks at them anyway. Around they come, Queenie still leading the way, and holding a little gray jar in her hand. Slots Three through Seven are unmanned and I could see her wondering between Stokes and me, but Stokesie with his usual luck draws an old party[9] in baggy gray pants who stumbles up with four giant cans of pineapple juice (what do these bums *do* with all that pineapple juice? I've often asked myself) so the girls come to me. Queenie puts down the jar and I take it into my fingers icy cold. Kingfish Fancy Herring Snacks in Pure Sour Cream: 49¢. Now her hands are empty, not a ring or a bracelet, bare as God made them, and I wonder where the money's coming from. Still with that prim look she lifts a folded dollar bill out of the hollow at the center of her nubbled pink top. The jar went heavy in my hand. Really, I thought that was so cute.

---

[1] varicose:静脉曲张的。
[2] freeloaders:原意为"吃白食的人",这里指挖开路面修理下水道的工人,注意文中"I"的轻蔑口吻。
[3] joints:原意是"(羊、牛等)带骨的大块腿肉",这里指姑娘们的大腿。作者用这个词一是体现了McMahon的屠夫身份,二是表达了一种幽默感。
[4] pinball machine:弹球戏机。
[5] tunnel:弹球戏机上的槽,这里指超级市场里的过道。
[6] the Caribbean Six, Tony Martin Sings:乐队名。
[7] gunk:肮脏的货色。
[8] wax:唱片。
[9] party:(俚)家伙。

Then everybody's luck begins to run out. Lengel comes in from haggling with[1] a truck full of cabbages on the lot and is about to scuttle into that door marked MANAGER behind which he hides all day when the girls touch his eye. Lengel's pretty dreary, teaches Sunday school and the rest, but he doesn't miss that much. He comes over and says, "Girls, this isn't the beach."

Queenie blushes, though maybe it's just a brush of sunburn I was noticing for the first time, now that she was so close. "My mother asked me to pick up a jar of herring snacks." Her voice kind of startled me, the way voices do when you see the people first, coming out so flat and dumb yet kind of tony[2], too, the way it ticked over "pick up" and "snacks." All of a sudden I slid right down her voice into her living room. Her father and the other men were standing around in ice-cream coats[3] and bow ties and the women were in sandals picking up herring snacks on toothpicks off a big plate and they were all holding drinks the color of water with olives and sprigs of mint in them. When my parents have somebody over they get lemonade and if it's a real racy affair Schlitz[4] in tall glasses with "They'll Do It Every Time" cartoons stencilled on.

"That's all right," Lengel said. "But this isn't the beach." His repeating this struck me as funny, as if it had just occurred to him, and he had been thinking all these years the A & P was a great big dune[5] and he was the head lifeguard. He didn't like my smiling—as I say he doesn't miss much—but he concentrates on giving the girls that sad Sunday-school-superintendent stare[6].

Queenie's blush is no sunburn now, and the plump one in plaid, that I liked better from the back—a really sweet can—pipes up, "We weren't doing any shopping. We just came in for the one thing."

"That makes no difference," Lengel tells her, and I could see from the way his eyes went that he hadn't noticed she was wearing a two-piece before. "We want you decently dressed when you come in here."

"We are decent," Queenie says suddenly, her lower lip pushing, getting sore now that she remembers her place, a place from which the crowd that runs the A & P must look pretty crummy[7]. Fancy Herring Snacks flashed in her very blue eyes.

"Girls, I don't want to argue with you. After this come in here with your shoulders covered. It's our policy." He turns his back. That's policy for you. Policy is what the kingpins[8] want. What the others want is juvenile delinquency.

---

[1] haggling with:讨价还价。
[2] tony:时髦的。
[3] ice-cream coats:乳白色的上衣。
[4] Schlitz:啤酒名。
[5] dune:沙丘。
[6] Sunday-school-superintendent stare:主日学校学监的目光。
[7] getting sore now... pretty crummy:她十分恼火,想起了自己的社会地位,比起她来,那些经营A&P超市的人当然算不了什么。
[8] kingpins:原意为"中心人物"、"重要人物"。这里指像Lengel那样的经理。

All this while, the customers had been showing up with their carts but, you know, sheep, seeing a scene, they had all bunched up on Stokesie, who shook open a paper bag as gently as peeling a peach, not wanting to miss a word. I could feel in the silence everybody getting nervous, most of all Lengel, who asks me, "Sammy, have you rung up this purchase?"

I thought and said "No" but it wasn't about that I was thinking. I go through the punches, 4, 9, GROC, TOT[1]—it's more complicated than you think, and after you do it often enough, it begins to make a little song, that you hear words to, in my case "Hello (*bing*) there, you (*gung*) hap-py pee-pul (*splat*)"—the splat being the drawer flying out. I uncrease the bill, tenderly as you may imagine, it just having come from between the two smoothest scoops of vanilla[2] I had ever known were there, and pass a half and a penny into her narrow pink palm, and nestle the herrings in a bag and twist its neck and hand it over, all the time thinking.

The girls, and who'd blame them, are in a hurry to get out, so I say "I quit" to Lengel quick enough for them to hear, hoping they'll stop and watch me, their unsuspected hero. They keep right on going, into the electric eye[3]; the door flies open and they flicker across the lot to their car, Queenie and Plaid and Big Tall Goony-Goony (not that as raw material she was so bad), leaving me with Lengel and a kink in his eyebrow[4].

"Did you say something, Sammy?"

"I said I quit."

"I thought you did."

"You didn't have to embarrass them."

"It was they who were embarrassing us."

I started to say something that came out "Fiddle-de-doo[5]." It's a saying of my grand-mother's, and I know she would have been pleased.

"I don't think you know what you're saying," Lengel said.

"I know you don't," I said. "But I do." I pull the bow at the back of my apron and start shrugging it off my shoulders. A couple customers that had been heading for my slot begin to knock against each other, like scared pigs in a chute[6].

Lengel sighs and begins to look very patient and old and gray. He's been a friend of my parents for years. "Sammy, you don't want to do this to your Mom and Dad," he tells me. It's true, I don't. But it seems to me that once you begin a gesture it's fatal not to go through with it. I fold the apron, "Sammy" stitched in red on the pocket, and put

[1] GROC, TOT：grocery, total 两词的缩写。
[2] it just having come... scoops of vanilla：这张钞票可是从最柔滑的香草冰激凌似的酥胸中间掏出来的。
[3] the electric eye：电子监视器。
[4] a kink in his eyebrow：眉毛拧成了一个结。
[5] fiddle-de-doo：胡说！
[6] chute：让牲畜并排通过的狭栏，牲畜通道。

it on the counter, and drop the bow tie on top of it. The bow tie is theirs, if you've ever wondered. "You'll feel this for the rest of your life," Lengel says, and I know that's true, too, but remembering how he made that pretty girl blush makes me so scrunchy[1] inside I punch the No Sale tab and the machine whirs "pee-pul" and the drawer splats out. One advantage to this scene taking place in summer, I can follow this up with a clean exit, there's no fumbling around getting your coat and galoshes[2], I just saunter into the electric eye in my white shirt that my mother ironed the night before, and the door heaves itself open, and outside the sunshine is skating around on the asphalt.

I look around for my girls, but they're gone, of course. There wasn't anybody but some young married screaming with her children about some candy they didn't get by the door of a powder-blue Falcon station wagon[3]. Looking back in the big windows, over the bags of peat moss[4] and aluminum lawn furniture stacked on the pavement, I could see Lengel in my place in the slot, checking the sheep through. His face was dark gray and his back stiff, as if he'd just had an injection of iron, and my stomach kind of fell as I felt how hard the world was going to be to me hereafter.

1961

赏 析

《A&P》最初发表于《纽约客》，后收入《鸽羽及其他故事》。在故事里，19岁的小伙子萨米是超市收银员，有一天，三个身穿比基尼的姑娘来逛商场，因"着装不雅"被经理伦格尔赶出去，萨米打抱不平，愤然辞职，然而，等他出到店外寻找这三位姑娘时，她们已无影无踪，只剩下他孤独一人。

作品从两个方面反映了人们对现实的不满。年轻的萨米厌烦自己的工作，对每天与之打交道的中产阶级顾客毫无尊敬，把他们比作"推着手推车的绵羊"、"吓坏了的猪挤在槽道里"。他对三个着装出格的姑娘极为欣赏，用超市里的商品来描述她们的性感，说其中一个姑娘"看上去像软软的罐头，下面是两块月牙形面包"，另一个的"脸长得像草莓"。不过，在他和伦格尔发生正面冲突之前，这种厌烦还只是藏在心里。与之相比，三位姑娘与现实的格格不入要明显得多。在美国保守的50年代，她们敢穿比基尼逛超市，令萨米耳目一新。超市是一个城市最大众化的公共场合，最能反映一个社会的主流价值观和道德规范取向。三个姑娘的穿着与绵羊一般的大众截然不同，她们逆着人流浏览商品，而且敢于和经理这位保守思想的代表争辩，她们的穿着、言行和遭遇反映了美国19世纪著名思想家爱默生的名言，"谁要做真正的人，就不能做一个顺民"。

厄普代克借故事人物之间的冲突来批评美国沉闷的50年代，不过他思想相对保守，喜欢用"YES,BUT"的模式来讲故事，他对社会的批评是委婉的，反叛是温和的。姑娘们虽然据理力争，但还是被经理赶出了超市；萨米在勇敢一番后，前途茫茫，这都表现了厄普代克的这一思想。

小说采用第一人称，让萨米成为主人公兼叙述者，使读者更易观察、体会一个青年人的心理

---

[1] scrunchy: 又拼作 crunchy, 感到别扭。这个词源于 crunch, (美俚)危境。
[2] galoshes: (冬天穿的)高筒皮靴。
[3] Falcon station wagon: Falcon 牌客货两用车。
[4] peat moss: 泥炭沼，用作养花种树的肥料。

变化。同时,口语化和幽默的风格拉近了读者和人物的距离。

相关评论

John Updike's "A & P": A Return to "Araby"
Walter Wells

John Updike's penchant[1] for appropriating great works of literature and giving them contemporary restatement in his own fiction is abundantly documented—as is the fact that, among his favorite sources, James Joyce looms large.

With special affinity[2] for *Dubliners*, Updike has, by common acknowledgment, written at least one short story that strongly resembles the acclaimed "Araby," not only in plot and theme, but in incidental detail. That story, the 1960 "You'll Never Know, Dear, How Much I Love You"—like "Araby"—tells the tale of a poor, romantically infatuated[3] young boy who, though obstructed by parental slowness, journeys with innocent urgency, coins in hand, to a seemingly magical carnival—only to find there, behind its facades, just a sleazy[4], money grasping, sexually tinged reality that frustrates and embitters him. Both stories draw on the Christian imagery of Bunyan's *Vanity Fair* episode to trace a modern boy's passage from innocence to experience, and to expose some of the pains and complexities of that passage. Notwithstanding *Araby*'s cachet[5] as one of the great short stories in the English language, at least two critics have found "You'll Never Know, Dear" to be "a far more complex story."

What remains unacknowledged, I think, is that shortly after writing "You'll Never Know, Dear," Updike made a second fictional excursion to *Araby*. This time he transformed Joyce's latter-day *Vanity Fair*, not into a cheaply exotic destination for a starry-eyed youngster, but into the richly resonant single setting for an older adolescent's sad tale: a tale of the modern supermarket. The resulting story, since its publication in 1962, has been Updike's most frequently anthologized: the popular "A & P." Updike even signals his intention for us at the outset, giving his story a title that metrically echoes Joyce's: Araby... A & P. (Grand Union or Safeway would not suffice.)

Like "Araby," "A & P" is told after the fact by a young man now much the wiser, presumably, for his frustrating infatuation with a beautiful but inaccessible girl whose allure[6] excites him into confusing his sexual impulses for those of honor and chivalry. The self-delusion in both cases leads quickly to an emotional fall.

At 19, Updike's protagonist, Sammy, is a good bit older than Joyce's—at the

---

[1] penchant:偏爱;强烈的倾向。
[2] affinity:密切的关系。
[3] infatuated:迷恋的,醉心于。
[4] sleazy:肮脏的,庸俗的。
[5] cachet:声望。
[6] allure:吸引力;诱惑。

opposite end of adolescence, it would seem. While in Joyce's boy we readily believe such confusion between the gallant and profane, I think we needn't assume that Sammy is likewise unable to distinguish between the two quite normal impulses. His attraction to the girl in the aisle is certainly far more anatomically and less ambiguously expressed than that of Joyce's boy to Mangan's sister. But it is Beauty that confounds the issue. When human aesthetics come into play, when the object of a young man's carnal desire also gratifies[1] him aesthetically, that is when the confusion arises. In Irish-Catholic Dublin of the 1890s, such youthful beauty not surprisingly invokes analogies between Mangan's sister and the Queen of Heaven (though the swinging of her body and "the soft rope of her hair tossing from side to side" [Joyce], which captivate the boy, hint at something less spiritual than Madonna worship). And while beauty's benchmarks[2] in Sammy's more secular mid-century America are more anatomical than spiritual, Updike does have Sammy call his young *femme fatal*[3] "Queenie," and he does make her the center of a "trinity" of sorts, showing her two friends at one point "huddling against her for relief" ("A & P").

Once smitten, both young protagonists become distracted, agitated, disoriented. Joyce's turns impatient "with the serious work of life." His teacher accuses him of idling. His heart leaps, his thoughts wander, his body responds "like a harp" to the words and gestures of Mangan's sister, which run "like fingers ... upon the wires." Similarly, Updike's young hero can't remember, from the moment he spots Queenie in the aisle, which items he has rung up on the cash register.

Even details in the two stories are similar, Updike clearly taking his cues from "Araby." Both boys are excited by specified *whiteness* about the girls—Joyce's boy by "the white curve of her neck" and "the white border of her petticoat" in the glow of Dublin lamplight, Sammy by the "long white prima-donna legs" ("A & P") and the white shoulders to which he refers repeatedly. "Could there," he wonders, "have been anything whiter than those shoulders?" Joyce's boy also observes a nimbus surrounding Mangan's sister, "her figure defined by the light from the half-opened door." True, Mangan's sister comports herself[4] more humbly than her American counterpart. Queenie walks, heavy-heeled and head high, with the haughty pride of the affluent, secularized American upper middle class. But her enticing whiteness, in Updike's sly parody, is also given a luminous, halo-like quality: "around the top of the cloth," says Sammy of the bathing suit that "had slipped a little on her... there was this shining rim."

Both girls, remote as they are from their ardent admirers, also engage in some subtly seductive posturing. In the supermarket aisle, Queenie turns so slowly that

---

[1] gratifies:使满足。
[2] benchmark:基准点,标准。
[3] *femme fatal*:法语为 femme fatale,妖女,祸水红颜(尤指引诱男人堕落的女人)。
[4] comports herself:她的举止。comport oneself:举止,即以一种特殊方式行为或表现。

Sammy's stomach is made to "rub the inside of his apron." It's the same sensation, we suspect, that Joyce's protagonist feels when Mangan's sister "turns the silver bracelet round and round her wrist" and bows her head toward him in the lamplight in front of her door. Queenie bows to no one, but the "clear bare plane of the top of her chest… is like a dented sheet of metal tilted in the light" ("A & P"). Her beauty, too, like that of Mangan's sister, is incandescent[1] as it inclines toward her aspiring young knight.

Source: *Studies in Short Fiction* 30.2 (Spring 1993): p127 – 133.

问题与思考

1. Pay attention to how artfully the author arranges details to set the story in an ordinary supermarket. What does this close attention to detail contribute to the story?
2. What is the dramatic conflict in the story? When does it become apparent? What is the climax of the story?
3. How fully does Updike draw the character of Sammy? What characteristic does Sammy show? Why does Sammy quit his job? Is he any less a hero for wanting the girls to notice his heroism?
4. Of what value to the story is the carefully detailed portrait of Queenie, the leader of the three girls?
5. What do you understand from the conclusion of the story? What does Sammy mean when he realizes "how hard the world was going to be… hereafter"?

阅读链接

1. http://www.life123.com/arts-culture/american-authors/john-updike/famous-john-updike-short-stories.shtml:厄普代克的四部著名短篇小说集简介。
2. http://www.brainyquote.com/quotes/authors/j/john_updike.html:厄普代克的名言辑录。
3. http://www.bookrags.com/studyguide-rabbitrun:《兔子,跑吧》的分章介绍和评论。

---

[1] incandescent:灿烂的,耀眼的。

3. 人物(Characters)

　　人物指文艺作品描写的人的形象。叙事性文艺作品大多是通过人物的相互关系和人物的活动来刻画人物性格、塑造人物形象。美国作家亨利·詹姆斯将人物和情节视为一个硬币的两面,人物决定情节,情节展现人物,二者相辅相成。

　　在小说里,人物像真实生活中的人,尤其在现实主义小说里,作家从生活中撷取大量细节,用以突出人物的真实感。然而,小说中的人物毕竟是作家想象力的产物,有别于现实生活中的人。他们尽管有真实感,但却是虚构的;他们具有人类复杂的个性,但常常是人性某一方面的代表;他们生活在故事中,不能与真实生活中的人完全等同。在小说里,主要人物居于情节结构的中心位置,往往最能表达主题思想。次要人物的功能是发展情节、衬托主要人物或帮助提炼主题。长篇小说的主要人物和次要人物没有定数,短篇小说因人物较少,主要人物和次要人物的划分相对明确。

　　英国小说家福斯特在《小说面面观》中将小说人物分为两类:扁型人物(flat character)和圆型人物(round character)。扁型人物也叫二维人物,是"围绕一个单独的概念或素质创造出来的……真正的扁型人物可以用一句话来概括"。[1]因此,扁型人物只有一个特质,从头到尾都如此,没有发展变化。圆型人物是三维的、变化的——他们在生活中尤其是挫折中学到东西,受到启蒙,走向成长或堕落。在长篇小说中,扁型人物和圆型人物是并存的,各有其作用。一些以情节为中心的通俗小说如侦探小说、冒险小说塑造的通常都是扁型人物。但是,不能因此简单地认为圆型人物比扁型人物好,塑造扁型的人物还是圆型的人物,要视创作意图和主题而定。如果作家想清晰、有力地表达某一思想,那么他会塑造极少变化的扁型人物,这样才不至于模糊主题。在《暴力的使用》中,冲突的双方没有名字,也没有针对他们个人的详细描写,因为冲突才是故事的中心。人物简单,有助于读者专心思考"使用暴力"的多维涵蕴。如果作者要展现人的个性,那么他会塑造圆型人物。理查德·赖特的《即将成人》描写黑人男孩戴夫·桑德斯痛苦的成长。戴夫从渴望得到一枝枪,终于得到枪,到因为枪而闯祸,被当众羞辱,最后在愤怒中爬上火车离家出走。在这一过程中,他从一个只会纠缠妈妈的大男孩成为一个走向独立生活的男人。在海明威的《士兵之家》中,从战场上回来的哈罗德·克雷伯很难融入家庭和周围的生活中,母亲要求他安定下来好好过日子,他最终做出让步。在这一痛苦转变的过程中,克雷伯认识了生活,也了解了自我。

　　刻画人物主要有两种手法:展示(showing)和讲述(telling)。展示是直接描写人物外在的言行和内在的思想,让读者自己进行评判。现代主义小说在对展示进行的实验中发展出"意识流"(stream of consciousness)手法。意识流表现的是人物内心纷乱无序的思绪,缺乏逻辑性和连贯性,以此挖掘个体行为的动机、道德意识和思想意识。在凯瑟琳·安·波特的《被抛弃的韦罗瑟尔奶奶》中,临终前的韦罗瑟尔奶奶在时而清醒时而昏迷中回忆当年遭未婚夫抛弃,回忆生活的艰辛。在她混乱的意识中,时间和空间变得无序:过去与现在混为一体,死者与生者彼此混淆。这种碎片性使读者生动地了解到韦罗瑟尔奶奶一生所经历的沧桑。如果作家在创作中使用讲

---

[1] Foster, op. cit., p.63.

述手法,那么他/她的"声音"会常常出现故事中,对人物的动机、品质和行为进行解释或评论。现实主义小说常采用这种手法。霍桑的《拉帕奇尼医生之女》有许多地方正面评价贝雅特里齐的美丽和善良,解释乔万尼为贝雅特里齐吸引后的种种行为及其动机。

从艺术价值来看,上面提到的所有手法谈不上孰优孰劣,优秀的作家会博采众长,综合利用,以求传情达意。我们在分析人物形象时,要从外到内进行全面的思考,关注作者是如何通过艺术手段把人物的外在形象、言行和内在的情感、思想有机地结合在一起。

Ernest Hemingway (1899—1961)

作者简介

厄内斯特·海明威(Ernest Hemingway,1899—1961)生于美国伊利诺州芝加哥附近的奥克帕克,父亲是医生,母亲是音乐家。父亲经常带他去打猎和钓鱼,海明威因此亲近大自然,一直非常喜爱户外运动。高中毕业后他在《堪萨斯城星报》当见习记者。1917年,他以救护车司机的身份赴法国参加第一次世界大战,后去意大利,在那里身负重伤。战后他成为《多伦多星报》的自由撰稿人、编辑和驻外记者,1920年搬到芝加哥,成为一份月刊的副编辑。在芝加哥,他遇到美国著名作家舍伍德·安德森,得到他的指点。1921年海明威以《多伦多星报》记者的身份常驻巴黎,在那里得到美国著名作家格特鲁德·斯泰因和诗人庞德的帮助,最终形成了自己独特的简洁文风。此后,他发表一系列小说,蜚声文坛,1954年他以中篇小说《老人与海》(The Old Man and the Sea,1952)及一生的文学成就获得诺贝尔文学奖。1961年,深受疾患困扰的海明威像他父亲30年前所做的那样,开枪自杀,终年62岁。

文学创作

海明威是美国最具影响力的小说家之一,20世纪20年代"迷惘的一代"(The Lost Generation)的重要代表。贯穿其作品的重要主题是"硬汉精神"。海明威塑造了一系列硬汉形象来体现其"重压下的优雅"这一信念,这些硬汉包括《太阳照样升起》(The Sun Also Rises,1926)中勇于笑对人生的一战士兵巴恩斯和被拳击手一次次打倒在地但一次次顽强站起来的斗牛士罗梅罗,《丧钟为谁而鸣》(For Whom the Bell Tolls,1940)中在西班牙内战中为掩护游击队和情人平安转移而从容赴死的志愿兵乔丹,而《老人与海》中的老渔民圣地亚哥则达到了这一硬汉形象的顶峰。圣地亚哥出海84天没打到鱼,第85天捕到了一条大马林鱼,却又被鲨鱼夺走了。他明知打不过鲨鱼,却拼死作战,他说,"人不是为失败而生的,一个人可以被毁灭,但不能被打败。"这句话常被引来阐释海明威式的"硬汉精神"。

海明威文风独特,自成一家。他用词俭省,极少修饰,句式简短,对话简洁,但这种简洁绝不等于简单,相反,简洁的背后意蕴无穷,耐人寻味。海明威自己曾用"冰山原则"来描述这种近似新闻报道的写实风格,"冰山的移动之所以雄伟壮观,是因为它只有1/8浮在水面上。"他的短篇小说是这一风格的典型体现,主要集子有《在我们这个时代》(*In Our Time*,1925)、《第五纵队及最早的49个故事》(*The Fifth Column and the First Forty-Nine Stories*,1938)、《尼克·亚当斯故事集》(*The Nick Adams Stories*,1972)等。

作　　品

Soldier's Home

Krebs went to the war from a Methodist[1] college in Kansas. There is a picture which shows him among his fraternity brothers[2], all of them wearing exactly the same height and style collar. He enlisted in the Marines in 1917 and did not return to the United States until the second division[3] returned from the Rhine[4] in the summer of 1919.

There is a picture which shows him on the Rhone with two German girls and another corporal[5]. Krebs and the corporal look too big for their uniforms. The German girls are not beautiful. The Rhine does not show in the picture.

By the time Krebs returned to his home town in Oklahoma the greeting of heroes was over. He came back much too late. The men from the town who had been drafted[6] had all been welcomed elaborately on their return. There had been a great deal of hysteria[7]. Now the reaction had set in.[8] People seemed to think it was rather ridiculous for Krebs to be getting back so late, years after the war was over.

At first Krebs, who had been at Belleau Wood, Soissons, the Champagne, St.

---

[1] Methodist:卫理公会的。卫理公会为基督教一派别。
[2] his fraternity brothers:这里指他教会学校里的同学。fraternity:一群因背景、职业、兴趣或嗜好相似而走在一起的人。
[3] division:(军事用语)师。
[4] the Rhine:莱茵河。莱茵河流经德国,这里代指德国。
[5] corporal:(军)下士。
[6] drafted:(美)征兵。
[7] hysteria:这里指欣喜若狂的人们热烈欢迎胜利凯旋的士兵。
[8] the reaction had set in:这里指人们对归来的士兵和战争不再感兴趣。

Mihiel and in the Argonne[1] did not want to talk about the war at all. Later he felt the need to talk but no one wanted to hear about it. His town had heard too many atrocity stories to be thrilled by actualities. Krebs found that to be listened to at all he had to lie, and after he had done this twice he, too, had a reaction against the war and against talking about it. A distaste for everything that had happened to him in the war set in because of the lies he had told. All of the times that had been able to make him feel cool and clear inside himself when he thought of them; the times so long back when he had done the one thing, the only thing for a man to do, easily and naturally, when he might have done something else, now lost their cool, valuable quality and then were lost themselves.

His lies were quite unimportant lies and consisted in attributing to himself things other men had seen, done or heard of, and stating as facts certain apocryphal[2] incidents familiar to all soldiers. Even his lies were not sensational at the pool room. His acquaintances, who had heard detailed accounts of German women found chained to machine guns in the Argonne and who could not comprehend, or were barred by their patriotism from interest in, any German machine gunners who were not chained, were not thrilled by his stories.

Krebs acquired the nausea in regard to experience that is the result of untruth or exaggeration, and when he occasionally met another man who had really been a soldier and they talked a few minutes in the dressing room at a dance he fell into the easy pose of the old soldier among other soldiers: that he had been badly, sickeningly frightened all the time. In this way he lost everything.

During this time, it was late summer, he was sleeping late in bed, getting up to walk down town to the library to get a book, eating lunch at home, reading on the front porch until he became bored and then walking down through the town to spend the hottest hours of the day in the cool dark of the pool room. He loved to play pool.

In the evening he practiced on his clarinet[3], strolled down town, read and went to bed. He was still a hero to his two young sisters. His mother would have given him breakfast in bed if he had wanted it. She often came in when he was in bed and asked him to tell her about the war, but her attention always wandered. His father was non-committal[4].

Before Krebs went away to the war he had never been allowed to drive the family motor car. His father was in the real estate business and always wanted the car to be at his command when he required it to take clients out into the country to show them a piece of farm property. The car always stood outside the First National Bank building

---

[1] Belleau Wood, Soissons, the Champagne, St. Mihiel and in the Argonne:均为法国地名。第一次世界大战期间，这些地方都曾发生过战斗。
[2] apocryphal:假冒的,不足为信的。
[3] clarinet:单簧管。
[4] non-committal:情感、态度等不确定的。

where his father had an office on the second floor. Now, after the war, it was still the same car.

Nothing was changed in the town except that the young girls had grown up. But they lived in such a complicated world of already defined alliances and shifting feuds[1] that Krebs did not feel the energy or the courage to break into it. He liked to look at them, though. There were so many good-looking young girls. Most of them had their hair cut short. When he went away only little girls wore their hair like that or girls that were fast[2]. They all wore sweaters and shirt waists with round Dutch collars. It was a pattern. He liked to look at them from the front porch as they walked on the other side of the street. He liked to watch them walking under the shade of the trees. He liked the round Dutch collars above their sweaters. He liked their silk stockings and flat shoes. He liked their bobbed hair and the way they walked.

When he was in town their appeal to him was not very strong. He did not like them when he saw them in the Greek's ice cream parlor. He did not want them themselves really. They were too complicated. There was something else. Vaguely he wanted a girl but he did not want to have to work to get her. He would have liked to have a girl but he did not want to have to spend a long time getting her. He did not want to get into the intrigue and the politics[3]. He did not want to have to do any courting. He did not want to tell any more lies. It wasn't worth it.

He did not want any consequences[4]. He did not want any consequences ever again. He wanted to live along without consequences. Besides he did not really need a girl. The army had taught him that. It was all right to pose as though you had to have a girl. Nearly everybody did that. But it wasn't true. You did not need a girl. That was the funny thing. First a fellow boasted how girls mean nothing to him, that he never thought of them, that they could not touch him. Then a fellow boasted that he could not get along without girls, that he had to have them all the time, that he could not go to sleep without them.

That was all a lie. It was all a lie both ways. You did not need a girl unless you thought about them. He learned that in the army. Then sooner or later you always got one. When you were really ripe for a girl you always got one. You did not have to think about it. Sooner or later it could come. He had learned that in the army.

Now he would have liked a girl if she had come to him and not wanted to talk. But here at home it was all too complicated. He knew he could never get through it all again. It was not worth the trouble. That was the thing about French girls and German girls. There was not all this talking. You couldn't talk much and you did not need to

---

[1] defined alliances and shifting feuds:这里指姑娘们在选择男朋友方面已有了自己的好恶。
[2] fast:放荡的。
[3] the intrigue and the politics:这里指为赢得姑娘的欢心所施展的伎俩。
[4] consequences:这里指他的身份和他撒的关于战争的小谎言所产生的效应。

talk. It was simple and you were friends. He thought about France and then he began to think about Germany. On the whole he had liked Germany better. He did not want to leave Germany. He did not want to come home. Still, he had come home. He sat on the front porch.

He liked the girls that were walking along the other side of the street. He liked the look of them much better than the French girls or the German girls. But the world they were in was not the world he was in. He would like to have one of them. But it was not worth it. They were such a nice pattern. He liked the pattern. It was exciting. But he would not go through all the talking. He did not want one badly enough. He liked to look at them all, though. It was not worth it. Not now when things were getting good again.

He sat there on the porch reading a book on the war. It was a history and he was reading about all the engagements[1] he had been in. It was the most interesting reading he had ever done. He wished there were more maps. He looked forward with a good feeling to reading all the really good histories when they would come out with good detail maps. Now he was really learning about the war. He had been a good soldier. That made a difference.

One morning after he had been home about a month his mother came into his bedroom and sat on the bed. She smoothed her apron.

"I had a talk with your father last night, Harold," she said, "and he is willing for you to take the car out in the evenings."

"Yeah?" said Krebs, who was not fully awake. "Take the car out? Yeah?"

"Yes. Your father has felt for some time that you should be able to take the car out in the evenings whenever you wished but we only talked it over last night."

"I'll bet you made him," Krebs said.

"No. It was your father's suggestion that we talk the matter over."

"Yeah. I'll bet you made him," Krebs sat up in bed.

"Will you come down to breakfast, Harold?" his mother said.

"As soon as I get my clothes on," Krebs said.

His mother went out of the room and he could hear her frying something downstairs while he washed, shaved and dressed to go down into the dining-room for breakfast. While he was eating breakfast, his sister brought in the mail.

"Well, Hare[2]," she said. "You old sleepy-head. What do you ever get up for?"

Krebs looked at her. He liked her. She was his best sister.

"Have you got the paper?" he asked.

She handed him *The Kansas City Star* and he shucked off[3] its brown wrapper and

---

[1] engagements:指战斗。
[2] Hare:Harold 的昵称。
[3] shucked off:剥去。

opened it to the sporting page. He folded *The Star* open and propped it against the water pitcher with his cereal dish to steady it, so he could read while he ate.

"Harold," his mother stood in the kitchen doorway. "Harold, please don't muss up the paper. Your father can't read his *Star* if its been mussed."

"I won't muss it," Krebs said.

His sister sat down at the table and watched him while he read.

"We're playing indoor over at school this afternoon," she said. "I'm going to pitch."

"Good," said Krebs. "How's the old wing?"

"I can pitch better than lots of the boys. I tell them all you taught me. The other girls aren't much good."

"Yeah?" said Krebs.

"I tell them all you're my beau[1]. Aren't you my beau, Hare?"

"You bet."

"Couldn't your brother really be your beau just because he's your brother?"

"I don't know."

"Sure you know. Couldn't you be my beau, Hare, if I was old enough and if you wanted to?"

"Sure. You're my girl now."

"Am I really your girl?"

"Sure."

"Do you love me?"

"Uh, huh."

"Do you love me always?"

"Sure."

"Will you come over and watch me play indoor?"

"Maybe."

"Aw, Hare, you don't love me. If you loved me, you'd want to come over and watch me play indoor."

Krebs' mother came into the dining-room from the kitchen. She carried a plate with two fried eggs and some crisp bacon on it and a plate of buckwheat[2] cakes.

"You run along, Helen," she said. "I want to talk to Harold."

She put the eggs and bacon down in front of him and brought in a jug of maple syrup for the buckwheat cakes. Then she sat down across the table from Krebs.

"I wish you'd put down the paper a minute, Harold," she said.

Krebs took down the paper and folded it.

"Have you decided what you are going to do yet, Harold?" his mother said, taking

---

[1] beau:情人。
[2] buckwheat:荞麦。

off her glasses.

"No," said Krebs.

"Don't you think it's about time?" His mother did not say this in a mean way[1]. She seemed worried.

"I hadn't thought about it," Krebs said.

"God has some work for every one to do," his mother said. "There can be no idle hands in His Kingdom."

"I'm not in His Kingdom," Krebs said.

"We are all of us in His Kingdom."

Krebs felt embarrassed and resentful as always.

"I've worried about you too much, Harold," his mother went on. "I know the temptations you must have been exposed to. I know how weak men are. I know what your own dear grandfather, my own father, told us about the Civil War and I have prayed for you. I pray for you all day long, Harold."

Krebs looked at the bacon fat hardening on his plate.

"Your father is worried, too," his mother went on. "He thinks you have lost your ambition, that you haven't got a definite aim in life. Charley Simmons, who is just your age, has a good job and is going to be married. The boys are all settling down; they're all determined to get somewhere; you can see that boys like Charley Simmons are on their way to being really a credit to the community[2]."

Krebs said nothing.

"Don't look that way, Harold," his mother said. "You know we love you and I want to tell you for your own good how matters stand. Your father does not want to hamper your freedom. He thinks you should be allowed to drive the car. If you want to take some of the nice girls out riding with you, we are only too pleased. We want you to enjoy yourself. But you are going to have to settle down to work, Harold. Your father doesn't care what you start in at. All work is honorable as he says. But you've got to make a start at something. He asked me to speak to you this morning and then you can stop in and see him at his office."

"Is that all?" Krebs said.

"Yes. Don't you love your mother, dear boy?"

"No," Krebs said.

His mother looked at him across the table. Her eyes were shiny. She started crying.

"I don't love anybody," Krebs said.

It wasn't any good. He couldn't tell her, he couldn't make her see it. It was silly to have said it. He had only hurt her. He went over and took hold of her arm. She was crying with her head in her hands.

---

[1] in a mean way: 随口说出的。
[2] being really a credit to the community: 为社区带来荣誉和赞许的人。

"I didn't mean it," he said. "I was just angry at something. I didn't mean I didn't love you."

His mother went on crying. Krebs put his arm on her shoulder.

"Can't you believe me, mother?"

His mother shook her head.

"Please, please, mother. Please believe me."

"All right," his mother said chokily. She looked up at him. "I believe you, Harold."

Krebs kissed her hair. She put her face up to him.

"I'm your mother," she said. "I held you next to my heart when you were a tiny baby."

Krebs felt sick and vaguely nauseated.

"I know, Mummy," he said. "I'll try and be a good boy for you."

"Would you kneel and pray with me, Harold?" his mother asked.

They knelt down beside the dining-room table and Krebs's mother prayed.

"Now, you pray, Harold," she said.

"I can't," Krebs said.

"Try, Harold."

"I can't."

"Do you want me to pray for you?"

"Yes."

So his mother prayed for him and then they stood up and Krebs kissed his mother and went out of the house. He had tried so to keep his life from being complicated. Still, none of it had touched him. He had felt sorry for his mother and she had made him lie. He would go to Kansas City and get a job and she would feel all right about it. There would be one more scene maybe before he got away. He would not go down to his father's office. He would miss that one. He wanted his life to go smoothly. It had just gotten going that way. Well, that was all over now, anyway. He would go over to the schoolyard and watch Helen play indoor baseball.

1925

赏 析

对战争有切肤之痛的海明威在《太阳照样升起》、《永别了,武器》、《丧钟为谁而鸣》等长篇小说和《大二心河》、《在另一个国家》等短篇小说中关注这样一个问题:战争对人意味着什么?战争是如何对一个人的身心造成伤害的?人如何面对这样的创伤?这也是短篇小说《士兵之家》的主题。为此,作者不动声色地为主人公哈罗德·克雷伯安排了一连串的对比。战前,他就读于教会学校,是个有信仰的人;从战场回来后,他拒绝承认上帝,拒绝祈祷。战前,他有志趣相投的学友;战后,他过着几近隐居的生活。在战争中,他很容易与德国或法国姑娘相处;回到家乡,他却连爱的能力和兴趣都失去了。试想,如果一个年轻人连爱情都觉得索然寡味,那么他的生活还有多少意义?战争不一定夺人性命,但会使之失去信仰;战争不一定使人身体残废,却很有可能令他心灵残废。相比之下,后者也许更为可怕。

　　回家后的克雷伯觉得生活变得复杂了,他无法适应,也不愿迁就,只能百无聊赖地过日子,连他喜爱的妹妹的球赛也不想去看。更糟的是,作为惨烈的第一次世界大战的幸存者,克雷伯本应庆幸自己活了下来,应该开始新生活,但他却陷入了行尸走肉的空虚状态。克雷伯的另一个问题是,他无法完全做到身在嚣尘,心在桃源,自顾自地生活。为了安慰母亲和妹妹,他一而再地撒谎,却又为此感到恶心。

　　尽管克雷伯生活空虚,但他还是打算面对现实,离开家乡,开始工作。这在一定程度上体现了海明威的"重压下的优雅"这一观念。然而,海明威又暗示,这仅仅是克雷伯的想法而已,他的未来依然难以预测。这一开放性的结尾表明,战争的阴影难以消弭。在这一点上,《士兵之家》比海明威其他几部主题类似的作品在基调上要阴暗一些。

　　作品很好地体现了海明威言简意赅的"冰山"风格,如克雷伯与母亲的对话句式十分简单,他的一句"I'm not in His Kingdom"就把自己"哀莫大于心死"的心态和战争对人性的影响突显得淋漓尽致。

相关评论

Lies in Hemingway's "Soldier's Home"
Ruben De Bardemaeker

　　Upon returning to his home town, wanting to talk about his war experiences, "Krebs found that to be listened to at all he had to lie." Having moved from the Methodist college in Kansas to the war in Europe and then home again, Krebs cannot retrieve[1] the sense of fitting in so tellingly illustrated by the story's opening snapshot. The setting of postwar Europe differs so greatly from homey Oklahoma that it becomes impossible to speak the truth about the war. Krebs moves from the "pattern" of college to the pattern of war back to the pattern of home, but he has lost his talent for uniformity[2]. Krebs's life in Oklahoma is patterned, but does not fit in with the local ethos[3]:

> ... he was sleeping late in bed, getting up to walk down town to the library to get a book, eating lunch at home, reading on the front porch until he became bored and then walking down through the town to spend the hottest hours of the day in the cool dark of the pool room. He loved to play pool. In the evening he practised on his clarinet, strolled down town, read and went to bed.

　　Clearly, our soldier's home is beset with[4] fewer extremes than Belleau Wood and

---

[1] retrieve:重新得到,找回。
[2] uniformity:一致性,这里指融入主流生活。
[3] ethos:精神特质,社会风气。
[4] is beset with:被……包围;为……所困扰。

Soissons, and its inhabitants seem scarcely interested in the truth about the war. Even Krebs' parents show no real interest in their son's recent experiences: "[His mother] often came in when he was in bed and asked him to tell her about the war, but her mind always wandered. His father was non-committal."

The "quite unimportant lies" that Krebs finds himself compelled to tell have a curious effect on him: "A distaste for everything that had happened to him in the war set in because of the lies he had told"—a distaste evolving into "the nausea in regard to experience that is the result of untruth or exaggeration." At this stage, Krebs is in the process of losing whatever positive memories he may have had about his time in Europe—for it becomes clear that not all was miserable there, especially after the war had finished.

Krebs' growing distaste for his own war memories is emblematized in the way he interacts with former fellow-soldiers:

> ... when he occasionally met another man who had really been a soldier and they talked a few minutes in the dressing room at a dance he fell into the easy *pose* of the old soldier among other soldiers: that he had been badly, sickeningly frightened all the time. In this way he lost everything. (my italics)

That Krebs is obliged to *pose* even in the company of people with whom he shares parts of his past illustrates the extent to which views of the past are tainted by the present. Past experiences become embedded in the pattern of the present, encapsulated[1] in a narrative that adapts itself to present circumstances, not facts in the past. Memories, then, as soon as they are actualized and "presented" in the form of narrative, acquire a performative value. Memory needs to be re-enacted or, rather, reconfigured in language to become intelligible within the discourse of the present. As Peter Messent has observed, this is a transition that Harold Krebs is not capable of making:

> Belleau Wood has rendered his mother's pious language and framework of conventional belief a nonsense. The world now contingent to Krebs is one from which he is absolutely disconnected—whose language and values he cannot share.

Krebs, then, has come undone, or "lost everything," because he is not in touch with home, or does not feel at home in Oklahoma, and because this present unease taints his past, rather than vice versa. Paradoxically, Krebs' past actions do not give him a particular status (such as "war hero") within the present regime; instead, the present alters Krebs' very memory of the past. In the extreme case of Harold Krebs, there is such a disconnect between the war and his American home that his narrative about the

---

[1] encapsulated: 用概括的话来表达; 概述。

past war cannot be accommodated in the present.

With regard to "Soldier's Home," John McKenna and David Raabe, inspired by "temperament theory," boldly claim: "Language is an abstraction. Talk can never substitute for the event itself." But what the story really shows is that language and talk are necessary in order to preserve an event as a factor in one's self, in one's narrative identity. The tragedy of Harold Krebs, then, lies not in having to talk or having to lie, but in being unable to *translate* experiences into the paradigm(s) expected in small-town USA. One may even suggest that it is this inability to translate the past into a past-as-present that causes Krebs' passivity and apparent disaffectedness.

Source: *Hemingway Review* 27.1 (Fall 2007): p55 – 73.

问题与思考

1. What are the outstanding traits of Harold Krebs' character? Does Hemingway give his anti-hero any motivation to withdraw from the mainstream of life?
2. Compare Harold with the other characters in the story. What are the conflicts between Harold and his family, or even the community he lives in?
3. What is revealed through the conversation between Harold and his mother? Why is this revelation important to the characterization of Harold?
4. What is the story's point of view? Discuss its appropriateness.

阅读链接

1. http://www.hemingwayhome.com/HTML/main_menu.html:配图介绍海明威生活的方方面面。
2. http://en.wikipedia.org/wiki/The_Complete_Short_Stories_of_Ernest_Hemingway:海明威短篇小说代表作梗概介绍。
3. http://www.cliffsnotes.com/study_guide/literature/Hemingway-s-Short-Stories.id-10.html:包括海明威生平、短篇小说的大意及简要分析,小说人物的介绍。

Katherine Anne Porter (1890—1980)

作者简介

凯瑟琳·安·波特（Catherine Anne Porter，1890—1980）出生于美国得克萨斯州印第安河市一个天主教家庭，是美国著名作家欧·亨利的远亲。她两岁丧母，由祖母抚养，在南方的农场度过童年，没有受过多少正规教育。16岁时波特离开学校结了婚，并随丈夫皈依罗马天主教。她在芝加哥、纽约等地做过演员、歌手、记者等。1917年，波特开始了她漫长的创作生涯，为刊物写书评、剧评和社会新闻。1919年她去纽约，主要创作儿童故事，并为电影公司做宣传工作，一直到1937年。期间去过欧洲和墨西哥，并在旅居墨西哥时参加了左翼政治活动。40年代末到50年代末，她在美国斯坦福大学等几所大学任教，其独特的教风受到学生的欢迎。波特把一生献给了文学。1980年，她以90岁的高龄去世。

文学创作

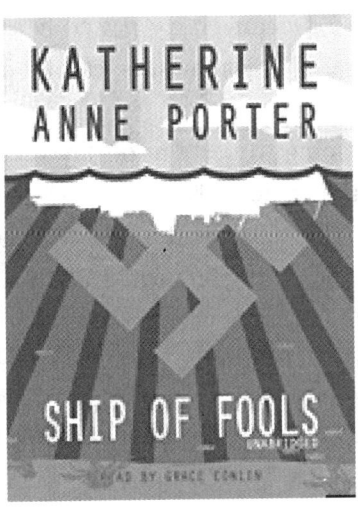

波特是20世纪上半叶美国著名的短篇小说文体家。也许是因为她创作数量不多，直到第二次大战后才在美国文坛上出名，获得过普利策奖和全国图书奖。她的主要作品有短篇小说集《盛开的犹大花及其他故事》(*Flowering Judas and Other Stories*，1930)、《灰白马、灰白骑手》(*Pale Horse，Pale Rider*，1939)和《斜塔及其他故事》(*The Leaning Tower and Other Stories*，1944)。她唯一的长篇小说《愚人船》(*Ship of Fools*，1962)受到广泛好评，是当年的畅销书。

波特的短篇小说有些以她在墨西哥的生活经历为蓝本，有些则是美国南方生活的写照。她善于将自身经历赋予地方色彩、时代特征和历史的厚度，三部短篇小说集被认为是短篇小说的典范，成功地展示了她生动细致的艺术风格。波特还往往着眼于追寻一种具有很强感染力的社会意识,如中篇小说《中午酒》(*Noon Wine*,1937)描写了农庄主汤普生和抓捕逃犯的哈奇为了自己的私利而发生争斗,汤普生杀死哈奇,自己也因忍受不了精神的折磨而自杀。波特指出,这篇小说的创作意图是揭示文明社会表面的平静下涌动着暴力,涌动着"一种最痛苦的混乱,一种道德和情感的混乱"。

作为心理小说家,波特具有意识流大师弗吉尼亚·伍尔芙和普鲁斯特的深度,这表现在她对决定人之行为的"无意识"的洞察。她擅长不动声色的客观描写,善用象征和神话背景,时不时将白描与"意识流"巧妙结合,将人物的情感刻画得栩栩如生。

作　　品

The Jilting of Granny Weatherall

She[1] flicked her wrist neatly out of Doctor Harry's pudgy[2] careful fingers and pulled the sheet up to her chin. The brat ought to be in knee breeches. Doctoring around the country with spectacles on his nose![3] "Get along now. Take your schoolbooks and go. There's nothing wrong with me."

Doctor Harry spread a warm paw[4] like a cushion on her forehead where the forked green vein danced and made her eyelids twitch. "Now, now, be a good girl, and we'll have you up in no time."

"That's no way to speak to a woman nearly eighty years old just because she's down. I'd have you respect your elders, young man."

"Well, Missy, excuse me." Doctor Harry patted her cheek. "But I've got to warn you, haven't I? You're a marvel, but you must be careful or you're going to be good and sorry[5]."

"Don't tell me what I'm going to be. I'm on my feet now, morally speaking. It's Cornelia. I had to go to bed to get rid of her."

Her bones felt loose, and floated around in her skin, and Doctor Harry floated like a balloon around the foot of the bed. He floated and pulled down his waistcoat, and swung his glasses on a cord. "Well, stay where you are, it certainly can't hurt you."

"Get along and doctor your sick," said Granny Weatherall. "Leave a well[6] woman alone. I'll call for you when I want you... Where were you forty years ago when I pulled through[7] milk-leg and double pneumonia? You weren't even born. Don't let Cornelia

---

[1] She:指 Granny Weatherall。80 高龄的 Granny Weatherall 已在弥留之际,她躺在女儿 Cornelia 家中,迷迷糊糊地想到了一生中的往事。整篇故事用意识流手法叙述了 Granny Weatherall 临死前断断续续的回忆及与之交织在一起的她对环境的反应。

[2] pudgy:短而胖的。

[3] The brat ought... on his nose:这小子该穿上短腿马裤。他居然鼻子上架着眼镜在乡间出诊! 注意这两句话的轻蔑口吻。

[4] paw:指医生厚实的手掌。

[5] be good and sorry: be very sorry。good and...:(口) very or altogether。

[6] well:健康的。

[7] pulled through:度过难关,恢复健康。

lead you on," she shouted, because Doctor Harry appeared to float up to the ceiling and out. "I pay my own bills, and I don't throw my money away on nonsense!"

She meant to wave good-by, but it was too much trouble. Her eyes closed of themselves, it was like a dark curtain drawn around the bed. The pillow rose and floated under her, pleasant as a hammock in a light wind. She listened to the leaves rustling outside the window. No, somebody was swishing newspapers; no, Cornelia and Doctor Harry were whispering together. She leaped broad awake,[1] thinking they whispered in her ear.

"She was never like this, *never* like this!" "Well, what can we expect?" "Yes, eighty years old..."

Well, and what if she was? She still had ears. It was like Cornelia to whisper around doors. She always kept things secret in such a public way. She was always being tactful and kind. Cornelia was dutiful; that was the trouble with her. Dutiful and good: "So good and dutiful," said Granny, "that I'd like to spank her." She saw herself spanking Cornelia and making a fine job of it[2].

"What'd you say, mother?"

Granny felt her face tying up in hard knots.

"Can't a body think, I'd like to know?"

"I thought you might like something."

"I do. I want a lot of things. First of, go away and don't whisper."

She lay and drowsed, hoping in her sleep that the children would keep out and let her rest a minute. It had been a long day. Not that she was tired. It was always pleasant to snatch a minute now and then. There was always so much to be done, let me see: tomorrow.

Tomorrow was far away and there was nothing to trouble about. Things were finished somehow when the time came; thank God there was always a little margin over for peace[3]; then a person could spread out the plan of life and tuck in the edges orderly. It was good to have everything clean and folded away, with the hair brushes and tonic bottles sitting straight on the white, embroidered linen; the day started without fuss and the pantry shelves[4] laid out with rows of jelly glasses and brown jugs and white stone-china[5] jars with blue whirligigs and words painted on them: coffee, tea, sugar, ginger, cinnamon, allspice; and the bronze clock with the lion on top nicely dusted off. The dust that lion could collect in twenty-four hours![6] The box in the attic with all those letters tied up, well, she'd have to go through that tomorrow. All those

---

[1] She leaped broad awake: 她猛然坐起身来，完全清醒了。
[2] making a fine job of it: 狠狠地打。
[3] a little margin over for peace: 一点享受安宁的时间。
[4] the pantry shelves: 放餐具的架子。
[5] stone-china: 产于英国的石制品。
[6] The dust that lion... in twenty-four hours!: 一昼夜那狮子身上可积了不少灰尘！

letters—George's letters and John's letters and her letters to them both—lying around for the children to find afterwards made her uneasy. Yes, that would be tomorrow's business. No use to let them know how silly she had been once.

While she was rummaging around she found death in her mind[1] and it felt clammy and unfamiliar. She had spent so much time preparing for death there was no need for bringing it up again. Let it take care of itself for now. When she was sixty she had felt very old, finished, and went around making farewell trips to see her children and grandchildren, with a secret in her mind: This was the very last of your mother, children! Then she made her will and came down with a long fever. That was all just a notion like a lot of other things, but it was lucky too, for she had once and for all got over the idea of dying for a long time. Now she couldn't be worried. She hoped she had better sense now. Her father had lived to be one hundred and two years old and had drunk a noggin[2] of strong hot toddy[3] on his last birthday. He told the reporters it was his daily habit, and he owed his long life to that. He had made quite a scandal and was very pleased about it. She believed she'd just plague Cornelia a little.

"Cornelia! Cornelia!" No footsteps, but a sudden hand on her cheek. "Bless you, where have you been?"

"Here, Mother."

"Well, Cornelia, I want a noggin of hot toddy."

"Are you cold, darling?"

"I'm chilly, Cornelia. Lying in bed stops the circulation. I must have told you a thousand times."

Well, she could just hear Cornelia telling her husband that Mother was getting a little childish and they'd have to humor her. The thing that most annoyed her was that Cornelia thought she was deaf, dumb, and blind. Little hasty glances and tiny gestures tossed around here and over her head saying, "Don't cross her, let her have her way, she's eighty years old," and she sitting there as if she lived in a thin glass cage. Sometimes granny almost made up her mind to pack up and move back to her own house where nobody could remind her every minute that she was old. Wait, wait, Cornelia, till your own children whisper behind your back!

In her day she had kept a better house and had got more work done. She wasn't too old yet for Lydia[4] to be driving eighty miles for advice when one of the children jumped the track, and Jimmy[5] still dropped in and talked things over: "Now, Mammy, you've a good business head, I want to know what you think of this?" Old. Cornelia couldn't change the furniture around without asking. Little things, little

---

[1] she found death in her mind：她想到了死。
[2] Noggin：小瓷杯或茶杯。
[3] toddy：柠檬威士忌甜酒（加热过的酒精、水和柠檬的混合物）。
[4] Lydia：拟为 Granny Weatherall 的另一个女儿。
[5] Jimmy：拟为 Granny Weatherall 的儿子。

things! They had been so sweet when they were little. Granny wished the old days were back again with the children young and everything to be done over. It had been a hard pull, but not too much for her. When she thought of all the food she had cooked, and all the clothes she had cut and sewed, and all the gardens she had made—well, the children showed it. There they were, made out of her, and they couldn't get away from that. Sometimes she wanted to see John[1] again and point to them and say, Well, I didn't do so badly, did I? But that would have to wait. That was for tomorrow. She used to think of him as a man, but now all the children were older than their father, and he would be a child beside her if she saw him now. It seemed strange and there was something wrong in the idea. Why, he couldn't possibly recognize her. She had fenced in a hundred acres once, digging the post holes herself and clamping the wires with just a negro boy to help. That changed a woman. John would be looking for a young woman with a peaked Spanish comb[2] in her hair and the painted fan. Digging post holes changed a woman. Riding country roads in the winter when women had their babies was another thing: sitting up nights with sick horses and sick negroes and sick children and hardly ever losing one. John, I hardly ever lost one of them! John would see that in a minute, that would be something he could understand, she wouldn't have to explain anything!

It made her feel like rolling up her sleeves and putting the whole place to rights[3] again. No matter if Cornelia was determined to be everywhere at once, there were a great many things left undone on this place. She would start tomorrow and do them. It was good to be strong enough for everything, even if all you made melted and changed and slipped under your hands, so that by the time you finished you almost forgot what you were working for. What was it I set out to do? She asked herself intently, but she could not remember. A fog rose over the valley, she saw it marching across the creek swallowing the trees and moving up the hill like an army of ghosts. Soon it would be at the near edge of the orchard, and then it was time to go in and light the lamps. Come in, children, don't stay out in the night air.

Lighting the lamps had been beautiful. The children huddled up to her and breathed like little calves waiting at the bars in the twilight. Their eyes followed the match and watched the flame rise and settle in a blue curve, then they moved away from her. The lamp was lit, they didn't have to be scared and hang on to mother any more. Never, never, never more. God, for all my life, I thank Thee. Without Thee, my God, I could never have done it. Hail, Mary, full of grace.[4]

I want you to pick all the fruit this year and see nothing is wasted. There's always someone who can use it. Don't let good things rot for want of using. You waste life

---

[1] John: Granny Weatherall 的丈夫。
[2] Spanish comb: 一种梳齿很长的梳子,常作为装饰插在妇女的发髻间。
[3] putting the whole place to rights: 把整个屋子收拾好。
[4] Hail, Mary, full of grace: (天主教徒在祈祷开始时说)万福玛利亚,宽厚仁慈的圣母!

when you waste good food. Don't let things get lost. It's bitter to lose things. Now, don't let me get to thinking, not when I'm tired and taking a little nap before supper...

The pillow rose about her shoulders and pressed against her heart and the memory was being squeezed out of it: oh, push down the pillow, somebody: it would smother her if she tried to hold it. Such a fresh breeze blowing and such a green day with no threats in it[1]. But he[2] had not come, just the same. What does a woman do when she has put on the white veil and set out the white cake for a man and he doesn't come? She tried to remember. No, I swear he never harmed me but in that. He never harmed me but in that... and what if he did? There was the day, the day, but a whirl of dark smoke rose and covered it, crept up and over into the bright field where everything was planted so carefully in orderly rows. That was hell, she knew hell when she saw it. For sixty years she had prayed against remembering him and against losing her soul in the deep pit of hell[3], and now the two things were mingled in one and the thought of him was a smoky cloud from hell that moved and crept in her head when she had just got rid of Doctor Harry and was trying to rest a minute. Wounded vanity, Ellen,[4] said a sharp voice in the top of her mind. Don't let your wounded vanity get the upper hand of you. Plenty of girls get jilted[5]. You were jilted, weren't you? Then stand up to it. Her eyelids wavered and let in streamers of blue-gray light like tissue paper over her eyes. She must get up and pull the shades down or she'd never sleep. She was in bed again and the shades were not down. How could that happen? Better turn over, hide from the light, sleeping in the light gave you nightmares. "Mother, how do you feel now?" and a stinging wetness on her forehead. But I don't like having my face washed in cold water!

Hapsy[6]? George? Lydia? Jimmy? No, Cornelia and her features were swollen and full of little puddles. "They're coming, darling, they'll all be here soon." Go wash your face, child, you look funny.

Instead of obeying, Cornelia knelt down and put her head on the pillow. She seemed to be talking but there was no sound. "Well, are you tongue-tied? Whose birthday is it? Are you going to give a party?"

Cornelia's mouth moved urgently in strange shapes. "Don't do that, you bother me, daughter."

"Oh no, Mother. Oh, no..."

Nonsense. It was strange about children. They disputed your every word. "No what, Cornelia?"

---

[1] such a green... threats in it: 这么风和日丽的天气不会有什么变化。
[2] he: 指 George, Granny Weatherall 年轻时的第一个未婚夫。他与 Granny Weatherall 订下了婚期,结婚那一天他却没来。下面的一部分即叙述了这件事。
[3] she had prayed against... pit of hell: 她祈祷不要再想他(George),不要让自己的灵魂落到地狱的深渊。
[4] Ellen: Granny Weatherall 的名字。
[5] get jilted: 遭到抛弃。
[6] Hapsy: 拟为 Granny Weatherall 的另一个女儿,亦可能是她想象中的孩子。

"Here's Doctor Harry."

"I won't see that boy again. He left just five minutes ago."

"That was this morning, Mother. It's night now. Here's the nurse."

"This is Doctor Harry, Mrs. Weatherall. I never saw you look so young and happy!"

"Ah, I'll never be young again—but I'd be happy if they'd let me lie in peace and get rested."

She thought she spoke up loudly, but no one answered. A warm weight on her forehead, a warm bracelet on her wrist, and a breeze went on whispering, trying to tell her something.[1] A shuffle of leaves in the everlasting hand of God, He blew on them and they danced and rattled. "Mother, don't mind, we're going to give you a little hypodermic[2]." "Look here, daughter, how do ants get in this bed? I saw sugar ants yesterday." Did you send for Hapsy too?

It was Hapsy she really wanted. She had to go a long way back through a great many rooms to find Hapsy standing with a baby on her arm. She seemed to herself to be Hapsy also, and the baby on Hapsy's arm was Hapsy and himself and herself, all at once, and there was no surprise in the meeting. Then Hapsy melted from within and turned flimsy as gray gauze and the baby was a gauzy shadow, and Hapsy came up close and said, "I thought you'd never come," and looked at her very searchingly and said, "You haven't changed a bit!" They leaned forward to kiss, when Cornelia began whispering from a long way off, "Oh, is there anything you want to tell me? Is there anything I can do for you?"

Yes, she had changed her mind after sixty years and she would like to see George. I want you to find George. Find him and be sure to tell him I forgot him. I want him to know I had my husband just the same and my children and my house like any other woman. A good house too and a good husband that I loved and fine children out of him. Better than I had hoped for even. Tell him I was given back everything he took away and more. Oh, no, oh, God, no, there was something else besides the house and the man and the children. Oh, surely they were not all? What was it? Something not given back... Her breath crowded down under her ribs and grew into a monstrous frightening shape with cutting edges; it bored up into her head, and the agony was unbelievable: Yes, John, get the Doctor now, no more talk, my time has come.[3]

When this one was born it should be the last. The last. It should have been born first, for it was the one she had truly wanted. Everything came in good time. Nothing left out, left over. She was strong, in three days she would be as well as ever. Better. A woman needed milk in her to have her full health.

---

[1] A warm weight... tell her something:有人用温暖的手按着她的额头,握着她的手腕,柔声细语地对她讲了什么。作者用 weight, bracelet, breeze 作了形象化的比喻。

[2] hypodermic:皮下注射。

[3] my time has come:我要临产了。Granny Weatherall 回忆她年轻时分娩的情景。

"Mother, do you hear me?"

"I've been telling you—"

"Mother, Father Connolly[1]'s here."

"I went to Holy Communion only last week. Tell him I'm not so sinful as all that."

"Father just wants to speak with you."

He could speak as much as he pleased. It was like him to drop in and inquire about her soul as if it were a teething baby[2], and then stay on for a cup of tea and a round of cards and gossip. He always had a funny story of some sort, usually about an Irishman who made his little mistakes and confessed them, and the point lay in some absurd thing he would blurt out in the confessional showing his struggles between native piety and original sin. Granny felt easy about her soul. Cornelia, where are your manners? Give Father Connolly a chair. She had her secret comfortable understanding with a few favorite saints who cleared a straight road to God for her. All as surely signed and sealed as the papers for the new Forty Acres[3]. Forever heirs and assigns forever. Since the day the wedding cake was not cut, but thrown out and wasted. The whole bottom of the world dropped out, and there she was blind and sweating with nothing under her feet and the walls falling away. His hand had caught her under the breast, she had not fallen, there was the freshly polished floor with the green rug on it, just as before. He had cursed like a sailor's parrot and said, "I'll kill him for you." Don't lay a hand on him, for my sake leave something to God[4]. "Now, Ellen, you must believe what I tell you…"

So there was nothing, nothing to worry about anymore, except sometimes in the night one of the children screamed in a nightmare, and they both hustled out and hunting for the matches and calling, "There, wait a minute, here we are!" John, get the doctor now, Hapsy's time has come. But there was Hapsy standing by the bed in a white cap. "Cornelia, tell Hapsy to take off her cap. I can't see her plain."

Her eyes opened very wide and the room stood out like a picture she had seen somewhere. Dark colors with the shadows rising towards the ceiling in long angles. The tall black dresser gleamed with nothing on it but John's picture, enlarged from a little one, with John's eyes very black when they should have been blue. You never saw him, so how do you know how he looked? But the man insisted the copy was perfect, it was very rich and handsome. For a picture, yes, but it's not my husband. The table by the bed had a linen cover and a candle and a crucifix. The light was blue from Cornelia's silk lampshades. No sort of light at all, just frippery. You had to live forty years with kerosene lamps to appreciate honest electricity. She felt very strong and she saw Doctor

---

[1] Father Connolly:天主教习俗,病人临终前,神父要为他祝福或由病人向神父忏悔,祈求上帝的宽恕。

[2] a teething baby:出乳牙的婴儿。

[3] Forty Acres:拟为 Granny Weatherall 的农场名。

[4] leave something to God:让上帝去对付吧(指惩罚 George)。

Harry with a rosy nimbus[1] around him.

"You look like a saint, Doctor Harry, and I vow that's as near as you'll ever come to it."

"She's saying something."

"I heard you Cornelia. What's all this carrying-on?"

"Father Connolly's saying—"

Cornelia's voice staggered and jumped like a cart in a bad road. It rounded corners and turned back again and arrived nowhere. Granny stepped up in the cart very lightly and reached for the reins, but a man sat beside her and she knew him by his hands, driving the cart. She did not look in his face, for she knew without seeing, but looked instead down the road where the trees leaned over and bowed to each other and a thousand birds were singing a Mass. She felt like singing too, but she put her hand in the bosom of her dress and pulled out a rosary, and Father Connolly murmured Latin in a very solemn voice and tickled her feet. My God, will you stop that nonsense? I'm a married woman. What if he did run away and leave me to face the priest by myself? I found another a whole world better.[2] I wouldn't have exchanged my husband for anybody except St. Michael[3] himself, and you may tell him that for me with a thank you in the bargain[4].

Light flashed on her closed eyelids, and a deep roaring shook her. Cornelia, is that lightning? I hear thunder. There's going to be a storm. Close all the windows. Call the children in... "Mother, here we are, all of us." "Is that you Hapsy?" "Oh, no, I'm Lydia. We drove as fast as we could." Their faces drifted above her, drifted away. The rosary fell out of her hands and Lydia put it back. Jimmy tried to help, their hands fumbled together, and granny closed two fingers around Jimmy's thumb. Beads wouldn't do, it must be something alive. She was so amazed her thoughts ran round and round. So, my dear Lord, this is my death and I wasn't even thinking about it. My children have come to see me die. But I can't, it's not time. Oh, I always hated surprises. I wanted to give Cornelia the amethyst set[5]—Cornelia, you're to have the amethyst set, but Hapsy's to wear it when she wants, and, Doctor Harry, do shut up. Nobody sent for you. Oh, my dear Lord, do wait a minute. I meant to do something about the Forty Acres, Jimmy doesn't need it and Lydia will later on, with that worthless husband of hers. I meant to finish the alter cloth and send six bottles of wine to Sister Borgia for her dyspepsia[6]. I want to send six bottles of wine to Sister Borgia, Father Connolly, now don't let me forget.

---

[1] a rosy nimbus: 一个玫瑰色光环。
[2] I found another a whole world better: 我找到了另一个更好的人(指John)。
[3] St. Michael: 是《圣经》中的持刀天使,曾征服魔鬼撒旦,也是天主教徒崇拜的一位圣人。
[4] in the bargain: 外加,另外。
[5] the amethyst set: 一套紫水晶首饰。
[6] dyspepsia: 消化不良。

Cornelia's voice made short turns and tilted over and crashed. "Oh, mother, oh, mother, oh, mother…"

"I'm not going, Cornelia. I'm taken by surprise. I can't go."

You'll see Hapsy again. What bothered her? "I thought you'd never come." Granny made a long journey outward, looking for Hapsy. What if I don't find her? What then? Her heart sank down and down, there was no bottom to death, she couldn't come to the end of it. The blue light from Cornelia's lampshade drew into a tiny point in the center of her brain, it flickered and winked like an eye, quietly it fluttered and dwindled. Granny laid curled down within herself, amazed and watchful, staring at the point of light that was herself; her body was now only a deeper mass of shadow in an endless darkness and this darkness would curl around the light and swallow it up. God, give a sign!

For a second time there was no sign. Again no bridegroom and the priest in the house. She could not remember any other sorrow because this grief wiped them all away. Oh, no, there's nothing more cruel than this—I'll never forgive it. She stretched herself with a deep breath and blew out the light.

1930

赏 析

《被遗弃的韦瑟罗尔奶奶》是一篇有深度、有意蕴的意识流小说,它奠定了波特作为短篇小说重要作家的地位。

意识流小说20世纪初兴起于西方,是现代派小说一个重要的类型,其特点是打破传统小说直线发展的情节结构,通过自由联想来组织故事和表现人的意识活动,在时间上常常是过去、现在、将来相互交叉或重叠。波特在《被遗弃的韦瑟罗尔奶奶》中采用了意识流小说创作手法。故事开始,躺在床上的女主人公韦瑟罗尔奶奶依然头脑清醒,和医生开玩笑,渐渐地,她意识变得模糊,陷于断断续续的回忆中,她曲折的生活轨迹在过去与现实的纠缠交错中一点点浮现出来:新婚之日被未婚夫乔治抛弃,后来与约翰结婚,丈夫不幸英年早逝,她一人抚养孩子,管理农场。"韦瑟罗尔"这个名字(Weatherall)意为饱经沧桑。韦瑟罗尔奶奶在漫长的一生中两次被抛弃,一是男人(婚姻),二是上帝(死亡)。她一辈子想忘掉抛弃她的乔治,但终究没有做到。这时,"一阵黑烟旋起,盖住了它,弥漫过来,飘进明亮的田野。田野里是精心耕种、排列整齐的庄稼。那是地狱,她一看就知道那是地狱。"这阵黑烟,以及贯穿整个故事的明暗对比,象征突如其来的灾难,改变了她原来期待的美好生活。韦瑟罗尔奶奶面对逆境,坚强地生活。支撑她生活下去的是对上帝的信念。不过当死亡临近,上帝并未出现,她对上帝的求助转化为失望。

作者通过展现韦瑟罗尔奶奶临终前浮现在脑海的思绪,使读者可以直接深入人物的内心世界,并且通过他/她的眼光看待一切,这样容易产生认同感,对韦瑟罗尔尔奶奶产生同情。句式的变化契合人物身体状况的变化,韦瑟罗尔尔奶奶清醒时,用的是有条理的长句,到故事结尾,则改用缺乏连贯性的短句来表现她濒临死亡时呼吸急促,思维混乱。故事结束时,韦瑟罗尔奶奶意识到自己被上帝遗弃,一如她一生奋力掌握自己命运,她用最后一口气,自己吹灭了生命之光,这一结尾揭示了韦瑟罗尔奶奶的坚强性格。

相关评论

The Problem of Atheistic[1] Interpretations
Bruce A. French

A few critics assume that there is no god and that therefore Granny is bound to be grievously disappointed when she dies. James William Johnson's essay, entitled "Another Look at Katherine Anne Porter," implies this atheistic interpretation: "The Jilting of Granny Weatherall' shows a dying old woman, stood up by the God she had supposed to exist, just as she had been jilted by an earthly finance' [*sic*] and forced to live a life of disappointment and compensation". Johnson also speaks of "the Everlasting Nay," the "thing 'most cruel of all', which in its enormity transcends all other sorrows—the obliteration of hope." Johnson, however, does not make a thematic connection between the two jiltings; for him, the one does not lead to the other.

Edward G. Schwartz takes a similar but vaguer atheistic stance regarding the possibility of people being able to achieve spiritual salvation: "The dying grandmother in 'The Jilting of Granny Weatherall' achieves *a final awful illumination* through her last confused reveries[2]" (italics added). It does not seem likely that Schwartz's "final awful illumination" refers to Granny's realization that memories of George are still painful. She has been continually aware of the pain for sixty years. Nor does it seem that the word "illumination" could refer to her realization that God is simply not going to reward her for a life's job well done. What Schwartz probably means by "a final awful illumination" is that, after a life filled with psychological suffering and hard work, Granny realizes that there is no God to reward her for having weathered all. For Granny, such an illumination would, of course, be "final" and "awful."

A third critic, William Nance, also takes the atheistic approach as he explains Ellen's failure both with George and with god on the basis of a childish romanticism: "The Divine Bridegroom, like the earthly one, proves to have been a romantic dream, but Granny's courage will do her no good after this delusion."

Joann P. Cobb, in an essay entitled "Pascal's Wager and Two Modern Losers", interprets the bleak ending, like Hendrick and Nance, atheistically. She feels the context of the story asserts: "God is not." But this bald assertion is never supported by details from the story.

However, such atheistic readings of the story's ending are irrelevant to the thematically important details of the story. If the reader assumes the non-existence of a transcendent God in a transcendent heaven, then the entire pathos[3] of the story rests

---
[1] atheistic:无神论的。
[2] reveries:回忆;幻想。
[3] pathos:伤感。

on the irony created by that extra-textual assumption. However, the story has significant pathos long before its last few lines. None of these details leading up to the end indicates that Ellen's life will have been in vain simply because there is no transcendent God to reward a life of virtue. Why then is Granny jilted by God? Why is Granny's soul condemned to "hell"?

The Problem of Salvation Through Faith, Good Works, and Middle-Class Virtues

Darlene Harbour Unrue's answer to the question regarding the fate of Granny's soul focuses on Ellen's vain efforts to save herself through the systems and patterns of religion:

> Porter's darkest discourse on ineffectual religion occurs in "The Jilting of Granny Weatherall." Granny's religion could be any other religion, but Catholicism served Porter's theme best because of its refined and elaborate structure. Structure is inherently important to Granny, who has spent her life looking for *truth* through systems and patterns, and it is the failure of systematic religion that is terrifyingly dramatized in her dying hour... In the final instance, the bridegroom is unmistakably Christ—and she has not found the *meaning* focused through His life that her religion has promised and which she expected to have before she died. (italics added)

Unrue's use of the words "truth" and "meaning" have scant relevance to the story as crafted by Porter. Although Granny is outwardly a Roman Catholic, she has her own way of trying to deal with her spiritual problems. Her interactions with Doctor Harry, Father Connolly, and others show that she hardly knows what sin is. The main concern of her adult life has been to heal her broken heart, to get past the pain of George's having jilted her. She is irritable with the priest because he wants to speak with her:

> He could speak as much as he pleased. It was like him to drop in and inquire about her soul as if it were a teething baby... He always had a funny story... usually about an Irishman who made his little mistakes and confessed them, and the point lay in some absurd thing he would blurt out in the confessional showing his struggles between native piety and original sin. Granny felt easy about her soul... She had her secret comfortable understanding with few favorite saints who cleared a straight road to God for her.

With this understanding in place, this agreement with the saints, Granny has spent the sixty years of her adult life focusing on the practical problems of daily life. She has become an expert in solving those problems, and in her own eyes she does not make "little mistakes" which need to be confessed. No doubt she is always right in such practical matters. Her middle-class, self-righteous morality can be summed up in her comment to Doctor Harry: "I pay my own bills, and I don't throw my money away on nonsense." But, of course, such a position, despite its obvious satisfactions, has little to do with the spiritual condition of Granny's soul. And despite the obvious pleasures and satisfactions that Granny refers to on her deathbed, the story still ends on a note of utter spiritual darkness. This darkness, Unrue says, is the "ultimate agony that is created when one pins one's faith on formal systems or on an external order that is not natural to one's spirit." This idea has merit, but wording it this way does not help the reader see its relationship to the story as Porter tells it. The reason for Granny's damnation must be sought elsewhere and not in her failure to find "truth" and "meaning" in the systems and patterns of religion and of everyday living that she sets up in her life. The question "Why spiritual damnation?" still remains.

For most readers, Granny appears to have a strong faith both in her religion and in her God: she feels "easy about her soul." When she is thinking about her children and about her hard life, she says something to herself that also implies a great reliance on her religious faith: "God, for all my life I thank Thee. Without Thee, my God, I could never have done it. Hail Mary, full of grace." At another time, as Granny lies there on her bed, thoughts of death come into her mind, and she thinks confidently: "She had spent so much time preparing for death there was no need for bringing it up again. Let it take care of itself now." And when Cornelia tells her that Father Connolly has come to see her, Granny says, "I went to Holy Communion only last week. Tell him I'm not so sinful as all that."

The reader is also informed that Granny's life has been filled with good works:

> Granny wished the old days were back again with the children young and everything to be done over. It had been a hard pull, but not too much for her. When she thought of all the food she had cooked, and all the clothes she had cut and sewed, and all the gardens she had made—well, the children showed it.

In general, Granny feels good about her role as mother and about her success with her children; she would like for John to see them and know that "she didn't do so badly" in raising them by herself. Her good works extended beyond her immediate family. She remembers "riding country roads in the winter when women had their babies... sitting up nights with sick horses and sick negroes (sic) and sick children and hardly ever losing one." We also know that she was working on an altar cloth for her church and that she had meant to "send six bottles of wine to Sister Borgia for her dyspepsia."

No doubt, for Granny, during her adult years, cleanliness—as well as orderliness—was next to godliness:

> It was good to have everything clean and folded away, with the hair brushes and tonic bottles sitting straight on the white embroidered linen... the pantry shelves laid out with rows of jelly glasses on them: coffee, tea, sugar, ginger, cinnamon, allspice; and the bronze clock with the lion on top nicely dusted off. The dust that lion could collect in twenty-four hours!

George Hendrick in his book *Katherine Anne Porter*, sees the dusty lion as a reference to James' "The Beast in the Jungle": "that is, the disorder which she

(Granny), like Sophia Jane, constantly had to fight." However, the thematic significance of the dusty lion has less to do with fighting ordinary household dust and disorder than with fighting the disorder that built up in Granny's soul when she was not busy doing something: "Don't let things get lost. It's bitter to lose things. Now, don't let me get to thinking, not when I'm tired." One can call Granny's busy-ness "constructive avoidance": she wanted to avoid the painful thoughts of George. Dusting the bronze lion every day was obviously not an important task in running the farm efficiently or raising the children well. (The dust-free lion functions in a manner similar to the always-wet top of the kitchen table in Eudora Welty's story "Livvie." Livvie's life is so empty that she has nothing better to do than wipe off the kitchen table one more time.) Such compulsive behavior as lion-dusting has become such a deep-seated part of Granny's way of life that, even while she lies there on her deathbed, she looks around at Cornelia's house and says to herself: "No matter if Cornelia was determined to be everywhere at once, there were a great many things left undone on this place. She would start tomorrow and do them." All of this—Granny's concern for her children, for her hired help, for her farm animals, and for the farm itself; her concern for orderliness and cleanliness; and her concern for others—indicates that Granny sees herself as having been a responsible person who knew what her duty was and did it.

Most important, however, was her sense of duty to herself as a woman. This was the central motivating force in her life: her sacred, God-given duty as a woman was to marry a man, have children, and raise them well in a well-kept house. The reader can believe her when she says to herself on her deathbed: "...I had my husband just the same and my children and my house *like any other woman*. A good house too and a good husband that I loved and fine children out of him. Better than I hoped for even" (italics added). Granny is convinced that she has performed these "God-given" duties as well as anybody could have expected her to do so, given the extenuating[1] circumstances of her life. Clearly, she has had to work hard at living the good life, and it is no wonder that as death approaches and she sees no sign from God, she says, "Oh, no, there's nothing more cruel than this—I'll never forgive it." She feels that God or His saints have not lived up to their end of the bargain, have not done their part of the "secret comfortable understanding."

Source: *Essays in Arts and Sciences* 24 (Oct. 1995): p63 – 76.

问题与思考

1. What are the outstanding traits of Granny Weatherall? What is her attitude toward life? Does she have any regret in her life? What does the name "Weatherall" tell us

---

[1] extenuating: 情有可原的。

about her?
2. In what ways does Porter characterize Granny Weatherall? How effective is the author's method?
3. Compare Granny Weatherall with Elisa in Steinbeck's "The Chrysanthemums". Both stories were written in the 1930's. What is revealed concerning women and their position in life?
4. Discuss the arrangement of the actions in the story. How does Porter treat the past and the present? And how does she make the reader aware of the distinction?

阅读链接

1. http://www.answers.com/topic/katherine-anne-porter：对波特生平的详细介绍，重要作品的主要内容和作品目录。
2. http://www.csustan.edu/english/reuben/pal/chap7/porter.html：对波特创作的详细介绍，研究波特作品的文章目录及研究问题。
3. http://www.lib.umd.edu/Guests/KAP：凯瑟琳·安·波特学会，包括新闻、会议和出版物。

Richard Wright (1908—1960)

作者简介

理查德·赖特(Richard Wright，1908—1960)生于美国密西西比州纳齐兹镇附近的一个种植园，祖父是奴隶，父亲是种植园工人，后弃家出走，母亲患病，家庭贫困。赖特在亲戚家和孤儿院里度过童年，15岁起独立谋生，1927年来到芝加哥找工作，但大萧条使他不得不靠救济金生活。赖特在芝加哥开始接触马克思主义，并于1933年加入美国共产党，写下了大量的革命诗歌。1937年他去纽约，任美国共产党机关报《工人日报》哈莱姆区的编辑。赖特成名后，于1946年迁居巴黎，次年加入法国国籍，此后他游历欧洲、亚洲和非洲，同时继续文学创作和社会活动。1960年11月他因心脏病去世，终年52岁。为纪念赖特对美国社会和文学作出的贡献，美国于2009年发行了一枚面值61分的邮票。

文学创作

赖特是美国20世纪杰出的黑人作家，他的文学创作包括长篇小说、短篇故事、戏剧和诗歌等，主要作品有短篇小说集《汤姆叔叔的孩子》(*Uncle Tom's Children*，1938)、长篇小说《土生子》(*Native Son*，1940)和自传体小说《黑孩子》(*Black Boy*，1945)。

《汤姆叔叔的孩子》是赖特的第一部作品，收录了四篇故事，主要运用自然主义手法描写了美国南方农村白人与黑人之间残酷的冲突，表现了美国黑人精神上受压迫、身体上受奴役的生存状况。该书一经出版，立刻获得评论界的好评。代表作《土生子》使赖特一跃成为享誉美国文坛的作家。小说以30年代的芝加哥为背景，描写了家境清贫的黑人青年别格·托马斯因在无意中杀死了富有的白人小姐而逃跑、被捕和处死的经过。小说获得畅销,后被改编成戏剧在百老汇上演,并拍成电影。赖特在《土生子》中力图说明:黑人的野蛮凶残既非天性也非民族性,而是美国社会制度使然。《黑孩子》生动讲述了赖特在种族隔离的二三十年代的成长历程,记录了他在身体上和精神上遭受的许多苦难。赖特的另一部短篇小说集是在他去世后出版的《八个人》(*Eight Men*,1961),其中的《地下人》("The Man Who Lived Underground")被认为是他50年代最重要的作品之一。

无论是小说还是非小说,赖特的创作主题鲜明,即"以深刻的笔触和充满激情的描述再现了挣扎在贫困、恐惧、耻辱和仇恨之中的黑人生活情景",批判了种族歧视现象和种族隔离政策。他准确地描写了黑人的形象及其在白人种族压迫下的扭曲心理,从而成为美国"抗议小说"的代表作家。

作　　品

The Man Who Was Almost a Man

Dave struck out across the fields,[1] looking homeward through paling light. Whut's the use talkin wid 'em niggers[2] in the field? Anyhow, his mother was putting supper on the table. Them niggers can't understan nothing[3]. One of these days he was going to get a gun and practice shooting, then they couldn't talk to him as though he were a little boy. He slowed, looking at the ground. Shucks, Ah ain't scareda them even ef they are biggern me![4] Aw, Ah know whut Ahma[5] do. Ahm going by ol Joe's sto n git[6] that Sears Roebuck catlog[7] n look at them guns. Mebbe Ma will lemme[8] buy one when she gits mah pay from ol man Hawkins.[9] Ahma beg her t gimme [10]some money. Ahm ol ernough[11] to hava[12] gun. Ahm seventeen. Almost a man. He strode, feeling his long loose-jointed limbs. Shucks, a man oughta hava little gun aftah[13] he done worked hard

---

[1] struck out across the fields:迈步走过田野。
[2] Whut's the use talkin wid 'em niggers...? = what's the use talking with those niggers...? em:them,等于these或those。黑人英语里常将th念成d,将ing念成in,将you念成yuh,将字尾的t、d音吃掉。
[3] nothing = anything;黑人英语常用双重否定来表示否定。
[4] Shucks, Ah ain't scareda… biggern me! = Shucks, I am not scared of them even if they are bigger than me; shucks:感叹词,表示失望、不快等情绪。
[5] Ahma = I am to.
[6] by ol Joe's sto n git = by old Joe's store and get.
[7] catlog = catalogue.
[8] Mebbe Ma will lemme = Maybe Ma will let me.
[9] gits mah pay from ol man Hawkins = gets my pay from old man Hawkins.
[10] t gimme = to give me.
[11] ernough = enough.
[12] hava = have a.
[13] aftah = after.

all day.

He came in sight of Joe's store. A yellow lantern glowed on the front porch. He mounted steps and went through the screen door, hearing it bang behind him. There was a strong smell of coal oil and mackerel fish.[1] He felt very confident until he saw fat Joe walk in through the rear door, then his courage began to ooze.

"Howdy, Dave! Whutcha want?"[2]

"How yuh, Mistah[3] Joe? Aw, Ah don wana buy nothing. Ah jus wanted t see ef yuhd lemme look at tha catlog erwhile[4]."

"Sure! You wanna see it here?"

"Nawsuh[5]. Ah wans[6] t take it home wid me. Ah'll bring it back termorrow when Ah come in from the fiels."

"You planning on buying something?"

"Yessuh[7]."

"Your ma lettin you have your own money now?"

"Shucks. Mistah Joe, Ahm gittin t be a man like anybody else!"

Joe laughed and wiped his greasy white face with a red bandanna[8].

"Whut you plannin on buyin?"

Dave looked at the floor, scratched his head, scratched his thigh, and smiled. Then he looked up shyly.

"Ah'll tell yuh, Mistah Joe, ef yuh promise yuh won't tell."

"I promise."

"Waal[9], Ahma buy a gun."

"A gun? Whut you want with a gun?"

"Ah wanna keep it."

"You ain't nothing but a boy. You don't need a gun."

"Aw, lemme have the catalog, Mistah Joe. Ah'll bring it back."

Joe walked through the rear door. Dave was elated. He looked around at barrels of sugar and flour. He heard Joe coming back. He craned his neck to see if he were bringing the book. Yeah, he's got it. Gawddog[10], he's got it!

"Here, but be sure you bring it back. It's the only one I got."

---

[1] mackerel fish: 鲭鱼。
[2] Howdy, Dave! Whutcha want? = How do you do, Dave? What do you want?
[3] Mistah = Mister.
[4] erwhile = a while.
[5] Nawsuh = No, sir.
[6] wans = want; 黑人英语里常将现在时第三人称单数加 s 的规律用错。
[7] Yessuh = Yes, sir.
[8] bandanna: 印花大手帕。
[9] Waal = Well.
[10] Gawddog = Good dog.

"Sho[1], Mistah Joe."

"Say, if you wanna buy a gun, why don't you buy one from me? I gotta gun to sell."

"Will it shoot?"

"Sure it'll shoot."

"Whut kind is it?"

"Oh, it's kinda old... a left-hand Wheeler[2]. A pistol. A big one."

"Is it got bullets in it?"

"It's loaded."

"Kin[3] Ah see it?"

"Where's your money?"

"Whut yuh wan fer[4] it?"

"I'll let you have it for two dollars."

"Just two dollahs? Shucks, Ah could buy tha when Ah git mah pay."

"I'll have it here when you want it."

"Awright[5], suh. Ah be in fer it."

He went through the door, hearing it slam again behind him. Ahma git some money from Ma n buy me a gun! Only two dollahs! He tucked the thick catalogue under his arm and hurried.

"Where yuh been, boy?" His mother held a steaming dish of black-eyed peas.[6]

"Aw, Ma, Ah jus stopped down the road t talk wid the boys."

"Yuh know bettah t keep suppah waitin.[7]"

He sat down, resting the catalogue on the edge of the table.

"Yuh git up from there and git to the well n wash yosef[8]! Ah ain feedin no hogs in mah house!"

She grabbed his shoulder and pushed him. He stumbled out of the room, then came back to get the catalogue.

"Whut this?"

"Aw, Ma, it's jusa[9] catlog."

"Who yuh git it from?"

"From Joe, down at the sto."

---

[1] Sho = Sure.

[2] Wheeler：一种手枪的牌子。

[3] Kin = Can.

[4] fer = for.

[5] Awright = All right.

[6] black-eyed peas：豇豆。

[7] Yuh know bettah t keep supppah waitin = You know better to keep supper waiting.

[8] yosef = yourself.

[9] jusa = just a.

"Waal, thas good. We kin use it in the outhouse[1]."

"Naw, Ma." He grabbed for it. "Gimme ma catlog, Ma." She held onto it and glared at him.

"Quit hollerin[2] at me! Whut's wrong wid yuh? Yuh crazy?"

"But Ma, please. It ain't mine! It's Joe's! He tol me t bring it back t im termorrow."

She gave up the book. He stumbled down the back steps, hugging the thick book under his arm. When he had splashed water on his face and hands, he groped back to the kitchen and fumbled in a corner for the towel. He bumped into a chair; it clattered to the floor. The catalogue sprawled at his feet. When he had dried his eyes he snatched up the book and held it again under his arm. His mother stood watching him.

"Now, ef yuh gonna act a fool over that ol book, Ah'll take it n burn it."

"Naw, Ma, please."

"Waal, set down n be still!"

He sat down and drew the oil lamp close. He thumbed page after page, unaware of the food his mother set on the table. His father came in. Then his small brother.

"Whutcha got there, Dave?" his father asked.

"Jusa catlog," he answered, not looking up.

"Yeah, here they is[3]!" His eyes glowed at blue-and-black revolvers. He glanced up, feeling sudden guilt. His father was watching him. He eased the book under the table and rested it on his knees. After the blessing was asked,[4] he ate. He scooped up peas and swallowed fat meat without chewing. Buttermilk helped to wash it down. He did not want to mention money before his father. He would do much better by cornering his mother when she was alone. He looked at his father uneasily out of the edge of his eye.

"Boy, how come yuh don quit foolin wid tha book n eat yo suppah?"

"Yessuh."

"How you n ol man Hawkins gitten erlong[5]?"

"Can't yuh hear? Why don yuh lissen? Ah ast yu how wuz[6] yuh n ol man Hawkins gittin erlong?"

"Oh, swell, Pa. Ah plows mo[7] lan than anybody over there."

"Waal, yuh oughta keep yo[8] mind on whut yuh doin."

"Yessuh."

---

[1] outhouse:厕所。
[2] hollerin = hollering.
[3] is = are.
[4] the blessing was asked:指饭前祈祷。
[5] erlong = along.
[6] Why don yuh lissen? Ah ast yuh how wuz = Why don't you listen? I asked you how was...
[7] mo = more.
[8] yo = your.

He poured his plate full of molasses[1] and sopped it up slowly with a chunk of cornbread. When his father and brother had left the kitchen, he still sat and looked again at the guns in the catalogue, longing to muster courage enough to present his case to his mother. Lawd[2], ef Ah only had tha pretty one! He could almost feel the slickness of the weapon with his fingers. If he had a gun like that he would polish it and keep it shining so it would never rust. N Ah'd keep it loaded, by Gawd!

"Ma?" His voice was hesitant.

"Hunh?"

"Ol man Hawkins give yuh mah money yit[3]?"

"Yeah, but ain't no usa[4] yuh thinking bout[5] throwin nona it erway. Ahm keeping tha money sos[6] yuh kin have cloes[7] to go to school this winter."

He rose and went to her side with the open catalogue in his palms. She was washing dishes, her head bent low over a pan. Shyly he raised the book. When he spoke, his voice was husky, faint.

"Ma, Gawd knows Ah wans one of these."

"One of whut?" she asked, not raising her eyes.

"One of these," he said again, not daring even to point. She glanced up at the page, then at him with wide eyes.

"Nigger, is yuh gone plumb[8] crazy?"

"Aw, Ma—"

"Git outta here! Don yuh talk t me bout no gun! Yuh a fool!"

"Ma, Ah kin buy one fer two dollahs."

"Not ef Ah knows it, yuh ain't!"

"But yuh promised me one—"

"Ah don care what Ah promised! Yuh ain't nothing but a boy yit!"

"Ma, ef yuh lemme buy one Ah'll *never* ast yuh fer nothing no mo."

"Ah tol yuh t git outta here! Yuh ain't gonna toucha[9] penny of tha money fer no gun! Thas how come Ah has Mistah Hawkins t pay yo wages t me, cause[10] Ah knows yuh ain't got no sense."

"But, Ma, we needa gun. Pa ain't got no gun. We needa gun in the house. Yuh kin never tell whut might happen."

---

[1] molasses:糖蜜,糖浆。
[2] Lawd = Lord.
[3] yit = yet.
[4] usa = use of.
[5] bout = about.
[6] sos = so.
[7] cloes = clothes.
[8] plumb = absolutely.
[9] toucha = touch a.
[10] cause = because.

"Now don yuh try to maka fool outta[1] me, boy! Ef we did hava gun, yuh wouldn't have it!"

He laid the catalogue down and slipped his arm around her waist.

"Aw, Ma, Ah done[2] worked hard alla[3] summer n am ast yuh fer nothing, is Ah, now?"

"Thas whut yuh spose[4] t do!"

"But Ma, Ah wans a gun. Yuh kin lemme have two dollahs outta mah money. Please, Ma. I kin give it to Pa... Please, Ma! Ah loves yuh, Ma."

When she spoke her voice came soft and low.

"Whut yu wan wida gun, Dave? Yuh don need no gun. Yuh'll git in trouble. N ef yo pa jus thought Ah let yuh have money t buy a gun he'd hava fit."

"Ah'll hide it, Ma. It am but two dollahs."

"Lawd, chil[5], whut's wrong wid yuh?"

"Am nothin wrong. Ma. Ahm almos a man now. Ah wans a gun."

"Who gonna sell yuh a gun?"

"Ol Joe at the sto."

"N it don cos[6] but two dollahs?"

"Thas all, Ma. Jus two dollahs. Please, Ma."

She was stacking the plates away; her hands moved slowly, reflectively Dave kept an anxious silence. Finally, she turned to him.

"Ah'll let yuh git tha gun ef yuh promise me one thing."

"Whut's tha, Ma?"

"Yuh bring it straight back t me, yuh hear? It be fer Pa."

"Yessum![7] Lemme go now, Ma."

She stooped, turned slightly to one side, raised the hem of her dress, rolled down the top of her stocking, and came up with a slender wad of bills.

"Here," she said. "Lawd knows yuh don need no gun. But yer pa does. Yuh bring it right back t me, yuh hear? Ahma put it up. Now ef yuh don, Ahma have yuh pa lick yuh so hard yuh won fergit it.[8]"

"Yessum."

He took the money, ran down the steps, and across the yard.

"Dave! Yuuuuuh Daaaaave!"

---

[1] outta = out of.
[2] done = have.
[3] alla = all the.
[4] spose = suppose.
[5] chil = child.
[6] cos = cost.
[7] Yessum = Yes, mum.
[8] lick yuh so hard yuh won fergit it = flog you so hard you won't forget it.

He heard, but he was not going to stop now. "Now, Lawd!"

The first movement he made the following morning was to reach under his pillow for the gun. In the gray light of dawn he held it loosely, feeling a sense of power. Could kill a man with a gun like this. Kill anybody, black or white. And if he were holding his gun in his hand, nobody could run over him; they would have to respect him. It was a big gun, with a long barrel and a heavy handle. He raised and lowered it in his hand, marveling at its weight.

He had not come straight home with it as his mother had asked; instead he had stayed out in the fields, holding the weapon in his hand, aiming it now and then at some imaginary foe. But he had not fired it; he had been afraid that his father might hear. Also he was not sure he knew how to fire it.

To avoid surrendering the pistol he had not come into the house until he knew that they were all asleep. When his mother had tiptoed to his bedside late that night and demanded the gun, he had first played possum;[1] then he had told her that the gun was hidden outdoors, that he would bring it to her in the morning. Now he lay turning it slowly in his hands. He broke it, took out the cartridges, felt them, and then put them back.

He slid out of bed, got a long strip of old flannel from a trunk, wrapped the gun in it, and tied it to his naked thigh while it was still loaded. He did not go in to breakfast. Even though it was not yet daylight, he started for Jim Hawkins' plantation. Just as the sun was rising he reached the barns where the mules and plows were kept.

"Hey! That you, Dave?"

He turned. Jim Hawkins stood eying him suspiciously.

"What're yuh doing here so early?"

"Ah didn't know Ah wuz gittin up so early, Mistah Hawkins. Ah wuz fixin t hitch up ol Jenny[2] n take her t the fiels."

"Good. Since you're so early, how about plowing that stretch down by the woods?"

"Suits me, Mistah Hawkins."

"O.K. Go to it!"

He hitched Jenny to a plow and started across the fields. Hot dog! This was just what he wanted. If he could get down by the woods, he could shoot his gun and nobody would hear. He walked behind the plow, hearing the traces creaking, feeling the gun tied tight to his thigh.

When he reached the woods, he plowed two whole rows before he decided to take out the gun. Finally, he stopped, looked in all directions, then untied the gun and held it in his hand. He turned to the mule and smiled.

"Know whut this is, Jenny? Naw, yuh wouldn know! Yuhs jusa ol mule! Anyhow,

---

[1] played possum:(口)装死,装傻。
[2] hitch up ol Jenny:给骡子套上犁;Jenny:骡子名。

this is a gun, n it kin shoot, by Gawd!"

He held the gun at arm's length. Whut t hell, Ahma shoot this thing! He looked at Jenny again.

"Lissen here, Jenny! When Ah pull this ol trigger, Ah don wan yuh t run n acka[1] fool now!"

Jenny stood with head down, her short ears pricked straight. Dave walked off about twenty feet, held the gun far out from him at arm's length, and turned his head. Hell, he told himself, Ah am afraid. The gun felt loose in his fingers; he waved it wildly for a moment. The he shut his eyes and tightened his forefinger. Bloom! A report half deafened him and he thought his right hand was torn from his arm. He heard Jenny whinnying and galloping over the field, and he found himself on his knees, squeezing his fingers hard between his legs. His hand was numb; he jammed it into his mouth, trying to warm it, trying to stop the pain. The gun lay at his feet. He did not quite know what had happened. He stood up and stared at the gun as though it were a living thing. He gritted his teeth and kicked the gun. Yuh almos broke mah arm! He turned to look for Jenny; she was far over the fields, tossing her head and kicking wildly.

"Hol on there, ol mule!"

When he caught up with her she stood trembling, walling[2] her big white eyes at him. The plow was far away; the traces had broken. Then Dave stopped short, looking, not believing. Jenny was bleeding. Her left side was red and wet with blood. He went closer. Lawd, have mercy! Wondah did[3] Ah shoot this mule? He grabbed for Jenny's mane. She flinched, snorted, whirled, tossing her head.

"Hol on now! Hol on."

Then he saw the hole in Jenny's side, right between the ribs. It was round, wet, red. A crimson stream streaked down the front leg, flowing fast. Good Gawd! Ah wuzn't shootin at tha mule. He felt panic. He knew he had to stop that blood, or Jenny would bleed to death. He had never seen so much blood in all his life. He chased the mule for half a mile, trying to catch her. Finally she stopped, breathing hard, stumpy tail half arched. He caught her mane and led her back to where the plow and gun lay. Then he stopped and grabbed handfuls of damp black earth and tried to plug the bullet hole. Jenny shuddered, whinnied, and broke from him.

"Hol on! Hol on now!"

He tried to plug it again, but blood came anyhow. His fingers were hot and sticky. He rubbed dirt into his palms, trying to dry them. Then again he attempted to plug the bullet hole; but Jenny shied away, kicking her heels high. He stood helpless. He had to do something. He ran at Jenny; she dodged him. He watched a red stream of blood flow

---

[1] acka = act as.

[2] walling: 紧闭。

[3] Wondah did = wonder I did.

down Jenny's leg and form a bright pool at her feet.

"Jenny...Jenny," he called weakly.

His lips trembled. She's bleeding t death! He looked in the direction of home, wanting to go back, wanting to get help. But he saw the pistol lying in the damp black clay. He had a queer feeling that if he only did something, this would not be; Jenny would not be there bleeding to death.

When he went to her this time, she did not move. She stood with sleepy, dreamy eyes; and when he touched her she gave a low-pitched whinny and knelt to the ground, her front knees slopping in blood.

"Jenny...Jenny..." he whispered.

For a long time she held her neck erect; then her head sank, slowly. Her ribs swelled with a mighty heave and she went over.[1]

Dave's stomach felt empty, very empty. He picked up the gun and held it gingerly between his thumb and forefinger. He buried it at the foot of a tree. He took a stick to cover the pool of blood with dirt—but what was the use? There was Jenny lying with her mouth open and her eyes walled and glassy. He could not tell Jim Hawkins he had shot his mule. But he had to tell something. Yeah, Ah'll tell em Jenny started gittin wil[2] n fell on the joint of the plow... But that would hardly happen to a mule. He walked across the field slowly, head down.

It was sunset. Two of Jim Hawkins' men were over near the edge of the woods digging a hole in which to bury Jenny. Dave was surrounded by a knot of people, all of whom were looking down at the dead mule.

"I don't see how in the world it happened," said Jim Hawkins for the tenth time.

The crowd parted and Dave's mother, father, and small brother pushed into the center.

"Where Dave?" his mother called. "There he is," said Jim Hawkins. His mother grabbed him.

"Whut happened, Dave? Whut yuh done?"

"Nothin."

"C mon,[3] boy, talk," his father said.

Dave took a deep breath and told the story he knew nobody believed.

"Waal," he drawled[4]. "Ah brung ol Jenny down here sos Ah could do mah plowin. Ah plowed bout two rows, just like yuh see." He stopped and pointed at the long rows of upturned earth. 'Then somethin musta been wrong wid ol Jenny. She wouldn ack right a-tall.[5] She started snortin n kickin her heels. Ah tried t hol her, but

---

[1] went over: 死了。
[2] gitting wil = getting wild.
[3] C mon = Come on.
[4] drawled: 慢吞吞地说。
[5] ack right a-tall = act right at all.

she pulled erway, rearm n goin in. Then when the point of the plow was stickin up in the air, she swung erroun[1] n twisted herself back on it... She stuck herself n started t bleed. N fo Ah could do anything, she wuz dead."

"Did you ever hear of anything like that in all your life?" asked Jim Hawkins.

There were white and black standing in the crowd. They murmured. Dave's mother came close to him and looked hard into his face. "Tell the truth, Dave," she said.

"Looks like a bullet hole to me," said one man.

"Dave, whut yuh do wid the gun?" his mother asked.

The crowd surged in, looking at him. He jammed his hands into his pockets, shook his head slowly from left to right, and backed away. His eyes were wide and painful.

"Did he hava gun?" asked Jim Hawkins.

"By Gawd, Ah tol yuh tha wuz a gun wound," said a man, slapping his thigh.

His father caught his shoulders and shook him till his teeth rattled.

"Tell whut happened, yuh rascal! Tell whut happened!"

Dave looked at Jenny's stiff legs and began to cry.

"Whut yuh do wid tha gun?" his mother asked.

"What wuz he doin wida gun?" his father asked.

"Come on and tell the truth," said Hawkins. "Ain't nobody going to hurt you..."

His mother crowded close to him.

"Did yuh shoot tha mule, Dave?"

Dave cried, seeing blurred white and black faces.

"Ahh ddinn gggo tt sshooot hher... Ah ssswear ffo Gawd Ahh ddin... Ah wuz a-tryin t sssee ef the old gggun would sshoot—"

"Where yuh git the gun from?" his father asked.

"Ah got it from Joe, at the sto."

"Where yuh git the money?"

"Ma give it t me."

"He kept worryin me, Bob. Ah had t. Ah tol im[2] t bring the gun right back t me. ... It was fer yuh, the gun."

"But how yuh happen to shoot that mule?" asked Jim Hawkins.

"Ah wuzn shootin at the mule, Mistah Hawkins. The gun jumped when Ah pulled the trigger... N fo Ah knowed anythin Jenny was there a-bleedin."

Somebody in the crowd laughed. Jim Hawkins walked close to Dave and looked into his face.

"Well, looks like you have bought you a mule, Dave."

"Ah swear fo Gawd, Ah didn go t kill the mule, Mistah Hawkins!"

"But you killed her!"

---

[1] erroun = around.
[2] im = him.

All the crowd was laughing now. They stood on tiptoe and poked heads over one another's shoulders.

"Well, boy, looks like yuh done bought a dead mule! Hahaha!"

"Am tha ershame[1]."

"Hohohohoho."

Dave stood, head down, twisting his feet in the dirt.

"Well, you needn't worry about it, Bob," said Jim Hawkins to Dave's father. "Just let the boy keep on working and pay me two dollars a month."

"Whut yuh wan fer yo mule, Mistah Hawkins?" Jim Hawkins screwed up his eyes.

"Fifty dollars."

"Whut yuh do wid tha gun?" Dave's father demanded. Dave said nothing.

"Yuh wan me t take a tree n beat yuh till yuh talk!"

"Nawsuh!"

"Whut yuh do wid it?"

"Ah throwed it erway."

"Where?"

"Ah... Ah throwed it in the creek."

"Waal, c mon home. N firs thing in the mawnin[2] git to tha creek n fin tha gun."

"Yessuh."

"Whut yuh pay fer it?"

"Two dollahs."

"Take tha gun n git yo money back n carry it to Mistah Hawkins, yuh hear? N don fergit Ahma lam[3] you black bottom good fer this! Now march yosef on home, suh!"

Dave turned and walked slowly. He heard people laughing. Dave glared, his eyes welling with tears. Hot anger bubbled in him. Then he swallowed and stumbled on.

That night Dave did not sleep. He was glad that he had gotten out of killing the mule so easily, but he was hurt. Something hot seemed to turn over inside him each time he remembered how they had laughed. He tossed on his bed, feeling his hard pillow. N Pa says he's gonna beat me... He remembered other beatings, and his back quivered. Naw, Ah sho don wan im t beat me tha way no mo. Dam em all! Nobody ever gave him anything. All he did was work. They treat me like a mule, n then they beat me. He gritted his teeth. N Ma had t tell on[4] me.

Well, if he had to, he would take old man Hawkins that two dollars. But that meant selling the gun. And he wanted to keep that gun. Fifty dollars for a dead mule.

He turned over, thinking how he had fired the gun. He had an itch to fire it again.

---

[1] erashame = a shame.
[2] N firs thing in the mawnin = And the first thing in the morning.
[3] lam:lambast,狠狠地打。
[4] tell on:告发,泄密。

Ef other men kin shoota gun, by Gawd, Ah kin! He was still, listening. Mebbe they all sleepin now. The house was still. He heard the soft breathing of his brother. Yes, now!

He would go down and get that gun and see if he could fire it! He eased out of bed and slipped into overalls.

The moon was bright. He ran almost all the way to the edge of the woods. He stumbled over the ground, looking for the spot where he had buried the gun. Yeah, here it is. Like a hungry dog scratching for a bone, he pawed it up. He puffed his black cheeks and blew dirt from the trigger and barrel. He broke it and found four cartridges unshot.

He looked around; the fields were filled with silence and moonlight. He clutched the gun stiff and hard in his fingers. But, as soon as he wanted to pull the trigger, he shut his eyes and turned his head. Naw, Ah can't shoot wid mah eyes closed n mah head turned.

With effort he held his eyes open; then he squeezed. *Blooooom*! He was stiff, not breathing. The gun was still in his hands. Dammit, he'd done it! He fired again. Blooooom! He smiled. Bloooom! Blooooom! Click, click. There! It was empty. If anybody could shoot a gun, he could. He put the gun into his hip pocket and started across the fields.

When he reached the top of a ridge he stood straight and proud in the moonlight, looking at Jim Hawkins' big white house, feeling the gun sagging in his pocket. Lawd, ef Ah had just one mo bullet Ah'd taka[1] shot at tha house. Ah'd like t scare ol man Hawkins jusa little...Jusa enough t let im know Dave Saunders is a man.

To his left the road curved, running to the tracks of the Illinois Central. He jerked his head, listening. From far off came a faint hoooof-hoooof; hoooof-hoooof...He stood rigid. Two dollahs a mont[2]. Les see now... Tha means it'll take bout two years. Shucks! Ah'll be dam[3]!

He started down the road, toward the tracks. Yeah, here she[4] comes! He stood beside the track and held himself stiffly. Here she comes, erroun the ben...C mon, yuh slow poke! C mon! He had his hand on his gun; something quivered in his stomach. Then the train thundered past, the gray and brown box cars rumbling and clinking. He gripped the gun tightly; then he jerked his hand out of his pocket. Ah betcha[5] Bill wouldn't do it! Ah betcha. ...The cars slid past, steel grinding upon steel. Ahm ridin yuh ternight, so hep me Gawd! He was hot all over. He hesitated just a moment; then he grabbed, pulled atop of a car, and lay flat. He felt his pocket; the gun was still there. Ahead the long rails were glinting in the moonlight, stretching away, away to

---

[1] taka = take a.
[2] mont = month.
[3] dam = damned.
[4] she:指火车。
[5] betcha = bet you.

somewhere, somewhere where he could be a man...

1961

赏 析

  短篇小说《即将成人》收在《八人行》中。在故事里,黑人男孩戴夫急于拥有一把枪,他对母亲软磨硬泡,终于如愿。他高高兴兴带着枪,赶着白人雇主的骡子去耕地。耕了一阵子后,他忍不住要试一试打枪的感觉,便开了一枪,没料到打死了骡子。戴夫非常害怕,撒谎以求自保,但没有成功。他遭到围观者的嘲笑,白人雇主要求他父母赔一大笔钱。晚上戴夫难以入眠,跑到野地里,愤怒地打完枪里所有子弹后,跳上北去的火车,离开了家乡。

  故事的主题是成长,戴夫从拥有枪到失去枪,是他从"即将成人"到"成人"的过程。起初,戴夫相信,只要拥有一把枪,就能赢得尊敬,不再害怕任何人。但他获得枪的办法是像个小孩子那样缠着母亲。在误杀骡子后,他处理问题的办法也是幼稚的,先是试图用泥巴糊住骡子的枪伤,接着又编了一个"谁也不相信的"谎言。戴夫本想通过拥有枪来证明自己是个男子汉,结果惹来羞辱:父亲当众责骂他,人们嘲笑他,白人雇主霍金斯趁机索要高价赔偿。

  在成长小说中,重大的挫折往往是人物成长的催化剂。戴夫决定离家出走,表面看是为了逃避还钱,为了不挨父亲打,实际上是因为他感受到了自己作为一个人的尊严受到了极大伤害。他终于看清了,"他们只让他干活,当他是一头骡子,然后就揍他,他的牙齿咬得格格响。"他想朝霍金斯的房子开枪,"只想让他知道戴夫·桑德斯是个男子汉"。有尊严感是一个人成长的标志之一。戴夫离开家乡,暗示他踏上了独自成长的历程。

  在小说里,枪不但是人物成长的重要象征,还有作者没有点明的社会意义。故事的时间背景是20世纪20年代,当时的美国南方对黑人来说是个危险之地,数以千计的黑人因小罪过或没有证实的"罪行"而被白人暴徒处以私刑。赖特曾把这些故事纳入他一部没完成的小说中,在故事开始前,主人公听说邻县的一个黑人劳工被处以私刑。从这一点看,《即将成人》隐含了赖特创作的一贯主题,即反种族暴力。

  故事采用黑人的口语,很有亲切感;通过动作来展现主人公的心态变化,生动形象。

相关评论

Domestic Prey: Richard Wright's Parody of the Hunt Tradition in "The Man Who Was Almost a Man"

John E. Loftis

  For a people living in a new and unsettled land, variations on the archetype of the young hero who achieves manhood by hunting and slaying a wild beast came early and naturally as a literary theme. American writers have consistently dramatized the threat of the wilderness as an element in their heroes' *rites du passage*.[1] The courageous and

---

[1] *rites du passage*:标志一个人某个成长阶段的仪式(如成年礼)。

determined Natty Bumpo, the Deerslayer,[1] is still an All-American hero and a model for the heroes of later generations. Captain Ahab,[2] equally courageous in his madness, is perhaps the archetype in its demonic or perverted form. Modern writers continue the tradition: Hemingway with Francis Macomber[3] and Faulkner with, particularly, Ike McCaslin[4]. In American literature, however, the hunt is a European and thus white tradition, and its heroic and mythic dimensions hardly seem available to black American writers—unless used ironically to underscore the gulf between the chivalrous[5] white hero and the black field hand or urban outcast. But when deftly handled, this problematic theme becomes an artistic asset[6] for the black writer: the hunt can embody the hero's maturation[7] at the same time that its parodic implications dramatize the disparity[8] between black and white possibilities of growth and development in American society. The initiation story can thus criticize the society within which it occurs in a uniquely effective way, as it does in Richard Wright's "The Man Who Was Almost a Man."

To clarify the precise nature of Wright's parody of the hunt tradition, I would like to compare it with Faulkner's story of Ike McCaslin's initiation[9] in "The Old People." I am not arguing here that Wright is directly parodying Faulkner or that there is any direct connection at all between the two stories, but for several reasons, Faulkner's story is a useful and logical one to represent the normative, mainstream pattern of the hunt in American literature in a comparison with Wright. First, the stories are contemporaneous: Faulkner's story was first published in *Harper's Magazine* in September 1940; Wright's had appeared only nine months earlier, in January 1940, in *Harper's Bazaar*. In addition, the thematic and geographical similarities between the two stories invite comparison, while the ethnic and cultural differences between the authors and the stories suggest new areas of interpretation, especially for Wright's story. Most important, Faulkner's story offers a double initiation where the successful hunt itself serves almost as a preliminary to the more important, more mysterious initiation of the vision of the ancestor-buck. Because he is reaching beyond the simple hunt-as-initiation, Faulkner relies particularly heavily on the tradition itself to inform his initial hunt with meaning and thus becomes especially representative of that tradition.

Initiations occur within personal, social, and literary contexts, and Wright's parody

---

[1] Natty Bumpo, the Deerslayer:杀鹿人纳迪·班波,美国小说家詹姆斯·费尼莫尔·库珀(1789—1851)笔下最有名的人物,美国文学中西部牛仔的原型。
[2] Captain Ahab:亚哈船长。美国小说家赫尔·麦尔维尔(1819—1891)长篇小说《白鲸》(1851)中的主人公。
[3] Francis Macomber:海明威短篇小说《弗朗西斯·麦康伯短暂的幸福生活》中的男主人公。
[4] Ike McCaslin:美国作家威廉·福克纳小说《三角洲之歌》里的人物。
[5] chivalrous:(男人或其行为)(尤指对女性)有礼的,殷勤的,骑士风度的。
[6] asset:资产;有价值(或有用)的人或物。
[7] maturation:成熟。
[8] disparity:差异。
[9] initiation:(通过正式手续或秘密仪式)加入;首次启动,开始进入(成年等)。

of the hunt-as-initiation exploits the differences between those contexts for his hero, a seventeen-year-old black field hand, and the pattern as it develops for most white heroes, like Ike McCaslin. The fact of initiation is, of course, a partial creation of individual identity, and identity is closely bound to names and naming. Fenimore Cooper's Deerslayer, for example, receives his name from his prowess[1] as a hunter, although his initiation involves the killing of a man, not just an animal. In "the Old People," Ike McCaslin's name is not only a given name, it is a part of a larger web of identity with implications for larger meanings in the story. His father, Carothers McCaslin, was an old man when Ike was born, and his present guardian is his cousin McCaslin Edmonds. As these interlocking names suggest, a great deal of the story investigates Ike's hereditary background to establish his relationship to the white, black, and Indian communities of which he is a part. His initiation, then, solidifies a complex of relationships to family, community, and heritage.

Dave, on the other hand, has only his given name as the story opens. He has family—mother, father, brother—but neither their given names nor the family name is provided until late in the story. And when we finally learn that Dave's surname is Saunders, the fact is presented not just as information but as something significant that Dave has earned and has had to assert, to claim. After successfully firing his pistol and just before hopping the freight train out of Mississippi, Dave looks at Jim Hawkins' "big white house" and thinks to himself, "Lawd, ef Ah had just one mo bullet Ah'd taka shot at tha house. Ah'd like t scare ol man Hawkins jusa little…Jusa enough t let im know Dave Saunders is a man"; his assertion of his name is identical with his assertion of his manhood. Only now that he has mastered the pistol that had caused his apparent disaster, just before the ultimate assertion of abandoning his family and immediate social setting, can Dave rightfully claim the identity that is associated with his own name. Dave must earn that which is a complex given for Ike McCaslin.

Source: *Studies In Short Fiction* 23.4 (Fall 1986): p437-442.

问题与思考

1. What relationship between the black and the white is revealed in the story?
2. What kind of boy is Dave? How does Wright characterize him before the accident? Is there any change in Dave's character after the accident? What is it? What does the gun represent in the story?
3. Why do you think the story is titled "The Man Who Was Almost a Man"?
4. To what extent is the accidental shooting of the mule crucial to Dave's departure from home? Does it merely hasten him on a course he would in any case have followed?

---

[1] prowess: 高超的技艺；非凡的才能。

5．What sort of future for Dave is implied by the last paragraph?

阅读链接

1. http：//en.wikipedia.org/wiki/Native_Son：对《土生子》的介绍和评论总结。
2. http：//www.olemiss.edu/mwp/dir/wright_richard：对理查德·赖特的全面介绍、作品目录和相关链接。
3. http：//archive.itvs.org/richardwright：对《黑孩子》的介绍。

Truman Capote (1924—1984)

作者简介

　　杜鲁门·卡波特（Truman Capote，1924—1984）生于美国南方的新奥尔良，四岁时父母离异，由母亲的亲戚抚养成人。卡波特天资聪慧，还没上学便开始广泛阅读，11岁开始写小说，并迷上了写作，高中时为学校的文学刊物和校报撰稿。18岁他到著名的《纽约客》杂志社打工，1944年据说因冒犯了著名诗人弗罗斯特而遭解雇。不久《小姐》杂志刊登他的短篇小说《米丽亚姆》，引起兰登书屋编辑的注意，21岁他成为兰登书屋签约作家。20世纪50年代他将自己的作品改编成剧本和音乐剧。卡波特除写作之外的另一爱好是社交，他热衷于参加和举办各种聚会，是纽约名流派对圈子里的活跃分子。六七十年代他生活无度，沉迷于毒品和酒精，常进出疗养院。由于其"非虚构小说"《冷血》未能获得普利策奖和全国图书奖，卡波特一度感到消沉。80年代，他的健康状况恶化，不得不住院治疗，并退出纽约社交圈，文学创作也变得断断续续。1984年8月卡波特在朋友家猝死，终年59岁。

文学创作

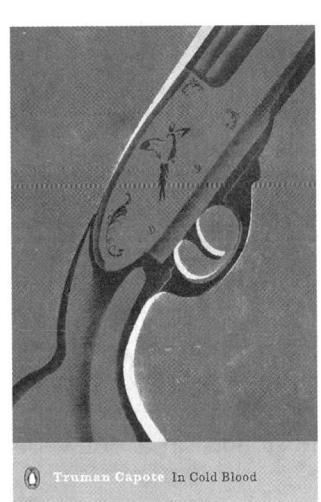

　　卡波特是美国当代著名的南方小说家。17岁起就经常在《纽约客》、《大西洋月刊》等名刊上发表作品。他的第一部长篇小说《其他的声音，其他的房间》(*Other Voices, Other Rooms*，1948)讲述一个敏感的男孩痛苦的成长经历，该小说一举登上《纽约时报》的畅销书榜。长篇小说《草竖琴》(*The Grass Harp*，1951)以回忆的方式和喜剧的色彩书写了一对老处女姐妹分而又合的感人故事。中篇小说《蒂凡尼早餐》(*Breakfast at Tiffany's*，1958)于1961年被改编成电影，奥黛丽·赫本的出色表演使该片成为经典。不过，真正奠定卡波特文坛地位的则是长篇作品《冷血》

(*In Cold Blood*,1966),它集传统小说的想象力与新闻报道的纪实性于一身,开创了美国"非虚构小说"(non-fiction novel)的先河。该书出版后,占据畅销书榜首长达一年之久,隔年改编为同名电影,获得成功。

卡波特的短篇小说同样有名,主要收在《夜之树及其他故事》(*A Tree of Night and Other Stories*,1949)等集子中。《米丽亚姆》("Miriam")和《关上最后一扇门》("Shut a Final Door")分别获得美国短篇小说最高奖欧·亨利小说奖。批评家倾向于把卡波特的小说分为两类,"白日"类和"黑夜"类。前者的故事常发生在公共场合,展示一种积极的社会状态,采用第一人称叙事、口语化的语言,且幽默有加。后者关注的是人复杂的内心世界,展现人的孤独和隔阂,采用第三人称叙事和客观化的语言,现实与梦幻界限模糊。两类作品各有魅力。

作 品

Miriam

For several years, Mrs. H. T. Miller had lived alone in a pleasant apartment (two rooms with kitchenette) in a remodeled brownstone near the East River[1]. She was a widow: Mr. H. T. Miller had left a reasonable amount of insurance. Her interests were narrow, she had no friends to speak of, and she rarely journeyed farther than the corner grocery. The other people in the house never seemed to notice her: her clothes were matter-of-fact[2], her hair iron-gray, clipped and casually waved; she did not use cosmetics, her features were plain and inconspicuous, and on her last birthday she was sixty-one. Her activities were seldom spontaneous: she kept the two rooms immaculate[3], smoked an occasional cigarette, prepared her own meals and tended a canary[4].

Then she met Miriam. It was snowing that night. Mrs. Miller had finished drying the supper dishes and was thumbing through an afternoon paper when she saw an advertisement of a picture playing at a neighborhood theater. The title sounded good, so she struggled into her beaver coat, laced her galoshes and left the apartment, leaving one light burning in the foyer[5]: she found nothing more disturbing than a sensation of darkness.

The snow was fine, falling gently, not yet making an impression on the pavement. The wind from the river cut only at street crossings. Mrs. Miller hurried, her head bowed, oblivious as a mole burrowing a blind path[6]. She stopped at a drugstore and bought a package of peppermints.

---

[1] a remodeled brownstone near the East River:离东河不远的一栋改建过的褐色沙石楼房。the East River:在纽约市。

[2] her clothes were matter-of-fact:她的穿着讲究实际,平淡无味。

[3] immaculate:一尘不染。

[4] canary:金丝雀。

[5] foyer:门厅。

[6] oblivious as...a blind path:像在暗道里打洞的鼹鼠,不理会周围的一切(只低头向前走)。

A long line stretched in front of the box office; she took her place at the end. There would be (a tired voice groaned) a short wait for all seats. Mrs. Miller rummaged in her leather handbag till she collected exactly the correct change for admission. The line seemed to be taking its own time and looking around for some distraction, she suddenly became conscious of a little girl standing under the edge of the marquee.

Her hair was the longest and strangest Mrs. Miller had ever seen: absolutely silver-white, like an albino[1]'s. It flowed waist-length in smooth, loose lines. She was thin and fragilely constructed. There was a simple, special elegance in the way she stood with her thumbs in the pockets of a tailored plum-velvet coat[2].

Mrs. Miller felt oddly excited, and when the little girl glanced toward her, she smiled warmly. The little girl walked over and said, "Would you care to do me a favor?"

"I'd be glad to, if I can," said Mrs. Miller.

"Oh, it's quite easy. I merely want you to buy a ticket for me; they won't let me in otherwise. Here, I have the money." And gracefully she handed Mrs. Miller two dimes and a nickel.

They went into the theater together. An usherette directed them to a lounge; in twenty minutes the picture would be over[3].

"I feel just like a genuine criminal," said Mrs. Miller gaily, as she sat down. "I mean that sort of thing's against the law, isn't it? I do hope I haven't done the wrong thing. Your mother knows where you are, dear? I mean she does, doesn't she?"

The little girl said nothing. She unbuttoned her coat and folded it across her lap. Her dress underneath was prim and dark blue. A gold chain dangled about her neck, and her fingers, sensitive and musical-looking, toyed with it. Examining her more attentively, Mrs. Miller decided the truly distinctive feature was not her hair, but her eyes: they were hazel[4], steady, lacking any childlike quality whatsoever and, because of their size, seemed to consume her small face[5].

Mrs. Miller offered a peppermint. "What's your name, dear?"

"Miriam," she said, as though, in some curious way, it were information already familiar.

"Why, isn't that funny—my name' Miriam, too. And it's not a terribly common name either. Now, don't tell me your last name's Miller!"

"Just Miriam."

"But isn't that funny?"

"Moderately," said Miriam, and rolled the peppermint on her tongue.

Mrs. Miller flushed and shifted uncomfortably. "You have such a large vocabulary

---

[1] albino:生白化病的人。
[2] a tailored plum-velvet coat:一件做工考究的梅红色丝绒外套。
[3] in twenty minutes... would be over:这里指上一场电影还有20分钟就结束。
[4] hazel:浅褐色的。
[5] seemed to consume her small face:仿佛遮盖了她小巧的脸庞。

for such a little girl."

"Do I?"

"Well, yes," said Mrs. Miller, hastily changing the topic to "Do you like the movies?"

"I really wouldn't know," said Miriam. "I've never been before."

Women began filling the lounged; the rumble of the newsreel bombs exploded in the distance[1]. Mrs. Miller rose, tucking her purse under her arm. "I guess I'd better be running now if I want to get a seat," she said. "It was nice to have met you."

Miriam nodded ever so slightly.

It snowed all week. Wheels and footsteps moved soundlessly on the street, as if the business of living continued secretly behind a pale but impenetrable curtain. In the falling quiet there was no sky or earth, only snow lifting in the wind, frosting the window glass, chilling the rooms, deadening and hushing the city. At all hours it was necessary to keep a lamp lighted, and Mrs. Miller lost track of the days: Friday was no different from Saturday and on Sunday she went to the grocery, closed, of course.

That evening she scrambled eggs and fixed a bowl of tomato soup. Then, after putting on a flannel robe and cold-creaming her face, she propped herself up in bed with a hot-water bottle under her feet. She was reading the *Times* when the doorbell rang. At first she thought it must be a mistake and whoever it was would go away. But it rang and rang and settled to a persistent buzz. She looked at the clock: a little after eleven; it did not seem possible, she was always asleep by ten.

Climbing out of bed, she trotted barefoot across the living room. "I'm coming, please be patient." The latch was caught; she turned it this way and that way and the bell never paused an instant. "Stop it," she cried. The bolt gave way and she opened the door an inch. "What in heaven's name[2]?"

"Hello," said Miriam.

"Oh... why, hello," said Mrs. Miller, stepping hesitantly into the hall. "You're that little girl."

"I thought you'd never answer, but I kept my finger on the button; I know you were home. Aren't you glad to see me?"

Mrs. Miller did not know what to say. Miriam, she saw, wore the same plum-velvet coat and now she had also a beret[3] to match; her white hair was braided in two shining plaits and looped at the ends with enormous white ribbons.

"Since I've waited so long, you could at least let me in," she said.

"It's awfully late..."

Miriam regarded her blankly. "What difference does that make? Let me in. It's

[1] the rumble of... in the distance: 远处传来新闻纪录片中炸弹爆炸的隆隆声。
[2] What in heaven's name?: 你究竟要干什么?
[3] beret: 贝雷帽。

cold out here and I have on a silk dress." Then, with a gentle gesture, she urged Mrs. Miller aside and passed into the apartment.

She dropped her coat and beret on a chair. She was indeed wearing a silk dress. White silk. White silk in February. The skirt was beautifully pleated and the sleeves long; it made a faint rustle as she strolled about the room. "I like your place," she said. "I like the rug, blue's my favorite color." She touched a paper rose in a vase on the coffee table. "Imitation," she commented wanly. "How sad. Aren't imitation sad?" She seated herself on the sofa, daintily spreading her skirt.

"What do you want?" asked Mrs. Miller.

"Sit down," said Miriam. "It makes me nervous to see people stand."

Mrs. Miller sank to a hassock[1]. "What do you want?" she repeated.

"You know, I don't think you're glad I came."

For a second time Mrs. Miller was without an answer; her hand motioned vaguely. Miriam giggled and pressed back on a mound of chintz pillows[2]. Mrs. Miller observed that the girl was less pale than she remembered; her cheeks were flushed.

"How did you know where I lived?"

Miriam frowned. "That's no question at all. What's your name? What's mine?"

"But I'm not listed in the phone book."

"Oh, let's talk about something else."

Mrs. Miller said, "Your mother must be insane to let a child like you wander around at all hours of the night—and in such ridiculous clothes. She must be out of her mind."

Miriam got up and moved to a corner where a covered bird cage hung from a ceiling chain. She peeked beneath the cover. "It's a canary," she said. "Would you mind if I woke him? I'd like to hear him sing."

"Leave Tommy alone," said Mrs. Miller, anxiously. "Don't you dare wake him."

"Certainly," said Miriam. "But I don't see why I can't hear him sing." And then, "Have you anything to eat? I'm starving! Even milk and a jam sandwich would be fine."

"Look," said Mrs. Miller, arising from the hassock, "Look—if I made some nice sandwiches will you be a good child and run along home? It's past midnight, I'm sure."

"It's snowing," reproached Miriam. "And cold and dark."

"Well, you shouldn't have come here to begin with," said Mrs. Miller, struggling to control her voice. "I can't help the weather. If you want anything to eat you'll have to promise to leave."

Miriam brushed a braid against her cheek. Her eyes were thoughtful, as if weighing the proposition. She turned toward the bird cage. "Very well," she said, "I promise."

How old is she? Ten? Eleven? Mrs. Miller, in the kitchen, unsealed a jar of strawberry preserves and cut four slices of bread. She poured a glass of milk and paused

---

[1] hassock:跪垫,藤垫。
[2] chintz pillows:闪光印花布面的靠枕。

to light a cigarette. *And why has she come?* Her hand shook as she held the match, fascinated, till it burned her finger. The canary was singing; singing as he did in the morning and at no other time. "Miriam," she called, "Miriam, I told you not to disturb Tommy." There was no answer. She called again; all she heard was the canary. She inhaled the cigarette and discovered she had lighted the cork-tip end[1] and—oh, really, she mustn't lose her temper.

She carried the food in on a tray and set it on the coffee table. She saw first that the bird cage still wore its night cover. And Tommy was singing. It gave her a queer sensation. And no one was in the room. Mrs. Miller went through an alcove[2] leading to her bedroom; at the door she caught her breath.

"What are you doing?" she asked.

Miriam glanced up and in her eyes there was a look that was not ordinary. She was standing by the bureau, a jewel case opened before her. For a minute she studied Mrs. Miller, forcing their eyes to meet, and she smiled. "There's nothing good here," she said. "But I like this." Her hand held a cameo brooch[3]. "It's charming."

"Suppose—perhaps you'd better put it back," said Mrs. Miller, feeling suddenly the need of some support. She leaned against the door frame; her head was unbearably heavy, pressure weighted the rhythm of her heartbeat. The light seemed to flutter defectively. "Please, child—a gift from my husband..."

"But it's beautiful and I want it," said Miriam. *"Give it to me."*

As she stood, striving to shape a sentence which would somehow save the brooch, it came to Mrs. Miller there was no one to whom she might turn; she was alone; a fact that had not been among her thoughts for a long time. Its sheer emphasis was stunning[4]. But here in her own room in the hushed snow-city were evidences she could not ignore or, she knew with startling clarity, resist.

Miriam ate ravenously, and when the sandwiches and milk were gone, her fingers made cobweb movements over the plate, gathering crumbs. The cameo gleamed on her blouse, the blonde profile[5] like a trick reflection of its wearer. "That was very nice," she sighed, "though now an almond cake or a cherry would be ideal. Sweets are lovely, don't you think?"

Mrs. Miller was perched precariously on the hassock, smoking a cigarette. Her hair net had slipped lopsided and loose strands straggled down her face. Her eyes were stupidly concentrated on nothing and her cheeks were mottled in red patches, as though a fierce slap had left permanent marks.

"Is there a candy—a cake?"

---

[1] the cork-tip end:香烟有过滤嘴的那一端。
[2] alcove:房间里凹进去的部分。这里指连接客厅与卧室的过道。
[3] a cameo brooch:一枚浮雕宝石胸针。
[4] Its sheer emphasis was stunning:这完完全全的孤单无援令人窒息。
[5] blonde profile:金发女郎的侧面像。

Mrs. Miller tapped ash on the rug. Her head swayed slightly as she tried to focus her eyes. "You promised to leave if I made the sandwiches," she said.

"Dear me, did I?"

"It was a promise and I'm tired and I don't feel well as all."

"Mustn't fret," said Miriam. "I'm only teasing."

She picked up her coat, slung it over her arm, and arranged her beret in front of a mirror. Presently she bent close to Mrs. Miller and whispered, "Kiss me good night."

"Please—I'd rather not," said Mrs. Miller.

Miriam lifted a shoulder, arched an eyebrow. "As you like," she said, and went directly to the coffee table, seized the vase containing the paper roses, carried it to where the hard surface of the floor lay bare, and hurled it downward. Glass sprayed in all directions and she stamped her foot on the bouquet.

Then slowly she walked to the door, but before closing it she looked back to Mrs. Miller with slyly innocent curiosity.

Mrs. Miller spent the next day in bed, rising once to feed the canary and drink a cup of tea; she took her temperature and had none, yet her dreams were feverishly agitated; their unbalanced mood lingered even as she lay staring wide-eyed at the ceiling. One dream threaded through the others like an elusively mysterious theme in a complicated symphony[1], and the scenes it depicted were sharply outlined, as though sketched by a hand of gifted intensity[2]: a small girl, wearing a bridal gown and a wreath of leaves, led a gray procession down a mountain path, and among them there was unusual silence till a woman at the rear asked, "Where is she taking us?" "No one knows," said an old man marching in front. "But isn't she pretty?" volunteered a third voice. "Isn't she like a frost flower... so shining and white?"

Tuesday morning she woke up feeling better; harsh slats of sunlight, slanting through Venetian blinds[3], shed a disrupting light on her unwholesome fancies. She opened the window to discover a thawed, mild-as-spring day; a sweep of clean new clouds crumpled against a vastly blue, out-of-season sky; and across the low line of rooftops she could see the river and smoke curving from tugboat stacks in a warm wind. A great silver truck plowed the snow-blanked street, its machine sound humming in the air.

After straightening[4] the apartment, she went to the grocer's, cashed a check and continued to Schrafft's where she ate breakfast and chatted happily with the waitress. Oh, it was a wonderful day—more like a holiday—and it would be so foolish to go home.

---

[1] One dream threaded... a complicated symphony: 梦一个接一个, 像一首结构复杂的交响曲的神秘主题, 令人难以捉摸。

[2] a hand of gifted intensity: 一只具有天才表现力的手。

[3] Venetian blinds: 软百叶帘。

[4] straightening: 打扫。

She boarded a Lexington Avenue bus and rode up to Eighty-sixth Street; it was here that she had decided to do a little shopping.

She had no idea what she wanted or needed, but she idled along, intent only upon the passers-by, brisk and preoccupied, who gave her a disturbing sense of separateness.

It was while waiting at the corner of Third Avenue that she saw the man: an old man, bowlegged[1] and stooped under an armlord of bulging packages; he wore a shabby brown coat and a checkered cap. Suddenly she realized they were exchanging a smile; there was nothing friendly about this smile, it was merely two cold flickers of recognition. But she was certain she had never seen him before.

He was standing next to an El pillar[2], and as she crossed the street he turned and followed. He kept quite close; from the corner of her eye she watched his reflection wavering on the shopwindows.

Then in the middle of the block she stopped and faced him. He stopped also and cocked his head, grinning. But what could she say? Do? Here, in broad daylight, on Eighty-sixth Street? It was useless and, despising her own helplessness, she quickened her steps.

Now Second Avenue is a dismal street, made from scraps and ends; part cobblestone, part asphalt, part cement; and its atmosphere of desertion is permanent. Mrs. Miller walked five blocks without meeting anyone, and all the while the steady crunch of his footfalls in the snow stayed near. And when she came to a florist's shop, the sound was still with her. She hurried inside and watched through the glass door as the old man passed; he kept his eyes straight ahead and didn't slow his pace, but he did one strange-telling thing: he tipped his cap.

"Six white ones, did you say?" asked the florist. "Yes," she told him, "white roses." From there she went to a glassware store and selected a vase, presumably a replacement for the one Miriam had broken, though the price was intolerable and the vase itself (she thought,) grotesquely vulgar. But a series of unaccountable purchases had began, as if by prearranged plan; a plan of which she had not the least knowledge or control.

She bought a bag of glazed cherries[3], and at a place called the Knicker-bocker Bakery she paid forty cents for six almond cakes.

Within the last hour the weather had turned cold again; like blurred lenses, winter clouds cast a shade over the sun, and the skeleton of an early dusk colored the sky; a damp mist mixed with the wind and the voices of a few children who romped high on mountains of gutter snow seemed lonely and cheerless. Soon the first flake fell, and when Mrs. Miller reached the brownstone house, snow was falling in a swift screen and

---

[1] bowlegged:弓形腿。
[2] El pillar:高架铁道的支撑柱。El 即 elevated railroad。
[3] glazed cherries:浇了糖浆的樱桃。

foot tracks vanished as they were printed.

The white roses were arranged decoratively in the vase. The glazed cherries shone on a ceramic plate. The almond cakes, dusted with sugar, awaited a hand. The canary fluttered on its swing and picked at a bar of seed.

At precisely five the doorbell rang, Mrs. Miller *knew* who it was. The hem of her house-coat trailed as she crossed the floor. "Is that you?" she called.

"Naturally," said Miriam, the word resounding shrilly from the hall. "Open this door."

"Go away," said Mrs. Miller.

"Please hurry... I have a heavy package."

"Go away," said Mrs. Miller. She returned to the living room, lighted a cigarette, sat down and calmly listened to the buzzer: on and on and on. "You might as well leave. I have no intention of letting you in."

Shortly the bell stopped. For possibly ten minutes Mrs. Miller did not move. Then, hearing no sound, she concluded Miriam had gone. She tiptoed to the door and opened it a sliver; Miriam was half-reclining atop a cardboard box with a beautiful French doll cradled in her arms.

"Really, I thought you were never coming," she said peevishly. "Here, help me get this in, it's awfully heavy."

It was not spell-like compulsion that Mrs. Miller felt, but rather a curious passivity[1], she brought in the box, Miriam and the doll. Miriam curled up on the sofa, not troubling to remove her coat or beret, and watched disinterestedly as Mrs. Miller dropped the box and stood trembling, trying to catch her breath.

"Thank you," she said. In the daylight she looked pinched and drawn, her hair less luminous. The French doll she was loving wore an exquisite powdered wig and its idiot glass eyes sought solace in Miriam's. "I have a surprise," she continued. "Look into my box."

Kneeling, Mrs. Miller parted the flaps and lifted out another doll; then a blue dress which she recalled as the one Miriam had worn that first night at the theater; ad of the remainder she said, "It's all clothes. Why?"

"Because I've come to live with you," said Miriam, twisting a cherry stem. "Wasn't it nice of you to buy me the cherries...?"

"But you can't! For God's sake go away—go away and leave me alone!"

"... and the roses and the almond cakes? How really wonderfully generous. You know, these cherries are delicious. The last place I lived was with an old man; he was terribly poor and we never had good things to eat. But I think I'll be happy here." She paused to snuggle her doll closer. "Now, if you'll just show me where to put my things..."

Mrs. Miller's face dissolved into a mask of ugly red lines; she began to cry, and it

---

[1] It was not... a curious passivity: Mrs. Miller 并没觉得非要服从不可,她只是受了好奇心的驱使。

was an unnatural, tearless sort of weeping, as though, not having wept for a long time, she had forgotten how. Carefully she edged backward till she touched the door.

She fumbled through the hall and down the stairs to a landing below. She pounded frantically on the door of the first apartment she came to; a short, red-headed man answered and she pushed past him. "Say, what the hell is this?" he said. "Anything wrong, lover?" asked a young woman who appeared from the kitchen, drying her hands. And it was to her that Mrs. Miller turned.

"Listen," she cried, "I'm ashamed behaving this way but—well, I'm Mrs. H. T. Miller and I live upstairs and..." She pressed her hands over her faces. "It sounds so absurd..."

The woman guided her to a chair, while the man excitedly rattled pocket change[1]. "Yeah?"

"I live upstairs and there's a little girl visiting me, and I suppose that I'm afraid of her. She won't leave and I can't make her and—she's going to do something terrible. She's already stolen my cameo, but she's about to do something worse—something terrible!"

The man asked, "Is she a relative, huh?"

Mrs. Miller shook her head. "I don't know who she is. Her name's Miriam, but I don't know for certain who she is."

"You gotta calm down, honey," said the woman, stroking Mrs. Miller's arm. "Harry, he'll tend this kid. Go on, lover." And Mrs. Miller said, "The door's open—5A."

After the man left, the woman brought a towel and bathed Mrs. Miller's face. "You're very kind," Mrs. Miller said. "I'm sorry to act like such a fool, only this wicked child..."

"Sure, honey," consoled the woman. "Now, you better take it easy."

Mrs. Miller rested her head in the crook of her arm; she was quiet enough to be asleep. The woman turned a radio dial; a piano and a husky voice filled the silence and the woman, taping her foot, kept excellent time. "Maybe we oughta[2] go up to," she said.

"I don't want to see her again. I don't want to be anywhere near her."

"Uh huh, but what you shoulda[3] done, you shoulda called a cop."

Presently they heard the man on the stairs. He strode into the room frowning and scratching the back of his neck. "Nobody there," he said, honestly embarrassed. "She musta beat it[4]."

---

[1] rattled pocket change:把口袋里的硬币弄得叮当直响。
[2] oughta = ought to.
[3] shoulda = should have.
[4] beat it:(俚)逃走。

"Harry, you're a jerk[1]," announced the woman. "We been sitting here the whole time and we woulda seen—" she stopped abruptly, for the man's glance was sharp.

"I looked all over," he said, "and there just ain't nobody there. Nobody, understand?"

"Tell me," said Mrs. Miller, rising, "tell me, did you see a large box? Or a doll?"

"No, ma'am, I didn't."

And the woman, as if delivering a verdict, said, "Well, for cryinoutloud…"

Mrs. Miller entered her apartment softly; she walked to the center of the room and stood quite still. No, in a sense it had not changed; the roses, the cakes, and the cherries were in place. But this was an empty room, emptier than if the furnishings and familiars[2] were not present, lifeless and petrified as a funeral parlor. The sofa loomed before her with a new strangeness: its vacancy had a meaning that would have been less penetrating and terrible had Miriam been curled on it. She gazed fixedly at the space where she remembered setting the box and, for a moment, the hassock spun desperately. And she looked through the window; surely the river was real, surely snow was falling—but then, one could not be certain witness to anything: Miriam, so vividly *there*—and yet, where was she? Where, where?

As though moving in a dream, she sank to a chair. The room was losing shape; it was dark and getting darker and there was nothing to be done about it; she could not lift her hand to light a lamp.

Suddenly, closing her eyes, she felt an upward surge, like a diver emerging from some deeper, greener depth. In times of terror or immense distress, there are moments when the mind waits, as though for a revelation, while a skein of calm is woven over thought[3]; it is like a sleep, or a supernatural trance[4]; and during this lull one is aware of a force of quiet reasoning; well, what if she had never known a girl named Miriam? That she had been foolishly frightened on the street? In the end, like everything else, it was of no importance. For the only thing she had lost to Miriam was her identity, but now she knew she had found again the person who lived in this room, who cooked her own meals, who owned a canary, who was someone she could trust and believe in: Mrs. H. T. Miller.

Listening in contentment, she became aware of a double sound; a bureau drawer opening and closing; she seemed to hear it long after completion—opening and closing. Then gradually, the harshness of it was replaced by the murmur of a silk dress and this, delicately faint, was moving nearer and swelling in intensity till the walls trembled with the vibration and the room was caving under a wave of whispers. Mrs. Miller stiffened

---

[1] a jerk:(美俚)笨蛋,傻瓜。
[2] familiars:原意为"熟悉的伴侣",这里指每天与 Mrs. Miller 为伴的物品。
[3] a skein of calm is woven over thought:一丝平静与思绪交织起来。
[4] trance:恍惚,昏睡状态。

and opened her eyes to a dull, direct stare.

"Hello," said Miriam.

1949

赏　析

　　1946 年,卡波特凭借短篇小说《米丽亚姆》获得了欧·亨利小说奖,成为美国文坛新秀。在故事里,61 岁的寡妇米勒太太独居在纽约一幢不起眼的公寓楼里,过着平淡而舒适的日子。在一个看电影的雪夜,她认识了一个和自己同名的小女孩米丽亚姆。此后,米丽亚姆几次不请自到,闯入米勒太太的屋子,并提出无礼的要求。米勒太太绝望之下,向邻居求助。邻居到她屋里查看,却没发现任何人。米勒太太回到屋里,坐到椅子上陷入沉思。恍惚之中,她睁开双眼,却发现米丽亚姆就站在她面前。

　　卡波特的不少故事可归类为"荒诞故事",他常用的一个技巧就是将怪异因素引入熟悉的日常生活场景中。他喜欢情节的模糊性,任其发展,却不作出解释。米丽亚姆就是这样的怪异因素,她无来由地侵入米勒太太平静的生活,米勒太太的反应由迷惑、愤怒,到绝望、惊恐,最后精神崩溃。对米丽亚姆的来历和目的,作者没有明确交代,于是出现了这样的疑问,米丽亚姆和那个邂逅老人是不是米勒夫人自己臆想出来的,代表了她内心的恐惧? 米勒太太和米丽亚姆同名,暗示她们是母女,被抛弃的米丽亚姆前来复仇? 米丽亚姆是米勒太太的另一自我,是她极力压抑又无法拒绝的潜意识? 或者,米丽亚姆代表无常的厄运,会突然造访我们,而我们无力抗拒,也无法对之进行理性的解释? 这些读解各有道理,有一点可以肯定,那就是《米丽亚姆》表现了现代都市人生活的孤独状态。小说里现实与梦幻交错在一起,故事从现实主义不知不觉滑向超现实主义,情节变得越来越离奇。这似乎暗示,在我们熟悉的日常生活中会有无名的威胁和危险不期而至,我们的理性世界总会受到非理性的冲击。这或许就是这篇小说受到关注的原因之一。

相关评论

Madness in Truman Capote's "Miriam"
Amanda Flinner

　　Truman Capote was just eighteen-years old when *Mademoiselle* magazine published his first short story, "Miriam," in 1945. Looking back on his career, Capote claimed to have enjoyed his earlier work, except for this very first piece. He recalled the story of Mrs. H. T. Miller and her persistent child stalker "a good stunt[1], but nothing more," yet his critics saw a stroke of genius in the young writer, an observation that was solidified with his internationally acclaimed first novel *Other Voices, Other Rooms* in 1948.

"Miriam" and Mrs. H. T. Miller

　　Mrs. H. T. Miller is a mild-mannered widow who lives a solitary life within the comforts of a simple daily routine—a routine that's about to be shattered upon a chance

---
[1] stunt:惊人的表演。

meeting with a precocious child. She spots the striking young girl standing beneath a marquee[1] amidst a throng of theatre-goers and is soon agreeing to buy her a ticket so she can see the movie. Mrs. Miller learns that her name is Miriam—coincidentally her own first name—and soon becomes uneasy with her adult-like directness and vocabulary.

Her wide, hazel eyes reflect a haunting, almost inhuman vacancy. She manages to penetrate Mrs. Miller's orderly existence and drives her to madness with her persistent presence and unusual demands. While Mrs. Miller is a plain woman, content with simple pleasures, Miriam is a stunning child who commands the finest quality in everything from her white silk dresses to the silk bows tied in her silvery, flowing hair. She shuns Mrs. Miller's bouquet of paper roses ("aren't imitations sad?") and drops hints for treats like almond cakes and cherries. The final blow comes when Mrs. Miller catches Miriam riffling through her jewelry.

"There's nothing good here," Miriam claims, but manages to pick out the one item that holds sentimental value to Mrs. Miller, a cameo brooch that was a gift from her late husband. Miriam demands to keep the cameo, and it's soon pinned on her silken chest.

Teetering[2] Into Madness

Just after her first meeting with Miriam, Mrs. Miller's orderly life starts to crumble. Days start to blend together in a dull stretch. She visits the grocer on a Sunday, a day that she knows it will be closed. Even the weather seems to bend to Miriam's will and shifts to unseasonable warmth. She's plagued throughout the night by terrifying dreams, and for the first time, she sees her own loneliness. Miriam's presence serves to illuminate her solitary life, increasing her terror when realizes there's no one to turn to for help. She is at the mercy of Miriam, a merciless child who is no child at all. Her helplessness comes to a head when Miriam arrives on her doorstep with a heavy box stuffed with clothes and dolls, announcing her intention to move in with Mrs. Miller.

Is Miriam Real?

Mrs. Miller questions her own sanity when Miriam and her box vanish after she flees to obtain help from her bewildered neighbors. Indeed, is Mrs. Miller insane? The lonely widow leads a solitary life with little to no interests, and no one to take care of but her canary. Her entire identity is wrapped up in being "Mrs. H. T. Miller," though her husband has long been dead. We only learn her first name upon her initial meeting with Miriam; is it more than a coincidence that they share a first name?

Why, in an anxious crowd of bustling people, did no one else notice the unusual child with striking features? Even the usherette[3] makes no comment as she leads

---

[1] marquee:(装于剧院或旅馆等大型建筑物入口处的)延伸遮篷,大天篷。
[2] teeter:蹒跚而行。
[3] usherette:女引座员。

"them" to a lounge. Miriam also never reveals how she found Mrs. Miller's apartment, claiming "That's no question at all. What's your name? What's Mine?" Why does Mrs. Miller, feeling a surge of joy, endeavor to buy the very things she knows Miriam desires—almond cakes, glazed cherries, real white roses—and then act horrified when her guest arrives?

Is Miriam, the source of Mrs. Miller's terror, a creation of her own mind borne out of years of loneliness and unacknowledged despair? Capote leaves us to wonder as Miriam again looms over Mrs. Miller at the close of his haunting tale.

Source: http://americanfiction.suite101.com/article.cfm/madness_in_truman_capotes_miriam(Aug 25, 2009).

问题与思考

1. Is it significant that Mrs. Miller is also named Miriam? Why? What changes does the appearance of Miriam bring to Mrs. Miller's life? What is the theme of the story?
2. How do you trust or distrust Mrs. Miller's perception of things? Do you think Mrs. Miller to be mentally unstable and Miriam to be the creation of her mind? Or do you consider Miriam to be a figure that makes trouble to Mrs. Miller?
3. What elements of the supernatural power do you find in the story? In what way is Miriam portrayed strange and mysterious? And in what way does Miriam appear to be an ordinary and willful child?
4. How do you understand the event that the old man pursues Mrs. Miller? Is there any connection between his behavior and the appearance of Miriam at Mrs. Miller apartment in the evening?
5. Discuss the author's description of the setting for the story. How effective do they create the atmosphere for the whole story?

阅读链接

1. http://www.imdb.com/name/nm0001986：卡波特所有改编成电影的作品的目录及影片信息。
2. http://www.google.com/search?q=truman+capote&hl=en&newwindow=1&sa=G&tbs=tl:1&tbo=u&ei=lm9GTOLIBJKGvAOP-uHGAg&oi=timeline_result&ct=title&resnum=18&ved=0CEkQ5wIwEQ：收集了当年报道卡波特的主要新闻短讯。
3. http://www.google.com/images?hl=en&q=truman+capote&um=1&ie=UTF-8&source=univ&ei=93BGTLrtI4jovQOdorzRAw&sa=X&oi=image_result_group&ct=title&resnum=4&ved=0CCMQsAQwAw：卡波特的照片集。

4. 视角(Point of View)

　　视角是"叙述者"(narrator)呈现故事的角度,我们通过他/她观察人物,跟踪情节,形成和发展观点。视角常常隐含了叙述者对事件和人物的态度和立场。叙述视角决定作品的构成方式,也决定读者对作品感受和接受的方式。在所有的小说要素中,最基本、同时又是最复杂的当属视角。

　　叙述视角有多种分类,最常见的是分为第一人称视角和第三人称视角。在第一人称视角中,叙述者参与事件的程度又不同。有时叙述者可能同时是主人公,如《A & P》和《集市》;也可能只是作为观察者或报告者的次要人物,如《献给爱米丽的玫瑰》,这种视角也叫"第一人称参与者"(first-person participant)或"第一人称观察者"(first-person observer);叙述者也可能不参与事件,只转述他人提供的故事。一般而言,第一人称视角比第三人称的客观叙述更能使读者身临其境地感受人物情感的动荡和内心世界的丰富多彩。叙述者有时是作者的化身,但在更多场合下是他/她的面具,我们不能想当然地把叙述者等同于作者。由于第一人称叙述限于某一人物的视角,我们又必须区分叙述者的有限视角和不可靠叙述者对事件的扭曲。在舍伍德·安德森的《我是个傻瓜》中,主人公以第一人称有限视角坦率地讲述了自己的愚蠢,有效地展示了年轻的主人公痛苦的示爱经历。

　　在第三人称视角中,叙述者不参与事件,只用名字或代词称呼人物,读者只闻其音不见其人。第三人称视角分为以下三种:

　　1. 全知视角(Omniscient)　　作者选择全知视角,有如无所不知的上帝,可以随意进入任何人物的内心世界,描写其外在形象、言语和行为,可以自由地解释人物的所思所想,也可以从任何人物的角度来讲述事件。《A & P》、《盲人》、《魔桶》采用的是这一视角。全知视角视野开阔,叙事明晰,可适时变化,一般适用于人物众多、情节复杂的题材。

　　2. 客观视角(Objective)　　在这一视角中,叙述者不能自由进入任何人物的内心世界,他像一架照相机时时跟踪人物,如实地报告行为,记录对话;只描写,不加评论;只是呈现,任由读者自己去甄别、评判。海明威的短篇小说多用这一视角。在本书中,《好人难寻》、《苍蝇》、《即将成人》、《米丽亚姆》采用的是这一视角。客观视角是一种直观的叙述,可以生动地展示事件和行为,有效地制造悬念,同时布下有意义的"空白",促使读者去思考,去参与文本意义的生产。弗兰纳里·奥康纳在《好人难寻》中对奶奶和"不合时宜的人"这两个人物几乎不作任何评论,只是"客观地"详细描写他们的对话和行为,在不知不觉中促使读者对人物作出判断,而人物从头到尾也在作判断。

　　3. 有限全知视角(Limited omniscience)　　这一视角居于全知视角和客观视角之间。作者站在某一人物身后,从他肩头观察一切,有时对此人物的内心状态进行描写。因为单一人物的认知有限,而他的视角又控制着读者的视角,因而读者对其他人物的动机知之有限。这个人物看到什么,读者也只能看到什么。在莱辛的《屋顶丽人》中,叙述者从三个工人的视角观察在屋顶晒太阳的年轻女人,生动描写了男性的心理反应,但对女性的内心世界只字不提。莱辛巧妙地运用第三人称有限全知视角,将视角的局限性转变为男性观念的局限性,以实现其社会批评的目的。

在实际的创作中,即便是短篇小说这样篇幅有限、结构单一的体裁,作家也常常是综合各种视角,以取得理想的叙述效果。例如《青春》结合双重第一人称叙述,第一次是在开头,用"我们"引出主要叙述者马洛,第二次以马洛的口吻讲故事,而马洛同时又是所讲故事的主要参与者,这样读者对事件既保持客观审视的距离,又有身临其境的认同感。要把握视角,我们首先要找到叙述的声音(叙述者),其次要找到这个声音所提供的材料(人物和情节),最后找出作者希望我们对这些材料采取的态度,我们对人物和场景该有的感觉。要理解视角,读者对叙述声音要敏感,对素材要有洞察力。

Sherwood Anderson (1876—1941)

作者简介

舍伍德·安德森(Sherwood Anderson,1876—1941)出生在美国中西部俄亥俄州的克莱德镇,父亲是马具制作商,在工业化时代,生意越来越萧条,不得不经常搬家。为贴补家用,安德森14岁就辍学,在农场、商店和赛马场打过各种各样的零工。1898年美国西班牙战争爆发,他参加了俄亥俄州国民警卫队,退役后在威腾堡学院短暂读书(1899—1900),后去芝加哥找了一份撰写广告的工作。结婚后,安德森携妻回到俄亥俄州,创办了美国商人公司,空余时间从事文学创作。根据他自己的说法,1912年11月28日,他正向一位速记员口授材料,突然停下,径直离开了办公室,不知去向。四天后,他突然在克利夫兰市出现,衣衫褴褛,已记不起自己是谁。安德森后来恢复了记忆,这一事件说明他必须改变自己的生活。1913年初他卖掉了在俄亥俄州的公司,来到芝加哥,加入那里的文人圈子,成为一位职业作家。他直到40岁时才出版第一部长篇小说《温迪·麦克弗森的儿子》(Windy McPherson's Son,1916)。20年代,安德森经常旅行,这一段时间也是他创作的高峰期。安德森的死极其偶然,1941年,他在一次鸡尾酒告别宴会上因误吞牙签而死于腹膜炎,享年65岁。

文学创作

安德森是美国20世纪早期著名的小说家,在美国文学史上占有重要的地位。福克纳、海明威、斯坦贝克、塞林格等当代作家都深受他的影响,海明威曾说:"他是我们所有人的老师"。马尔科姆·考利指出,安德森是"作家的作家,在他那一代中,只有他对后一代的风格和视野都产生了影响。"

安德森最为知名的是短篇小说,包括《小镇畸人》(Winesburg, Ohio, 1919)、《鸡蛋的胜利》(The Triumph of the Egg, 1921)、《马与人》(Horses and Men, 1923)和《林中之死》(Death in the Woods, 1933)等集子。他的长篇小说不多,主要有《穷白人》(Poor White, 1920)和《暗笑》(Dark Laughter, 1925)。安德森生活在美国快速奔向现代化的时代,他的作品反映了一种矛盾的心态:一方面留恋过去恬静的生活方式,对时代的变革感到困扰,另一方面深知变革对社会进步的作用,对未来又抱有希望。前者反映在《小镇畸人》中,人与人之间缺乏正常交流,人情冷漠,心境孤独。后者反映在《穷白人》中一心一意努力建设新城市的土木工和发明家等形象中。

在风格上,安德森依然走写实之路,但与传统的现实主义不同,他不再只关注外部世界和生活表象,而是转向人物内心的精神世界,特别是那些不善于表达自己的小人物的迷茫,以及年轻一代毁灭性的激情,这是安德森对美国小说的一大贡献。他的另一贡献是口语风格。安德森继承了马克·吐温的口语体,但他的口语体不是"土得掉渣"的方言土语,而是经过提炼的美国西部乡村的口语体,明晰优美,流畅易懂,还表现出令人忍俊不禁,又令人深思的灰色幽默。

作 品

I'm a Fool

It was a hard jolt[1] for me, one of the most bitterest I ever had to face. And it all came about through my own foolishness too. Even yet sometimes, when I think of it, I want to cry or swear or kick myself. Perhaps, even now, after all this time,[2] there will be a kind of satisfaction in making myself look cheap by telling of it.

It began at three o'clock one October afternoon as I sat in the grandstand at the fall trotting and pacing meet at Sandusky,[3] Ohio.

To tell the truth, I felt a little foolish that I should be sitting in the grandstand at all. During the summer before I had left my home town with Harry Whitehead and, with a nigger named Burt, had taken a job as swipe[4] with one of the two horses Harry was campaigning through the fall race meets that year. Mother cried and my sister Mildred, who wanted to get a job as a school teacher in our town that fall, stormed and scolded about the house all during the week before I left. They both thought it something disgraceful that one of our family should take a place as a swipe with race horses. I've an idea Mildred thought my taking the place would stand in the way of her

---

[1] jolt: 吃惊,惊讶。
[2] after all this time: 过了这么长时间之后。
[3] the grandstand... meet at Sandusky: 桑达斯基秋季赛马会的大看台。trotting 指快步马赛,pacing 指溜蹄步马赛。桑达斯基在俄亥俄州北部。
[4] swipe: 马夫。

getting the job she'd been working so long for.

But after all I had to work, and there was no other work to be got. A big lumbering[1] fellow of nineteen couldn't just hang around the house and I had got too big to mow people's lawns and sell newspapers. Little chaps who could get next to people's sympathies by their sizes[2] were always getting jobs away from me. There was one fellow who kept saying to everyone who wanted a lawn mowed or a cistern[3] cleaned, that he was saving money to work his way through college, and I used to lay awake nights thinking up ways to injure him without being found out. I kept thinking of wagons running over him and bricks falling on his head as he walked along the street. But never mind him.[4]

I got the place with Harry and I liked Burt fine. We got along splendid together. He was a big nigger with a lazy sprawling body and soft, kind eyes, and when it came to a fight he could hit like Jack Johnson[5]. He had Bucephalus[6], a big black pacing stallion that could do 2.09 or 2.10, if he had to, and I had a little gelding[7] named Doctor Fritz that never lost a race all fall when Harry wanted him to win.

We set out from home late in July in a box car with the two horses and after that, until late November, we kept moving along to the race meets and the fairs. It was a peachy[8] time for me, I'll say that. Sometimes now I think that boys who are raised regular in houses, and never have a fine nigger like Burt for best friend, and go to high schools and college, and never steal anything, or get drunk a little, or learn to swear from fellows who know how, or come walking up in front of a grandstand in their shirt sleeves and with dirty horsy pants on when the races are going on and the grandstand is full of people all dressed up—what's the use of talking about it? Such fellows don't know nothing at all.[9] They've never had no opportunity.

But I did. Burt taught me how to rub down a horse[10] and put the bandages on after a race and steam a horse out[11] and a lot of valuable things for any man to know. He could wrap a bandage on a horse's leg so smooth that if it had been the same color you would think it was his skin, and I guess he'd have been a big driver too and got to the top like Murphy and Walter Cox and the others if he hadn't been black.

---

[1] lumbering:笨拙的,动作迟缓的。
[2] Little chaps who... by their sizes:那些家伙因为个头小,容易博得人们的同情。
[3] cistern:水池。
[4] But never mind him:不提他了。注意这篇小说的口语化风格。主人公仿佛就坐在你身边,与你聊起他的往事。
[5] Jack Johnson:约翰逊(1878—1946),美国拳击手,世界重量级冠军(1908—1915)。
[6] Bucephalus:亚历山大大帝的战马。现用来指马。
[7] gelding:骟马。
[8] peachy:(美俚)极好的。
[9] Such fellows... nothing at all:这里 nothing = anything;下句中 no opportunity = any opportunity。主人公的英语不规范,表明他受教育不多。
[10] rub down a horse:给马梳洗。
[11] steam a horse out:遛马。

Gee whizz![1] it was fun. You got to a county seat town, maybe say on a Saturday or Sunday, and the fair began the next Tuesday and lasted until Friday afternoon. Doctor Fritz would be, say in the 2.25 trot on Tuesday afternoon and on Thursday afternoon Bucephalus would knock'em cold in the "free-for-all" pace.[2] It left you a lot of time to hang around and listen to horse talk, and see Burt knock some yap[3] cold that got too gay, and you'd find out about horses and men and pick up a lot of stuff you could use all the rest of your life, if you had some sense and salted down what you heard and felt and saw.

And then at the end of the week when the race meet was over, and Harry had run home to tend up to his livery stable business,[4] you and Burt hitched the two horses to carts and drove slow and steady across country to the place for the next meeting, so as to not overheat the horses, etc., etc., you know.

Gee whizz! Gosh amighty![5] the nice hickory-nut and beechnut and oaks and other kinds of trees along the roads, all brown and red, and the good smells, and Burt singing a song that was called Deep River, and the country girls at the windows of houses and everything. You can stick your colleges up your nose for all me.[6] I guess I know where I got my education.

Why, one of those little burgs[7] of towns you come to on the way, say now on a Saturday afternoon, and Burt says, "Let's lay up here." And you did.

And you took the horses to a livery stable and fed them, and you got your good clothes out of a box and put them on.

And the town was full of farmers gaping, because they could see you were race horse people, and the kids maybe never see a nigger before and was afraid and run away when the two of us walked down their main street.

And that was before prohibition[8] and all that foolishness, and so you went into a saloon, the two of you, and all the yaps come and stood around, and there was always someone pretended he was horsy[9] and knew things and spoke up and began asking questions, and all you did was to lie and lie all you could about what horses you had, and I said I owned them, and then some fellow said, "Will you have a drink of whiskey" and Burt knocked his eye out[10] the way he could say, offhand like, "Oh well, all right, I'm

---

[1] Gee whizz!:(俚)哎呀!(表示惊奇。)
[2] knock'em cold in the "free-for-all" pace:在赛马大会上将对手全部击败。knock'em cold = knock them cold; free-for-all 指任何人(这里指马)都可以参加的比赛。
[3] yap:(美俚)乡巴佬。
[4] tend up to his livery stable business:处理他的马房事务。
[5] Gosh amighty! = God almighty! 全能的上帝呀! Gosh 是 God 的委婉语。
[6] You can stick... for all me:为得到我这样的经历,你可以拒绝上大学。
[7] burgs:(美口)小镇。
[8] prohibition:这里指 1920—1933 年间美国的禁酒法案和措施。
[9] horsy:显出赛马行家的样子。
[10] Burt knocked his eye out:Burt 令他印象十分深刻。

agreeable to a little nip[1]. I'll split a quart with you." Gee whizz!

But that isn't what I want to tell my story about. We got home late in November and I promised mother I'd quit the race horses for good. There's a lot of things you've got to promise a mother because she don't know any better.

And so, there not being any work in our town any more than when I left there to go to the races, I went off to Sandusky and got a pretty good place taking care of horses for a man who owned a teaming and delivery and storage and coal and real estate business there. It was a pretty good place with good eats[2], and a day off each week, and sleeping on a cot in a big barn, and mostly just shovelling in hay and oats to a lot of big good-enough skates of horses[3] that couldn't have trotted a race with a toad. I wasn't dissatisfied and I could send money home.

And then, as I started to tell you, the fall races come to Sandusky and I got the day off and I went. I left the job at noon and had on my good clothes and my new brown derby hat[4] I'd just bought the Saturday before, and a stand-up collar.

First of all I went downtown and walked about with the dudes[5]. I've always thought to myself, "Put up a good front" and so I did it. I had forty dollars in my pocket and so I went into the West House, a big hotel, and walked up to the cigar stand. "Give me three twenty-five cent cigars," I said. There was a lot of horsemen and strangers and dressed-up people from other towns standing around in the lobby and in the bar, and I mingled amongst them. In the bar there was a fellow with a cane and a Windsor tie[6] on, that it made me sick to look at him. I like a man to be a man and dress up, but not to go put on that kind of airs. So I pushed him aside, kind of rough, and had me a drink of whisky. And then he looked at me, as though he thought maybe he's get gay[7], but he changed his mind and didn't say anything. And then I had another drink of whisky, just to show him something, and went out and had a hack[8] out to the races, all to myself, and when I got there I bought myself the best seat I could get up in the grand stand, but didn't go in for any of these boxes. That's putting on too many airs.

And so there I was, sitting up in the grand stand as gay as you please and looking down on the swipes coming out with their horses, and with their dirty horsy pants on and the horse blankets swung over their shoulders, same as I had been doing all the year before. I liked one thing about the same as the other, sitting up there and feeling grand and being down there and looking up at the yaps and feeling grander and more important

---

[1] nip:一小口。
[2] eats:食物,饭菜。
[3] skates of horses:一群驽马。
[4] derby hat:(美)圆顶礼帽。
[5] dudes:花花公子,纨绔子弟。
[6] Windsor tie:一种打成松散蝴蝶结式的宽领带。
[7] get gay:恼怒。
[8] hack:出租马车。

too.

One thing's about as good as another, if you take it just right. I've often said that.

Well, right in front of me, in the grandstand that day, there was a fellow with a couple of girls and they was about my age. The young fellow was a nice guy all right. He was the kind maybe that goes to college and then comes to be a lawyer or maybe a newspaper editor or something like that, but he wasn't stuck on[1] himself. There are some of that kind are all right and he was one of the ones.

He had his sister with him and another girl and the sister looked around over his shoulder, accidental at first, not intending to start anything—she wasn't that kind—and her eyes and mine happened to meet.

You know how it is. Gee, she was a peach! She had on a soft dress, kind of a blue stuff and it looked carelessly made, but was well sewed and made and everything. I knew that much. I blushed when she looked right at me and so did she. She was the nicest girl I've ever seen in my life. She wasn't stuck on herself and she could talk proper grammar without being like a school teacher or something like that. What I mean is, she was O.K. I think maybe her father was well-to-do, but not rich to make her chesty[2] because she was his daughter, as some are. Maybe he owned a drug store or a dry-goods store in their home town, or something like that. She never told me and I never asked.

My own people are all O.K. too when you come to that. My grandfather was Welsh and over in the old country, in Wales he was—but never mind that.

The first heat[3] of the first race come off and the young fellow setting there with the two girls left them and went down to make a bet. I knew what he was up to, but he didn't talk big and noisy and let everyone around know he was a sport[4] as some do. He wasn't that kind. Well, he come back and I heard him tell the two girls what horse he'd bet on, and when the heat was trotted they all half got to their feet and acted in the excited, sweaty way people do when they've got money down on a race, and the horse they bet on is up there pretty close at the end, and they think maybe he'll come on with a rush, but he never does because he hasn't got the old juice in him, come right down to it.

And then, pretty soon, the horses came out for the 2.18 pace and there was a horse in it I knew. He was a horse Bob French had in his string[5] but Bob didn't own him. He was a horse owned by a Mr. Mathers down at Marietta[6], Ohio.

This Mr. Mathers had a lot of money and owned some coal mines or something, and

---

[1] stuck on:(俚)被(异性)迷住。
[2] chesty:骄傲的,自负的。
[3] heat:(比赛中的一次)竞赛、预赛。
[4] a sport:赌徒,以体育赛事作赌之人。
[5] in his string:在马厩里。
[6] Marietta:玛丽埃塔,在俄亥俄州桑达斯基以南。

he had a swell place out in the country, and he was stuck on race horses, but was a Presbyterian[1] or something, and I think more than likely his wife was one too, maybe a stiffer one than himself. So he never raced his horses hisself[2], and the story round the Ohio race tracks was that when one of his horses got ready to go to the races he turned him over to Bob French and pretended to his wife he was sold.

So Bob had the horses and he did pretty much as he pleased and you can't blame Bob, at least I never did. Sometimes he was out to win and sometimes he wasn't. I never cared much about that when I was swiping a horse. What I did want to know was that my horse had the speed and could go out in front if you wanted him to.

And, as I'm telling you, there was Bob in this race with one of Mr. Mathers' horses, was named About Ben Ahem or something like that, and was fast as a streak[3]. He was a gelding and had a mark of 2.21, but could step in .08 or .09.

Because when Burt and I were out, as I've told you, the year before, there was a nigger Burt knew, worked for Mr. Mathers, and we went out there one day when we didn't have no race on at the Marietta Fair and our boss Harry was gone home.

And so everyone was gone to the fair but just this one nigger and he took us all through Mr. Mathers' swell house and he and Burt tapped a bottle of wine Mr. Mathers had hid in his bedroom, back in a closet, without his wife knowing, and he showed us this Ahem horse. Burt was always stuck on being a driver but didn't have much chance to get to the top, being a nigger, and he and the other nigger gulped that whole bottle of wine and Burt got a little lit up.[4]

So the nigger let Burt take this About Ben Ahem and step him a mile in a track Mr. Mathers had all to himself, right there on the farm. And Mr. Mathers had one child, a daughter, kinda sick and not very good looking, and she came home and we had to hustle and get About Ben Ahem stuck back in the barn.

I'm only telling you to get everything straight. At Sandusky, that afternoon I was at the fair, this young fellow with the two girls was fussed, being with the girls and losing his bet. You know how a fellow is that way. One of them was his girl and the other his sister. I had figured that out.

"Gee whizz," I says to myself, "I'm going to give him the dope[5]."

He was mighty nice when I touched him on the shoulder. He and the girls were nice to me right from the start and clear to the end. I'm not blaming them.

And so he leaned back and I give him the dope on About Ben Ahem. "Don't bet a cent on this first heat because he'll go like an oxen hitched to a plow, but when the first

---

[1] Presbyterian:长老会教徒。
[2] hisself = himself.
[3] as a streak:像一道闪电。
[4] got a little lit up:喝得有点醉了。
[5] dope:(赛马术语)给马喝的兴奋剂。这里指给那个下赌注的人一点好消息。

heat is over go right down and lay on your pile.[1]" That's what I told him.

Well, I never saw a fellow treat any one swelter. There was a fat man sitting beside the little girl, that had looked at me twice by this time, and I at her, and both blushing, and what did he do but have the nerve to turn and ask the fat man to get up and change places with me so I could set with his crowd.

Gee whizz, craps amighty.[2] There I was. What a chump[3] I was to go and get gay up there in the West House bar, and just because that dude was standing there with a cane and that kind of a necktie on, to go and get all balled up[4] and drink that whiskey, just to show off.

Of course she would know, me setting right beside her and letting her smell of my breath. I could have kicked myself right down out of that grandstand and all around that race track and made a faster record than most of the skates of horses they had there that year.

Because that girl wasn't any mutt[5] of a girl. What wouldn't I have give right then for a stick of chewing gum to chew, or a lozenger, or some liquorice,[6] or most anything. I was glad I had those twenty-five cent cigars in my pocket and right away I give that fellow one and lit one myself. Then that fat man got up and we changed places and there I was, plunked[7] right down beside her.

They introduced themselves and the fellow's best girl he had with him was named Miss Elinor Woodbury, and her father was a manufacturer of barrels from a place called Tiffin[8], Ohio. And the fellow himself was named Wilbur Wessen and his sister was Miss Lucy Wessen.

I suppose it was their having such swell names got me off my trolley[9]. A fellow, just because he has been a swipe with a race horse and works taking care of horses for a man in the teaming, delivery, and storage business, isn't any better or worse than anyone else. I've often thought that, and said it too.

But you know how a fellow is. There's something in that kind of nice clothes, and the kind of nice eyes she had, and the way she had looked at me, awhile before, over her brother's shoulder, and me looking back at her, and both of us blushing.

I couldn't show her up for a boob,[10] could I?

I made a fool of myself, that's what I did. I said my name was Walter Mathers from

---

[1] lay on your pile:拿你那堆钱打赌。
[2] craps amighty = craps almighty,真是个了不起的赌注。craps指掷骰子赌博。
[3] chump:笨蛋,傻瓜。
[4] get all balled up:给弄昏了头。get/be all balled up:(俚),弄糊涂了。
[5] mutt:笨蛋。
[6] lozenger, or some liquorice:菱形糖片或甘草。
[7] plunked:扑通落下,重重掉下。
[8] Tiffin:蒂芬,在俄亥俄州。
[9] got me off my trolley:疯了。
[10] I couldn't show her up for a boob:我不能在她面前显得像个傻瓜。

Marietta, Ohio, and then I told all three of them the smashingest lie you ever heard. What I said was that my father owned the horse About Ben Ahem and that he had let him out to this Bob French for racing purposes, because our family was proud and had never gone into racing that way, in our own name, I mean. Then I had got started and they were all leaning over and listening, and Miss Lucy Wessen's eyes were shining, and I went the whole hog.[1]

I told about our place down at Marietta, and about the big stables and the grand brick house we had on a hill, up above the Ohio River, but I knew enough not to do it in no bragging way. What I did was to start things and then let them drag the rest out of me. I acted just as reluctant to tell as I could. Our family hasn't got any barrel factory, and, since I've known us, we've always been pretty poor, but not asking anything of anyone at that, and my grandfather, over in Wales—but never mind that.

We set there talking like we had known each other for years and years, and I went and told them that my father had been expecting maybe this Bob French wasn't on the square,[2] and had sent me up to Sandusky on the sly to find out what I could.

And I bluffed[3] it through I had found out all about the 2.18 pace, in which About Ben Ahem was to start.

I said he would lose the first heat by pacing like a lame cow and then he would come back and skin'em alive[4] after that. And to back up what I said I took thirty dollars out of my pocket and handed it to Mr. Wilbur Wessen and asked him, would he mind, after the first heat, to go down and place it on About Ben Ahem for whatever odds he could get. What I said was that I didn't want Bob French to see me and none of the swipes.

Sure enough the first heat come off and About Ben Ahem went off his stride up the back stretch and looked like a wooden horse or a sick one and come in to be last. Then this Wilbur Wessen went down to the betting place under the grandstand and there I was with the two girls, and when that Miss Woodbury was looking the other way once, Lucy Wessen kinda[5], with her shoulder you know, kinda touched me. Not just tucking down, I don't mean. You know how a woman can do. They get close, but not getting gay either. You know what they do. Gee whizz.

And then they give me a jolt. What they had done, when I didn't know, was to get together, and they had decided Wilbur Wessen would bet fifty dollars, and the two girls had gone and put in ten dollars each, of their own money too. I was sick then, but I was sicker later.

About the gelding, About Ben Ahem, and their winning their money, I wasn't worried a lot about that. It come out O. K. Ahem stepped the next three heats like a

---

[1] went the whole hog:(俚)完全接受她。
[2] on the square:诚实地。
[3] bluffed:欺骗,作假。
[4] skin'em alive:彻底击败(其他赛马)。
[5] kinda = kind of,有几分。

bushel of spoiled eggs going to market before they could be found out, and Wilbur Wessen had got nine to two for the money. There was something else eating at me.

Because Wilbur come back after he had bet the money, and after that he spent most of his time talking to that Miss Woodbury, and Lucy Wessen and I was left alone together like on a desert island. Gee, if I'd only been on the square or if there had been any way of getting myself on the square. There ain't any Walter Mathers, like I said to her and them, and there hasn't ever been one, but if there was, I bet I'd go to Marietta, Ohio, and shoot him tomorrow.

There I was, big book that I am. Pretty soon the race was over, and Wilbur had gone down and collected our money, and we had a hack downtown, and he stood us a swell supper at the West House, and a bottle of champagne beside.

And I was with that girl and she wasn't saying much, and I wasn't saying much either. One thing I know. She wasn't stuck on me because of the lie about my father being rich and all that. There's a way you know... Craps amighty. There's a kind of girl you see just once in your life, and if you don't get busy and make hay, then you're gone for good and all, and might as well go jump off a bridge. They give you a look from inside of them somewhere, and it ain't no vamping,[1] and what it means is—you want that girl to be your wife, and you want nice things around her like flowers and swell clothes, and you want her to have the kids you're going to have, and you want good music played and no ragtime[2]. Gee whizz.

There's a place over near Sandusky, across a kind of bay, and it's called Cedar Point. And after we had supper we went over to it in a launch[3], all by ourselves. Wilbur and Miss Lucy and that Miss Woodbury had to catch a ten o'clock train back to Tiffin, Ohio, because, when you're out with girls like that, you can't get careless and miss any trains and stay out all night, like you can with some kinds of Janes[4].

And Wilbur blowed himself to the launch and it cost him fifteen cold plunks[5], but I wouldn't never have knew if I hadn't listened. He wasn't no tin horn kind[6] of a sport.

Over at the Cedar Point place, we didn't stay around where there was a gang of common kind of cattle[7] at all.

There was big dance halls and dining places for yaps, and there was a beach you could walk along and get where it was dark, and we went there.

She didn't talk hardly at all and neither did I, and I was thinking how glad I was my

---

[1] it ain't no vamping = it isn't vamping;没有任何挑逗的意思。vamp:指女子(用色相)引诱男子。
[2] ragtime:拉格泰姆,美国一种以2/4节拍为基础的爵士乐,节奏很强。
[3] launch:游艇。
[4] Janes:(俚)姑娘或妇女。
[5] plunks:(美俚)一元银(纸)币。
[6] tin horn kind:(美俚)那种吹牛的人。
[7] cattle:卑鄙的家伙,贱骨头。

mother was all right, and always made us kids learn to eat with a fork at table, and not swill soup, and not be noisy and rough like a gang you see around a race track that way.

Then Wilbur and his girl went away up the beach and Lucy and I sat down in a dark place, where there was some roots of old trees the water had washed up, and after that the time, till we had to go back in the launch and they had to catch their trains, wasn't nothing at all. It went like winking your eye.

Here's how it was. The place we were setting in was dark, like I said, and there was the roots from that old stump sticking up like arms, and there was a watery smell, and the night was like—as if you could put your hand out and feel it—so warm and soft and dark and sweet like an orange.

I most cried and I most swore and I most jumped up and danced, I was so mad and happy and sad.

When Wilbur come back from being alone with his girl, and she saw him coming, Lucy she says, "We got to go to the train now," and she was most crying too, but she never knew nothing I knew, and she couldn't be so all busted up.[1] And then, before Wilbur and Miss Woodbury got up to where we was, she put her face up and kissed me quick and put her head up against me and she was all quivering and—Gee whizz.

Sometimes I hope I have cancer and die. I guess you know what I mean. We went in the launch across the bay to the train like that, and it was dark too. She whispered and said it was like she and I could get out of the boat and walk on the water, and it sounded foolish, but I knew what she meant.

And then quick we were right at the depot, and there was a big gang of yaps, the kind that goes to the fairs, and crowded and milling around like cattle, and how could I tell her? "It won't be long because you'll write and I'll write to you." That's all she said.

I got a chance like a hay barn afire. A swell chance I got.

And maybe she would write me, down at Marietta that way, and the letter would come back, and stamped on the front of it by the U.S.A. "there ain't any such guy," or something like that, whatever they stamp on a letter that way.

And me trying to pass myself off for a big-bug[2] and a swell—to her, as decent a little body as God ever made. Craps amighty—a swell chance I got!

And then the train come in, and she got on it, and Wilbur Wessen, he come and shook hands with me, and that Miss Woodbury was nice too and bowed to me, and I at her, and the train went and I busted out[3] and cried like a kid.

Gee, I could have run after that train and made Dan Patch look like a freight train after a wreck but, socks amighty, what was the use? Did you ever see such a fool?

I'll bet you what—if I had an arm broke right now or a train had run over my foot—

---

[1] busted up: 分手，告别。
[2] a big-bug: (俚)大人物。
[3] busted out: 一下失控了。

I wouldn't go to no doctor at all. I'd go set down and let her hurt and hurt—that's what I'd do.

I'll bet you what—if I hadn't a drunk that booze[1] I'd a never been such a boob as to go tell such a lie—that couldn't never be made straight to a lady like her.

I wish I had that fellow right here that had on a Windsor tie and carried a cane. I'd smash him for fair[2]. Gosh darn his eyes.[3] He's a big fool—that's what he is.

And if I'm not another you just go find me one and I'll quit working and be a bum and give him my job. I don't care nothing for working, and earning money, and saving it for no such boob as myself.

1922

赏　析

《我是个傻瓜》是安德森小说中唯一被改编成电影的作品。它用第一人称和松散的口吻讲述了十九岁的马夫安迪赛马场上短暂的看台情缘。安迪用挣来的钱把自己打扮成有钱人，到大看台上观看赛马，没多久就喜欢上前排的姑娘露西，为赢得芳心，他谎称自己是当地富翁马特斯先生的儿子。露西似乎也喜欢他，临别时提出要给他写信，信会寄到马特斯先生家，安迪煞费苦心，最终却自食其果。

撒谎是故事的中心情节。不仅安迪撒谎，露西的哥哥温布尔也撒谎。温布尔来自中产阶级，修养良好，谈吐有礼，连安迪也看出他"将来能当个律师，要不就是报纸编辑什么的"。安迪一张口就是蹩脚的语法和乡音土语（如他把赛马的名字"Abou Ben Adhere"说成"About Ben Ahem"），温布尔不可能看不出他低等的出身。温布尔之所以向安迪示好，其实是想从他那里套到赛马的信息，结果的确赚了一笔钱。因此，《我是个傻瓜》既是一个爱情故事，也是一个金钱的故事。身份低下的安迪对上层社会怀着矛盾的心理，一方面，他对那个手拿拐杖、打着蝴蝶结式宽领带的绅士十分不顺眼，声称"看着他我就恶心"，粗鲁地对待他，可在追求爱情时，安迪又不惜大话连篇，把自己吹嘘成有钱人。安迪以金钱为诱饵（透露赛马信息，吹嘘自己是富家子弟），想钓上爱情，进而成为上流社会的一员，没想到被温布尔愚弄了一番。不过，温布尔的精明直到故事结尾也没点破，只让读者逐渐明白，这个故事以喜剧和突转的形式生动表现了一个年轻人的梦想如何在瞬间破灭。

小说最突出的风格是口语化，简朴的俚语和粗话。不过，简朴不等于简单，如小说中出现频率最高的"...whiz"至少表达了主人公四种不同的情感：高兴、惊奇、痛悔和爱情。小说还以印象式的描述，以悲喜剧的格调表现青少年成长的困境。

相关评论

Who's a fool? A Rereading of Sherwood Anderson's "I'm a Fool"
Tom Hansen

How can Anderson's critics disagree so completely that they hardly seem to be

---

[1] Booze：酒。
[2] for fair：(口)肯定地。
[3] Gosh darn his eyes：他那双该死的眼睛！darn 为 damn 的委婉语。

commenting on the same story? Perhaps they are not. Some of them—Howe, Schevill, and Simpson and Nevins most obviously—do not adequately distinguish between the teller and the tale. They seem insufficiently aware of what the narrator himself is utterly unaware of: that a teller shapes and slants[1] the story he tells; that—given the naivete and defensiveness of this particular narrator—the teller IS the tale. Of all Anderson's critics, only Charles Child Walcutt examines the point of view of the story, but his overriding[2] consideration is Anderson's technique of literary impressionism. Using the story to illustrate this technique, Walcutt never seems to immerse himself in the particulars of the story, never closely attends to the particular limitations and idiosyncracies of this particular narrator. Yet these limitations and idiosyncracies, far from being colorful incidentals, are so central to the story that without them it degenerates into little more than a variation on the tired, old formula of boy meets girl, boy falls in love with girl, boy loses girl.

The Monterey Home Video of "I'm A Fool," which objectifies the narrator to the point where he is no longer the teller of his tale but merely its protagonist—whose overwhelming experience of first love unfolds before us on the screen—manages to reduce the story to what Howe, Schevill, and Simpson and Nevins believe it already is: a bittersweet tale of adolescent love found and then lost, starring Ron Howard as the racetrack swipe (a groomer of horses and general factotum[3]) who decides, one day, to dress up like those fancy swells who sit in the grandstand and place bets on horses and smoke expensive cigars. Up in the grandstand, he meets Wilbur Wessen, Wilbur's fiance Elinor Woodbury, and Wilbur's sister Lucy. The swipe is so taken with Lucy and so desperate to make a good impression on her—in fact, on all three of them—that he spins a web of glorious lies about the many horses his supposedly well-to-do father owns and the big house he lives in and, by implication, the comfortable moneyed life to which he is accustomed. A few hours later, when he realizes that Lucy is as smitten with him as he is with her, he is too ashamed to confess the truth: that he is merely a stable worker who feeds, cares for, and cleans up after horses. When it is time for the trio to catch their train back home from Sandusky to Tiffin, Lucy, a vision of shy beauty played by Amy Irving in the video, tells the swipe that she will write to him—that is, to Walter Mathers, the fictitious character whose identity he has assumed and whose address he gives her. Convinced that she will no longer care for him when her letter to the nonexistent Walter Mathers is returned and she then realizes what a fool he has made of her—but too ashamed, here and now in the story, to tell her the truth by confessing who he really is and to declare how much he really loves her—he realizes that they will never

---

[1] slants: 使有倾向性,使有偏向性。
[2] overriding: 最重要的。
[3] factotum: 杂役,打杂的人。

see each other again. He is so inwardly despondent[1] and she is so outwardly radiant—not knowing that her newfound romance is already over—that our hearts go out to both of them. Poor sad swipe. Poor sweet Lucy.

No wonder Howe and Schevill dismiss this story as being insignificant. But the sentimental Monterey Home Video version is not the story Anderson wrote. In Anderson's story, we see nothing for ourselves. Everything is told to us by the swipe, who reveals—as do all naive narrators—much he is unaware of. He has no idea how great an inferiority complex he has or how childish he is, for "a big lumbering fellow of nineteen," to blame others for problems he has inadvertantly created himself. He likes the free and easy life of cussing[2]—"Gee whizz! Gosh amighty!" but his boyish attempt at swearing in the real language of men reveals how far he is from speaking that language and, by implication, how far he is from being a man and, by further implication, how far he is from perceiving things as they actually are—and now and then drinking and smoking and stealing, and generally keeping company with horses and men who work with horses. He is fatherless, for reasons unspecified in the story, and his mother and sister, acutely aware that their lower-middle-class status falls short of the middle-class respectability to which they aspire, are disappointed in his lack of ambition. He refuses to look for a more respectable job, declaring unashamedly—and repeatedly throughout the story—his belief in his own self-worth. On the other hand, well aware that most people with middle-class values look down upon the lowly occupation of a swipe, he also doubts his own self-worth. Caught in this inner conflict of class values, he cannot bring himself to be himself in the presence of middle-class people—for fear that they, who so greatly impress him, will reject him for not being more like them. Hence his pretense, to the trio in the grandstand, of being Walter Mathers, son of a well-to-do horse breeder.

Clearly, then, this is not just a story of adolescent infatuation, of young love frustrated even at the very moment it is fully reciprocated[3].

Is it, in fact, reciprocated at all? Is Miss Lucy Wessen really fooled by his assumed identity? Is anyone in this story duped[4] by this phony Walter Mathers—other, that is, than the duper himself, who is so far from being the super duper he believes himself to be that he is, instead, a duper duped?

Source: Hansen, Tom. "Who's a fool? A rereading of Sherwood Anderson's 'I'm a Fool'." *The Midwest Quarterly* 38.4 (1997): 372.

[1] despondent: 沮丧的，消沉的。
[2] cussing: (口)说粗口话。
[3] reciprocated: 互给，交换，回报。
[4] duped: 欺骗，愚弄。

问题与思考

1. From what point of view does Anderson tell this story? Does the narrator of "I'm a Fool" seem a boy—a native innocent narrator—or a mature man looking through a boy's eyes?
2. What is the regret of the narrator? That has he recognized in his rather painful experience?
3. Note the plot of the story. It has a long exposition about his previous experience with horse racing. What is the function of the long exposition? How does it help to create the atmosphere of the story? How does it help the reader to understand the character of the story?

阅读链接

1. http://sherwoodandersonfoundation.org：舍伍德·安德森基金会，主要栏目有如何争取研究资助、安德森生平介绍、作品目录、评论，以及安德森的照片。
2. http://www.gradesaver.com/winesburg-ohio/study-guide/related-links：包括《小镇畸人》的文本、论文、论坛、学习指导等多个链接。
3. http://www.enotes.com/death-woods：《林中之死》的故事梗概和学习指导。

Flannery O'Connor (1925—1964)

作者简介

弗兰纳里·奥康纳(Flannery O'Connor,1925—1964)出生于美国南方佐治亚州港口城市萨凡纳,是家里唯一的孩子。15岁时父亲死于家族遗传病红斑狼疮。1945年奥康纳毕业于佐治亚州女子学院,并获得研究生奖学金,进入著名的依阿华大学作家培训班,得到当时美国文坛上一些名家的指点,并崭露文学才华。1951年她被诊断出患上和父亲同样的绝症,回到位于佐治亚州米尔吉维尔祖辈留下的农场。医生预计她只能再活五年,但她在与疾病的搏斗中过着充实的生活,延长了自己的生命。奥康纳在农场饲养孔雀、鸡鸭的同时,创作了20多篇短篇小说和两部长篇小说,收集天主教神学的书籍,有时还做关于信念和文学的演讲,或作长途旅行。奥康纳终身未婚,只与母亲相伴,她去世时年仅39岁。

文学创作

奥康纳被公认为是继福克纳之后美国南方最杰出的小说家,评论界称她的早逝是"自斯科特·菲茨杰拉尔德去世以来美国文坛最重大的损失"。奥康纳生命短暂,并不高产,只出版了两部长篇小说,《慧血》(*Wise Blood*,1952)和《暴力将它夺走》(*The Violent Bear It Away*,1960),和31篇短篇小说,但文学成就很高:1957年她获得欧·亨利短篇小说奖,2009年,《弗兰纳里·奥康纳小说全集》获得美国国家图书奖60年来唯一的最佳小说奖。

《慧血》的主人公黑兹是一个宗教狂,要在佐治亚州一个边远地区建立一个"没有基督的神圣教会",他为此而流浪、杀人并把自己的双眼弄瞎,用自残的方式进行赎罪。奥康纳称之为一部关于身不由己的基督徒的滑稽故事,但其主题却是严肃的。在《暴力将它夺走》中,自封为先知的梅森的侄孙弗朗西斯仿照先人的做法,在湖里为自己的白痴表弟施洗,却淹死了他。弗朗西斯最后放火烧了自己的林子。故事充满怪诞和恐怖,却不失诙谐。奥康纳的短篇小说更为有名,收在《好人难寻》(*A Good Man Is Hard to Find*,1955)和《上升的一切必然汇聚》(*Everything That Rises Must Converge*,1965)两个集子里。名篇有《好人难寻》、《善良的乡下人》("Good Country People")、《河流》("The River")、《最后审判日》("Judgment Day")等。

奥康纳以其家乡为背景,塑造了一系列怪诞的南方乡村人物,他们都鲜有正常的人格和行为,只在一个没有上帝的自我世界里漂荡。她继承了南方哥特小说的风格,故事时而诡谲阴郁,时而轻松幽默。死亡和暴力是其作品的显著特征,它们既是罪孽的体现,也是救赎的必由之路,这反映了她的罗马天主教信仰,以及对道德和伦理的关注。奥康纳的作品语言简练,经常采用南方的本土口语。

作 品

A Good Man Is Hard To Find

The grandmother didn't want to go to Florida. She wanted to visit some of her connections in east Tennessee and she was seizing at every chance to change Bailey's mind. Bailey was the son she lived with, her only boy. He was sitting on the edge of his chair at the table, bent over the orange sports section of the Journal. "Now look here, Bailey," she said, "see here, read this," and she stood with one hand on her thin hip and the other rattling the newspaper at his bald head. "Here this fellow that calls himself The Misfit is aloose from the Federal Pen[1] and headed toward Florida and you read here what it says he did to these people. Just you read it. I wouldn't take my children in any direction with a criminal like that aloose in it. I couldn't answer to my conscience if I did."

Bailey didn't look up from his reading so she wheeled around then and faced the children's mother, a young woman in slacks[2], whose face was as broad and innocent as a cabbage and was tied around with a green head-kerchief that had two points on the top like rabbit's ears. She was sitting on the sofa, feeding the baby his apricots out of a jar. "The children have been to Florida before," the old lady said. "You all ought to take them somewhere else for a change so they would see different parts of the world and be broad. They never have been to east Tennessee."

The children's mother didn't seem to hear her but the eight-year-old boy, John

---

[1] the Federal Pen:the Federal Penitentiary 的简称,即联邦监狱。
[2] slacks:宽松的裤子,便裤。

Wesley, a stocky child with glasses, said, "If you don't want to go to Florida, why dontcha[1] stay at home?" He and the little girl, June Star, were reading the funny papers on the floor.

"She wouldn't stay at home to be queen for a day," June Star said without raising her yellow head.

"Yes and what would you do if this fellow, The Misfit, caught you?" the grandmother asked.

"I'd smack his face," John Wesley said.

"She wouldn't stay at home for a million bucks," June Star said. "Afraid she'd miss something. She has to go everywhere we go."

"All right, Miss," the grandmother said. "Just remember that the next time you want me to curl your hair."

June Star said her hair was naturally curly.

The next morning the grandmother was the first one in the car, ready to go. She had her big black valise that looked like the head of a hippopotamus[2] in one corner, and underneath it she was hiding a basket with Pitty Sing[3], the cat, in it. She didn't intend for the cat to be left alone in the house for three days because he would miss her too much and she was afraid he might brush against one of her gas burners and accidentally asphyxiate[4] himself. Her son, Bailey, didn't like to arrive at a motel with a cat.

She sat in the middle of the back seat with John Wesley and June Star on either side of her. Bailey and the children's mother and the baby sat in front and they left Atlanta[5] at eight forty-five with the mileage on the car at 55890. The grandmother wrote this down because she thought it would be interesting to say how many miles they had been when they got back. It took them twenty minutes to reach the outskirts of the city.

The old lady settled herself comfortably, removing her white cotton gloves and putting them up with her purse on the shelf in front of the back window. The children's mother still had on slacks and still had her head tied up in a green kerchief, but the grandmother had on a navy blue straw sailor hat with a bunch of white violets on the brim and a navy blue dress with a small white dot in the print. Her collars and cuffs were white organdy trimmed with lace and at her neckline she had pinned a purple spray of

---

[1] dontcha = don't you.
[2] hippopotamus:河马。
[3] Pitty Sing:英国作曲家 Sir Arthur Sulliven(1842—1900)与英国歌词作家 Sir William Gilbert (1836—1911)共同创作的轻歌剧《天皇》(The Mikada,1885)中一个人物的名字。
[4] asphyxiate:窒息。
[5] Atlanta:亚特兰大,美国佐治亚州首府。

cloth violets containing a sachet.[1] In case of an accident, anyone seeing her dead on the highway would know at once that she was a lady.

She said she thought it was going to be a good day for driving, neither too hot nor too cold, and she cautioned Bailey that the speed limit was fifty-five miles an hour and that the patrolmen hid themselves behind billboards[2] and small clumps of trees and sped out after you before you had a chance to slow down. She pointed out interesting details of the scenery: Stone Mountain[3]; the blue granite that in some places came up to both sides of the highway; the brilliant red clay banks slightly streaked with purple; and the various crops that made rows of green lace-work on the ground. The trees were full of silver-white sunlight and the meanest of them sparkled. The children were reading comic magazines and their mother had gone back to sleep.

"Let's go through Georgia fast so we won't have to look at it much," John Wesley said.

"If I were a little boy," said the grandmother, "I wouldn't talk about my native state that way. Tennessee has the mountains and Georgia has the hills."

"Tennessee is just a hillbilly[4] dumping ground," John Wesley said, "and Georgia is a lousy state too."

"You said it,[5]" June Star said.

"In my time," said the grandmother, folding her thin veined fingers, "children were more respectful of their native states and their parents and everything else. People did right then. Oh look at the cute little pickaninny[6]!" she said and pointed to a Negro child standing in the door of a shack. "Wouldn't that make a picture, now?" she asked and they all turned and looked at the little Negro out of the back window. He waved.

"He didn't have any britches[7] on," June Star said.

"He probably didn't have any," the grandmother explained. "Little niggers in the country don't have things like we do. If I could paint, I'd paint that picture," she said.

The children exchanged comic books.

The grandmother offered to hold the baby and the children's mother passed him over the front seat to her. She set him on her knee and bounced him and told him about the things they were passing. She rolled her eyes and screwed up her mouth and stuck her leathery thin face into his smooth bland one. Occasionally he gave her a faraway smile. They passed a large cotton field with five or six graves fenced in the middle of it,

---

[1] Her collars and... containing a sachet:镶花边的领子和袖口全是白玻璃纱做的,领口上还别着一枝带香囊的紫罗兰布花。
[2] billboards:(广告等)招贴板。
[3] Stone Mountain:佐治亚州亚特兰大市附近一处著名景观。石山的一面山体上雕刻了美国内战期间南部联邦的著名人物:Jefferson Davis, Robert E. Lee 和 Stonewall Jackson。
[4] hillbilly:(美俚)乡巴佬,特指居住在美国南部山区的农民。
[5] You said it:说得一点没错。
[6] pickaninny:黑人小孩,也可拼作 piccaninny。
[7] britches:(口)裤子,同 beeches。

like a small island. "Look at the graveyard!" the grandmother said, pointing it out. "That was the old family burying ground. That belonged to the plantation."

"Where's the plantation?" John Wesley asked.

"Gone With the Wind,[1]" said the grandmother. "Ha. Ha."

When the children finished all the comic books they had brought, they opened the lunch and ate it. The grandmother ate a peanut butter sandwich and an olive and would not let the children throw the box and the paper napkins out the window. When there was nothing else to do they played a game by choosing a cloud and making the other two guess what shape it suggested. John Wesley took one the shape of a cow and June Star guessed a cow and John Wesley said, no, an automobile, and June Star said he didn't play fair, and they began to slap each other over the grandmother.

The grandmother said she would tell them a story if they would keep quiet. When she told a story, she rolled her eyes and waved her head and was very dramatic. She said once when she was a maiden lady she had been courted by a Mr. Edgar Atkins Teagarden from Jasper, Georgia. She said he was a very good-looking man and a gentleman and that he brought her a watermelon every Saturday afternoon with his initials cut in it, E. A. T. Well, one Saturday, she said, Mr. Teagarden brought the watermelon and there was nobody at home and he left it on the front porch and returned in his buggy[2] to Jasper, but she never got the watermelon, she said, because a nigger boy ate it when he saw the initials, E. A. T. ! This story tickled John Wesley's funny bone and he giggled and giggled but June Star didn't think it was any good. She said she wouldn't marry a man that just brought her a watermelon on Saturday. The grandmother said she would have done well to marry Mr. Teagarden because he was a gentle man and had bought Coca-Cola stock when it first came out and that he had died only a few years ago, a very wealthy man.

They stopped at The Tower for barbecued sandwiches. The Tower was a part stucco[3] and part wood filling station and dance hall set in a clearing outside of Timothy[4]. A fat man named Red Sammy Butts ran it and there were signs stuck here and there on the building and for miles up and down the highway saying, TRY RED SAMMY'S FAMOUS BARBECUE. NONE LIKE FAMOUS RED SAMMY'S! RED SAM! THE FAT BOY WITH THE HAPPY LAUGH. A VETERAN! RED SAMMY'S YOUR MAN!

Red Sammy was lying on the bare ground outside The Tower with his head under a

---

[1] Gone With the Wind：《飘》，即美国女作家玛格丽特·米切尔（Margaret Mitchell，1900—1949）发表于1936年的长篇小说，描写美国南北战争前后南方佐治亚州地区人民的生活及种植园的衰落。老祖母用小说的名字表达"一切都随风而去"的意思。
[2] buggy：轻便马车。
[3] stucco：拉毛水泥。
[4] Timothy：蒂莫西，佐治亚州小镇。

truck while a gray monkey about a foot high, chained to a small chinaberry tree[1], chattered nearby. The monkey sprang back into the tree and got on the highest limb as soon as he saw the children jump out of the car and run toward him.

Inside, The Tower was a long dark room with a counter at one end and tables at the other and dancing space in the middle. They all sat down at a board table next to the nickelodeon[2] and Red Sam's wife, a tall burnt-brown woman with hair and eyes lighter than her skin, came and took their order. The children's mother put a dime in the machine and played "The Tennessee Waltz", and the grandmother said that tune always made her want to dance. She asked Bailey if he would like to dance but he only glared at her. He didn't have a naturally sunny disposition like she did and trips made him nervous. The grandmother's brown eyes were very bright. She swayed her head from side to side and pretended she was dancing in her chair. June Star said play something she could tap to so the children's mother put in another dime and played a fast number[3] and June Star stepped out onto the dance floor and did her tap routine.

"Ain't she cute?" Red Sam's wife said, leaning over the counter. "Would you like to come be my little girl?"

"No I certainly wouldn't," June Star said. "I wouldn't live in a broken-down place like this for a million bucks!" and she ran back to the table.

"Ain't she cute?" the woman repeated, stretching her mouth politely.

"Ain't you ashamed?" hissed the grandmother.

Red Sam came in and told his wife to quit lounging on the counter and hurry up with these people's order. His khaki trousers reached just to his hip bones and his stomach hung over them like a sack of meal swaying under his shirt. He came over and sat down at a table nearby and let out a combination sigh and yodel[4]. "You can't win," he said. "You can't win," and he wiped his sweating red face off with a gray handkerchief. "These days you don't know who to trust," he said. "Ain't that the truth?"

"People are certainly not nice like they used to be," said the grandmother.

"Two fellers come in here last week," Red Sammy said, "driving a Chrysler. It was a old beat-up car but it was a good one and these boys looked all right to me. Said they worked at the mill and you know I let them fellers charge the gas they bought? Now why did I do that?"

"Because you're a good man!" the grandmother said at once.

"Yes'm[5], I suppose so," Red Sam said as if he were struck with this answer.

His wife brought the orders, carrying the five plates all at once without a tray, two in each hand and one balanced on her arm. "It isn't a soul in this green world of God's

---

[1] chinaberry tree:楝树。
[2] nickelodeon = jukebox,投币式自动点唱机。
[3] a fast number:一首快节奏的曲子。Number:(音乐术语)节奏。
[4] yodel:(指瑞士等国家的山里人)用常声和假声反复咏唱的一种曲子。这里形容 Sam 的叹息声。
[5] Yes'm = Yes, madam.

that you can trust," she said. "And I don't count nobody out of that, not nobody," she repeated, looking at Red Sammy.

"Did you read about that criminal, The Misfit, that's escaped?" asked the grandmother.

"I wouldn't be a bit surprised if he didn't attact[1] this place right here," said the woman. "If he hears about it being here, I wouldn't be none surprised to see him. If he hears it's two cent in the cash register, I wouldn't be a tall surprised if he …"

"That'll do," Red Sam said. "Go bring these people their Co'-Colas," and the woman went off to get the rest of the order.

"A good man is hard to find," Red Sammy said. "Everything is getting terrible. I remember the day you could go off and leave your screen door unlatched. Not no more."

He and the grandmother discussed better times. The old lady said that in her opinion Europe was entirely to blame for the way things were now. She said the way Europe acted you would think we were made of money and Red Sam said it was no use talking about it, she was exactly right. The children ran outside into the white sunlight and looked at the monkey in the lacy chinaberry tree. He was busy catching fleas on himself and biting each one carefully between his teeth as if it were a delicacy.

They drove off again into the hot afternoon. The grandmother took cat naps and woke up every few minutes with her own snoring. Outside of Toombsboro[2] she woke up and recalled an old plantation that she had visited in this neighborhood once when she was a young lady. She said the house had six white columns across the front and that there was an avenue of oaks leading up to it and two little wooden trellis arbors[3] on either side in front where you sat down with your suitor after a stroll in the garden. She recalled exactly which road to turn off to get to it. She knew that Bailey would not be willing to lose any time looking at an old house, but the more she talked about it, the more she wanted to see it once again and find out if the little twin arbors were still standing. "There was a secret panel[4] in this house," she said craftily, not telling the truth but wishing that she were, "and the story went that all the family silver was hidden in it when Sherman[5] came through but it was never found…"

"Hey!" John Wesley said. "Let's go see it! We'll find it! We'll poke all the woodwork and find it! Who lives there? Where do you turn off at? Hey Pop, can't we turn off there?"

"We never have seen a house with a secret panel!" June Star shrieked. "Let's go to

---

[1] attact = attack.
[2] Toombsboro:图姆斯伯勒,佐治亚州一城市。
[3] two little wooden trellis arbors:两座木格子小凉亭。Arbor 又拼作 arbour。
[4] panel:(建筑)夹板墙。
[5] Sherman:谢尔曼(William T. Sherman,1820—1891),美国南北战争期间北方联邦军队将领,1864 年底率军攻占佐治亚州亚特兰大市,使该地区遭到浩劫。他的名字在南方一直遭到诅咒。

the house with the secret panel! Hey Pop[1], can't we go see the house with the secret panel!"

"It's not far from here, I know," the grandmother said. "It wouldn't take over twenty minutes."

Bailey was looking straight ahead. His jaw was as rigid as a horseshoe. "No," he said.

The children began to yell and scream that they wanted to see the house with the secret panel. John Wesley kicked the back of the front seat and June Star hung over her mother's shoulder and whined desperately into her ear that they never had any fun even on their vacation, that they could never do what THEY wanted to do. The baby began to scream and John Wesley kicked the back of the seat so hard that his father could feel the blows in his kidney.

"All right!" he shouted and drew the car to a stop at the side of the road. "Will you all shut up? Will you all just shut up for one second? If you don't shut up, we won't go anywhere."

"It would be very educational for them," the grandmother murmured.

"All right," Bailey said, "but get this: this is the only time we're going to stop for anything like this. This is the one and only time."

"The dirt road that you have to turn down is about a mile back," the grandmother directed. "I marked it when we passed."

"A dirt road," Bailey groaned.

After they had turned around and were headed toward the dirt road, the grandmother recalled other points about the house, the beautiful glass over the front doorway and the candle-lamp in the hall. John Wesley said that the secret panel was probably in the fireplace.

"You can't go inside this house," Bailey said. "You don't know who lives there."

"While you all talk to the people in front, I'll run around behind and get in a window," John Wesley suggested.

"We'll all stay in the car," his mother said.

They turned onto the dirt road and the car raced roughly along in a swirl of pink dust. The grandmother recalled the times when there were no paved roads and thirty miles was a day's journey. The dirt road was hilly and there were sudden washes[2] in it and sharp curves on dangerous embankments. All at once they would be on a hill, looking down over the blue tops of trees for miles around, then the next minute, they would be in a red depression with the dust-coated trees looking down on them.

"This place had better turn up in a minute,[3]" Bailey said, "or I'm going to turn

---

[1] Pop: (俚)爸爸。
[2] washes: 水洼。
[3] This place had... in a minute: 这地方最好马上出现。

around."

The road looked as if no one had traveled on it in months.

"It's not much farther," the grandmother said and just as she said it, a horrible thought came to her. The thought was so embarrassing that she turned red in the face and her eyes dilated and her feet jumped up, upsetting her valise in the corner. The instant the valise moved, the newspaper top she had over the basket under it rose with a snarl and Pitty Sing, the cat, sprang onto Bailey's shoulder.

The children were thrown to the floor and their mother, clutching the baby, was thrown out the door onto the ground; the old lady was thrown into the front seat. The car turned over once and landed right-side-up in a gulch[1] off the side of the road. Bailey remained in the driver's seat with the cat gray-striped with a broad white face and an orange nose clinging to his neck like a caterpillar.

As soon as the children saw they could move their arms and legs, they scrambled out of the car, shouting, "We've had an ACCIDENT!" The grandmother was curled up under the dashboard, hoping she was injured so that Bailey's wrath would not come down on her all at once. The horrible thought she had had before the accident was that the house she had remembered so vividly was not in Georgia but in Tennessee.

Bailey removed the cat from his neck with both hands and flung it out the window against the side of a pine tree. Then he got out of the car and started looking for the children's mother. She was sitting against the side of the red gutted ditch, holding the screaming baby, but she only had a cut down her face and a broken shoulder. "We've had an ACCIDENT!" the children screamed in a frenzy of delight.

"But nobody's killed," June Star said with disappointment as the grandmother limped out of the car, her hat still pinned to her head but the broken front brim standing up at a jaunty angle and the violet spray hanging off the side. They all sat down in the ditch, except the children, to recover from the shock. They were all shaking.

"Maybe a car will come along," said the children's mother hoarsely.

"I believe I have injured an organ," said the grandmother, pressing her side, but no one answered her. Bailey's teeth were clattering. He had on a yellow sport shirt with bright blue parrots designed in it and his face was as yellow as the shirt. The grandmother decided that she would not mention that the house was in Tennessee.

The road was about ten feet above and they could see only the tops of the trees on the other side of it. Behind the ditch they were sitting in there were more woods, tall and dark and deep. In a few minutes they saw a car some distance away on top of a hill, coming slowly as if the occupants were watching them. The grandmother stood up and waved both arms dramatically to attract their attention. The car continued to come on slowly, disappeared around a bend and appeared again, moving even slower, on top of

---

[1] gulch:干沟。

the hill they had gone over. It was a big black battered hearse-like[1] automobile. There were three men in it.

It came to a stop just over them and for some minutes, the driver looked down with a steady expressionless gaze to where they were sitting, and didn't speak. Then he turned his head and muttered something to the other two and they got out. One was a fat boy in black trousers and a red sweat shirt with a silver stallion embossed on the front of it. He moved around on the right side of them and stood staring, his mouth partly open in a kind of loose grin. The other had on khaki pants and a blue striped coat and a gray hat pulled down very low, hiding most of his face. He came around slowly on the left side. Neither spoke.

The driver got out of the car and stood by the side of it, looking down at them. He was an older man than the other two. His hair was just beginning to gray and he wore silver-rimmed spectacles that gave him a scholarly look. He had a long creased face and didn't have on any shirt or undershirt. He had on blue jeans that were too tight for him and was holding a black hat and a gun. The two boys also had guns.

"We've had an ACCIDENT!" the children screamed.

The grandmother had the peculiar feeling that the bespectacled man was someone she knew. His face was as familiar to her as if she had known him all her life but she could not recall who he was. He moved away from the car and began to come down the embankment, placing his feet carefully so that he wouldn't slip. He had on tan and white shoes and no socks, and his ankles were red and thin. "Good afternoon," he said. "I see you all had you a little spill."

"We turned over twice!" said the grandmother.

"Once", he corrected. "We seen it happen. Try their car and see will it run, Hiram," he said quietly to the boy with the gray hat.

"What you got that gun for?" John Wesley asked. "Whatcha gonna[2] do with that gun?"

"Lady," the man said to the children's mother, "would you mind calling them children to sit down by you? Children make me nervous. I want all you all to sit down right together there where you're at."

"What are you telling US what to do for?" June Star asked.

Behind them the line of woods gaped like a dark open mouth. "Come here," said their mother.

"Look here now," Bailey began suddenly, "we're in a predicament! We're in..."

The grandmother shrieked. She scrambled to her feet and stood staring. "You're The Misfit!" she said. "I recognized you at once!"

"Yes'm," the man said, smiling slightly as if he were pleased in spite of himself to

---

[1] hearse-like: 像一辆灵柩车似的。
[2] Whatcha gona = What you got to.

be known, "but it would have been better for all of you, lady, if you hadn't of reckernized me."

Bailey turned his head sharply and said something to his mother that shocked even the children. The old lady began to cry and The Misfit reddened.

"Lady," he said, "don't you get upset. Sometimes a man says things he doesn't mean. I don't reckon he meant to talk to you thataway[1]."

"You wouldn't shoot a lady, would you?" the grandmother said and removed a clean handkerchief from her cuff and began to slap at her eyes with it.

The Misfit pointed the toe of his shoe into the ground and made a little hole and then covered it up again. "I would hate to have to," he said.

"Listen," the grandmother almost screamed, "I know you're a good man. You don't look a bit like you have common blood. I know you must come from nice people!"

"Yes mam[2]," he said, "finest people in the world." When he smiled he showed a row of strong white teeth. "God never made a finer woman than my mother and my daddy's heart was pure gold," he said. The boy with the red sweat shirt had come around behind them and was standing with his gun at his hip. The Misfit squatted down on the ground. "Watch them children, Bobby Lee," he said. "You know they make me nervous." He looked at the six of them huddled together in front of him and he seemed to be embarrassed as if he couldn't think of anything to say. "Ain't a cloud in the sky," he remarked, looking up at it. "Don't see no sun but don't see no cloud neither."

"Yes, it's a beautiful day," said the grandmother. "Listen," she said, "you shouldn't call yourself The Misfit because I know you're a good man at heart. I can just look at you and tell."

"Hush!" Bailey yelled. "Hush! Everybody shut up and let me handle this!" He was squatting in the position of a runner about to sprint forward[3] but he didn't move.

"I pre-chate[4] that, lady," The Misfit said and drew a little circle in the ground with the butt of his gun.

"It'll take a half a hour to fix this here car," Hiram called, looking over the raised hood of it.

"Well, first you and Bobby Lee get him and that little boy to step over yonder with you," The Misfit said, pointing to Bailey and John Wesley. "The boys want to ask you something," he said to Bailey. "Would you mind stepping back in them woods there with them?"

"Listen," Bailey began, "we're in a terrible predicament! Nobody realizes what this is," and his voice cracked. His eyes were as blue and intense as the parrots in his shirt

---

[1] thataway = that way.
[2] mam = madam.
[3] a runner about to sprint forward: (棒球中)向前全速奔跑的跑垒者; sprint: 全速奔跑。
[4] pre-chate = appreciate.

and he remained perfectly still.

The grandmother reached up to adjust her hat brim as if she were going to the woods with him but it came off in her hand. She stood staring at it and after a second she let it fall on the ground. Hiram pulled Bailey up by the arm as if he were assisting an old man. John Wesley caught hold of his father's hand and Bobby Lee followed. They went off toward the woods and just as they reached the dark edge, Bailey turned and supporting himself against a gray naked pine trunk, he shouted, "I'll be back in a minute, Mamma, wait on me!"

"Come back this instant!" his mother shrilled but they all disappeared into the woods.

"Bailey Boy!" the grandmother called in a tragic voice but she found she was looking at The Misfit squatting on the ground in front of her. "I just know you're a good man," she said desperately. "You're not a bit common!"

"Nome, I ain't a good man," The Misfit said after a second as if he had considered her statement carefully, "but I ain't the worst in the world neither. My daddy said I was a different breed of dog from my brothers and sisters. 'You know,' Daddy said, 'It's some that can live their whole life out without asking about it and it's others has to know why it is, and this boy is one of the latters. He's going to be into everything!'" He put on his black hat and looked up suddenly and then away deep into the woods as if he were embarrassed again. "I'm sorry I don't have on a shirt before you ladies," he said, hunching his shoulders slightly. "We buried our clothes that we had on when we escaped and we're just making do until we can get better. We borrowed these from some folks we met," he explained.

"That's perfectly all right," the grandmother said. "Maybe Bailey has an extra shirt in his suitcase."

"I'll look and see terrectly[1]," The Misfit said.

"Where are they taking him?" the children's mother screamed.

"Daddy was a card[2] himself," The Misfit said. "You couldn't put anything over on him.[3] He never got in trouble with the Authorities though. Just had the knack of handling them."

"You could be honest too if you'd only try," said the grandmother. "Think how wonderful it would be to settle down and live a comfortable life and not have to think about somebody chasing you all the time."

The Misfit kept scratching in the ground with the butt of his gun as if he were thinking about it. "Yes'm, somebody is always after you," he murmured.

The grandmother noticed how thin his shoulder blades were just behind his hat

---

[1] terrectly = directly.
[2] card: 精明的人。
[3] You couldn't put anything over on him: 你作弄不了他。

because she was standing up looking down on him. "Do you ever pray?" she asked.

He shook his head. All she saw was the black hat wiggle between his shoulder blades. "Nome," he said.

There was a pistol shot from the woods, followed closely by another. Then silence. The old lady's head jerked around. She could hear the wind move through the tree tops like a long satisfied insuck of breath. "Bailey Boy!" she called.

"I was a gospel singer for a while," The Misfit said. "I been most everything. Been in the arm service both land and sea, at home and abroad, been twict[1] married, been an undertaker, been with the railroads, plowed Mother Earth, been in a tornado, seen a man burnt alive oncet[2]," and he looked up at the children's mother and the little girl who were sitting close together, their faces white and their eyes glassy; "I even seen a woman flogged," he said.

"Pray, pray," the grandmother began, "pray, pray..."

"I never was a bad boy that I remember of," The Misfit said in an almost dreamy voice, "but somewheres along the line I done[3] something wrong and got sent to the penitentiary. I was buried alive," and he looked up and held her attention to him by a steady stare.

"That's when you should have started to pray," she said. "What did you do to get sent to the penitentiary that first time?"

"Turn to the right, it was a wall," The Misfit said, looking up again at the cloudless sky. "Turn to the left, it was a wall. Look up it was a ceiling, look down it was a floor. I forget what I done, lady. I set[4] there and set there, trying to remember what it was I done and I ain't recalled it to this day. Oncet in a while, I would think it was coming to me, but it never come."

"Maybe they put you in by mistake," the old lady said vaguely.

"None," he said. "It wasn't no mistake. They had the papers on me."

"You must have stolen something," she said.

The Misfit sneered slightly. "Nobody had nothing I wanted," he said. "It was a head-doctor at the penitentiary said what I had done was kill my daddy but I known that for a lie. My daddy died in nineteen ought nineteen of the epidemic flu[5] and I never had a thing to do with it. He was buried in the Mount Hopewell Baptist churchyard and you can go there and see for yourself."

"If you would pray," the old lady said, "Jesus would help you."

"That's right," The Misfit said.

---

[1] twict = twice.
[2] oncet = once.
[3] done = did.
[4] set = sat.
[5] in nineteen ought nineteen of the epidemic flu:这里指发生在1918至1919年间的全球性流感,导致美国当时约50万人死亡。

"Well then, why don't you pray?" she asked trembling with delight suddenly.

"I don't want no hep[1]," he said. "I'm doing all right by myself."

Bobby Lee and Hiram came ambling back from the woods. Bobby Lee was dragging a yellow shirt with bright blue parrots in it.

"Thow[2] me that shirt, Bobby Lee," The Misfit said. The shirt came flying at him and landed on his shoulder and he put it on. The grandmother couldn't name what the shirt reminded her of. "No, lady," The Misfit said while he was buttoning it up, "I found out the crime don't matter. You can do one thing or you can do another, kill a man or take a tire off his car, because sooner or later you're going to forget what it was you done and just be punished for it."

The children's mother had begun to make heaving noises as if she couldn't get her breath. "Lady," he asked, "would you and that little girl like to step off yonder with Bobby Lee and Hiram and join your husband?"

"Yes, thank you," the mother said faintly. Her left arm dangled helplessly and she was holding the baby, who had gone to sleep, in the other. "Hep that lady up, Hiram," The Misfit said as she struggled to climb out of the ditch, "and Bobby Lee, you hold onto that little girl's hand."

"I don't want to hold hands with him," June Star said. "He reminds me of a pig."

The fat boy blushed and laughed and caught her by the arm and pulled her off into the woods after Hiram and her mother.

Alone with The Misfit, the grandmother found that she had lost her voice. There was not a cloud in the sky nor any sun. There was nothing around her but woods. She wanted to tell him that he must pray. She opened and closed her mouth several times before anything came out. Finally she found herself saying, "Jesus. Jesus," meaning, Jesus will help you, but the way she was saying it, it sounded as if she might be cursing.

"Yes'm," The Misfit said as if he agreed. "Jesus shown everything off balance. It was the same case with Him as with me except He hadn't committed any crime and they could prove I had committed one because they had the papers on me. Of course," he said, "they never shown me my papers. That's why I sign myself now. I said long ago, you get you a signature and sign everything you do and keep a copy of it. Then you'll know what you done and you can hold up the crime to the punishment and see do they match and in the end you'll have something to prove you ain't been treated right. I call myself The Misfit," he said, "because I can't make what all I done wrong fit what all I gone through in punishment."

There was a piercing scream from the woods, followed closely by a pistol report. "Does it seem right to you, lady, that one is punished a heap[3] and another ain't

---

[1] hep = help.
[2] thow = throw.
[3] a heap of = a heap.

punished at all?"

"Jesus!" the old lady cried. "You've got good blood! I know you wouldn't shoot a lady! I know you come from nice people! Pray! Jesus, you ought not to shoot a lady. I'll give you all the money I've got!"

"Lady," The Misfit said, looking beyond her far into the woods, "there never was a body that give the undertaker a tip."

There were two more pistol reports and the grandmother raised her head like a parched old turkey hen crying for water and called, "Bailey Boy, Bailey Boy!" as if her heart would break.

"Jesus was the only One that ever raised the dead," The Misfit continued, "and He shouldn't have done it. He shown everything off balance. If He did what He said, then it's nothing for you to do but thow away everything and follow Him, and if He didn't, then it's nothing for you to do but enjoy the few minutes you got left the best way you can by killing somebody or burning down his house or doing some other meanness to him. No pleasure but meanness," he said and his voice had become almost a snarl.

"Maybe He didn't raise the dead," the old lady mumbled, not knowing what she was saying and feeling so dizzy that she sank down in the ditch with her legs twisted under her.

"I wasn't there so I can't say He didn't," The Misfit said. "I wisht[1] I had of been there," he said, hitting the ground with his fist. "It ain't right I wasn't there because if I had of been there I would of known. Listen lady," he said in a high voice, "if I had of been there I would of known and I wouldn't be like I am now." His voice seemed about to crack and the grandmother's head cleared for an instant. She saw the man's face twisted close to her own as if he were going to cry and she murmured, "Why you're one of my babies. You're one of my own children!" She reached out and touched him on the shoulder. The Misfit sprang back as if a snake had bitten him and shot her three times through the chest. Then he put his gun down on the ground and took off his glasses and began to clean them.

Hiram and Bobby Lee returned from the woods and stood over the ditch, looking down at the grandmother who half sat and half lay in a puddle of blood with her legs crossed under her like a child's and her face smiling up at the cloudless sky.

Without his glasses, The Misfit's eyes were red-rimmed and pale and defenseless-looking. "Take her off and thow her where you thown[2] the others," he said, picking up the cat that was rubbing itself against his leg.

"She was a talker, wasn't she?" Bobby Lee said, sliding down the ditch with a yodel.

"She would of been a good woman," The Misfit said, "if it had been somebody

---

[1] wisht = wished.

[2] thown = threw.

there to shoot her every minute of her life."

"Some fun!" Bobby Lee said.

"Shut up, Bobby Lee," The Misfit said. "It's no real pleasure in life."

1953

赏析

《好人难寻》是奥康纳最为知名的短篇小说。它概括了奥康纳的创作特点：以幽默的笔触反衬暴力的惊心，精心勾画人物以强调她的宗教信仰。在这个震撼人心的故事里，这一信仰指的是人如何能获得上帝的圣恩(divine grace)。奥康纳认为，圣恩在人物的生活之外，是一瞬间的顿悟，而这一顿悟常常在自己或他人的死亡中到来。在杀人者和被杀者当中，也许只有老太太在临死前获得了这样的圣恩。她看到家人一个个被枪杀，只想到自己怎么活下去。一旦她看到获救无望，便向"不合时宜的人"伸出手去，想把这个杀人者看作是自己的孩子，这时，她的自私之心消失，得到了天恩。作者似乎在暗示，圣恩无所不在，它同样会降临到那些令人讨厌的人身上。

《好人难寻》是一个旅行故事，它以死亡为终结。在西方文学中，旅行往往代表了人物的成长，但这种成长通常不是身体的或年龄的，而是心理的和精神的。老太太开始认为打扮体面就是淑女，她假怀宗教的虔诚，实则有种族歧视心理，且自视甚高，直到临死前，她才明白死亡与圣恩的关系。从宗教信仰的无知到顿悟，这是老太太的成长。对另一个主要人物"不合时宜的人"来说，杀害老太太及其一家究竟是预示他最终也得到了拯救，还是暗示这是一个不可能有拯救的世界？这是作者留给读者思考的问题。

视角是这篇作品的一个重要特征。作者采用第三人称叙事，在有限的全知视角(the limited total omniscience)和全知视角(the total omniscience)之间滑行，大部分事件是从老太太的视角来观察的，如"她清楚贝莱不想花时间去看什么老屋……"、"她可不想让这只猫独自在家里呆上三天……"，同时也从客观的角度来描述一部分事件。老太太的有限视角既暗示她的自我中心，又帮助读者深入她的内心世界；全知视角则提供必要的故事背景，解释事件，增加戏剧性。二者相辅相成，使读者既了解人物的所作所为，又可深思其意义。

《好人难寻》的笔调轻松，具有喜剧色彩，但是骇人听闻的凶杀事件不能不引起读者心灵上的震撼和对现实的思考。

相关评论

Interpretation of the Names in "A Goodman Is Hard to Find"
Anonymous

This story is a travel narrative, but neither east Tennessee nor Florida is the destination toward which this family rides. There are foreshadowing and symbolic suggestions of other levels of meaning than the literal ones from early on in the story, for which the reader may see the references to the possibility of the grandmother's cat dying if she leaves it at home, dressing up for a drive lest she die in a highway accident, and noticing the five or six graves in a field. Then, the family stops at the infernal RED SAMMY'S, near Toombsboro, where horrors, both real and suggested, abound: the "burnt brown" owner's wife, and the animal guard all are reminders of a Dante-Inferno[1] landscape. Finally, of course, the family dies when they meet a group who emerges from "a big black battered hearse-like automobile."

So, if Toombsboro is a suggestive name, are there other names that have suggested levels of meaning? Probably, since O'Connor's appropriation of external realities to suggest other levels of meaning extends to the names in the story: John Wesley, founder of Methodism, is in this story a bespectacled child with a lively, argumentative mind; June Star is possibly a tribute to all the Junes who got last billing[2] in second-feature films[3] of the 1930s and '40s; Bailey seems to confer upon the father a kind of Southern Everyman status. Then there are characters with, significantly, no name: the children's mother seems more vegetable[4] than human with her "broad and innocent" face like a "cabbage and was tied around with a green head-kerchief that had two points on the top like rabbit's ears."

Among all the characters in the work, The Misfit is such an important and strange character that he's bound to mean something. What is it? The Misfit suggests many levels of interpretation, some of them suggesting a parallel with John Wesley, the child, some of them suggesting spiritual levels of meaning, and others stemming from The Misfit's need for literal proof.

First, the grandmother makes a gesture of inclusion toward The Misfit, calling him her son which compels him to shoot her. Why does this inclusion into a family upset him so much? At the beginning of the story, we learn about the grandmother that "Bailey was the son she lived with," suggesting the possibility of another son. Later she warns him about The Misfit. At the end of the story, these postural details—both Bailey and The Misfit squatted down on the ground—recur. After Bailey is shot, The Misfit is wearing his "yellow shirt with bright blue parrots in it."

Secondly, why is he called a misfit? O'Connor shows that The Misfit's tendency to take things literally is the theological heart of the problem. Growing up in the Bible Belt[5], where children are named after John Wesley[6] and the Bible is taken literally, The Misfit cut his ties to his family by asking too many questions. Now, he is defined by his adversarial stance toward the world and its wisdom. Like the child, John Wesley, who is desperate to open the secret panel in the fireplace of the grandmother's mythical

---

[1] Dante-Inferno: Dante,但丁(1265—1321),意大利诗人,所作长诗《神曲》(*Divine Comedy*)描绘了地狱(Inferno)的可怕景象。
[2] got last billing: 在演员表上排最后,指最不重要的角色。
[3] second-feature films: 重映片。
[4] vegetable: 生活呆板单调的人。
[5] the Bible Belt: 圣经带,尤指美国南部和中西部基督教新教徒基要主义普及的一些地区。
[6] John Wesley: 约翰·卫斯理(1703—1791)英国宗教领袖。他创建了卫理公会(1738年)。

white mansion, The Misfit wants to make experience intelligible. He wants to actually see, hear, taste, touch; he needs literal proof of things and ideas.

The grandmother keeps throwing the name of Jesus at The Misfit, not understanding that his profound alienation stems from his inability to subscribe to the shallow beliefs to which the grandmother has paid lip service[1] all her life. His need for verification traps him in an inadequate "rational" view of the world. He does not know about what O'Connor speaks of as "the mystery of faith that allows one to know the truth that has never been seen." He is one of what is called O'Connor's "flawed prophets," as he has a depth of experience as shown in his listing of occupations—gospel singing, undertaking, plowing "Mother Earth," being in a tornado, seeing a man burnt and a woman flogged—that goes far beyond the banal experience of his victims. Sensitive and psychotic, he has the spiritual insight to recognize that true belief throws "everything off balance."

Then, is the murder of the grandmother and her family a prelude to The Misfit's eventual salvation, as O'Connor may hint, or is the story a vision of a world without redemptive possibilities? Perhaps O'Connor would agree that the "silver stallion embossed on the front of" the red sweatshirt worn by one of The Misfit's henchmen[2] is a mass-marketed replica of the pale horse on which Death sits in the book of Revelation (6.8), the Christian's ultimate source of mystical symbols open to multiple and mutually contradictory interpretations. O'Connor's story, like the Bible itself, like all religious experience, defies pat[3] analysis and for today's readers (consciously post-modern or not) remains open to interpretation.

Source: http://images.schoolinsites.com/SiSFiles/Schools/AL/DothanCitySchools/NorthviewHigh/Uploads/DocumentsCategories/Documents/A%20Good%20Man%20is%20Hard%20to%20Find.doc. (2010-10-2)

问题与思考

1. What do you understand to be Flannery O'Connor's opinion of the grandmother? What conventional, social and religious values does the grandmother represent? How are they exposed in the story?
2. Summarise the character of The Misfit. What does he represent? What kind of philosophy does he convey in his justifying his actions? What does he mean when he says that Jesus "thrown everything off balance"?
3. Explain the function of the other family members in the story. Through her description of the grandmother and her family members, what kind of tone does

---

[1] paid lip service: 嘴上说得好听，却没有实际行动。
[2] henchmen: 追随者，帮凶。
[3] pat: 现成的，早已准备好了的。

O'Connor create in the story?
4. Which parts of the story are realistic and which parts are fanciful or improbable? What is accomplished by the mixture of realistic and unrealistic elements?
5. What is the theme of the story? What attitudes does O'Connor reveal towards "good and evil"?

阅读链接

1. http://mediaspecialist.org/on.html：包括奥康纳的生平、评论文章和相关链接。
2. http://www.cyberpat.com/essays/flan.html：奥康纳的作品介绍和作品引文。
3. http://flanneryoconnor.net：奥康纳导学导研。

Doris Lessing (1919—　)

作者简介

多丽丝·莱辛(Doris Lessing,1919—　)出生于伊朗,父母都是英格兰人。5岁时她随父母迁居非洲南罗得西亚(今津巴布韦)。父亲经营农场,但很不成功,生活窘迫,家庭气氛阴郁。作为逃避,少年莱辛大量阅读欧洲现实主义文学作品,并很早就离家工作。1937年她去索尔兹伯里当了一名电话接线员。第一次婚姻失败后她加入了"左翼读书俱乐部",并很快嫁给了俱乐部的负责人、来自德国的马克思主义者弗里德·莱辛,这次婚姻于1949年也走到了尽头。同年,她留下两个孩子在非洲,带着小儿子去伦敦追求文学事业。莱辛早年参加过英国共产党,积极投入左派政治活动,是一位有社会责任心的作家。1950年,长篇小说《野草在歌唱》(*The Grass Is Singing*)问世,使她一举成名。1962年出版的《金色笔记本》(*The Golden Notebook*)进一步巩固了她的文学地位。莱辛于1999年获封为英国名誉勋爵,2007年获诺贝尔文学奖,时年87岁,是诺贝尔文学奖历史上年纪最大的获奖者。她至今笔耕不辍。

文学创作

莱辛被誉为继弗吉尼亚·伍尔芙之后英国最伟大的女性作家,在其漫长的创作生涯中,发表了20多部长篇小说,还写了不少短篇小说、诗歌、戏剧、回忆录、歌剧等。

莱辛的成名作《野草在歌唱》以现实主义风格讲述一位白人农场主的妻子被黑人男仆杀死的故事,反映了非洲殖民地的种族矛盾。五部曲《暴力的孩子们》(*The Children of Violence*, 1952—1969)是一部女性成长小说,它"以诚实细腻的笔触和颇有印象主义色彩的写实风格展示了一位在罗得西亚长大的白人青年妇女的人生求索",作品源于莱辛早年在非洲的亲身经历,涉及妇女的出路、种族关系以及战后的政治生活。莱辛公认的最高成就是长篇小说《金色笔记本》，讲述的是小说家安娜·沃尔夫的经历，深刻剖析一位当代女性的精神世界。为了从不同角度分析自己的问题，安娜分别在黑、红、黄、蓝四个笔记本上记录不同的内容。最后，她找到了完整的自我，用新的笔记本(金色笔记)"记下我的一切"。在 1979—1983 年间，莱辛发表了一系列总名为《天舟座老人星：历史档案》的"太空小说"，内容集历史、科学、政治、神话、寓言于一体，以科幻的形式写出了对人类历史和命运的思考与忧虑。80 年代中期以来，莱辛的创作又回到现实主义的传统。

在短篇小说方面，莱辛同样高产，她的 50 多篇作品收入八个集子，主要有《一个男人和两个女人》(*A Man and Two Women*，1963)、《黑色圣母》(*The Black Madonna*，1966)、《杰克·奥克尼的诱惑》(*Temptation of Jack Orkney and Other Stories*，1972)和《幸存者回忆录》(*The Memoirs of a Survivor*，1975)。

莱辛立足于人和社会，以文学的方式反映和思考人和社会的真实状况，她将心理内省与政治分析、社会记录和女性主义成功地结合起来，因此诺贝尔文学奖颁奖词称她是"女性经验的史诗作者，以其怀疑、激情和卓识远见来审视一个分裂的文明"。

作　　品

A Woman on a Roof

It was during the week of hot sun, that June.

Three men were at work on the roof, where the leads[1] got so hot they had the idea of throwing water on to cool them. But the water steamed, then sizzled; and they make jokes about getting an egg from some woman in the flats under the flats under them, to poach[2] it for their dinner. By two it was not possible to touch the guttering[3] they were replacing, and they speculated about what workmen did in regularly hot countries. Perhaps they should borrow kitchen gloves[4] with the egg? They were all a bit dizzy, not used to the heat; and they shed[5] their coats and stood side by side squeezing themselves into a foot-wide patch of shade against a chimney, careful to keep their feet in the thick socks and boots out of the sun. There was a fine view across several acres of roofs. Not far off a man sat in a deck chair reading the newspapers. Then they saw her, between chimneys, about fifty yards away. She lay face down on a brown blanket. They could see the top part of her: black hair, flushed solid back, arms spread out.

"She's stark naked," said Stanley, sounding annoyed.

---

[1] the leads：(英)铅皮屋顶。
[2] poach：水煮(荷包蛋)。
[3] guttering：檐沟。
[4] kitchen gloves：(防烫的)棉手套。
[5] shed：脱掉。

Harry, the oldest, a man of about forty-five, said: "Looks like it."

Young Tom, seventeen, said nothing, but he was excited and grinning.

Stanley said: "Someone'll report her if she doesn't watch out."

"She thinks no one can see," said Tom, craning his head all ways to see more.

At this point the woman, still lying prone, brought her two hands up behind her shoulders with the ends of a scarf in them, tied it behind her back, and sat up. She wore a red scarf tied around her breasts and brief red bikini pants. This being the first day of the sun she was white, flushing red. She sat smoking, and did not look up when Stanley let out a wolf whistle[1]. Harry said: "Small things amuse small minds," leading the way back to their part of the roof, but it was scorching[2]. Harry said: "Wait, I'm going to rig up[3] some shade," and disappeared down the skylight[4] into the building. Now that he'd gone Stanley and Tom went to the farthest point they could to peer at the woman. She had moved, and all they could see were two pink legs stretched on the blanket. They whistled and shouted but the legs did no move. Harry came back with a blanket and shouted: "Come on, then." He shouted irritated with them. They clambered[5] back to him and he said to Stanley: "What about your missus[6]?"—preserving his independence. Tom said nothing, but his mind was full of the nearly naked woman. Harry slung the blanket, which he had borrowed from a friendly woman downstairs, from the stem of a television aerial to a row of chimney-pots[7]. This shade fell across the piece of gutter they had to replace. But the shade kept moving, they had to adjust the blanket, and not much progress was made. At last some of the heat left the roof, and they worked fast, making up for lost time. First Stanley, then Tom, made a trip to the end of the roof to see the woman. "She's on her back," Stanley said, adding a jest which made Tom snicker,[8] and the older man smile tolerantly. Tom's report was that she hadn't moved, but it was a lie. He wanted to keep what he had seen to himself: he had caught her in the act of rolling down the little red pants over her hips, till they were no more than a small triangle. She was on her back, fully visible, glistening with oil[9].

Next morning, as soon as they came up, they went to look. She was already there, face down, arms spread out, naked except for the little red pants. She had turned brown in the night. Yesterday she was a scarlet-and-white woman, today she was a brown woman. Stanley let out a whistle. She lifted her head, startled, as if she'd been asleep, and looked straight over at them. The sun was in her eyes, she blinked and stared, then

---

[1] wolf whistle: (某些男子挑逗过路的美貌女子时吹出的)挑逗口哨, 亦可称做 wolf call。
[2] scorching: 灼热的。
[3] rig up: 匆忙准备。
[4] skylight: 天窗。
[5] clambered: 爬。
[6] missus: (伦敦方言) missis, 妻子, 太太。
[7] chimney-pots: 烟囱管帽, 亦可称做 chimney-pot hats。
[8] adding a jest which made Tom snicker: 加上一句俏皮话, 使 Tom 听了暗自发笑。
[9] oil: 这里指防晒护肤油。

she dropped her head again. At this gesture of indifference, they all three, Stanley, Tom and old Harry, let out whistle and yells. Harry was doing it in parody of the younger men, making fun of them, but he was also angry. They were all angry because of her utter indifference to the three men watching her.

"Bitch," said Stanley.

"She should ask us over," said Tom, snickering.

Harry recovered himself and reminded Stanley: "If she's married, her old man wouldn't like that."

"Christ," said Stanley virtuously, "if my wife lay about like that, for everyone to see, I'd soon stop her."

Harry said smiling: "How do you know, perhaps she's sunning herself at this very moment?"

"Not a chance, not on our roof." The safety of his wife put Stanley into a good humor, and they went to work. But today it was hotter than yesterday; and several times one or the other suggested they should tell Matthew, the foreman, and ask to leave the roof until the heat wave was over. But they didn't. There was work to be done in the basement of the big block of flats, but up here they felt free, on a different level from ordinary humanity shut in the streets or the buildings. A lot more people came out on to the roofs that day, for an hour at midday. Some married couples sat side by side in deck chairs, the women's legs stockingless and scarlet, the men in vests with reddening shoulders.

The woman stayed on her blanket, turning herself over and over. She ignored them, no matter what they did. When Harry went off to fetch more screws, Stanley said: "Come on." Her roof belonged to a different system of roofs, separated from theirs at one point by about twenty feet. It meant a scrambling climb from one level to another, edging along parapets[1], clinging to chimneys, while their big boots slipped and slithered, but at last they stood on a small square projecting roof looking straight down at her, close. She sat smoking reading a book. Tom thought she looked like a poster, or a magazine cover, with the blue sky behind her and her legs stretched out. Behind her a great crane[2] at work on a new building in Oxford Street[3] swung its black arm across roofs in a great arc. Tom imagined himself at work on the crane, adjusting the arm to swing over and pick her up and swing her back across the sky to drop her near him.

They whistled. She looked up at them, cool and remote, then went on reading. Again, they were furious. Or, rather, Stanley was. His sun-heated face was screwed into a rage as he whistled again and again, trying to make her look up. Young Tom

---

[1] parapet: (屋顶、露台等边上的)低矮短墙。
[2] crane: 起重机。
[3] Oxford Street: 牛津街,伦敦市中心的商业街。

stopped whistling. He stood beside Stanley, excited, grinning; but he felt as if he were saying to the woman: Don't associate me with him, for his grin was apologetic. Last night he had thought of the unknown woman before he slept, and she had been tender with him. This tenderness he was remembering as he shifted his feet by the jeering, whistling Stanley, and watched the indifferent, healthy brown woman a few feet off, with the gap that plunged to the street between them. Tom thought it was romantic, it was like being high on two hilltops. But there was a shout from Harry, and they clambered back. Stanley's face was hard, really angry. The boy kept looking at him and wondered why he hated the woman so much, for by now he loved her.

They played their little games with the blanket, trying to trap shade to work under; but again it was not until nearly four that they could work seriously, and they were exhausted, all three of them. They were grumbling about the weather by now. Stanley was in a thoroughly bad humor. When they made their routine trip to see the woman before they packed up for the day, she was apparently asleep, face down, her back all naked save for the scarlet triangle on her buttocks. "I've got a good mind to report her to the police," said Stanley, and Harry said: "What's eating you? What harm's she doing?"

"I tell you, if she was my wife!"

"But she isn't, is she?" Tom knew that Harry, like himself, was uneasy at Stanley's reaction. He was normally a sharp young man, quick at his work, making a lot of jokes, good company.

"Perhaps it will be cooler tomorrow," said Harry.

But it wasn't; it was hotter, if anything, and the weather forecast said the good weather would last. As soon as they were on the roof, Harry went over to see if the woman was there, and Tom knew it was to prevent Stanley going, to put off his bad humor. Harry had grownup children, a boy the same age as Tom, and the youth trusted and looked up to him.

Harry came back and said: "She's not there."

"I bet her old man has put his foot down,[1]" said Stanley, and Harry and Tom caught each other's eyes and smiled behind the young married man's back.

Harry suggested they should get permission to work in the basement, and they did, that day. But before packing up Stanley said: "Let's have a breath of fresh air." Again Harry and Tom smiled at each other as they followed Stanley up to the roof, Tom in the devout conviction that he was there to protect the woman from Stanley. It was about five-thirty, and a calm, full sunlight lay over the roofs. The great crane still swung its black arm from Oxford Street to above their heads. She was not there. Then there was a flutter of white from behind a parapet, and she stood up, in a belted, white dressing-grown. She had been there all day, probably, but on a different patch of roof, to hide

---

[1] I bet her... his foot down: 我打赌她老头子决不容许她这样。put one's foot down: (口)坚定地。

from them. Stanley did not whistle; he said nothing, but watched the woman bend to collect papers, books, cigarettes, then fold the blanket over her arm. Tom was thinking: If they weren't here, I'd go over and say... what? But he knew from his nightly dreams of her that she was kind and friendly. Perhaps she would ask him down to her flat? Perhaps ... He stood watching her disappear down the skylight. As she went, Stanley let out a shrill derisive yell; she started, and it seemed as if she nearly fell. She clutched to save herself, they could hear things falling. She looked straight at them, angry. Harry said, facetiously[1]: "Better be careful on those slippery ladders, love." Tom knew he said it to save her from Stanley, but she could not know it. She vanished, frowning. Tom was full of a secret delight, because he knew her anger was for the others, not for him.

"Roll on[2] some rain," said Stanley, bitter, looking at the blue evening sky.

Next day was cloudless, and they decided to finish the work in the basement. They felt excluded, shut in the grey cement basement fitting pipes, from the holiday atmosphere of London in a heat wave. At lunchtime they came up for some air, but while the married couples, and the men in shirt-sleeves or vests, were there, she was not there, either on her usual patch of roof or where she had been yesterday. They all, even Harry, clambered about, between chimney-pots, over parapets, the hot leads stinging their fingers. There was not a sign of her. They took off their shirts and vests and exposed their chests, feeling their feet sweaty and hot. They did not mention the woman. But Tom felt alone again. Last night she had him into her flat: it was big and had fitted white carpet and a bed with a padded white leather head-board. She wore a black filmy negligee[3] and her kindness to Tom thickened his throat as he remembered it. He felt she had betrayed him by not being there.

And again after work they climbed up, but still there was nothing to be seen of her. Stanley kept repeating that if it was as hot as this tomorrow he wasn't going to work and that's all there was to it. But they were all there next day. By ten the temperature was in the middle seventies,[4] and it was eighty long before noon. Harry went to the foreman to say it was impossible to work on the leads in that heat; but the foreman said there was nothing else he could put them on, and they'd have to. At midday they stood, silent, watching the skylight on her roof open, and then she slowly emerged in her white gown, holding a bundle of blanket. She looked at them, gravely, then went to the part of the roof where she was hidden from them. Tom was pleased. He felt she was more his when the other men couldn't see her. They had taken off their shirts and vests, but now they put them back again, for they felt the sun bruising their flesh. "She must have the hide

---

[1] facetiously: 开玩笑地。
[2] roll on: 这里指希望自己渴望之事快快到来。
[3] filmy negligee: 薄薄的女式长睡袍。
[4] in the middle seventies: 华氏70多度。

of a rhino,[1]" said Stanley, tugging at[2] guttering and swearing. They stopped work, and sat in the shade, moving around behind chimney stacks. A woman came to water a yellow window box[3] opposite them. She was middleaged, wearing a flowered summer dress. Stanley said to her: "We need a drink more than them." She smiled and said: "Better drop down to the pub quick, it'll be closing in a minute." They exchanged pleasantries[4], and she left them with a smile and a wave.

"Not like Lady Godiva,[5]" said Stanley. "She can give us a bit of a chat and a smile."

"You didn't whistle at *her*[6]," said Tom, reproving.

"Listen to him," said Stanley, "you didn't whistle, then?"

But the boy felt as if he hadn't whistled, as if only Harry and Stanley had. He was making plans, when it was time to knock off[7] work, to get left behind and somehow make his way over to the woman. The weather report said the hot spell was due to break,[8] so he had to move quickly. But there was no chance of being left. The other two decided to knock off work at four, because they were exhausted. As they went down, Tom quickly climbed a parapet and hoisted himself higher by pulling his weight up a chimney. He caught a glimpse of her lying on her back, her knees up, eyes closed, a brown woman lolling[9] in the sun. He slipped and clattered down, as Stanley looked for information: "She's gone down," he said. He felt as if he had protected her from Stanley, and that she must be grateful to him. He could feel the bond between the woman and himself.

Next day, they stood around on the landing below the roof, reluctant to climb up into the heat. The woman who had lent Harry the blanket came out and offered them a cup of tea. They accepted gratefully, and sat around Mrs. Pritchett's kitchen an hour or so, chatting. She was married to an airline pilot. A smart blonde, of about thirty, she had an eye for the handsome sharp-faced Stanley; and the two teased each other while Harry sat in a corner, watching, indulgent, though his expression reminded Stanley that he was married. And young Tom felt envious of Stanley's ease in badinage[10]; felt, too, that Stanley's getting off with Mrs. Pritchett left his romance with the woman on the roof safe and intact.

---

[1] the hide of a rhino:犀牛皮。这里是说她的皮肤经得起晒。
[2] tugging at:努力干活。
[3] to water a yellow window box:给黄色窗台上花箱里的花木浇水。
[4] pleasantries:打趣的话。
[5] Lady Godiva:这里指在屋顶晒日光浴的女人。Lady Godiva 是中世纪英国的一位贵族妇女,传说为使丈夫减免考文垂(Coventry)的苛捐杂税,她赤身裸体骑马从街上走过。裁缝 Tom 偷看了一眼,顿时遭到双目失明的报应。
[6] her:这里指浇花女人。
[7] knock off:(口)干完活儿。
[8] the hot spell was due to break:高温期快要结束。
[9] lolling:懒洋洋地躺着。
[10] badinage:(法语)开玩笑,取笑逗乐。

"I thought they said the heat wave'd break," said Stanley, sullen, as the time approached when they really would have to climb up into the sunlight.

"You don't like it, then?" asked Mrs. Pritchett.

"All right for some," said Stanley. "Nothing to do but lie about as if it was a beach up there. Do you ever go up?"

"Went up once," said Mrs. Pritchett. "But it's a dirty place up there, and it's too hot."

"Quite right too," said Stanley.

Then they went up, leaving the cool neat little flat and the friendly Mrs. Pritchett.

As soon as they were up they saw her. The three men looked at her, resentful at her ease in this punishing sun. Then Harry said, because of the expression on Stanley's face: "Come on, we've go to pretend to work, at least."

They had to wrench another length of guttering that ran beside a parapet out of its bed, so that they could replace it. Stanley took it in his two hands, tugged, swore, stood up. "Fuck it," he said, and sat down under a chimney. He lit a cigarette. "Fuck them," he said. "What do they think we are, lizards? I've got blisters all over my hands." Then he jumped up and climbed over the roof and stood with his back to them. He put his fingers either side of his mouth and let out a shrill whistle. Tom and Harry squatted, not looking at each other, watching him. They could just see the woman's head, the beginning of her brown shoulders. Stanley whistled again. Then he began stamping with his feet, and whistled and yelled and screamed at the woman, his face getting scarlet. He seemed quite mad, as he stamped and whistled, while the woman did not move, she did not move a muscle.

"Barmy[1]," said Tom.

"Yes," said Harry, disapproving.

Suddenly the older man came to a decision. It was, Tom knew, to save some sort of scandal or real trouble over the woman. Harry stood up and began packing tools into a length of oily cloth. "Stanley," he said, commanding. At first Stanley took no notice, but Harry said: "Stanley, we're packing it in, I'll tell Matthew."

Stanley came back, cheeks mottled, eyes glaring.

"Can't go on like this," said Harry. "It'll break in a day or so. I'm going to tell Matthew we've got sunstroke, and if he doesn't like it, it's too bad." Even Harry sounded aggrieved[2], Tom noted. The small, competent man, the family man with his grey hair, who was never at a loss, sounded really off balance. "Come on," he said, angry. He fitted himself into the open square in the roof, and went down, watching his feet on the ladder. Then Stanley went, with not a glance at the woman. Then Tom, who, his throat beating with excitement, silently promised her on a backward glance:

---

[1] barmy: (俚)不正常。

[2] aggrieved:愤愤不平的。

Wait for me, wait, I'm coming.

On the pavement Stanley said: "I'm going home." He looked white now, so perhaps he really did have sunstroke. Harry went off to find the foreman, who was at work on the plumbing of some flats down the street. Tom slipped back, not into the building they had been working on, but the building on whose roof the woman lay. He went straight up, no one stopping him. The skylight stood open, with an iron ladder leading up. He emerged on to the roof a couple of yards from her. She sat up, pushing back hair with both hand. The scarf across her breasts bound them tight, and brown flesh bulged around it. Her legs were brown and smooth. She stared at him in silence. The boy stood grinning, foolish, claiming the tenderness he expected from her.

"What do you want?" she asked.

"I ... I came to ... make your acquaintance," he stammered, grinning, pleading with her.

They looked at each other, the slight, scarlet-faced excited boy, and the serious, nearly naked woman. Then, without a word, she lay down on her brown blanket, ignoring him.

"You like the sun, do you?" he enquired of her glistening back.

Not a word. He felt panic, thinking of how she had held him in her arms, stroked his hair, brought him where he sat, lordly, in her bed, a glass of some exhilarating[1] liquor he had never tasted in life. He felt that if he knelt down, stroked her shoulders, her hair, she would turn and clasp him in her arms.

He said: "The sun's all right for you, isn't it?"

She raised her head, set her chin on two small fists, "Go away," she said. He did not move. "Listen," she said, in a slow reasonable voice, where anger was kept in check, though with difficulty; looking at him, her face weary with anger, "if you get a kick[2] out of seeing woman in bikinis, why don't you take a sixpenny bus ride to the Lido[3]? You'd see dozens of them, without all this mountaineering."

She hadn't understood him. He felt her unfairness pale him. He stammered: "But I like you, I've been watching you and ... "

"Thanks," she said, and dropped her face again, turned away from him.

She lay there. He stood there. She said nothing. She had simply shut him out. He stood, saying nothing at all, for some minutes. He thought: She'll have to say something if I stay. But the minutes went past, with no sign of them in her, except in the tension of her back, her thighs, her arms—the tension of waiting for him to go.

He looked up at the sky, where the sun seemed to spin in heat; and over the roofs where he and his mates had been earlier. He could see the heat quivering where they had

---

[1] exhilarating: 提神的。
[2] kick: (口) 刺激, 快感。
[3] Lido: 意大利威尼斯著名海滨浴场, 这里指伦敦海德公园(Hyde Park)的一个部分。

worked. And they expect us to work in these conditions! he thought, filled with righteous indignation. The woman hadn't moved. A bit of hot wind blew her black hair softly; it shone, and was iridescent[1]. He remembered how he had stroked it last night.

Resentment of her at last moved him off and away down the ladder, through the building, into the street. He got drunk then, in hatred of her.

Next day when he woke the sky was grey. He looked at the wet grey and thought, vicious: Well, that's fixed[2] you, hasn't it now? That's fixed you good and proper.

The three men were at work early on the cool leads, surrounded by damp drizzling roofs where no one came to sun themselves, black roofs, slimy with rain. Because it was cool now, they would finish the job that day, if they hurried.

1963

赏 析

《屋顶丽人》收入在莱辛的短篇小说集《一个男人和两个女人》中。这部集子主要关注现当代欧洲的生活和文化，主题涉及两性关系、身份危机、政治、历史和社会弊病。

《屋顶丽人》故事的时间跨度是六天。炎炎烈日下，三个工人在屋顶更换檐沟，他们每天都能看到一个年轻女人在不远的屋顶晒太阳（除了在地下室里干活的一天），他们数次挑逗她，却遭到冷遇。三个工人的年龄代表了人生的三个阶段：人到中年的哈里、新婚不久的斯坦利和年轻小伙子汤姆。他们代表了传统男性对女性的三种态度：哈里结婚已久，比较有家庭责任感；斯坦利有大男子主义思想，一旦被异性拒绝，便勃然大怒；汤姆对异性一见钟情，一味幻想。

从女性主义角度看，这个故事首先表现了父权社会对女性的监视和监管。晒太阳女子一直被男性"凝视（gaze）"，是男人评头品足的"物品"，成为"他者（the Other）"。他们一方面认为女性暴露身体有伤风化，要求自己的妻子严守妇道，一方面又挑逗女性，被拒绝后十分恼怒，这暗示男性把女性视为任由自己控制的对象。

其次，故事还表现了女性追求独立对男性造成的威胁感和不安，也表现了男性一旦发现自己的权威受到挑战，会有怎样激烈的反应，这一点在斯坦利身上表现得尤为明显。这个年轻女人只想在屋顶晒晒太阳，却成为男人性吸引的目标。当她以冷漠和我行我素来对抗时，又成为谩骂和仇恨的对象。男人（斯坦利）可以和女人（普里切特夫人）随意调情，却难以忍受女人对自己的不理睬。他们生她的气，不是因为她公然在屋顶这样空旷的场所展示自己的身体，而是因为她对他们的百般挑逗不理不睬。

故事里有两个值得注意的细节，一是"heat（炎热）"，它既指越来越高的气温，也暗示斯坦利越来越大的火气和汤姆越来越难以抑制的激情。另一个意象是比基尼。晒太阳姑娘穿比基尼，成为性吸引的重要因素。在厄普代克的短篇小说《A＆P》里，三个穿比基尼的姑娘到商场购物，引起轩然大波。在两个故事里，比基尼代表了20世纪60年代女性对传统社会规范的挑战。

---

[1] iridescent：闪闪发亮。
[2] fixed：(口)惩罚，修理。

相关评论

Mona Lisa on a Roof
Charmaine R. Berina

In Doris Lessing's "A Woman on a Roof," three workmen react differently towards a woman sunbathing on a roof. The men are Harry, who is in his mid-40s, Stanley, who is newly married, and Tom, who is 17. They are engaged in a jovial banter[1] when they spot a woman about fifty yards from where they are standing. She's on her back, face down on a brown blanket. Stanley is first to comment, "She's stark naked." Harry agrees, "Looks like it," while Tom cranes his neck so he can see more and replies, "She thinks no one can see." Stanley whistles, but the woman does not look up. She sits, smoking a cigarette.

This seems to be one of Lessing's most critically neglected stories. In fact, there are only a few written criticisms about it, and most of these focus on the different reactions of the three workmen. However, the woman, who is not named in the story, is also a very intriguing and interesting character. While many readers see her as an innocent—the sunbather who only wants to be left alone—there is evidence to show that she uses her sexuality through nonverbal communication to show power and privilege.

Sociological perspectives suggest that nonverbal communication is of particular importance to women because their socialization to docility[2] and passivity makes them likely targets for social control. Sexuality (masculinity or femininity) is not biologically determined but is part of social learning. In "Womanspeak and Manspeak," Nancy Henley, Mykol Hamilton, and Barrie Thorne have argued that while women's general bodily demeanor[3] must be restrained and restricted, and that their femininity is gauged[4] by how little (personal) space they take up. In contrast, masculinity is judged by males' expansiveness and the strength of their flamboyant[5] gestures. Thus males tend to fight for "greater territory" and to control greater personal space. Because the sunbathing woman is bikini-clad, which reveals the contours of her body, her sexuality becomes highly visible. Thus, the three men fight for her attention through flamboyant gestures of whistling, yelling or stomping their feet. However, no matter what they do, she refuses to respond the way the three workmen expect her to. Her utter indifference towards them earns her the title of "bitch." When they cannot get anything out of her, she makes them very angry. Stanley compares her to a middle-aged woman who comes to

---

[1] banter:善意地取笑,逗弄。
[2] docility:温顺,顺从。
[3] demeanor:行为,风度。
[4] gauged:测量,评估。
[5] flamboyant:夸张的。

the roof to water her plants: "*She's* not like Lady Godiva—she can give us a bit of a chat and a smile." This statement from Stanley proves that, despite their wolf whistling, they still expect the woman on the roof to be pleasant.

In an article titled "On Becoming Male," James Henslin says that males behave one way when they are among themselves and another way when they are with females. He calls this behavior "artificiality." Henslin points out that, because of this artificiality, men's exercises in manipulation are reinforced when they learn how to get what they want, whether that be an approving smile, a caress, a kiss, or more. However, no matter what the three workmen do, the woman on the roof remains indifferent, as if she does not even see them. Therefore, by employing nonverbal communication tactics—ignoring, reading a book, shifting body positions—she shows that, indeed, she is the one who has power over them. In fact, she is so powerful that her presence distracts the men from doing their work on time.

In addition, she expresses her privilege through nonverbal communication when she refuses to be intimidated from giving up her right to sunbathe on top of the roof. Edward Hall argues in "The Sounds of Silence" that nonverbal communication is significant in conveying feelings and attitudes. He says that nonverbal communication, though subtle, lies beyond even our own perception. Nonverbal communication "can communicate feelings of comfort and discomfort, trust and distrust, pleasure or tension, suspicions and a host of other feelings and concerns."

Source: http://facultystaff.vwc.edu/~cbellamy/Dream%20Child/Lessing-%20Martinez, Berina,Ciresi.htm. (2010-11-18)

问题与思考

1. Who tells the story? Does this narrator expose to the reader the mind of each character?
2. Imagine "A Woman on a Roof" told from the point of view of the sunbather herself. What do you think the story would lose or gain?
3. Who is the protagonist in the story? Explain your reason.
4. Note the setting in the story. What is the relationship between the hot weather and the behavior of the characters? Discuss the effectiveness of the descriptions of the heat wave.
5. Compare Tom with the boy in James Joyce's "Araby". What are the similarities between what happened to Tom and to the boy in "Araby"? What are the differences between Tom and the boy?
6. What do you think is the theme of the story? What do you think Doris Lessing wants to say about the relationship between men and women in modern society? Does she ever show any sympathy to the three men in the story? In what aspect?

阅读链接

1. http://dorislessing.org：包括莱辛的生平、作品目录和要旨介绍、评论文章、视频和图片。
2. http://www.dorislessing.org/thegolden.html：对《金色笔记本》的介绍和讨论。
3. http://www.dorislessing.org/childrenof.html：对五部曲《暴力的孩子们》的介绍。
4. http://en.wikipedia.org/wiki/Category:Short_stories_by_Doris_Lessing：对莱辛的短篇小说"Flight"和"Through the Tunnel"的评论。

5．象征(Symbol)

象征通常是指文学作品中通过某一特定的、容易引起联想的具体事物(象征物)来表现某种概念、思想或感情。可作为象征物的有物件、形象、行为、背景、人物和事件。象征以物征事，它并不直接表达意义，只暗示这一意蕴。象征的作用是深化主题，寄寓思想，令人回味。对短篇小说而言，象征的作用尤其重要，它丰富内涵，创造意境，意味深长，可弥补因篇幅短小可能造成的不足。

文学作品中的象征大致可分为两类：传统象征和个性化象征。传统的象征源于生活习俗和传统文化，为人民大众所熟知。如西方用十字架象征殉道和神圣，中国用红色象征喜庆，用鸳鸯象征爱情。传统象征在文学作品中常常出现，但文学作品真正引人入胜的是个性化象征。作家为了传情达意，广泛挖掘具象与抽象之间的联系，制造出适用于特定语境的象征。好的个性化象征新奇而不离奇，这是我们在阅读时要特别留意的。例如，《献给爱米丽的玫瑰》中爱米丽家那幢古旧但不失气派的大宅孤独地矗立在周围矮小的房屋群中，象征美国南方的旧传统走向衰落，也暗示这一传统对南方女性的束缚和压抑。在乔伊斯的《集市》中，题目"Araby"指的是集市，但又不仅仅指集市，因为"Araby"是"阿拉伯"的诗歌用词，让人联想到《天方夜谭》，含有幻想、浪漫之意味。

象征物和其象征意义之间的联系既不是天然给定的，也不是一成不变的，要由场合来确定，也就是说，上下文不同，同样的物体就会有不同的象征意义。这有两种情况，一是传统的象征在新的文本语境中衍生出新的意义。例如玫瑰在苏格兰诗人罗伯特·彭斯的名作《一朵红红的玫瑰》中象征纯洁美好的爱情。英国诗人威廉·布莱克在他的《病玫瑰》中同样写玫瑰，然而这里的玫瑰遭到虫子的侵袭，已不再是纯洁爱情的象征。在《献给爱米丽的玫瑰》中，玫瑰既代表爱米丽求而未得的爱情，又表示作者对这位不同寻常女性的敬意。另一种情况是一个象征在同一文本中因语境不同而生发出不同的个性化象征意义。霍桑的长篇小说《红字》中的红字"A"开始戴在被示众的海丝特的胸前，表示"通奸罪"(Adultery)。当海丝特以自己的勤劳、善良和坚韧不但继续生活下去，而且赢得人们的尊敬时，红字逐渐有了新的象征意义："能干"(Able)、"值得尊敬的"(Admirable)、"天使"(Angel)等。在斯坦贝克的《菊花》中，伊丽莎精心呵护的菊花同样有多重象征意义。它象征她平淡的生活、生命的活力和对真正爱情的向往。菊花被补锅匠抛弃路边，又象征她的希望和梦想破灭。

如果说物体或人是静态的象征，那么行为就是一种动态的象征。康拉德在《青春》中对艰难的航行和航海生活的细节进行了精彩的描写。叙述者马洛在故事一开始就提醒自己的听众："伙计们，你们知道有些航行像是为了阐明生活而安排的，它们是存在的象征。"因此，马洛的航行是对生活的理解的一个过程。在卡波特的《米丽亚姆》中，米丽亚姆用力踩踏纸玫瑰这一情节象征米勒太太在公寓里过的那种毫无生气的日子即将走向终结。

既然在文学作品中任何物体或行为都有可能成为象征物，那么我们在阅读过程中就应该持开放的心态，注意从象征的角度来解读文本，这比视而不见要好。作者常常提供线索来引导读者发现象征，有时是明确地或重复地提到与某一层意思有关的事物，有时在故事进程中积累暗示。忽视象征或拒绝思考象征会使我们错过故事的深层含义。不过，读者也不应该为寻找象征而变得过于敏感,而是对象征物及其意义之间的联系去进行理性的思考、自然的联想和有创意的想象。对象征的善读、滥读和误读没有明显的界线,但有一点是毫无疑问的,那就是象征的意义源于语境,我们读出来的象征意蕴要与整个作品的主旨和上下文语境相吻合,既不能与文本的语境相左,也不能无中生有。

Nathaniel Hawthorne (1804—1864)

作者简介

纳撒尼尔·霍桑(Nathaniel Hawthorne,1804—1864)出生于马萨诸塞州东北部港市萨勒姆,四岁时父亲去世,由母亲抚养成人。霍桑的一位祖先曾在1630年下令公开鞭挞一个贵格会女教徒,他的曾祖父主持了1692年萨勒姆女巫审判案。霍桑在23岁那年在自己的名字里加上一个"w",以示与祖辈划清界限。他在波多因大学读了四年书,1839至1841年在波士顿海关工作,投资布鲁克农场,在那里进行超验主义式社会实验,这些都开阔了他的眼界,为其文学创作打下基础。1853年,他的旧友富兰克林·皮尔斯当选美国总统,委任霍桑为驻利物浦领事。从那时到1860年,霍桑一直生活在英国和意大利。1860年他回到马萨诸塞州的康科德生活。美国内战爆发后,霍桑来到华盛顿,与林肯总统及其他名人见面。之后,霍桑的健康状况恶化,他坚持以旅行来康复身体,1864年5月,霍桑在睡眠中去世,终年60岁。

文学创作

霍桑是美国19世纪最伟大的作家之一,著有《红字》(*The Scarlet Letter*,1850)、《凶宅七角楼》(*The House of Seven Gables*,1851)、《福谷传奇》(*The Blithedale Romance*,1852)和《玉石雕像》(*The Marble Faun*,1860)等四部长篇小说,还创作了超过一百多篇的短篇小说、散文和随笔。霍桑的创作题材来自清教思想统治下的新英格兰生活,中心主题是罪过和邪恶乃人之天性,在表现手法上,他将充满象征的历史罗曼司和深刻的心理刻画结合起来。霍桑最重要的代表作是《红字》。医生齐林渥斯的妻子海丝特·白兰犯了通奸罪而受到示众的惩罚,在城外离群索居,满怀仇恨的齐林渥斯查出奸夫原来是城里有名的年轻牧师丁梅斯代尔。于是齐林渥斯接近他,折磨他。最后,丁梅斯代尔公开承认了自己的"罪恶",猝死在海丝特当年受辱的刑台上,齐林渥斯也因精神衰竭,不久死去,只有灵魂得到升华的海丝特安然面对未来。

霍桑和埃德加·爱伦·坡同为美国19世纪最重要的短篇小说家,两人将这一体裁提升至美国文学的重要特色之一,然而两人又各有特点,"霍桑虽然和坡一样运用一些超自然的元素,并且同样具有美学而不是宗教的基础,但不同的是,霍桑总是更关注伦理和哲学方面的思考和探索,这就使他的作品总是蕴含着令人回味不尽的深邃哲理。"霍桑的主要短篇小说集有《重讲一遍的故事》(*Twice-Told Tales*,1837)、《古屋青苔》(*Mosses from an Old Manse*,1846)和《雪人及其他重讲一遍的故事》(*The Snow-Image, and Other Twice-Told Tales*,1852),著名的作品有《好小伙布朗》("Young Goodman Brown")、《拉帕奇尼医生之女》("Rappaccini's Daughter")、《教长的黑面纱》("The Minister's Black Veil")等。

在艺术上,霍桑的作品结构严谨,意象丰富,基调阴郁。他擅长揭示人物的内心冲突和心理描写,称自己的作品是"心理罗曼司"。他善用象征,构思精巧的意象增添了作品的浪漫色彩,加深了寓意,但不乏神秘和晦涩。

 作 品

Rappaccini's Daughter

A young man, named Giovanni Guasconti, came, very long ago, from the more southern region of Italy, to pursue his studies at the University of Padua[1]. Giovanni, who had but a scanty supply of gold ducats[2] in his pocket, took lodgings in a high and gloomy chamber of an old edifice which looked not unworthy to have been the palace of a Paduan noble, and which, in fact, exhibited over its entrance the armorial bearings[3] of a family long since extinct. The young stranger, who was not unstudied in the great poem of his country, recollected that one of the ancestors of this family, and perhaps an occupant of this very mansion, had been pictured by Dante[4] as a partaker of the immortal agonies of his Inferno. These reminiscences and associations, together with the tendency to heartbreak natural to a young man for the first time out of his native sphere, caused Giovanni to sigh heavily as he looked around the desolate and ill-furnished apartment.

"Holy Virgin, signor[5]!" cried old Dame Lisabetta, who, won by the youth's remarkable beauty of person, was kindly endeavoring to give the chamber a habitable air, "What a sigh was that to come out of a young man's heart! Do you find this old mansion gloomy? For the love of Heaven, then, put your head out of the window, and

---

[1] Padua:帕多瓦,意大利东北部城市;the University of Padua 建于1222年。
[2] ducats:达克特,意大利当时通用的金币。
[3] armorial bearings:盾徽,纹章。
[4] Dante:但丁(1265—1321),意大利诗人、欧洲文艺复兴运动先驱,著有《神曲》,叙述维吉尔(Virgil)、贝雅特里齐(Beatrice)引导诗人游历地狱、炼狱和天国的故事。
[5] signor:(意大利语)先生。

you will see as bright sunshine as you have left in Naples[1]."

Guasconti mechanically did as the old woman advised, but could not quite agree with her that the Paduan sunshine was as cheerful as that of southern Italy. Such as it was, however, it fell upon a garden beneath the window and expended its fostering influences on a variety of plants, which seemed to have been cultivated with exceeding care.

"Does this garden belong to the house?" asked Giovanni.

"Heaven forbid, signor, unless it were fruitful of better pot herbs than any that grow there now," answered old Lisabetta. "No; that garden is cultivated by the own hands of Signor Giacomo Rappaccini, the famous doctor, who, I warrant him, has been heard of as far as Naples. It is said that he distils these plants into medicines that are as potent as a charm. Oftentimes you may see the signor doctor at work, and perchance the signora[2], his daughter, too, gathering the strange flowers that grow in the garden."

The old woman had now done what she could for the aspect of the chamber; and, commending the young man to the protection of the saints,[3] took her departure.

Giovanni still found no better occupation than to look down into the garden beneath his window. From its appearance, he judged it to be one of those botanic gardens which were of earlier date in Padua than elsewhere in Italy or in the world. Or, not improbably, it might once have been the pleasure-place of an opulent family; for there was the ruin of a marble fountain in the centre, sculptured with rare art, but so woefully shattered that it was impossible to trace the original design from the chaos of remaining fragments. The water, however, continued to gush and sparkle into the sunbeams as cheerfully as ever. A little gurgling sound ascended to the young man's window, and made him feel as if the fountain were an immortal spirit that sung its song unceasingly and without heeding the vicissitudes around it, while one century imbodied it in marble and another scattered the perishable garniture[4] on the soil. All about the pool into which the water subsided grew various plants, that seemed to require a plentiful supply of moisture for the nourishment of gigantic leaves, and in some instances, flowers gorgeously magnificent. There was one shrub in particular, set in a marble vase in the midst of the pool, that bore a profusion of purple blossoms, each of which had the lustre and richness of a gem; and the whole together made a show so resplendent that it seemed enough to illuminate the garden, even had there been no sunshine. Every portion of the soil was peopled with plants and herbs, which, if less beautiful, still bore tokens of assiduous care, as if all had their individual virtues, known to the scientific mind that fostered them. Some were placed in urns, rich with old carving, and others in common

---

[1] Naples: 那不勒斯, 意大利西南港市。
[2] signora: (意大利语) 太太, 小姐。
[3] commending the young man to the protection of the saints: 祈祷圣徒保佑这位年轻人。
[4] garniture: 装饰。

garden pots; some crept serpent-like along the ground or climbed on high, using whatever means of ascent was offered them. One plant had wreathed itself round a statue of Vertumnus[1], which was thus quite veiled and shrouded in a drapery of hanging foliage, so happily arranged that it might have served a sculptor for a study.

While Giovanni stood at the window he heard a rustling behind a screen of leaves, and became aware that a person was at work in the garden. His figure soon emerged into view, and showed itself to be that of no common laborer, but a tall, emaciated, sallow, and sickly-looking man, dressed in a scholar's garb of black. He was beyond the middle term of life, with gray hair, a thin, gray beard, and a face singularly marked with intellect and cultivation, but which could never, even in his more youthful days, have expressed much warmth of heart.

Nothing could exceed the intentness with which this scientific gardener examined every shrub which grew in his path: it seemed as if he was looking into their inmost nature, making observations in regard to their creative essence, and discovering why one leaf grew in this shape and another in that, and wherefore such and such flowers differed among themselves in hue and perfume. Nevertheless, in spite of this deep intelligence on his part, there was no approach to intimacy between himself and these vegetable existences. On the contrary, he avoided their actual touch or the direct inhaling of their odors with a caution that impressed Giovanni most disagreeably; for the man's demeanor was that of one walking among malignant influences, such as savage beasts, or deadly snakes, or evil spirits, which, should he allow them one moment of license[2], would wreak upon him some terrible fatality. It was strangely frightful to the young man's imagination to see this air of insecurity in a person cultivating a garden, that most simple and innocent of human toils, and which had been alike the joy and labor of the unfallen parents of the race. Was this garden, then, the Eden of the present world? And this man, with such a perception of harm in what his own hands caused to grow,—was he the Adam?

The distrustful gardener, while plucking away the dead leaves or pruning the too luxuriant growth of the shrubs, defended his hands with a pair of thick gloves. Nor were these his only armor. When, in his walk through the garden, he came to the magnificent plant that hung its purple gems beside the marble fountain, he placed a kind of mask over his mouth and nostrils, as if all this beauty did but conceal a deadlier malice; but, finding his task still too dangerous, he drew back, removed the mask, and called loudly, but in the infirm voice of a person affected with inward disease,—

"Beatrice! Beatrice!"

"Here am I, my father. What would you?" cried a rich and youthful voice from the window of the opposite house—a voice as rich as a tropical sunset, and which made

---

[1] Vertumnus:罗马神话中掌管四季变化、庭院和果树之神。
[2] license:自由行动;准许。

Giovanni, though he knew not why, think of deep hues of purple or crimson and of perfumes heavily delectable.[1] "Are you in the garden?"

"Yes, Beatrice," answered the gardener, "and I need your help."

Soon there emerged from under a sculptured portal[2] the figure of a young girl, arrayed with as much richness of taste as the most splendid of the flowers, beautiful as the day, and with a bloom so deep and vivid that one shade more would have been too much. She looked redundant with life, health, and energy; all of which attributes were bound down and compressed, as it were and girdled tensely, in their luxuriance, by her virgin zone.[3] Yet Giovanni's fancy must have grown morbid while he looked down into the garden; for the impression which the fair stranger made upon him was as if here were another flower, the human sister of those vegetable ones, as beautiful as they, more beautiful than the richest of them, but still to be touched only with a glove, nor to be approached without a mask. As Beatrice came down the garden path, it was observable that she handled and inhaled the odor of several of the plants which her father had most sedulously avoided.

"Here, Beatrice," said the latter, "see how many needful offices require to be done to our chief treasure. Yet, shattered as I am, my life might pay the penalty[4] of approaching it so closely as circumstances demand. Henceforth, I fear, this plant must be consigned to your sole charge."

"And gladly will I undertake it," cried again the rich tones of the young lady, as she bent towards the magnificent plant and opened her arms as if to embrace it. "Yes, my sister, my splendour, it shall be Beatrice's task to nurse and serve thee; and thou shalt reward her with thy kisses and perfumed breath, which to her is as the breath of life."

Then, with all the tenderness in her manner that was so strikingly expressed in her words, she busied herself with such attentions as the plant seemed to require; and Giovanni, at his lofty window, rubbed his eyes and almost doubted whether it were a girl tending her favorite flower, or one sister performing the duties of affection to another. The scene soon terminated. Whether Dr. Rappaccini had finished his labors in the garden, or that his watchful eye had caught the stranger's face, he now took his daughter's arm and retired. Night was already closing in; oppressive exhalations seemed to proceed from the plants and steal upward past the open window; and Giovanni, closing the lattice, went to his couch and dreamed of a rich flower and beautiful girl. Flower and maiden were different, and yet the same, and fraught with some strange peril in either shape.

But there is an influence in the light of morning that tends to rectify whatever errors

---

[1] perfumes heavily delectable:沁人肺腑的浓郁芳香。
[2] portal:入口;大门。
[3] virgin zone:地中海国家未婚女子扎的一种腰带。
[4] penalty:因自己的行为而带来的损失或苦难。

of fancy, or even of judgment, we may have incurred during the sun's decline, or among the shadows of the night, or in the less wholesome glow of moonshine. Giovanni's first movement, on starting from sleep, was to throw open the window and gaze down into the garden which his dreams had made so fertile of mysteries. He was surprised and a little ashamed to find how real and matter-of-fact an affair it proved to be, in the first rays of the sun which gilded the dew-drops that hung upon leaf and blossom, and, while giving a brighter beauty to each rare flower, brought everything within the limits of ordinary experience. The young man rejoiced that, in the heart of the barren city, he had the privilege of overlooking this spot of lovely and luxuriant vegetation. It would serve, he said to himself, as a symbolic language to keep him in communion with Nature. Neither the sickly and thoughtworn Dr. Giacomo Rappaccini, it is true, nor his brilliant daughter, were now visible; so that Giovanni could not determine how much of the singularity which he attributed to both was due to their own qualities and how much to his wonder-working fancy; but he was inclined to take a most rational view of the whole matter.

In the course of the day he paid his respects to Signor Pietro Baglioni, professor of medicine in the university, a physician of eminent repute to whom Giovanni had brought a letter of introduction. The professor was an elderly personage, apparently of genial nature, and habits that might almost be called jovial. He kept the young man to dinner, and made himself very agreeable by the freedom and liveliness of his conversation, especially when warmed by a flask or two of Tuscan wine. Giovanni, conceiving that men of science, inhabitants of the same city, must needs be on familiar terms with one another, took an opportunity to mention the name of Dr. Rappaccini. But the professor did not respond with so much cordiality as he had anticipated.

"Ill would it become[1] a teacher of the divine art of medicine," said Professor Pietro Baglioni, in answer to a question of Giovanni, "to withhold due and well-considered praise of a physician so eminently skilled as Rappaccini; but, on the other hand, I should answer it but scantily to my conscience[2] were I to permit a worthy youth like yourself, Signor Giovanni, the son of an ancient friend, to imbibe erroneous ideas respecting a man who might hereafter chance to hold your life and death in his hands. The truth is, our worshipful Dr. Rappaccini has as much science as any member of the faculty—with perhaps one single exception—in Padua, or all Italy; but there are certain grave objections to his professional character."

"And what are they?" asked the young man.

"Has my friend Giovanni any disease of body or heart, that he is so inquisitive about physicians?" said the professor, with a smile. "But as for Rappaccini, it is said of him—and I, who know the man well, can answer for its truth—that he cares infinitely more

---

[1] become:适合。
[2] I should answer it but scantily to my conscience:对此(赞扬),我深感有愧。

for science than for mankind. His patients are interesting to him only as subjects for some new experiment. He would sacrifice human life, his own among the rest, or whatever else was dearest to him, for the sake of adding so much as a grain of mustard seed to the great heap of his accumulated knowledge."

"Methinks[1] he is an awful man indeed," remarked Guasconti, mentally recalling the cold and purely intellectual aspect of Rappaccini. "And yet, worshipful professor, is it not a noble spirit? Are there many men capable of so spiritual a love of science?"

"God forbid," answered the professor, somewhat testily[2]; "at least, unless they take sounder views of the healing art than those adopted by Rappaccini. It is his theory that all medicinal virtues are comprised within those substances which we term vegetable poisons. These he cultivates with his own hands, and is said even to have produced new varieties of poison, more horribly deleterious[3] than Nature, without the assistance of this learned person, would ever have plagued the world withal[4]. That the signor doctor does less mischief than might be expected with such dangerous substances is undeniable. Now and then, it must be owned, he has effected, or seemed to effect, a marvellous cure; but, to tell you my private mind, Signor Giovanni, he should receive little credit for such instances of success,—they being probably the work of chance,—but should be held strictly accountable for his failures, which may justly be considered his own work."

The youth might have taken Baglioni's opinions with many grains of allowance had he known that there was a professional warfare of long continuance between him and Dr. Rappaccini, in which the latter was generally thought to have gained the advantage. If the reader be inclined to judge for himself, we refer him to certain black-letter tracts[5] on both sides, preserved in the medical department of the University of Padua.

"I know not, most learned professor," returned Giovanni, after musing on what had been said of Rappaccini's exclusive zeal for science,—"I know not how dearly this physician may love his art; but surely there is one object more dear to him. He has a daughter."

"Aha!" cried the professor, with a laugh. "So now our friend Giovanni's secret is out. You have heard of this daughter, whom all the young men in Padua are wild about, though not half a dozen have ever had the good hap[6] to see her face. I know little of the Signora Beatrice save that Rappaccini is said to have instructed her deeply in his science, and that, young and beautiful as fame reports her, she is already qualified to fill a professor's chair. Perchance her father destines her for mine! Other absurd rumors

---

[1] Methinks:〈古〉(无人称动词)窃以为,据敝人看来。
[2] testily:暴躁的;不耐烦的。
[3] deleterious:有害的,造成伤害的。
[4] withal:用,用以(用于句末)。
[5] black-letter tracts:黑体印刷体的小册子。
[6] hap:〈古〉机会;幸运。

there be, not worth talking about or listening to. So now, Signor Giovanni, drink off your glass of lachryma[1]."

Guasconti returned to his lodgings somewhat heated with the wine he had quaffed, and which caused his brain to swim with strange fantasies in reference to Dr. Rappaccini and the beautiful Beatrice. On his way, happening to pass by a florist's, he bought a fresh bouquet of flowers.

Ascending to his chamber, he seated himself near the window, but within the shadow thrown by the depth of the wall, so that he could look down into the garden with little risk of being discovered. All beneath his eye was a solitude. The strange plants were basking in the sunshine, and now and then nodding gently to one another, as if in acknowledgment of sympathy and kindred. In the midst, by the shattered fountain, grew the magnificent shrub, with its purple gems clustering all over it; they glowed in the air, and gleamed back again out of the depths of the pool, which thus seemed to overflow with colored radiance from the rich reflection that was steeped in it. At first, as we have said, the garden was a solitude. Soon, however,—as Giovanni had half hoped, half feared, would be the case,—a figure appeared beneath the antique sculptured portal, and came down between the rows of plants, inhaling their various perfumes as if she were one of those beings of old classic fable that lived upon sweet odors. On again beholding Beatrice, the young man was even startled to perceive how much her beauty exceeded his recollection of it; so brilliant, so vivid, was its character, that she glowed amid the sunlight, and, as Giovanni whispered to himself, positively illuminated the more shadowy intervals of the garden path. Her face being now more revealed than on the former occasion, he was struck by its expression of simplicity and sweetness,—qualities that had not entered into his idea of her character, and which made him ask anew what manner of mortal she might be. Nor did he fail again to observe, or imagine, an analogy between the beautiful girl and the gorgeous shrub that hung its gemlike flowers over the fountain,—a resemblance which Beatrice seemed to have indulged a fantastic humor[2] in heightening, both by the arrangement of her dress and the selection of its hues.

Approaching the shrub, she threw open her arms, as with a passionate ardor, and drew its branches into an intimate embrace—so intimate that her features were hidden in its leafy bosom and her glistening ringlets all intermingled with the flowers.

"Give me thy breath, my sister," exclaimed Beatrice; "for I am faint with common air. And give me this flower of thine, which I separate with gentlest fingers from the stem and place it close beside my heart."

With these words the beautiful daughter of Rappaccini plucked one of the richest blossoms of the shrub, and was about to fasten it in her bosom. But now, unless

---

[1] lachrymal:(用意大利南部生长的葡萄酿制的)甜味烈性葡萄酒。
[2] fantastic humor:心情起伏不定。

Giovanni's draughts of wine had bewildered his senses, a singular incident occurred. A small orange-colored reptile, of the lizard or chameleon[1] species, chanced to be creeping along the path, just at the feet of Beatrice. It appeared to Giovanni,—but, at the distance from which he gazed, he could scarcely have seen anything so minute,—it appeared to him, however, that a drop or two of moisture from the broken stem of the flower descended upon the lizard's head. For an instant the reptile contorted itself violently, and then lay motionless in the sunshine. Beatrice observed this remarkable phenomenon and crossed herself, sadly, but without surprise; nor did she therefore hesitate to arrange the fatal flower in her bosom. There it blushed, and almost glimmered with the dazzling effect of a precious stone, adding to her dress and aspect the one appropriate charm which nothing else in the world could have supplied. But Giovanni, out of the shadow of his window, bent forward and shrank back, and murmured and trembled.

"Am I awake? Have I my senses?" said he to himself. "What is this being? Beautiful shall I call her, or inexpressibly terrible?"

Beatrice now strayed carelessly through the garden, approaching closer beneath Giovanni's window, so that he was compelled to thrust his head quite out of its concealment in order to gratify the intense and painful curiosity which she excited. At this moment there came a beautiful insect over the garden wall; it had, perhaps, wandered through the city, and found no flowers or verdure[2] among those antique haunts of men until the heavy perfumes of Dr. Rappaccini's shrubs had lured it from afar. Without alighting on the flowers, this winged brightness seemed to be attracted by Beatrice, and lingered in the air and fluttered about her head. Now, here it could not be but that Giovanni Guasconti's eyes deceived him. Be that as it might, he fancied that, while Beatrice was gazing at the insect with childish delight, it grew faint and fell at her feet; its bright wings shivered; it was dead—from no cause that he could discern, unless it were the atmosphere of her breath. Again Beatrice crossed herself and sighed heavily as she bent over the dead insect.

An impulsive movement of Giovanni drew her eyes to the window. There she beheld the beautiful head of the young man—rather a Grecian than an Italian head, with fair, regular features, and a glistening of gold among his ringlets—gazing down upon her like a being that hovered in mid air. Scarcely knowing what he did, Giovanni threw down the bouquet which he had hitherto held in his hand.

"Signora," said he, "there are pure and healthful flowers. Wear them for the sake of Giovanni Guasconti."

"Thanks, signor," replied Beatrice, with her rich voice, that came forth as it were like a gush of music, and with a mirthful expression half childish and half woman-like.

---

[1] chameleon:变色蜥蜴。
[2] verdure:青葱的草木。

"I accept your gift, and would fain recompense it with this precious purple flower; but if I toss it into the air it will not reach you. So Signor Guasconti must even content himself with my thanks."

She lifted the bouquet from the ground, and then, as if inwardly ashamed at having stepped aside from her maidenly reserve[1] to respond to a stranger's greeting, passed swiftly homeward through the garden. But few as the moments were, it seemed to Giovanni, when she was on the point of vanishing beneath the sculptured portal, that his beautiful bouquet was already beginning to wither in her grasp. It was an idle thought; there could be no possibility of distinguishing a faded flower from a fresh one at so great a distance.

For many days after this incident the young man avoided the window that looked into Dr. Rappaccini's garden, as if something ugly and monstrous would have blasted his eyesight had he been betrayed into a glance. He felt conscious of having put himself, to a certain extent, within the influence of an unintelligible power by the communication which he had opened with Beatrice. The wisest course would have been, if his heart were in any real danger, to quit his lodgings and Padua itself at once; the next wiser, to have accustomed himself, as far as possible, to the familiar and daylight view of Beatrice—thus bringing her rigidly and systematically within the limits of ordinary experience. Least of all, while avoiding her sight, ought Giovanni to have remained so near this extraordinary being that the proximity and possibility even of intercourse should give a kind of substance and reality to the wild vagaries[2] which his imagination ran riot continually in producing. Guasconti had not a deep heart—or, at all events, its depths were not sounded now; but he had a quick fancy, and an ardent southern temperament, which rose every instant to a higher fever pitch. Whether or no Beatrice possessed those terrible attributes, that fatal breath, the affinity with those so beautiful and deadly flowers which were indicated by what Giovanni had witnessed, she had at least instilled a fierce and subtle poison into his system. It was not love, although her rich beauty was a madness to him; nor horror, even while he fancied her spirit to be imbued with the same baneful essence that seemed to pervade her physical frame; but a wild offspring of both love and horror that had each parent in it, and burned like one and shivered like the other. Giovanni knew not what to dread; still less did he know what to hope; yet hope and dread kept a continual warfare in his breast, alternately vanquishing one another and starting up afresh to renew the contest. Blessed are all simple emotions, be they dark or bright! It is the lurid[3] intermixture of the two that produces the illuminating blaze of the infernal regions.

Sometimes he endeavored to assuage the fever of his spirit by a rapid walk through

---

[1] maidenly reserve:少女的谨慎。
[2] wild vagaries:奇思怪想。
[3] lurid:苍白的,暗淡的。

the streets of Padua or beyond its gates; his footsteps kept time with the throbbings of his brain, so that the walk was apt to accelerate itself to a race. One day he found himself arrested; his arm was seized by a portly personage, who had turned back on recognizing the young man and expended much breath in overtaking him.

"Signor Giovanni! Stay, my young friend!" cried he. "Have you forgotten me? That might well be the case if I were as much altered as yourself."

It was Baglioni, whom Giovanni had avoided ever since their first meeting, from a doubt that the professor's sagacity would look too deeply into his secrets. Endeavoring to recover himself, he stared forth wildly from his inner world into the outer one and spoke like a man in a dream.

"Yes; I am Giovanni Guasconti. You are Professor Pietro Baglioni. Now let me pass!"

"Not yet, not yet, Signor Giovanni Guasconti," said the professor, smiling, but at the same time scrutinizing the youth with an earnest glance. "What! did I grow up side by side with your father? and shall his son pass me like a stranger in these old streets of Padua? Stand still, Signor Giovanni; for we must have a word or two before we part."

"Speedily, then, most worshipful professor, speedily," said Giovanni, with feverish impatience. "Does not your worship[1] see that I am in haste?"

Now, while he was speaking there came a man in black along the street, stooping and moving feebly like a person in inferior health. His face was all overspread with a most sickly and sallow hue, but yet so pervaded with an expression of piercing and active intellect that an observer might easily have overlooked the merely physical attributes and have seen only this wonderful energy. As he passed, this person exchanged a cold and distant salutation with Baglioni, but fixed his eyes upon Giovanni with an intentness that seemed to bring out whatever was within him worthy of notice. Nevertheless, there was a peculiar quietness in the look, as if taking merely a speculative, not a human interest, in the young man.

"It is Dr. Rappaccini!" whispered the professor when the stranger had passed. "Has he ever seen your face before?"

"Not that I know," answered Giovanni, starting at the name.

"He *has* seen you! He must have seen you!" said Baglioni, hastily. "For some purpose or other, this man of science is making a study of you. I know that look of his! It is the same that coldly illuminates his face as he bends over a bird, a mouse, or a butterfly, which, in pursuance of some experiment, he has killed by the perfume of a flower; a look as deep as Nature itself, but without Nature's warmth of love. Signor Giovanni, I will stake my life upon it, you are the subject of one of Rappaccini's experiments!"

"Will you make a fool of me?" cried Giovanni, passionately. "*That*, signor

---

[1] your worship: 阁下。

professor, were an untoward[1] experiment."

"Patience! patience!" replied the imperturbable professor. "I tell thee, my poor Giovanni, that Rappaccini has a scientific interest in thee. Thou hast fallen into fearful hands! And the Signora Beatrice,—what part does she act in this mystery?"

But Guasconti, finding Baglioni's pertinacity intolerable, here broke away, and was gone before the professor could again seize his arm. He looked after the young man intently and shook his head.

"This must not be," said Baglioni to himself. "The youth is the son of my old friend, and shall not come to any harm from which the arcane[2] of medical science can preserve him. Besides, it is too insufferable an impertinence in Rappaccini, thus to snatch the lad out of my own hands, as I may say, and make use of him for his infernal experiments. This daughter of his! It shall be looked to. Perchance, most learned Rappaccini, I may foil you where you little dream of it!"

Meanwhile Giovanni had pursued a circuitous route, and at length found himself at the door of his lodgings. As he crossed the threshold he was met by old Lisabetta, who smirked and smiled, and was evidently desirous to attract his attention; vainly, however, as the ebullition[3] of his feelings had momentarily subsided into a cold and dull vacuity. He turned his eyes full upon the withered face that was puckering itself into a smile, but seemed to behold it not. The old dame, therefore, laid her grasp upon his cloak.

"Signor! signor!" whispered she, still with a smile over the whole breadth of her visage, so that it looked not unlike a grotesque carving in wood, darkened by centuries. "Listen, signor! There is a private entrance into the garden!"

"What do you say?" exclaimed Giovanni, turning quickly about, as if an inanimate thing should start into feverish life. "A private entrance into Dr. Rappaccini's garden?"

"Hush! hush! not so loud!" whispered Lisabetta, putting her hand over his mouth. "Yes; into the worshipful doctor's garden, where you may see all his fine shrubbery. Many a young man in Padua would give gold to be admitted among those flowers."

Giovanni put a piece of gold into her hand.

"Show me the way," said he.

A surmise, probably excited by his conversation with Baglioni, crossed his mind, that this interposition of old Lisabetta might perchance be connected with the intrigue, whatever were its nature, in which the professor seemed to suppose that Dr. Rappaccini was involving him. But such a suspicion, though it disturbed Giovanni, was inadequate to restrain him. The instant that he was aware of the possibility of approaching Beatrice, it seemed an absolute necessity of his existence to do so. It mattered not

---

[1] untoward:怪异的;不适当的。
[2] arcane:奥秘,秘密。
[3] ebullition:突然爆发。

whether she were angel or demon; he was irrevocably within her sphere, and must obey the law that whirled him onward, in ever-lessening circles, towards a result which he did not attempt to foreshadow; and yet, strange to say, there came across him a sudden doubt whether this intense interest on his part were not delusory; whether it were really of so deep and positive a nature as to justify him in now thrusting himself into an incalculable position; whether it were not merely the fantasy of a young man's brain, only slightly or not at all connected with his heart.

He paused, hesitated, turned half about, but again went on. His withered guide led him along several obscure passages, and finally undid a door, through which, as it was opened, there came the sight and sound of rustling leaves, with the broken sunshine glimmering among them. Giovanni stepped forth, and, forcing himself through the entanglement of a shrub that wreathed its tendrils over the hidden entrance, stood beneath his own window in the open area of Dr. Rappaccini's garden.

How often is it the case that, when impossibilities have come to pass and dreams have condensed their misty substance into tangible realities, we find ourselves calm, and even coldly self-possessed, amid circumstances which it would have been a delirium of joy or agony to anticipate! Fate delights to thwart us thus. Passion will choose his own time to rush upon the scene, and lingers sluggishly behind when an appropriate adjustment of events would seem to summon his appearance. So was it now with Giovanni. Day after day his pulses had throbbed with feverish blood at the improbable idea of an interview with Beatrice, and of standing with her, face to face, in this very garden, basking in the Oriental sunshine of her beauty, and snatching from her full gaze the mystery which he deemed the riddle of his own existence. But now there was a singular and untimely equanimity within his breast. He threw a glance around the garden to discover if Beatrice or her father were present, and, perceiving that he was alone, began a critical observation of the plants.

The aspect of one and all of them dissatisfied him; their gorgeousness seemed fierce, passionate, and even unnatural. There was hardly an individual shrub which a wanderer, straying by himself through a forest, would not have been startled to find growing wild, as if an unearthly face had glared at him out of the thicket[1]. Several also would have shocked a delicate instinct by an appearance of artificialness indicating that there had been such commixture, and, as it were, adultery, of various vegetable species, that the production was no longer of God's making, but the monstrous offspring of man's depraved fancy, glowing with only an evil mockery of beauty. They were probably the result of experiment, which in one or two cases had succeeded in mingling plants individually lovely into a compound possessing the questionable and ominous character that distinguished the whole growth of the garden. In fine, Giovanni recognized but two or three plants in the collection, and those of a kind that he well

---

[1] thicket:灌木丛。

knew to be poisonous. While busy with these contemplations he heard the rustling of a silken garment, and, turning, beheld Beatrice emerging from beneath the sculptured portal.

Giovanni had not considered with himself what should be his deportment; whether he should apologize for his intrusion into the garden, or assume that he was there with the privity at least, if not by the desire, of Dr. Rappaccini or his daughter; but Beatrice's manner placed him at his ease, though leaving him still in doubt by what agency he had gained admittance. She came lightly along the path and met him near the broken fountain. There was surprise in her face, but brightened by a simple and kind expression of pleasure.

"You are a connoisseur in flowers, signor," said Beatrice, with a smile, alluding to the bouquet which he had flung her from the window. "It is no marvel, therefore, if the sight of my father's rare collection has tempted you to take a nearer view. If he were here, he could tell you many strange and interesting facts as to the nature and habits of these shrubs; for he has spent a lifetime in such studies, and this garden is his world."

"And yourself, lady," observed Giovanni, "if fame says true,—you likewise are deeply skilled in the virtues indicated by these rich blossoms and these spicy perfumes. Would you deign[1] to be my instructress, I should prove an apter scholar than if taught by Signor Rappaccini himself."

"Are there such idle rumors?" asked Beatrice, with the music of a pleasant laugh. "Do people say that I am skilled in my father's science of plants? What a jest is there! No; though I have grown up among these flowers, I know no more of them than their hues and perfume; and sometimes methinks I would fain[2] rid myself of even that small knowledge. There are many flowers here, and those not the least brilliant, that shock and offend me when they meet my eye. But pray, signor, do not believe these stories about my science. Believe nothing of me save what you see with your own eyes."

"And must I believe all that I have seen with my own eyes?" asked Giovanni, pointedly, while the recollection of former scenes made him shrink. "No, signora; you demand too little of me. Bid me believe nothing save what comes from your own lips."

It would appear that Beatrice understood him. There came a deep flush to her cheek; but she looked full into Giovanni's eyes, and responded to his gaze of uneasy suspicion with a queenlike haughtiness.

"I do so bid you, signor," she replied. "Forget whatever you may have fancied in regard to me. If true to the outward senses, still it may be false in its essence; but the words of Beatrice Rappaccini's lips are true from the depths of the heart outward. Those you may believe."

A fervor glowed in her whole aspect and beamed upon Giovanni's consciousness like

---

[1] deign:屈尊。
[2] fain:欣然,乐意。

the light of truth itself; but while she spoke there was a fragrance in the atmosphere around her, rich and delightful, though evanescent, yet which the young man, from an indefinable reluctance, scarcely dared to draw into his lungs. It might be the odor of the flowers. Could it be Beatrice's breath which thus embalmed her words with a strange richness, as if by steeping them in her heart[1]? A faintness passed like a shadow over Giovanni and flitted away; he seemed to gaze through the beautiful girl's eyes into her transparent soul, and felt no more doubt or fear.

The tinge of passion that had colored Beatrice's manner vanished; she became gay, and appeared to derive a pure delight from her communion with the youth not unlike what the maiden of a lonely island might have felt conversing with a voyager from the civilized world. Evidently her experience of life had been confined within the limits of that garden. She talked now about matters as simple as the daylight or summer clouds, and now asked questions in reference to the city, or Giovanni's distant home, his friends, his mother, and his sisters—questions indicating such seclusion, and such lack of familiarity with modes and forms, that Giovanni responded as if to an infant. Her spirit gushed out before him like a fresh rill[2] that was just catching its first glimpse of the sunlight and wondering at the reflections of earth and sky which were flung into its bosom. There came thoughts, too, from a deep source, and fantasies of a gemlike brilliancy, as if diamonds and rubies sparkled upward among the bubbles of the fountain. Ever and anon there gleamed across the young man's mind a sense of wonder that he should be walking side by side with the being who had so wrought upon his imagination, whom he had idealized in such hues of terror, in whom he had positively witnessed such manifestations of dreadful attributes,—that he should be conversing with Beatrice like a brother, and should find her so human and so maidenlike. But such reflections were only momentary; the effect of her character was too real not to make itself familiar at once.

In this free intercourse they had strayed through the garden, and now, after many turns among its avenues, were come to the shattered fountain, beside which grew the magnificent shrub, with its treasury of glowing blossoms. A fragrance was diffused from it which Giovanni recognized as identical with that which he had attributed to Beatrice's breath, but incomparably more powerful. As her eyes fell upon it, Giovanni beheld her press her hand to her bosom as if her heart were throbbing suddenly and painfully.

"For the first time in my life," murmured she, addressing the shrub, "I had forgotten thee."

"I remember, signora," said Giovanni, "that you once promised to reward me with one of these living gems for the bouquet which I had the happy boldness to fling to your feet. Permit me now to pluck it as a memorial of this interview."

---

[1] as if by steeping them in her heart:言词似乎在她内心深处浸润过。
[2] rill:小溪。

He made a step towards the shrub with extended hand; but Beatrice darted forward, uttering a shriek that went through his heart like a dagger. She caught his hand and drew it back with the whole force of her slender figure. Giovanni felt her touch thrilling through his fibres.

"Touch it not!" exclaimed she, in a voice of agony. "Not for thy life! It is fatal!"

Then, hiding her face, she fled from him and vanished beneath the sculptured portal. As Giovanni followed her with his eyes, he beheld the emaciated figure and pale intelligence of Dr. Rappaccini, who had been watching the scene, he knew not how long, within the shadow of the entrance.

No sooner was Guasconti alone in his chamber than the image of Beatrice came back to his passionate musings, invested with all the witchery that had been gathering around it ever since his first glimpse of her, and now likewise imbued with a tender warmth of girlish womanhood. She was human; her nature was endowed with all gentle and feminine qualities; she was worthiest to be worshipped; she was capable, surely, on her part, of the height and heroism of love. Those tokens which he had hitherto considered as proofs of a frightful peculiarity in her physical and moral system were now either forgotten, or, by the subtle sophistry of passion transmitted into a golden crown of enchantment, rendering Beatrice the more admirable by so much as she was the more unique.[1] Whatever had looked ugly was now beautiful; or, if incapable of such a change, it stole away and hid itself among those shapeless half ideas which throng the dim region beyond the daylight of our perfect consciousness.

Thus did he spend the night, not fell asleep until the dawn had begun to awake the slumbering flowers in Dr. Rappaccini's garden, whither Giovanni's dreams doubtless led him. Up rose the sun in his due season, and, flinging his beams upon the young man's eyelids, awoke him to a sense of pain. When thoroughly aroused, he became sensible of a burning and tingling agony in his hand—in his right hand—the very hand which Beatrice had grasped in her own when he was on the point of plucking one of the gemlike flowers. On the back of that hand there was now a purple print like that of four small fingers, and the likeness of a slender thumb upon his wrist.

Oh, how stubbornly does love,—or even that cunning semblance of love which flourishes in the imagination, but strikes no depth of root into the heart,—how stubbornly does it hold its faith until the moment comes when it is doomed to vanish into thin mist! Giovanni wrapped a handkerchief about his hand and wondered what evil thing had stung him, and soon forgot his pain in a reverie of Beatrice.

After the first interview, a second was in the inevitable course of what we call fate. A third; a fourth; and a meeting with Beatrice in the garden was no longer an incident in Giovanni's daily life, but the whole space in which he might be said to live; for the

---

[1] rendering Beatrice the more admirably by so much as she was the more unique: 贝雅特里齐越是与众不同,就越显得可爱。

anticipation and memory of that ecstatic hour made up the remainder. Nor was it otherwise with the daughter of Rappaccini. She watched for the youth's appearance, and flew to his side with confidence as unreserved as if they had been playmates from early infancy—as if they were such playmates still. If, by my unwonted[1] chance, he failed to come at the appointed moment, she stood beneath the window and sent up the rich sweetness of her tones to float around him in his chamber and echo and reverberate throughout his heart: "Giovanni! Giovanni! Why tarriest thou?[2] Come down!" And down he hastened into that Eden of poisonous flowers.

But, with all this intimate familiarity, there was still a reserve in Beatrice's demeanor, so rigidly and invariably sustained that the idea of infringing it scarcely occurred to his imagination.[3] By all appreciable signs, they loved; they had looked love with eyes that conveyed the holy secret from the depths of one soul into the depths of the other, as if it were too sacred to be whispered by the way; they had even spoken love in those gushes of passion when their spirits darted forth in articulated breath like tongues of long-hidden flame; and yet there had been no seal of lips, no clasp of hands, nor any slightest caress such as love claims and hallows. He had never touched one of the gleaming ringlets of her hair; her garment—so marked was the physical barrier between them—had never been waved against him by a breeze. On the few occasions when Giovanni had seemed tempted to overstep the limit, Beatrice grew so sad, so stern, and withal wore such a look of desolate separation, shuddering at itself, that not a spoken word was requisite to repel him. At such times he was startled at the horrible suspicions that rose, monster-like, out of the caverns of his heart and stared him in the face; his love grew thin and faint as the morning mist, his doubts alone had substance. But, when Beatrice's face brightened again after the momentary shadow, she was transformed at once from the mysterious, questionable being whom he had watched with so much awe and horror; she was now the beautiful and unsophisticated girl whom he felt that his spirit knew with a certainty beyond all other knowledge.

A considerable time had now passed since Giovanni's last meeting with Baglioni. One morning, however, he was disagreeably surprised by a visit from the professor, whom he had scarcely thought of for whole weeks, and would willingly have forgotten still longer. Given up as he had long been to a pervading excitement,[4] he could tolerate no companions except upon condition of their perfect sympathy with his present state of feeling. Such sympathy was not to be expected from Professor Baglioni.

The visitor chatted carelessly for a few moments about the gossip of the city and the university, and then took up another topic.

---

[1] unwonted:非同寻常的。
[2] Why tarriest thou? = Why tarries you? 你为什么姗姗来迟?
[3] the idea of infringing it scarcely occurred to his imagination:他简直想象不出她会放弃她那自我克制。
[4] Given up as he had long been to a pervading excitement:他一直处于情绪激动之中。

"I have been reading an old classic author lately," said he, "and met with a story that strangely interested me. Possibly you may remember it. It is of an Indian prince, who sent a beautiful woman as a present to Alexander the Great.[1] She was as lovely as the dawn and gorgeous as the sunset; but what especially distinguished her was a certain rich perfume in her breath—richer than a garden of Persian roses. Alexander, as was natural to a youthful conqueror, fell in love at first sight with this magnificent stranger; but a certain sage physician, happening to be present, discovered a terrible secret in regard to her."

"And what was that?" asked Giovanni, turning his eyes downward to avoid those of the professor.

"That this lovely woman," continued Baglioni, with emphasis, "had been nourished with poisons from her birth upward, until her whole nature was so imbued with them that she herself had become the deadliest poison in existence. Poison was her element of life. With that rich perfume of her breath she blasted the very air. Her love would have been poison—her embrace death. Is not this a marvellous tale?"

"A childish fable," answered Giovanni, nervously starting from his chair. "I marvel how your worship finds time to read such nonsense among your graver studies.[2]"

"By the by," said the professor, looking uneasily about him, "what singular fragrance is this in your apartment? Is it the perfume of your gloves? It is faint, but delicious; and yet, after all, by no means agreeable. Were I to breathe it long, methinks it would make me ill. It is like the breath of a flower; but I see no flowers in the chamber."

"Nor are there any," replied Giovanni, who had turned pale as the professor spoke; "nor, I think, is there any fragrance except in your worship's imagination. Odors, being a sort of element combined of the sensual and the spiritual, are apt to deceive us in this manner. The recollection of a perfume, the bare idea of it, may easily be mistaken for a present reality."

"Ay; but my sober imagination does not often play such tricks," said Baglioni; "and, were I to fancy any kind of odor, it would be that of some vile apothecary drug[3], wherewith my fingers are likely enough to be imbued. Our worshipful friend Rappaccini, as I have heard, tinctures[4] his medicaments with odors richer than those of Araby. Doubtless, likewise, the fair and learned Signora Beatrice would minister to her patients with draughts as sweet as a maiden's breath; but woe to him that sips them!"

---

[1] Alexander the Great:亚历山大大帝(356—323 BC),马其顿国王,先后征服希腊、埃及和波斯,并侵入印度,建立亚历山大帝国。
[2] I marvel how your worship finds time to read such nonsense among you graver studies:阁下忙于从事严肃的学术研究,竟还有时间看这种荒唐东西,真叫人诧异。
[3] vile apothecary drug:有毒药剂。
[4] tinctures:使有气味。

Giovanni's face evinced many contending emotions. The tone in which the professor alluded to the pure and lovely daughter of Rappaccini was a torture to his soul; and yet the intimation of a view of her character opposite to his own, gave instantaneous distinctness to a thousand dim suspicions, which now grinned at him like so many demons. But he strove hard to quell them and to respond to Baglioni with a true lover's perfect faith.

"Signor professor," said he, "you were my father's friend; perchance, too, it is your purpose to act a friendly part towards his son. I would fain feel nothing towards you save respect and deference; but I pray you to observe, signor, that there is one subject on which we must not speak. You know not the Signora Beatrice. You cannot, therefore, estimate the wrong—the blasphemy, I may even say—that is offered to her character by a light or injurious word."

"Giovanni! my poor Giovanni!" answered the professor, with a calm expression of pity, "I know this wretched girl far better than yourself. You shall hear the truth in respect to the poisoner Rappaccini and his poisonous daughter; yes, poisonous as she is beautiful. Listen; for, even should you do violence to my gray hairs, it shall not silence me. That old fable of the Indian woman has become a truth by the deep and deadly science of Rappaccini and in the person of the lovely Beatrice."

Giovanni groaned and hid his face.

"Her father," continued Baglioni, "was not restrained by natural affection from offering up his child in this horrible manner as the victim of his insane zeal for science; for, let us do him justice, he is as true a man of science as ever distilled his own heart in an alembic. What, then, will be your fate? Beyond a doubt you are selected as the material of some new experiment. Perhaps the result is to be death; perhaps a fate more awful still. Rappaccini, with what he calls the interest of science before his eyes, will hesitate at nothing."

"It is a dream," muttered Giovanni to himself; "surely it is a dream."

"But," resumed the professor, "be of good cheer, son of my friend. It is not yet too late for the rescue. Possibly we may even succeed in bringing back this miserable child within the limits of ordinary nature, from which her father's madness has estranged her. Behold this little silver vase! It was wrought by the hands of the renowned Benvenuto Cellini[1], and is well worthy to be a love gift to the fairest dame in Italy. But its contents are invaluable. One little sip of this antidote[2] would have rendered the most virulent poisons of the Borgias innocuous.[3] Doubt not that it will be as efficacious against those of Rappaccini. Bestow the vase, and the precious liquid within it, on your

---

[1] Benvenuto Cellini:切利尼(1500—1571),意大利佛罗伦萨金饰匠、雕塑家,其《帕尔修斯》是米开朗基罗之后佛罗伦萨最杰出的雕塑作品。

[2] antidote:解毒药。

[3] rendered the most virulent poisons of the Borgias innocuous:可使博尔吉亚家的剧毒药失效。the Borgias:博尔吉亚家族在15—16世纪意大利政坛上因不择手段达到目的而闻名。

Beatrice, and hopefully await the result."

Baglioni laid a small, exquisitely wrought silver vial on the table and withdrew, leaving what he had said to produce its effect upon the young man's mind.

"We will thwart Rappaccini yet," thought he, chuckling to himself, as he descended the stairs; "but, let us confess the truth of him, he is a wonderful man—a wonderful man indeed; a vile empiric, however, in his practice, and therefore not to be tolerated by those who respect the good old rules of the medical profession."

Throughout Giovanni's whole acquaintance with Beatrice, he had occasionally, as we have said, been haunted by dark surmises as to her character; yet so thoroughly had she made herself felt by him as a simple, natural, most affectionate, and guileless creature, that the image now held up by Professor Baglioni looked as strange and incredible as if it were not in accordance with his own original conception. True, there were ugly recollections connected with his first glimpses of the beautiful girl; he could not quite forget the bouquet that withered in her grasp, and the insect that perished amid the sunny air, by no ostensible agency save the fragrance of her breath. These incidents, however, dissolving in the pure light of her character, had no longer the efficacy of facts, but were acknowledged as mistaken fantasies, by whatever testimony of the senses they might appear to be substantiated. There is something truer and more real than what we can see with the eyes and touch with the finger. On such better evidence had Giovanni founded his confidence in Beatrice, though rather by the necessary force of her high attributes than by any deep and generous faith on his part. But now his spirit was incapable of sustaining itself at the height to which the early enthusiasm of passion had exalted it; he fell down, grovelling among earthly doubts, and defiled there with the pure whiteness of Beatrice's image. Not that he gave her up; he did but distrust. He resolved to institute some decisive test that should satisfy him, once for all, whether there were those dreadful peculiarities in her physical nature which could not be supposed to exist without some corresponding monstrosity of soul. His eyes, gazing down afar, might have deceived him as to the lizard, the insect, and the flowers; but if he could witness, at the distance of a few paces, the sudden blight of one fresh and healthful flower in Beatrice's hand, there would be room for no further question. With this idea he hastened to the florist's and purchased a bouquet that was still gemmed with the morning dew-drops.

It was now the customary hour of his daily interview with Beatrice. Before descending into the garden, Giovanni failed not to look at his figure in the mirror,—a vanity to be expected in a beautiful young man, yet, as displaying itself at that troubled and feverish moment, the token of a certain shallowness of feeling and insincerity of character. He did gaze, however, and said to himself that his features had never before possessed so rich a grace, nor his eyes such vivacity, nor his cheeks so warm a hue of superabundant life.

"At least," thought he, "her poison has not yet insinuated itself into my system. I am no flower to perish in her grasp."

With that thought he turned his eyes on the bouquet, which he had never once laid aside from his hand. A thrill of indefinable horror shot through his frame on perceiving that those dewy flowers were already beginning to droop; they wore the aspect of things that had been fresh and lovely yesterday. Giovanni grew white as marble, and stood motionless before the mirror, staring at his own reflection there as at the likeness of something frightful. He remembered Baglioni's remark about the fragrance that seemed to pervade the chamber. It must have been the poison in his breath! Then he shuddered—shuddered at himself. Recovering from his stupor, he began to watch with curious eye a spider that was busily at work hanging its web from the antique cornice of the apartment, crossing and recrossing the artful system of interwoven lines—as vigorous and active a spider as ever dangled from an old ceiling. Giovanni bent towards the insect, and emitted a deep, long breath. The spider suddenly ceased its toil; the web vibrated with a tremor originating in the body of the small artisan. Again Giovanni sent forth a breath, deeper, longer, and imbued with a venomous feeling out of his heart: he knew not whether he were wicked, or only desperate. The spider made a convulsive gripe with his limbs and hung dead across the window.

"Accursed! Accursed!" muttered Giovanni, addressing himself. "Hast thou grown so poisonous that this deadly insect perishes by thy breath?"

At that moment a rich, sweet voice came floating up from the garden.

"Giovanni! Giovanni! It is past the hour! Why tarriest thou? Come down!"

"Yes," muttered Giovanni again. "She is the only being whom my breath may not slay! Would that it might![1]"

He rushed down, and in an instant was standing before the bright and loving eyes of Beatrice. A moment ago his wrath and despair had been so fierce that he could have desired nothing so much as to wither her by a glance; but with her actual presence there came influences which had too real an existence to be at once shaken off: recollections of the delicate and benign power of her feminine nature, which had so often enveloped him in a religious calm; recollections of many a holy and passionate outgush of her heart, when the pure fountain had been unsealed from its depths and made visible in its transparency to his mental eye; recollections which, had Giovanni known how to estimate them, would have assured him that all this ugly mystery was but an earthly illusion, and that, whatever mist of evil might seem to have gathered over her, the real Beatrice was a heavenly angel. Incapable as he was of such high faith, still her presence had not utterly lost its magic. Giovanni's rage was quelled into an aspect of sullen insensibility. Beatrice, with a quick spiritual sense, immediately felt that there was a gulf of blackness between them which neither he nor she could pass. They walked on together, sad and silent, and came thus to the marble fountain and to its pool of water

---

[1] Would that it might! 假如她能被我的呼吸毒死，那倒好了！

on the ground, in the midst of which grew the shrub that bore gem-like blossoms. Giovanni was affrighted at the eager enjoyment—the appetite, as it were—with which he found himself inhaling the fragrance of the flowers.

"Beatrice," asked he, abruptly, "whence came this shrub?"

"My father created it," answered she, with simplicity.

"Created it! created it!" repeated Giovanni. "What mean you, Beatrice?"

"He is a man fearfully acquainted with the secrets of Nature," replied Beatrice; "and, at the hour when I first drew breath, this plant sprang from the soil, the offspring of his science, of his intellect, while I was but his earthly child. Approach it not!" continued she, observing with terror that Giovanni was drawing nearer to the shrub. "It has qualities that you little dream of. But I, dearest Giovanni,—I grew up and blossomed with the plant and was nourished with its breath. It was my sister, and I loved it with a human affection; for, alas! —hast thou not suspected it? —there was an awful doom."

Here Giovanni frowned so darkly upon her that Beatrice paused and trembled. But her faith in his tenderness reassured her, and made her blush that she had doubted for an instant.

"There was an awful doom," she continued, "the effect of my father's fatal love of science, which estranged me from all society of my kind. Until Heaven sent thee, dearest Giovanni, oh, how lonely was thy poor Beatrice!"

"Was it a hard doom?" asked Giovanni, fixing his eyes upon her.

"Only of late have I known how hard it was," answered she, tenderly. "Oh, yes; but my heart was torpid, and therefore quiet."

Giovanni's rage broke forth from his sullen gloom like a lightning flash out of a dark cloud.

"Accursed one!" cried he, with venomous scorn and anger. "And, finding thy solitude wearisome, thou hast severed me likewise from all the warmth of life and enticed me into thy region of unspeakable horror!"

"Giovanni!" exclaimed Beatrice, turning her large bright eyes upon his face. The force of his words had not found its way into her mind; she was merely thunderstruck.

"Yes, poisonous thing!" repeated Giovanni, beside himself with passion. "Thou hast done it! Thou hast blasted me! Thou hast filled my veins with poison! Thou hast made me as hateful, as ugly, as loathsome and deadly a creature as thyself—a world's wonder of hideous monstrosity! Now, if our breath be happily as fatal to ourselves as to all others, let us join our lips in one kiss of unutterable hatred, and so die!"

"What has befallen me?" murmured Beatrice, with a low moan out of her heart. "Holy Virgin, pity me, a poor heart-broken child!"

"Thou,—dost thou pray?" cried Giovanni, still with the same fiendish scorn. "Thy very prayers, as they come from thy lips, taint the atmosphere with death. Yes, yes; let us pray! Let us to church and dip our fingers in the holy water at the portal! They that come after us will perish as by a pestilence! Let us sign crosses in the air! It will be scattering curses abroad in the likeness of holy symbols!"

"Giovanni," said Beatrice, calmly, for her grief was beyond passion, "why dost thou join thyself with me thus in those terrible words? I, it is true, am the horrible thing thou namest me. But thou,—what hast thou to do, save with one other shudder at my hideous misery to go forth out of the garden and mingle with thy race, and forget there ever crawled on earth such a monster as poor Beatrice?"

"Dost thou pretend ignorance?" asked Giovanni, scowling upon her. "Behold! this power have I gained from the pure daughter of Rappaccini."

There was a swarm of summer insects flitting through the air in search of the food promised by the flower odors of the fatal garden. They circled round Giovanni's head, and were evidently attracted towards him by the same influence which had drawn them for an instant within the sphere of several of the shrubs. He sent forth a breath among them, and smiled bitterly at Beatrice as at least a score of the insects fell dead upon the ground.

"I see it! I see it!" shrieked Beatrice. "It is my father's fatal science! No, no, Giovanni; it was not I! Never! never! I dreamed only to love thee and be with thee a little time, and so to let thee pass away, leaving but thine image in mine heart; for, Giovanni, believe it, though my body be nourished with poison, my spirit is God's creature, and craves love as its daily food. But my father,—he has united us in this fearful sympathy. Yes; spurn me, tread upon me, kill me! Oh, what is death after such words as thine? But it was not I. Not for a world of bliss would I have done it."

Giovanni's passion had exhausted itself in its outburst from his lips. There now came across him a sense, mournful, and not without tenderness, of the intimate and peculiar relationship between Beatrice and himself. They stood, as it were, in an utter solitude, which would be made none the less solitary by the densest throng of human life. Ought not, then, the desert of humanity around them to press this insulated pair closer together? If they should be cruel to one another, who was there to be kind to them? Besides, thought Giovanni, might there not still be a hope of his returning within the limits of ordinary nature, and leading Beatrice, the redeemed Beatrice,[1] by the hand? O, weak, and selfish, and unworthy spirit, that could dream of an earthly union and earthly happiness as possible, after such deep love had been so bitterly wronged as was Beatrice's love by Giovanni's blighting words! No, no; there could be no such hope. She must pass heavily, with that broken heart, across the borders of Time—she must bathe her hurts in some fount of paradise, and forget her grief in the light of immortality, and *there* be well.

But Giovanni did not know it.

"Dear Beatrice," said he, approaching her, while she shrank away as always at his

---

[1] the redeemed Beatrice: 获得新生的贝雅特里齐。

approach, but now with a different impulse, "dearest Beatrice our fate is not yet so desperate. Behold! there is a medicine, potent, as a wise physician has assured me, and almost divine in its efficacy. It is composed of ingredients the most opposite to those by which thy awful father has brought this calamity upon thee and me. It is distilled of blessed herbs. Shall we not quaff it together, and thus be purified from evil?"

"Give it me!" said Beatrice, extending her hand to receive the little silver vial which Giovanni took from his bosom. She added, with a peculiar emphasis, "I will drink; but do thou await the result."

She put Baglioni's antidote to her lips; and, at the same moment, the figure of Rappaccini emerged from the portal and came slowly towards the marble fountain. As he drew near, the pale man of science seemed to gaze with a triumphant expression at the beautiful youth and maiden, as might an artist who should spend his life in achieving a picture or a group of statuary and finally be satisfied with his success. He paused; his bent form grew erect with conscious power; he spread out his hands over them in the attitude of a father imploring[1] a blessing upon his children; but those were the same hands that had thrown poison into the stream of their lives. Giovanni trembled. Beatrice shuddered nervously, and pressed her hand upon her heart.

"My daughter," said Rappaccini, "thou art no longer lonely in the world. Pluck one of those precious gems from thy sister shrub and bid thy bridegroom wear it in his bosom. It will not harm him now. My science and the sympathy between thee and him have so wrought within his system that he now stands apart from common men, as thou dost, daughter of my pride and triumph, from ordinary women. Pass on, then, through the world, most dear to one another and dreadful to all besides!"

"My father," said Beatrice, feebly,—and still as she spoke she kept her hand upon her heart,—"wherefore didst thou inflict this miserable doom upon thy child?"

"Miserable!" exclaimed Rappaccini. "What mean you, foolish girl? Dost thou deem it misery to be endowed with marvellous gifts against which no power nor strength could avail an enemy—misery, to be able to quell the mightiest with a breath—misery, to be as terrible as thou art beautiful? Wouldst thou, then, have preferred the condition of a weak woman, exposed to all evil and capable of none?"

"I would fain have been loved, not feared," murmured Beatrice, sinking down upon the ground. "But now it matters not. I am going, father, where the evil which thou hast striven to mingle with my being will pass away like a dream-like the fragrance of these poisonous flowers, which will no longer taint my breath among the flowers of Eden. Farewell, Giovanni! Thy words of hatred are like lead within my heart; but they, too, will fall away as I ascend. Oh, was there not, from the first, more poison in thy nature than in mine?"

To Beatrice,—so radically had her earthly part been wrought upon by Rappaccini's

---

[1] imploring:恳求,乞求。

skill,—as poison had been life, so the powerful antidote was death; and thus the poor victim of man's ingenuity and of thwarted nature, and of the fatality that attends all such efforts of perverted wisdom, perished there, at the feet of her father and Giovanni.

Just at that moment Professor Pietro Baglioni looked forth from the window, and called loudly, in a tone of triumph mixed with horror, to the thunderstricken man of science.

"Rappaccini! Rappaccini! and is *this* the upshot of your experiment!"

1844,1846

赏 析

《拉帕奇尼医生之女》以外国为背景,这在霍桑的作品中并不多见。在故事中,意大利东北部城市帕多瓦的名医拉帕奇尼精通药物学,他认为世事险恶,为了保护女儿贝雅特里齐,便用特制的毒草浸透其全身,使她无法与男性正常交往。年轻的乔万尼来本地求学,对纯洁美丽的贝雅特里齐产生好感,情愫暗生。两人交往的结果是,贝雅特里齐对爱情生活的美好希望被摧毁,还失去了生命。

评论家常把拉帕奇尼医生与霍桑的另一短篇小说《胎记》("The Birthmark",1843)中的天才科学家艾默以及《红字》里的齐林沃斯医生相提并论。三部作品都描绘了心灵阴暗的科学家及其所作所为的后果。为了追求知识或复仇,他们无视人性和道德。《拉帕奇尼医生之女》的特别之处在于,它刻画了两个这样的科学家:拉帕奇尼为了追求知识而不惜牺牲女儿的性命(也有人说他是为女儿谋安全、谋幸福);巴格里奥尼医生也是个堕落的科学家,他把解毒药给乔万尼,名义上是救贝雅特里齐,其实是为了打败竞争对手,而且不惜牺牲一位美丽纯洁少女的生命。

在艺术特色上,小说的结构是故事套故事,形成一明一暗两条线,明线是乔万尼与贝雅特里齐交往的故事,暗线是巴格里奥尼与拉帕奇尼的同行竞争。明线是科学实验,暗线是精神交流。在故事结尾,贝雅特里齐喝下解毒药,巴格里奥尼出现在乔万尼房间的窗前,贝雅特里齐从容赴死,两条线汇聚,引向悲剧性结局。

作为一篇浪漫主义之作,《拉帕奇尼医生之女》喜用象征,如乔万尼所住的旧楼弥漫着阴暗而神秘的氛围,暗示了故事的基调,也象征乔万尼的心灵。在西方文化中,"贝雅特里齐"这个名字象征纯洁和善良,作者用大理石喷泉来暗示她虽身体"残破(中毒)",但心灵如喷泉里纯净的水。毒药也是一种象征:故事里的主要人物都中了毒。如果说贝雅特里齐中的是体毒,那么其他人中的则是"心毒"。此外,花园、通向花园的暗门、拉帕奇尼医生的黑色衣服等也都具有与主题相关的象征意义。

相关评论

Giovanni Is a Failed Rescue
Terence Martin

Giovanni stumbles quite by chance into the role of redeemer or rescuer, the bringer of love. And he fails miserably, not through intent, not out of a conscious desire to do ill, but simply because he is a very ordinary and limited young man whose limitations are pointed up all the more explicitly by the exigencies[1] of a role that demands what he cannot give. When Beatrice first sees him from her garden, he is looking out from a window above; she beholds his beautiful head—"rather a Grecian than an Italian head, with fair, regular features, and a glistening of gold among his ringlets—gazing down upon her like a being that hovered in mid-air." The golden haired Giovanni, appearing, as it were, in mid-air, is endowed physically with all the attributes of the godlike hero who rescues the fair maiden from distress. Instinctively, "scarcely knowing what he did," he throws down to her a bouquet of flowers which he has purchased (instinctively?) shortly before.

In the terms set up by the narrative, Giovanni's first gesture toward Beatrice is natural and commendable[2]. Though Beatrice lives among the flowers in her garden, and though Giovanni's bouquet seems to be withering quickly as she disappears into her house, the bouquet is not redundant. Without knowing the secret of her poisonous garden world, Giovanni has bestowed with his fresh flowers a token antidote of the heart. But this is one of the few gestures of the heart that he ever makes to Beatrice.

Repeatedly, Hawthorne tells us of his shallowness and affectation. He "had not a deep heart, or, at all events, its depths were not sounded now; but he had a quick fancy." Allowed into the garden, Giovanni wonders momentarily if his intense interest in Beatrice "were not delusory"; could his interest, asks Hawthorne, be "merely the fantasy of a young man's brain, only slightly or not at all connected with his heart?" Again, Giovanni seems less in love than in the throes of[3] "that cunning semblance of love which flourishes in the imagination, but strikes no depth of root into the heart." When, after an interview with Baglioni, Giovanni buys a second bouquet of flowers, it is with the express purpose of testing Beatrice to see if she is what his senses proclaim her to be. And, before he goes into the garden for his final, fateful interview, he pauses to gaze at himself in a mirror, "a vanity to be expected in a beautiful young man, yet, as displaying itself at that troubled and feverish moment, the token of a certain shallowness of feeling and insincerity of character."

Giovanni, in short, lacks the depth of heart necessary to tender to Beatrice the love to which her spirit could respond. He vacillates[4] between faith and doubt, between the promptings of the heart and those of the fancy—and his alternating moods comprise the essential dramatic movement of the tale. He is not so much tricked or deluded as limited by his fancy, which blurs any profounder vision and makes it impossible for him to believe in Beatrice's spiritual beauty even though he has perceived its manifestations.

---

[1] exigencies: 紧急需要,迫切要求。
[2] commendable: 值得表扬的。
[3] in the throes of: 挣扎于。
[4] vacillates: 摇摆,犹豫不定。

Had he trusted in the heart rather than in the fancy he would have been reassured "that all this ugly mystery was but an earthly illusion," that despite the "mist of evil" surrounding her the real Beatrice was "a heavenly angel." But Giovanni is "incapable... of such high faith." When Beatrice says she had been lonely until heaven sent him, he turns angrily upon her, burying her with invective[1], calling her "a world's wonder of hideous monstrosity." And when she sadly explains the truth of her situation, a contrite Giovanni betrays the poverty of his heart one final time. Perhaps, he thinks, he can yet lead "the redeemed Beatrice" from the garden; putting his faith not in the heart but in a scientific antidote, he ministers the potion given him by Baglioni, and—compounding his emotional blindness—promises that it is "almost divine in its efficacy."

By listening to the advice of Signor Pietro Baglioni, Giovanni becomes unwittingly involved in the rivalry between this friend of his father and Rappaccini. Certainly the advice seems well meant; but in this tale things are not often what they seem. Rappaccini is a brilliant scientist, admits Baglioni, as good as any in Italy, "with perhaps one single exception." Although this cryptic[2] qualification is never explained, there can be little doubt that the "exception" is Baglioni himself. Baglioni goes on to expound Rappaccini's theory of medicine, to admit that with his vast knowledge of poisons Rappaccini undeniably "does less mischief than might be expected," and to admit further, albeit grudgingly, that he has, "now and then,... effected, or seemed to effect, a marvellous cure."

Then, in a statement that reflects heavily on the attitude of the speaker, he gives Giovanni his private opinion: Rappaccini "should receive little credit for such instances of success,—they being probably the work of chance,—but should be held strictly accountable for his failures, which may justly be considered his own work." The statement is so grossly onesided as to be humorous. And Hawthorne reinforces the certainty of bias by saying that Giovanni "might have taken Baglioni's opinions with many grains of allowance had he known that there was a professional warfare of long continuance between him and Dr. Rappaccini, in which the latter was generally thought to have gained the advantage." Yet this same Baglioni formulates what has come to be virtually the standard judgment of the mighty scientist: Rappaccini "cares infinitely more for science than for mankind," says Baglioni; his patients interest him only as subjects for experiments; and—most famous description of all—"he would sacrifice human life, his own among the rest, or whatever else was dearest to him, for the sake of adding so much as a grain of mustard seed to the great heap of his accumulated knowledge."

Source: *Twayne's United States Authors Series 75*. Boston: Twayne Publishers, 1983.

---

[1] invective: 非难。
[2] cryptic: 含义模糊的，神秘的。

问题与思考

1. Dante, the author of *Divine Comedy*, appears in the very beginning of the story. Is there any connection between Dante's Beatrice and Hawthorne's Beatrice?
2. Dr. Rappaccini's garden is compared to the "Eden of the present world" in the story. Discuss its implications.
3. How do you describe Dr. Rappaccini's character? What does he stand for?
4. In what way is the "shattered fountain" related to Beatrice?
5. What is the point of view of the story?

阅读链接

1. http://ibiblio.org/eldritch/nh/hawthorne.html：霍桑重要作品的搜索链接。
2. http://www.brainyquote.com/quotes/authors/n/nathaniel_hawthorne.html：来自霍桑作品的格言隽语。
3. http://en.wikipedia.org/wiki/Twice-Told_Tales：详细介绍《重讲一遍的故事》。
4. http://ibiblio.org/eldritch/nh/nhfilm.html：《红字》及霍桑其他作品的电影改编介绍。

D．H．Lawrence (1885—1930)

作者简介

D．H．劳伦斯(D. H. Law rence，1885—1930)出生于英国诺丁汉郡的一个矿工家庭。父亲性情暴躁，没有受过多少教育，但擅长讲故事，热爱自然，热情豪放；母亲则有良好的文化修养，举止文雅，感情细腻。她觉得自己屈尊下嫁给了一个矿工，对丈夫的粗暴和酗酒感到失望以至厌恶，于是将本应给予丈夫的全部热情化作强烈的母爱倾注在自己的儿子们身上。这种异乎寻常的母爱对劳伦斯的心理和成长产生了极大的影响。劳伦斯小学毕业时，成为当地第一个获得诺丁汉郡中学奖学金的学生。1906 年，他在一个初等学校担任三年代课教师后，进入诺丁汉学院学习教师专修课程，同时开始创作诗歌和小说。两年后，他到伦敦南部一所文法学校任教。1912 年 5 月，劳伦斯与他原来就读学院的一位教授的妻子弗丽达私奔到欧洲。第一次世界大战期间，他们居住在英国，可是弗丽达的德国国籍给劳伦斯带来不少麻烦。1919 年，劳伦斯携妻离开英国，从此开始漂泊天涯的旅行生活，到过锡兰(斯里兰卡)、澳大利亚、美国和墨西哥，并成为英国最好的游记作家之一。20 年代，打算移民美国的劳伦斯在新墨西哥州住了两年，最后定居在意大利北部弗罗伦萨附近。他长期健康不佳，但始终笔耕不止。1930 年劳伦斯在法国南部病逝，年仅 45 岁。

文学创作

劳伦斯是英国 20 世纪杰出的作家，创作涉及小说、诗歌、文学评论等，主要的长篇小说有《儿子与情人》(Sons and Lovers，1912)、《虹》(The Rainbow，1915)、《恋爱中的女人》(Women in

Love，1921)和《查泰莱夫人的情人》(*Lady Chatterley's Lover*，1928)，中短篇小说有十多集，名篇有《菊馨》("Odour of Chrysanthemums"，1914)、《马贩子的女儿》("The Horse Dealer's Daughter"，1917)、《木马赢家》("The Rocking-Horse Winner"，1926)等。

劳伦斯的主要作品都以英格兰中部诺丁汉一带的矿区和乡村为背景，其特征是将社会批判和心理探索这两个主题结合起来。《儿子与情人》描写矿工莫瑞尔一家在工业社会环境中的不幸遭遇和青年主人公保罗的成长和婚恋经历，具有自传色彩。《虹》讲述了布兰格温一家三代人的故事，特别是描写了代表第三代的厄秀拉对灵与肉完美统一的追求，《恋爱中的女人》是《虹》的续篇，诠释了完美的两性关系的理想。在劳伦斯看来，传统道德和工业文明扼杀人性，摆脱现代人精神空虚、文明枯萎困境的出路在于恢复人的自然本性。他在作品中表达的一贯思想是：使性爱回归到自然活泼的状态，建立和谐的两性关系，现代社会才有恢复生机的希望。因此，他热衷于"性描写"，通过主人公对性的体验和心理变化，写出他们肉体和精神的复苏过程。由于对两性关系的描写，劳伦斯的一些作品如《查泰莱夫人的情人》曾被列为禁书。劳伦斯从人性论角度表现和批判机械文明的冷酷无情，但在指责资本主义工业文明的罪恶的同时，他把社会的复杂性过于简单化了。

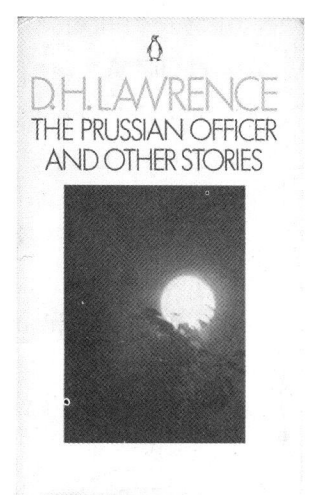

劳伦斯的小说有明显的现实主义和自然主义倾向，为深刻挖掘人物的无意识状态，他大量使用象征，如彩虹、鲜花、月亮、奔马等。此外，劳伦斯还善于根据人物身份和情节的需要恰当地使用方言。

作　　品

The Blind Man

Isabel Pervin was listening for two sounds—for the sound of wheels on the drive[1] outside and for the noise of her husband's footsteps in the hall. Her dearest and oldest friend，a man who seemed almost indispensable to her living，would drive up in the rainy dusk of the closing November day. The trap[2] had gone to fetch him from the station. And her husband，who had been blinded in Flanders[3]，and who had a disfiguring mark on his brow，would be coming in from the outhouses.

He had been home for a year now. He was totally blind. Yet they had been very happy. The Grange was Maurice's own place. The back was a farmstead[4]，and the Wernhams，who occupied the rear premises[5]，acted as farmers. Isabel lived with her husband in the handsome rooms in front. She and he had been almost entirely alone

---

[1] drive：(由住宅通向公路的)私人车道。
[2] trap：双轮轻便马车。
[3] Flanders：法兰德，欧洲北海沿岸地区。它包括法国北部部分地区、比利时的东、西法兰德省以及荷兰的泽兰省，是著名战略要地。第一次世界大战期间，协约国与德国的步兵曾在此激烈交战。
[4] farmstead：农舍及周围的农田。
[5] premises：建筑物及其土地。

together since he was wounded. They talked and sang and read together in a wonderful and unspeakable intimacy. Then she reviewed books for a Scottish newspaper, carrying on her old interest, and he occupied himself a good deal with the farm. Sightless, he could still discuss everything with Wernham, and he could also do a good deal of work about the place—menial work,[1] it is true, but it gave him satisfaction. He milked the cows, carried in the pails, turned the separator[2], attended to the pigs and horses. Life was still very full and strangely serene for the blind man, peaceful with the almost incomprehensible peace of immediate contact in darkness. With his wife he had a whole world, rich and real and invisible.

They were newly and remotely happy. He did not even regret the loss of his sight in these times of dark, palpable joy. A certain exultance swelled his soul.

But as time wore on, sometimes the rich glamour would leave them. Sometimes, after months of this intensity, a sense of burden overcame Isabel, a weariness, a terrible ennui[3], in that silent house approached between a colonnade of tall-shafted pines.[4] Then she felt she would go mad, for she could not bear it. And sometimes he had devastating fits of depression,[5] which seemed to lay waste his whole being. It was worse than depression—a black misery, when his own life was a torture to him, and when his presence was unbearable to his wife. The dread went down to the roots of her soul as these black days recurred. In a kind of panic she tried to wrap herself up still further in her husband. She forced the old spontaneous cheerfulness and joy to continue. But the effort it cost her was almost too much. She knew she could not keep it up. She felt she would scream with the strain, and would give anything, anything, to escape. She longed to possess her husband utterly; it gave her inordinate joy to have him entirely to herself. And yet, when again he was gone in a black and massive misery, she could not bear him, she could not bear herself; she wished she could be snatched away off the earth altogether, anything rather than live at this cost.

Dazed, she schemed for a way out. She invited friends, she tried to give him some further connection with the outer world. But it was no good. After all their joy and suffering, after their dark, great year of blindness and solitude and unspeakable nearness, other people seemed to them both shallow, prattling, rather impertinent.[6] Shallow prattle seemed presumptuous[7]. He became impatient and irritated, she was wearied. And so they lapsed into their solitude again. For they preferred it.

But now, in a few weeks' time, her second baby would be born. The first had died,

---

[1] menial work: 粗活。
[2] separator: 脱脂器。
[3] ennui: 厌倦；无聊。
[4] that silent house... tall-shafted pines: 那栋房子坐落在一排高大挺拔的松树之间，静悄悄的。
[5] fits of depression: 情绪一阵阵低落。
[6] other people... rattling, rather impertinent: 在他们看来，其他人都显得浅薄，吵吵嚷嚷，很没有礼貌。
[7] presumptuous: 傲慢，放肆。

an infant, when her husband first went out to France. She looked with joy and relief to the coming of the second. It would be her salvation. But also she felt some anxiety. She was thirty years old, her husband was a year younger. They both wanted the child very much. Yet she could not help feeling afraid. She had her husband on her hands, a terrible joy to her, and a terrifying burden. The child would occupy her love and attention. And then, what of Maurice? What would he do? If only she could feel that he, too, would be at peace and happy when the child came! She did so want to luxuriate[1] in a rich, physical satisfaction of maternity. But the man, what would he do? How could she provide for him, how avert those shattering black moods of his, which destroyed them both?

She sighed with fear. But at this time Bertie Reid wrote to Isabel. He was her old friend, a second or third cousin, a Scotchman, as she was a Scotchwoman. They had been brought up near to one another, and all her life he had been her friend, like a brother, but better than her own brothers. She loved him—though not in the marrying sense. There was a sort of kinship between them, an affinity. They understood one another instinctively. But Isabel would never have thought of marrying Bertie. It would have seemed like marrying in her own family.

Bertie was a barrister[2] and a man of letters, a Scotchman of the intellectual type, quick, ironical, sentimental, and on his knees before the woman he adored but did not want to marry. Maurice Pervin was different. He came of a good old country family—the Grange was not a very great distance from Oxford. He was passionate, sensitive, perhaps over-sensitive, wincing—a big fellow with heavy limbs and a forehead that flushed painfully. For his mind was slow, as if drugged by the strong provincial blood that beat in his veins. He was very sensitive to his own mental slowness, his feelings being quick and acute. So that he was just the opposite to Bertie, whose mind was much quicker than his emotions, which were not so very fine.

From the first the two men did not like each other. Isabel felt that they *ought* to get on together. But they did not. She felt that if only each could have the clue to the other there would be such a rare understanding between them. It did not come off, however. Bertie adopted a slightly ironical attitude, very offensive to Maurice, who returned the Scotch irony with English resentment, a resentment which deepened sometimes into stupid hatred.

This was a little puzzling to Isabel. However, she accepted it in the course of things. Men were made freakish[3] and unreasonable. Therefore, when Maurice was going out to France for the second time, she felt that, for her husband's sake, she must discontinue her friendship with Bertie. She wrote to the barrister to this effect. Bertram

---

[1] luxuriate: 沉溺。
[2] barrister: (可在高等法院出庭的)大律师;专门律师。
[3] freakish: 捉摸不定的。

Reid simply replied that in this, as in all other matters, he must obey her wishes, if these were indeed her wishes.

For nearly two years nothing had passed between the two friends. Isabel rather gloried in the fact; she had no compunction[1]. She had one great article of faith, which was, that husband and wife should be so important to one another, that the rest of the world simply did not count. She and Maurice were husband and wife. They loved one another. They would have children. Then let everybody and everything else fade into insignificance outside this connubial felicity.[2] She professed[3] herself quite happy and ready to receive Maurice's friends. She was happy and ready: the happy wife, the ready woman in possession. Without knowing why, the friends retired abashed and came no more. Maurice, of course, took as much satisfaction in this connubial absorption as Isabel did.

He shared in Isabel's literary activities, she cultivated a real interest in agriculture and cattle-raising. For she, being at heart perhaps an emotional enthusiast, always cultivated the practical side of life, and prided herself on her mastery of practical affairs. Thus the husband and wife had spent the five years of their married life. The last had been one of blindness and unspeakable intimacy. And now Isabel felt a great indifference coming over her, a sort of lethargy. She wanted to be allowed to bear her child in peace, to nod[4] by the fire and drift vaguely, physically, from day to day. Maurice was like an ominous thunder-cloud. She had to keep waking up to remember him.

When a little note came from Bertie, asking if he were to put up a tombstone to their dead friendship, and speaking of the real pain he felt on account of her husband's loss of sight, she felt a pang, a fluttering agitation of re-awakening. And she read the letter to Maurice.

"Ask him to come down," he said.

"Ask Bertie to come here!" she re-echoed.

"Yes—if he wants to."

Isabel paused for a few moments.

"I know he wants to—he'd only be too glad," she replied. "But what about you, Maurice? How would you like it?"

"I should like it."

"Well—in that case—But I thought you didn't care for him—"

"Oh, I don't know. I might think differently of him now," the blind man replied. It was rather abstruse to Isabel.

---

[1] compunction: 良心的责备。
[2] connubial felicity: 婚姻的幸福。
[3] professed: 声称。
[4] nod: 打瞌睡。

"Well, dear," she said, "if you're quite sure—"

"I'm sure enough. Let him come," said Maurice.

So Bertie was coming, coming this evening, in the November rain and darkness. Isabel was agitated, racked with[1] her old restlessness and indecision. She had always suffered from this pain of doubt, just an agonizing sense of uncertainty. It had begun to pass off,[2] in the lethargy of maternity. Now it returned, and she resented it. She struggled as usual to maintain her calm, composed, friendly bearing, a sort of mask she wore over all her body.

A woman had lighted a tall lamp beside the table, and spread the cloth. The long dining-room was dim, with its elegant but rather severe pieces of old furniture. Only the round table glowed softly under the light. It had a rich, beautiful effect. The white cloth glistened and dropped its heavy, pointed lace corners almost to the carpet, the china was old and handsome, creamy-yellow, with a blotched pattern of harsh red and deep blue,[3] the cups large and bell-shaped, the teapot gallant. Isabel looked at it with superficial appreciation.

Her nerves were hurting her. She looked automatically again at the high, uncurtained windows. In the last dusk she could just perceive outside a huge fir-tree swaying its boughs: it was as if she thought it rather than saw it. The rain came flying on the window panes. Ah, why had she no peace? These two men, why did they tear at her? Why did they not come—why was there this suspense?

She sat in a lassitude[4] that was really suspense and irritation. Maurice, at least, might come in—there was nothing to keep him out. She rose to her feet. Catching sight of her reflection in a mirror, she glanced at herself with a slight smile of recognition, as if she were an old friend to herself. Her face was oval and calm, her nose a little arched. Her neck made a beautiful line down to her shoulder. With hair knotted loosely behind, she had something of a warm, maternal look. Thinking this of herself, she arched her eyebrows and her rather heavy eyelids, with a little flicker of a smile, and for a moment her grey eyes looked amused and wicked, a little sardonic, out of her transfigured Madonna[5] face.

Then, resuming her air of womanly patience—she was really fatally self-determined—she went with a little jerk towards the door. Her eyes were slightly reddened.

She passed down the wide hall, and through a door at the end. Then she was in the farm premises. The scent of dairy, and of farm-kitchen, and of farm-yard and of leather

---

[1] racked with: 因……感到痛苦。
[2] pass off: 消失。
[3] with a blotched... deep blue: 鲜亮的红色和深蓝色点缀其上,构成图案。
[4] lassitude: 无精打采。
[5] Madonna: 圣母玛利亚。在这里作形容词,"像圣母玛利亚的"。

almost overcame her; but particularly the scent of dairy. They had been scalding out[1] the pans. The flagged passage[2] in front of her was dark, puddled[3] and wet. Light came out from the open kitchen door. She went forward and stood in the doorway. The farm-people were at tea, seated at a little distance from her, round a long, narrow table, in the centre of which stood a white lamp. Ruddy faces, ruddy hands holding food, red mouths working, heads bent over the tea-cups: men, land-girls, boys: it was tea-time, feeding-time. Some faces caught sight of her. Mrs. Wernham, going round behind the chairs with a large black teapot, halting slightly in her walk, was not aware of her for a moment. Then she turned suddenly.

"Oh, is it Madam!" she exclaimed. "Come in, then, come in! We're at tea." And she dragged forward a chair.

"No, I won't come in," said Isabel, "I'm afraid I interrupt your meal."

"No—no—not likely, Madam, not likely."

"Hasn't Mr. Pervin come in, do you know?"

"I'm sure I couldn't say! Missed him, have you, Madam?"

"No, I only wanted him to come in," laughed Isabel, as if shyly.

"Wanted him, did ye[4]? Get you, boy—get up, now—"

Mrs. Wernham knocked one of the boys on the shoulder. He began to scrape to his feet,[5] chewing largely.

"I believe he's in top stable," said another face from the table.

"Ah! No, don't get up. I'm going myself," said Isabel.

"Don't you go out of a dirty night like this. Let the lad go. Get along wi'ye,[6] boy," said Mrs. Wernham.

"No, no," said Isabel, with a decision that was always obeyed. "Go on with your tea, Tom. I'd like to go across to the stable, Mrs. Wernham."

"Did ever you hear tell!" exclaimed the woman.

"Isn't the trap late?" asked Isabel.

"Why, no," said Mrs. Wernham, peering into the distance at the tall, dim clock. "No, Madam—we can give it another quarter or twenty minutes yet, good—yes, every bit of a quarter."

"Ah! It seems late when darkness falls so early," said Isabel.

"It do, that it do. Bother the days, that they draw in so," answered Mrs. Wernham. "Proper miserable!"

"They are," said Isabel, withdrawing.

---

[1] scalding out: 烫洗。
[2] The flagged passage: 铺了石板的过道。
[3] puddled: 坑坑洼洼的。
[4] ye = you.
[5] scrape to his feet: 脚在地上蹭了一下,欠起身。
[6] wi'ye = will you.

She pulled on her overshoes, wrapped a large tartan shawl[1] around her, put on a man's felt hat, and ventured out along the causeways[2] of the first yard. It was very dark. The wind was roaring in the great elms behind the outhouses. When she came to the second yard the darkness seemed deeper. She was unsure of her footing. She wished she had brought a lantern. Rain blew against her. Half she liked it, half she felt unwilling to battle.

She reached at last the just visible door of the stable. There was no sign of a light anywhere. Opening the upper half,[3] she looked in: into a simple well of darkness. The smell of horses, and ammonia[4], and of warmth was startling to her, in that full night. She listened with all her ears, but could hear nothing save the night, and the stirring of a horse.

"Maurice!" she called, softly and musically, though she was afraid. "Maurice—are you there?"

Nothing came from the darkness. She knew the rain and wind blew in upon the horses, the hot animal life. Feeling it wrong, she entered the stable, and drew the lower half of the door shut, holding the upper part close. She did not stir, because she was aware of the presence of the dark hindquarters of the horses, though she could not see them, and she was afraid. Something wild stirred in her heart.

She listened intensely. Then she heard a small noise in the distance—far away, it seemed—the chink[5] of a pan, and a man's voice speaking a brief word. It would be Maurice, in the other part of the stable. She stood motionless, waiting for him to come through the partition door. The horses were so terrifyingly near to her, in the invisible.

The loud jarring of the inner door-latch made her start; the door was opened. She could hear and feel her husband entering and invisibly passing among the horses near to her, in darkness as they were, actively intermingled. The rather low sound of his voice as he spoke to the horses came velvety[6] to her nerves. How near he was, and how invisible! The darkness seemed to be in a strange swirl of violent life, just upon her. She turned giddy.

Her presence of mind made her call, quietly and musically:

"Maurice! Maurice—dea-ar!"

"Yes," he answered. "Isabel?"

She saw nothing, and the sound of his voice seemed to touch her.

"Hello!" she answered cheerfully, straining her eyes to see him. He was still busy, attending to the horses near her, but she saw only darkness. It made her almost

---

[1] tartan shawl:(苏格兰)格子花呢披肩。
[2] causeways:(通过低洼或潮湿地带的)堤道,砌道。
[3] the upper half:马厩的门通常分为上下两部分,可以分别打开。
[4] ammonia:氨气味(这里指牲口粪便的气味)。
[5] chink:(金属相碰时发出的)叮当声。
[6] velvety:(像天鹅绒那样)柔和的。

desperate.

"Won't you come in, dear?" she said.

"Yes, I'm coming. Just half a minute. Stand over—now! Trap's not come, has it?"

"Not yet," said Isabel.

His voice was pleasant and ordinary, but it had a slight suggestion of the stable to her. She wished he would come away. Whilst he was so utterly invisible she was afraid of him.

"How's the time?" he asked.

"Not yet six," she replied. She disliked to answer into the dark. Presently he came very near to her, and she retreated out of doors.

"The weather blows in here," he said, coming steadily forward, feeling for the doors. She shrank away. At last she could dimly see him.

"Bertie won't have much of a drive," he said, as he closed the doors.

"He won't indeed!" said Isabel calmly, watching the dark shape at the door.

"Give me your arm, dear," she said.

She pressed his arm close to her, as she went. But she longed to see him, to look at him. She was nervous. He walked erect, with face rather lifted, but with a curious tentative movement of his powerful, muscular legs. She could feel the clever, careful, strong contact of his feet with the earth, as she balanced against him. For a moment he was a tower of darkness to her, as if he rose out of the earth.

In the house-passage he wavered, and went cautiously, with a curious look of silence about him as he felt for the bench. Then he sat down heavily. He was a man with rather sloping shoulders, but with heavy limbs, powerful legs that seemed to know the earth. His head was small, usually carried high and light. As he bent down to unfasten his gaiters and boots he did not look blind. His hair was brown and crisp, his hands were large, reddish, intelligent, the veins stood out in the wrists; and his thighs and knees seemed massive. When he stood up his face and neck were surcharged with blood, the veins stood out on his temples. She did not look at his blindness.

Isabel was always glad when they had passed through the dividing door into their own regions of repose and beauty. She was a little afraid of him, out there in the animal grossness of the back. His bearing also changed, as he smelt the familiar, indefinable odour that pervaded his wife's surroundings, a delicate, refined scent, very faintly spicy. Perhaps it came from the potpourri[1] bowls.

He stood at the foot of the stairs, arrested, listening. She watched him, and her heart sickened. He seemed to be listening to fate.

"He's not here yet," he said. "I'll go up and change."

"Maurice," she said, "you're not wishing he wouldn't come, are you?"

---

[1] potpourri:(法语)百花香(放于壶内的干燥的花瓣和香料,用于熏房间)。

"I couldn't quite say," he answered. "I feel myself rather on the qui vive[1]."

"I can see you are," she answered. And she reached up and kissed his cheek. She saw his mouth relax into a slow smile.

"What are you laughing at?" she said roguishly.

"You consoling me," he answered.

"Nay," she answered. "Why should I console you? You know we love each other—you know *how* married we are! What does anything else matter?"

"Nothing at all, my dear."

He felt for her face, and touched it, smiling.

"*You're* all right, aren't you?" he asked, anxiously.

"I'm wonderfully all right, love," she answered. "It's you I am a little troubled about, at times."

"Why me?" he said, touching her cheeks delicately with the tips of his fingers. The touch had an almost hypnotizing effect[2] on her.

He went away upstairs. She saw him mount into the darkness, unseeing and unchanging. He did not know that the lamps on the upper corridor were unlighted. He went on into the darkness with unchanging step. She heard him in the bathroom.

Pervin moved about almost unconsciously in his familiar surroundings, dark though everything was. He seemed to know the presence of objects before he touched them. It was a pleasure to him to rock[3] thus through a world of things, carried on the flood in a sort of blood-prescience.[4] He did not think much or trouble much. So long as he kept this sheer immediacy of blood-contact with the substantial world he was happy, he wanted no intervention of visual consciousness. In this state there was a certain rich positivity, bordering sometimes on rapture. Life seemed to move in him like a tide lapping, and advancing, enveloping all things darkly. It was a pleasure to stretch forth the hand and meet the unseen object, clasp it, and possess it in pure contact. He did not try to remember, to visualize. He did not want to. The new way of consciousness substituted itself in him.

The rich suffusion of this state generally kept him happy, reaching its culmination in the consuming passion for his wife. But at times the flow would seem to be checked and thrown back. Then it would beat inside him like a tangled sea, and he was tortured in the shattered chaos of his own blood. He grew to dread this arrest, this throw-back, this chaos inside himself, when he seemed merely at the mercy of his own powerful and conflicting elements. How to get some measure of control or surety, this was the question. And when the question rose maddening in him, he would clench his fists as if

[1] on the qui vive：警戒着，时时提防着。qui vive：（法语）（哨兵的查问口令）谁？你是哪一边的？
[2] hypnotizing effect：催眠效果。
[3] rock：来回或左右轻晃或轻摆。
[4] a sort of blood-prescience：一种血性预言。

he would *compel* the whole universe to submit to him. But it was in vain. He could not even compel himself.

Tonight, however, he was still serene, though little tremors of unreasonable exasperation[1] ran through him. He had to handle the razor very carefully, as he shaved, for it was not at one with him,[2] he was afraid of it. His hearing also was too much sharpened. He heard the woman lighting the lamps on the corridor, and attending to the fire in the visitor's room. And then, as he went to his room he heard the trap arrive. Then came Isabel's voice, lifted and calling, like a bell ringing:

"Is it you, Bertie? Have you come?"

And a man's voice answered out of the wind:

"Hello, Isabell. There you are."

"Have you had a miserable drive? I'm so sorry we couldn't send a closed carriage. I can't see you at all, you know."

"I'm coming. No, I liked the drive—it was like Perthshire[3]. Well, how are you? You're looking fit as ever, as far as I can see."

"Oh, yes," said Isabel. "I'm wonderfully well. How are you? Rather thin, I think—"

"Worked to death—everybody's old cry. But I'm all right, Ciss. How's Pervin?—isn't he here?"

"Oh, yes, he's upstairs changing. Yes, he's awfully well. Take off your wet things; I'll send them to be dried."

"And how are you both, in spirits? He doesn't fret?"

"No—no, not at all. No, on the contrary, really. We've been wonderfully happy, incredibly. It's more than I can understand—so wonderful: the nearness, and the peace—"

"Ah! Well, that's awfully good news—"

They moved away. Pervin heard no more. But a childish sense of desolation had come over him, as he heard their brisk voices. He seemed shut out—like a child that is left out. He was aimless and excluded, he did not know what to do with himself. The helpless desolation came over him. He fumbled nervously as he dressed himself, in a state almost of childishness. He disliked the Scotch accent in Bertie's speech, and the slight response it found on Isabel's tongue. He disliked the slight purr[4] of complacency in the Scottish speech. He disliked intensely the glib way in which Isabel spoke of their happiness and nearness. It made him recoil. He was fretful and beside himself like a child, he had almost a childish nostalgia to be included in the life circle. And at the same

---

[1] exasperation:恼怒。
[2] it was not at one with him:不听他使唤。be at one:一致。
[3] Perthshire:佩思郡,苏格兰一风景胜地。
[4] purr:(尤指表达满意时)的轻声低语。

time he was a man, dark and powerful and infuriated by his own weakness. By some fatal flaw, he could not be by himself, he had to depend on the support of another. And this very dependence enraged him. He hated Bertie Reid, and at the same time he knew the hatred was nonsense, he knew it was the outcome of his own weakness.

He went downstairs. Isabel was alone in the dining-room. She watched him enter, head erect, his feet tentative. He looked so strong-blooded and healthy, and, at the same time, cancelled. Cancelled—that was the word that flew across her mind. Perhaps it was his scars suggested it.

"You heard Bertie come, Maurice?" she said.

"Yes—isn't he here?"

"He's in his room. He looks very thin and worn."

"I suppose he works himself to death."

A woman came in with a tray—and after a few minutes Bertie came down. He was a little dark man, with a very big forehead, thin, wispy hair,[1] and sad, large eyes. His expression was inordinately sad—almost funny. He had odd, short legs.

Isabel watched him hesitate under the door, and glance nervously at her husband. Pervin heard him and turned.

"Here you are, now," said Isabel. "Come, let us eat."

Bertie went across to Maurice.

"How are you, Pervin," he said, as he advanced.

The blind man stuck his hand out into space, and Bertie took it.

"Very fit. Glad you've come," said Maurice.

Isabel glanced at them, and glanced away, as if she could not bear to see them.

"Come," she said. "Come to table. Aren't you both awfully hungry? I am, tremendously."

"I'm afraid you waited for me," said Bertie, as they sat down.

Maurice had a curious monolithic[2] way of sitting in a chair, erect and distant. Isabel's heart always beat when she caught sight of him thus.

"No," she replied to Bertie. "We're very little later than usual. We're having a sort of high tea, not dinner. Do you mind? It gives us such a nice long evening, uninterrupted."

"I like it," said Bertie.

Maurice was feeling, with curious little movements, almost like a cat kneading[3] her bed, for his place, his knife and fork, his napkin. He was getting the whole geography of his cover into his consciousness. He sat erect and inscrutable, remote-seeming Bertie watched the static figure of the blind man, the delicate tactile

---

[1] wispy hair: 纤细的头发。
[2] monolithic: 稳如磐石的。
[3] kneading: 揉。

discernment of the large, ruddy hands, and the curious mindless silence of the brow, above the scar. With difficulty he looked away, and without knowing what he did, picked up a little crystal bowl of violets from the table, and held them to his nose.

"They are sweet-scented," he said. "Where do they come from?"

"From the garden—under the windows," said Isabel.

"So late in the year—and so fragrant! Do you remember the violets under Aunt Bell's south wall?"

The two friends looked at each other and exchanged a smile, Isabel's eyes lighting up.

"Don't I?" she replied. "*Wasn't* she queer!"

"A curious old girl," laughed Bertie. "There's a streak of freakishness in the family, Isabel."

"Ah—but not in you and me, Bertie," said Isabel. "Give them to Maurice, will you?" she added, as Bertie was putting down the flowers. "Have you smelled the violets, dear? Do! —they are so scented."

Maurice held out his hand, and Bertie placed the tiny bowl against his large, warm-looking fingers. Maurice's hand closed over the thin white fingers of the barrister. Bertie carefully extricated himself. Then the two watched the blind man smelling the violets. He bent his head and seemed to be thinking. Isabel waited.

"Aren't they sweet, Maurice?" she said at last, anxiously.

"Very," he said. And he held out the bowl. Bertie took it. Both he and Isabel were a little afraid, and deeply disturbed.

The meal continued. Isabel and Bertie chatted spasmodically. The blind man was silent. He touched his food repeatedly, with quick, delicate touches of his knife-point, then cut irregular bits. He could not bear to be helped. Both Isabel and Bertie suffered: Isabel wondered why. She did not suffer when she was alone with Maurice. Bertie made her conscious of a strangeness.

After the meal the three drew their chairs to the fire, and sat down to talk. The decanters[1] were put on a table near at hand. Isabel knocked the logs on the fire, and clouds of brilliant sparks went up the chimney. Bertie noticed a slight weariness in her bearing.

"You will be glad when your child comes now, Isabel?" he said.

She looked up to him with a quick wan smile.

"Yes, I shall be glad," she answered. "It begins to seem long. Yes, I shall be very glad. So will you, Maurice, won't you?" she added.

"Yes, I shall," replied her husband.

"We are both looking forward so much to having it," she said.

"Yes, of course," said Bertie.

---

[1] decanters:细颈酒瓶。

He was a bachelor, three or four years older than Isabel. He lived in beautiful rooms overlooking the river, guarded by a faithful Scottish man-servant. And he had his friends among the fair sex[1]—not lovers, friends. So long as he could avoid any danger of courtship or marriage, he adored a few good women with constant and unfailing homage, and he was chivalrously fond of quite a number. But if they seemed to encroach on him, he withdrew and detested them.

Isabel knew him very well, knew his beautiful constancy, and kindness, also his incurable weakness, which made him unable ever to enter into close contact of any sort. He was ashamed of himself, because he could not marry, could not approach women physically. He wanted to do so. But he could not. At the centre of him he was afraid, helplessly and even brutally afraid. He had given up hope, had ceased to expect any more that he could escape his own weakness. Hence he was a brilliant and successful barrister, also *litterateur*[2] of high repute, a rich man, and a great social success. At the centre he felt himself neuter[3], nothing.

Isabel knew him well. She despised him even while she admired him. She looked at his sad face, his little short legs, and felt contempt of him. She looked at his dark grey eyes, with their uncanny, almost childlike intuition, and she loved him. He understood amazingly—but she had no fear of his understanding. As a man she patronized him.

And she turned to the impassive, silent figure of her husband. He sat leaning back, with folded arms, and face a little uptilted. His knees were straight and massive. She sighed, picked up the poker, and again began to prod the fire, to rouse the clouds of soft, brilliant sparks.

"Isabel tells me," Bertie began suddenly, "that you have not suffered unbearably from the loss of sight."

Maurice straightened himself to attend, but kept his arms folded.

"No," he said, "not unbearably. Now and again one struggles against it, you know. But there are compensations."

"They say it is much worse to be stone deaf," said Isabel.

"I believe it is," said Bertie. "Are there compensations?" he added, to Maurice.

"Yes. You cease to bother about a great many things." Again Maurice stretched his figure, stretched the strong muscles of his back, and leaned backwards, with uplifted face.

"And that is a relief," said Bertie. "But what is there in place of the bothering? What replaces the activity?"

There was a pause. At length the blind man replied, as out of a negligent, unattentive thinking:

---

[1] the fair sex:女性。
[2] litterateur:(法语)文人。
[3] neuter:中性人。

"Oh, I don't know. There's a good deal when you're not active."

"Is there?" said Bertie. "What, exactly? It always seems to me that when there is no thought and no action, there is nothing."

Again Maurice was slow in replying.

"There is something," he replied. "I couldn't tell you what it is."

And the talk lapsed once more, Isabel and Bertie chatting gossip and reminiscence, the blind man silent.

At length Maurice rose restlessly, a big, obtrusive figure. He felt tight and hampered. He wanted to go away.

"Do you mind," he said, "if I go and speak to Wernham?"

"No—go along, dear," said Isabel.

And he went out. A silence came over the two friends. At length Bertie said:

"Nevertheless, it is a great deprivation[1], Cissie."

"It is, Bertie. I know it is."

"Something lacking all the time," said Bertie.

"Yes, I know. And yet—and yet—Maurice is right. There is something else, something *there*, which you never knew was there, and which you can't express."

"What is there?" asked Bertie.

"I don't know—it's awfully hard to define it—but something strong and immediate. There's something strange in Maurice's presence—indefinable—but I couldn't do without it. I agree that it seems to put one's mind to sleep. But when we're alone I miss nothing; it seems awfully rich, almost splendid, you know."

"I'm afraid I don't follow," said Bertie.

They talked desultorily[2]. The wind blew loudly outside, rain chattered on the window-panes, making a sharp, drum-sound, because of the closed, mellow-golden shutters inside. The logs burned slowly, with hot, almost invisible small flames. Bertie seemed uneasy, there were dark circles round his eyes. Isabel, rich with her approaching maternity, leaned looking into the fire. Her hair curled in odd, loose strands, very pleasing to the man. But she had a curious feeling of old woe in her heart, old, timeless night-woe.

"I suppose we're all deficient somewhere," said Bertie.

"I suppose so," said Isabel wearily.

"Damned, sooner or later."

"I don't know," she said, rousing herself. "I feel quite all right, you know. The child coming seems to make me indifferent to everything, just placid. I can't feel that there's anything to trouble about, you know."

"A good thing, I should say," he replied slowly.

---

[1] deprivation:丧失。

[2] desultorily:随意地,散漫地。

"Well, there it is. I suppose it's just Nature. If only I felt I needn't trouble about Maurice, I should be perfectly content—"

"But you feel you must trouble about him?"

"Well—I don't know—" She even resented this much effort.

The evening passed slowly. Isabel looked at the clock. "I say," she said. "It's nearly ten o'clock. Where can Maurice be? I'm sure they're all in bed at the back. Excuse me a moment."

She went out, returning almost immediately.

"It's all shut up and in darkness," she said. "I wonder where he is. He must have gone out to the farm—"

Bertie looked at her.

"I suppose he'll come in," he said.

"I suppose so," she said. "But it's unusual for him to be out now."

"Would you like me to go out and see?"

"Well—if you wouldn't mind. I'd go, but—" She did not want to make the physical effort.

Bertie put on an old overcoat and took a lantern. He went out from the side door. He shrank from the wet and roaring night. Such weather had a nervous effect on him: too much moisture everywhere made him feel almost imbecile[1]. Unwilling, he went through it all. A dog barked violently at him. He peered in all the buildings. At last, as he opened the upper door of a sort of intermediate barn, he heard a grinding noise, and looking in, holding up his lantern, saw Maurice, in his shirt-sleeves, standing listening, holding the handle of a turnip-pulper[2]. He had been pulping sweet roots, a pile of which lay dimly heaped in a corner behind him.

"That you, Wernham?" said Maurice, listening.

"No, it's me," said Bertie.

A large, half-wild grey cat was rubbing at Maurice's leg. The blind man stooped to rub its sides. Bertie watched the scene, then unconsciously entered and shut the door behind him. He was in a high sort of barn-place, from which, right and left, ran off the corridors in front of the stalled cattle. He watched the slow, stooping motion of the other man, as he caressed the great cat.

Maurice straightened himself.

"You came to look for me?" he said.

"Isabel was a little uneasy," said Bertie.

"I'll come in. I like messing about doing these jobs."

The cat had reared her sinister, feline[3] length against his leg, clawing at his thigh

---

[1] imbecile:愚笨。
[2] turnip-pulper:萝卜捣浆机。pulp:把……捣成浆状。
[3] feline:像猫一般的。

affectionately. He lifted her claws out of his flesh.

"I hope I'm not in your way at all at the Grange here," said Bertie, rather shy and stiff.

"My way? No, not a bit. I'm glad Isabel has somebody to talk to. I'm afraid it's I who am in the way. I know I'm not very lively company. Isabel's all right, don't you think? She's not unhappy, is she?"

"I don't think so."

"What does she say?"

"She says she's very content—only a little troubled about you."

"Why me?"

"Perhaps afraid that you might brood," said Bertie, cautiously.

"She needn't be afraid of that." He continued to caress the flattened grey head of the cat with his fingers. "What I am a bit afraid of," he resumed, "is that she'll find me a dead weight, always alone with me down here."

"I don't think you need think that," said Bertie, though this was what he feared himself.

"I don't know," said Maurice. "Sometimes I feel it isn't fair that she's saddled with[1] me." Then he dropped his voice curiously. "I say," he asked, secretly struggling, "is my face much disfigured? Do you mind telling me?"

"There is the scar," said Bertie, wondering. "Yes, it is a disfigurement. But more pitiable than shocking."

"A pretty bad scar, though," said Maurice.

"Oh, yes."

There was a pause.

"Sometimes I feel I am horrible," said Maurice, in a low voice, talking as if to himself. And Bertie actually felt a quiver of horror.

"That's nonsense," he said.

Maurice again straightened himself, leaving the cat.

"There's no telling," he said. Then again, in an odd tone, he added: "I don't really know you, do I?"

"Probably not," said Bertie.

"Do you mind if I touch you?"

The lawyer shrank away instinctively. And yet, out of very philanthropy, he said, in a small voice: "Not at all."

But he suffered as the blind man stretched out a strong, naked hand to him. Maurice accidentally knocked off Bertie's hat.

"I thought you were taller," he said, starting. Then he laid his hand on Bertie Reid's head, closing the dome of the skull in a soft, firm grasp, gathering it, as it were;

---

[1] saddled with:成为……负担,拖累。

then, shifting his grasp and softly closing again, with a fine, close pressure, till he had covered the skull and the face of the smaller man, tracing the brows, and touching the full, closed eyes, touching the small nose and the nostrils, the rough, short moustache, the mouth, the rather strong chin. The hand of the blind man grasped the shoulder, the arm, the hand of the other man. He seemed to take him, in the soft, travelling grasp.

"You seem young," he said quietly, at last.

The lawyer stood almost annihilated, unable to answer.

"Your head seems tender, as if you were young," Maurice repeated. "So do your hands. Touch my eyes, will you? —touch my scar."

Now Bertie quivered with revulsion. Yet he was under the power of the blind man, as if hypnotized. He lifted his hand, and laid the fingers on the scar, on the scarred eyes. Maurice suddenly covered them with his own hand, pressed the fingers of the other man upon his disfigured eye-sockets, trembling in every fibre, and rocking slightly, slowly, from side to side. He remained thus for a minute or more, whilst Bertie stood as if in a swoon[1], unconscious, imprisoned.

Then suddenly Maurice removed the hand of the other man from his brow, and stood holding it in his own.

"Oh, my God," he said, "we shall know each other now, shan't we? We shall know each other now."

Bertie could not answer. He gazed mute and terror-struck, overcome by his own weakness. He knew he could not answer. He had an unreasonable fear, lest the other man should suddenly destroy him. Whereas Maurice was actually filled with hot, poignant love, the passion of friendship. Perhaps it was this very passion of friendship which Bertie shrank from most.

"We're all right together now, aren't we?" said Maurice. "It's all right now, as long as we live, so far as we're concerned?"

"Yes," said Bertie, trying by any means to escape.

Maurice stood with head lifted, as if listening. The new delicate fulfilment of mortal friendship had come as a revelation and surprise to him, something exquisite and unhoped-for. He seemed to be listening to hear if it were real.

Then he turned for his coat.

"Come," he said, "we'll go to Isabel."

Bertie took the lantern and opened the door. The cat disappeared. The two men went in silence along the causeways. Isabel, as they came, thought their footsteps sounded strange. She looked up pathetically and anxiously for their entrance. There seemed a curious elation about Maurice. Bertie was haggard, with sunken eyes.

"What is it?" she asked.

"We've become friends," said Maurice, standing with his feet apart, like a strange

---

[1] swoon:晕厥。

colossus[1].

"Friends!" re-echoed Isabel. And she looked again at Bertie. He met her eyes with a furtive, haggard look; his eyes were as if glazed with misery.

"I'm so glad," she said, in sheer perplexity.

"Yes," said Maurice.

He was indeed so glad. Isabel took his hand with both hers, and held it fast.

"You'll be happier now, dear," she said.

But she was watching Bertie. She knew that he had one desire—to escape from this intimacy, this friendship, which had been thrust upon him. He could not bear it that he had been touched by the blind man, his insane reserve broken in. He was like a mollusk[2] whose shell is broken.

1922

赏 析

短篇小说《盲人》的主题是"孤独"和"交流",这体现在两组人物——伊莎贝拉和莫里斯,伯蒂和莫里斯——鲜明的对比中。表面上看,莫里斯与伊莎贝尔相亲相爱,但莫里斯的失明把夫妻俩隔绝在两个不同的世界里,莫里斯喜欢待在黑暗的马棚里,而伊莎贝尔总是待在明亮的屋子里。伊莎贝尔去马棚寻找丈夫时对黑暗满怀恐惧,而黑暗却是盲人非常习惯的。伊莎贝尔无法体会,当然也就难以理解盲人丈夫的世界,她只希望回到自己的世界里:"每次他们穿过那道隔门,回到自己宁静、漂亮的领地,伊莎贝尔总是很高兴。她有点儿怕他,怕他呆在后屋那个令人讨厌的牲畜栏里。"伊莎贝尔的远亲伯蒂和莫里斯的对比更为突出,从外貌到个性,到职业,两人都大相径庭。莫里斯高个子,两手阔大发红,双腿粗壮。伯蒂小个子,双手细白,两腿短小。莫里斯是个干粗活的农夫,伯蒂是个"文人"、"作家",只和语言、精神打交道。两组对比暗示了伯蒂的话,"我想我们多少都有些缺陷",这"缺陷"在三个人物身上表现不同:身体的残疾(莫里斯)、情感的缺失(伯蒂)和心灵的单调(伊莎贝尔)。他们都处在某种孤独中。

在小说末尾,莫里斯请伯蒂摸一摸自己的瞎眼和伤疤,他突然把手按在伯蒂的指尖上。这一有些莫名其妙又突如其来的动作有着深刻的含义:作为一个盲人,莫里斯渴望交流,而且是通过实实在在的"触摸"去交流。对劳伦斯来说,真正的交流和理解不是纯精神的,而需要物质作为媒介,是对物体的真实感知。这种即时的、直接的理解比视觉,甚至智力更接近真实的存在(authentic being)。伯蒂害怕交流,在被迫与莫里斯"接触"后,他委顿的神情暗示其自闭的灵魂最终被摧毁,而勇于去交流的莫里斯在精神上得到了拯救。

劳伦斯善于通过外部描写来刻画人物在心理上的挣扎。在故事结构上,看似平淡无奇的情节发展其实为结尾突然到来的高潮做了充分的铺陈,最后以一个隐喻结尾,令人深思。

---

[1] colossus:巨人。
[2] mollusk:软体动物。

相关评论

Character Transformations in D．H．Lawrence's "The Blind Man" And "Horse Dealer's Daughter"

Anonymous

In D. H. Lawrence's stories "The Blind Man" and "The Horse Dealer's Daughter," the reader watches as characters move from having something missing in their lives, to being truly whole.

Lawrence uses images of darkness to illustrate the emotions of his characters. In "The Blind Man," Isabel goes to look for Maurice and when she steps into the stable where he is, "The darkness seemed to be in a strange swirl of violent life". The darkness that swirled around Isabel is the darkness in which Maurice lives. The "Horse Dealer's Daughter", is also consumed in darkness, as seen in the description of the dwindling[1] town. The description reads like a disaster report on the five o'clock news: "across a shallow dip in the country, the small town was clustered like a smoldering ash, a tower, a spire, a heap of low, raw, extinct houses." To live in a town such as this, a person would become part of the "smoldering ash" as Mabel had. When Mabel was with her brothers she "sat on like one condemned," as they discussed her fate. She stayed quiet, working in the house because the family could no longer afford the hired help they once had. They could, in fact, no longer afford the horses that once brought them money. As the family breaks apart, with each sibling going his separate way, Mabel finds herself trapped by her emotions.

There is a great tension felt by each of Lawrence's characters. Mabel, in "The Horse Dealer's Daughter," and Maurice, in "The Blind Man," are excellent examples of this tension. Mabel's tension seems to remain an internal struggle, while Maurice's affects his wife greatly. After closer examination, it is apparent that Mabel's internal struggles become evident as she interacts with her brothers. She works in the kitchen and rarely answers them when they speak to her. She has pushed aside any traits she may have possessed and has become like a hired hand, going about her work, not speaking. Maurice's struggles are shown through his actions also. When Bertie and Isabel are talking after dinner, Maurice excuses himself. He seems uncomfortable in the situation and consequently retires himself to the darkness of the stable. It is not until Bertie goes out to look for him that Maurice confronts his emotions.

The characters of Maurice and Mabel move toward wholeness as they confront the emotions they have previously denied. Maurice meets Bertie and, in the moment that he touches Bertie's face, becomes whole. There is a connection between the two men, and

---

[1] dwindling: 逐渐缩小的。

even though the feeling is not mutual, Maurice feels that he has met a great friend. This friendship was the missing element in his life. For Mabel, the missing element was a relationship that allowed her to be herself. After walking into the pond to end her life, she is resurrected[1] by the doctor, who then becomes the center of the relationship she was searching for. Mabel asks for the doctor's love, and when he agrees to give her that love, she is once again the open caring person she has repressed.

Lawrence believes that "To be alive, to be man alive, to be whole man alive; that is the point." He shows this through the characters of his stories, especially Mabel in "The Horse Dealer's Daughter" and Maurice in "The Blind Man." These characters both undergo a transformation, ending with wholeness they did not possess before.

Source：http://www.123helpme.com/view.asp?id=57985(2010-8-2)

War Experience and Touch in "The Blind Man"
Nils Clausson

There is no reason to believe that my reading of "The Blind Man" is incompatible with a situated, contextualized, historical interpretation of the story. If I were to move from my reading of the story to an historical interpretation of it, I would begin by asking what strikes me as the most pertinent[2] question about Maurice's blindness: where did it come from? The answer, of course, is that Maurice "had been blinded in Flanders": "The Blind Man" in a post-War story and Maurice's (and Lawrence's) pursuit of an alternative to "the fribbling[3] intervention of mind, or moral, or what not" can be very precisely contextualized historically within Lawrence's reaction to the cataclysm[4] known as the Great War[5]. (The story was written in the months leading up to the Armistice[6] and completed a few weeks after it.) For Lawrence, the carnage[7] of the War was the logical outcome of "the crucifixion of the procreative body for the glorification of the spirit." The binary opposites in the story are not "suprahistorical[8]" but take on their precise "pragmatic and historical" meaning from a particular historical situation that profoundly shaped Lawrence's thought and writing. Maurice's emphasis on touch rather than speech as a form of communication arises directly from his experience of the War. His desperate need to believe that he has achieved intimacy with Bertie can be interpreted as an attempt to recreate after the War the same homosocial[9] bonding

---

[1] resurrected：复生。
[2] pertinent：相关的。
[3] fribbling：不重要的，无价值的。
[4] cataclysm：灾难，(社会政治的)大变动。
[5] the Great War：指第一次世界大战。
[6] the Armistice：停战，停战协定。
[7] carnage：(战场上的)残杀，大屠杀。
[8] suprahistorical：这里指脱离历史的。
[9] homosocial：同性社交的。

and intimacy, touch, which took place between soldiers in the trenches of Flanders and France during the War. For many of the soldiers who fought in the War, their experience was literally "unspeakable." Repeatedly they said that there was no point in talking to family and non-combatants about their experiences in the trenches because no one who was not there could possibly comprehend the War. Although we are not explicitly told that Bertie Reid did not serve in the War, the implication certainly is that he did not. Thus Maurice's failure to achieve intimacy with Bertie is historically contextualized. Ironically, the one thing that Maurice, Isabel and Bertie do not talk about in the story—the War—is the very thing that is responsible for Maurice's blindness in the first place. Queer and ironical, indeed!

Source: *College Literature*. 34.1（Winter 2007）: p106.

问题与思考

1. Why do you suppose the story is called "The Blind Man"? What is the symbolic significance of Maurice's blindness and the darkness which overshadows the whole story?
2. What psychological and emotional changes do the three major characters experience in the coming of Bertie, and in the "reconciliation" between Bertie and Maurice?
3. What are the dominant image patterns of the story? What is their function?
4. What does the story have to say about the nature of love? And about the relationship between men and women?
5. Lawrence often connects sight with intellect, and touch with instinct. Is "The Blind Man" a story of the conflict between them?

阅读链接

1. http://en.wikipedia.org/wiki/D._H._Lawrence#Death：劳伦斯生平、创作、文学评价及有关链接。
2. http://ebooks.adelaide.edu.au/l/lawrence/dh/prussian：短篇小说集《普鲁士官员及其他故事》的原文。
3. http://thinkexist.com/quotes/d.h._lawrence：劳伦斯作品中的名言隽语。
4. http://www.gradesaver.com/sons-and-lovers/study-guide/about：《儿子与情人》学习指导。

John Steinbeck (1902—1968)

作者简介

约翰·斯坦贝克(John Steinbeck,1902—1968)出生在加利福尼亚州的小镇萨利纳斯,在靠近太平洋的蒙特里市长大,这里成为他许多小说的背景。斯坦贝克的母亲是一名教师,在她的影响下,他很早就阅读了许多世界文学名著,并爱上了写作,经常给所在中学的报纸写文章。1920—1925年,斯坦贝克在斯坦福大学读书,但只去上他感兴趣的课。在此期间,他常到校外打工,认识了社会各色人群。斯坦贝克很早就知道自己会成为一名作家,他的关注点是普通人的生活。1925年他没有获得学位就离开了大学,前往纽约,在《纽约日报》当记者。不久又返回加州,投身到创作中。在美国参加第二次世界大战后,斯坦贝克以《纽约先驱论坛报》战地记者的身份去过英国、北非和意大利。1962年,他获诺贝尔文学奖。1966年初斯坦贝克作为纽约《新闻日报》的战地记者前往越南,之后返回美国继续文学创作。1968年,他健康恶化,同年12月因心脏病发作逝世,终年66岁。

文学创作

斯坦贝克虽创作于现代主义时期,但其作品却是多色调的,杂糅了地方色彩、现实主义、自然主义和浪漫主义。他的小说大都以其家乡萨利纳斯和蒙特里为背景,可归类于社会小说,多表现农业工人的经济问题,其中隐现的乡土气息淡化了说教的感觉,而多了几分亲切。斯坦贝克最出色的作品发表于20世纪30年代经济大萧条时期,主要有三部长篇小说:《胜负未决》(*In Dubious Battle*,1936)、《人与鼠》(*Of Mice and Men*,1937)和《愤怒的葡萄》(*The Grapes of Wrath*,1939)。《胜负未决》是斯坦贝克"工人三部曲"的第一部,描写了加利福尼亚托加斯山谷采果工人与农场主的斗争。在劳资双方的激烈交锋中,罢工组织者吉姆牺牲,但斗争依然在继续。《人与鼠》写的是两个流离失所的农业工人的故事,包含了种族主义、孤独、精神疾病和为个人独立而挣扎等主题。"工人三部曲"的最后一部《愤怒的葡萄》是斯坦贝克最广为人知的杰作,出版次年获普利策奖。它以俄克拉荷马州的乔德一家的痛苦经历为主线,讲述了"沙尘暴"移民在加利福尼亚州所遭遇的不公和屈辱。他们沿着公路向西部艰难行进,历经种种磨难。小说展现了大萧条时期美国农业方面的凄凉景象,具有史诗般的气势。

斯坦贝克的《煎饼坪》(*Tortilla Flat*,1935)以加利福尼亚蒙特里的派沙诺人(paisanos)生活为题材,书中主人公无忧无虑的生活方式表现了对中产阶级统治下的美国主流文化的反抗。散文《同查利旅行》(*Travels with Charley*,1962)描写了斯坦贝克和自己的爱犬在美国三个月的游历,这是迄今对美国最生动的描述之一。

斯坦贝克常采用民间故事的叙事形式,强调节奏和重复,以营造出诗意;而由对话串连起来的简洁描述,又显出戏剧的特点。

作　　品

The Chrysanthemums

　　The high gray-flannel fog of winter closed off the Salinas Valley[1] from the sky and from all the rest of the world. On every side it sat like a lid on the mountains and made of the great valley a closed pot. On the broad, level land floor the gang plows bit deep[2] and left the black earth shining like metal where the shares[3] had cut. On the foothill ranches across the Salinas River, the yellow stubble fields[4] seemed to be bathed in pale cold sunshine, but there was no sunshine in the valley now in December. The thick willow scrub[5] along the river flamed with sharp and positive yellow leaves.

　　It was a time of quiet and of waiting. The air was cold and tender. A light wind blew up from the southwest so that the farmers were mildly hopeful of a good rain before long; but fog and rain did not go together.

　　Across the river, on Henry Allen's foothill ranch there was little work to be done, for the hay was cut and stored and the orchards were plowed up to receive the rain deeply when it should come. The cattle on the higher slopes were becoming shaggy[6]

---

〔1〕 Salinas Valley:萨利纳斯山谷,在美国加州海岸山岭区,位于旧金山以南。斯坦贝克生于萨利纳斯城,常以萨利纳斯山谷作为故事发生的地点。
〔2〕 the gang plows bit deep:多铧犁深深地翻耕土地。bit:bite 的过去式,意为"耕,犁"。
〔3〕 shares:犁铧。
〔4〕 stubble fields:收获过后仍留下短谷茬的土地,亩茬地。
〔5〕 The thick willow scrub:浓密低矮的柳树丛。
〔6〕 shaggy:(头发、皮毛)长而厚的;蓬乱的。

and rough-coated.

Elisa Allen, working in her flower garden, looked down across the yard and saw Henry, her husband, talking to two men in business suits. The three of them stood by the tractor shed, each man with one foot on the side of the little Fordson[1]. They smoked cigarettes and studied the machine as they talked.

Elisa watched them for a moment and then went back to her work. She was thirty-five. Her face was lean and strong and her eyes were as clear as water. Her figure looked blocked and heavy in her gardening costume, a man's black hat pulled low down over her eyes, clod-hopper shoes,[2] a figured print dress[3] almost completely covered by a big corduroy apron[4] with four big pockets to hold the snips, the trowel and scratcher,[5] the seeds and the knife she worked with. She wore heavy leather gloves to protect her hands while she worked.

She was cutting down the old year's chrysanthemum stalks with a pair of short and powerful scissors. She looked down toward the men by the tractor shed now and then. Her face was eager and mature and handsome; even her work with the scissors was over-eager, over-powerful. The chrysanthemum stems seemed too small and easy for her energy.

She brushed a cloud of hair out of her eyes with the back of her glove, and left a smudge of earth on her cheek in doing it. Behind her stood the neat white farm house with red geraniums close-banked[6] around it as high as the windows. It was a hard-swept looking little house, with hard-polished windows, and a clean mud-mat on the front steps.

Elisa cast another glance toward the tractor shed. The strangers were getting into their Ford coupe.[7] She took off a glove and put her strong fingers down into the forest of new green chrysanthemum sprouts that were growing around the old roots. She spread the leaves and looked down among the close-growing stems. No aphids were there, no sowbugs or snails or cutworms.[8] Her terrier fingers[9] destroyed such pests before they could get started.

Elisa started at the sound of her husband's voice. He had come near quietly, and he leaned over the wire fence that protected her flower garden from cattle and dogs and chickens.

---

[1] Fordson：Fordson 牌小汽车。
[2] clod-hopper shoes：粗糙沉重的靴子，通常是农夫穿的。
[3] a figured print dress：一件有图案的印花布连衣裙。
[4] a big corduroy apron：一条大号灯芯绒围裙。
[5] the snips, the trowel and scratcher：(花匠用的)平头剪、泥铲和刮痕器。
[6] red geraniums close-banked：紧紧排成一行的红色天竺葵。
[7] Ford coupe：Ford 牌小汽车。
[8] aphids, sowbugs, cutworms：(虫)蚜虫，地鳖，夜盗蛾。
[9] terrier fingers：毫不留情的手指。terrier 是名词，意为"专为猎杀小动物而驯养的狗"，这里作形容词用。

"At it again," he said. "You've got a strong new crop[1] coming."

Elisa straightened her back and pulled on the gardening glove again. "Yes. They'll be strong this coming year." In her tone and on her face there was a little smugness.

"You've got a gift with things," Henry observed. "Some of those yellow chrysanthemums you had this year were ten inches across. I wish you'd work out in the orchard and raise some apples that big."

Her eyes sharpened. "Maybe I could do it, too. I've a gift with things, all right. My mother had it. She could stick anything in the ground and make it grow. She said it was having planters' hands that knew how to do it."

"Well, it sure works with flowers," he said.

"Henry, who were those men you were talking to?"

"Why, sure, that's what I came to tell you. They were from the Western Meat Company. I sold those thirty head of three-year-old steers[2]. Got nearly my own price, too."

"Good," she said. "Good for you."

"And I thought," he continued, "I thought how it's Saturday afternoon, and we might go into Salinas for dinner at a restaurant, and then to a picture show—to celebrate, you see."

"Good," she repeated. "Oh, yes. That will be good."

Henry put on his joking tone. "There's fights[3] tonight. How'd you like to go to the fights?"

"Oh, no," she said breathlessly. "No, I wouldn't like fights."

"Just fooling, Elisa. We'll go to a movie. Let's see. It's two now. I'm going to take Scotty[4] and bring down those steers from the hill. It'll take us maybe two hours. We'll go in town about five and have dinner at the Cominos Hotel. Like that?"

"Of course I'll like it. It's good to eat away from home."

"All right, then. I'll go get up a couple of horses."

She said, "I'll have plenty of time transplant some of these sets, I guess."

She heard her husband calling Scotty down by the barn. And a little later she saw the two men ride up the pale yellow hillside in search of the steers.

There was a little square sandy bed kept for rooting the chrysanthemums. With her trowel she turned the soil over and over, and smoothed it and patted it firm. Then she dug ten parallel trenches to receive the sets. Back at the chrysanthemum bed she pulled out the little crisp shoots, trimmed off the leaves of each one with her scissors and laid it on a small orderly pile.

---

[1] crop:这里指 Elisa 种的菊花。crop 一般指庄稼,Henry 却用它来指花;从作者安排的这个细节可以看出 Henry 对 Elisa 种花并不欣赏,也可看出他们的夫妻关系。
[2] steers:菜牛。
[3] fights:拳击赛。
[4] Scotty:Henry 农场上的帮手。

A squeak of wheels and plod of hoofs came from the road. Elisa looked up. The country road ran along the dense bank of willows and cottonwoods[1] that bordered the river, and up this road came a curious vehicle, curiously drawn. It was an old spring-wagon, with a round canvas top on it like the cover of a prairie schooner.[2] It was drawn by an old bay horse and a little grey-and-white burro[3]. A big stubble-bearded man sat between the cover flaps and drove the crawling team. Underneath the wagon, between the hind wheels, a lean and rangy mongrel dog[4] walked sedately. Words were painted on the canvas in clumsy, crooked letters. "Pots, pans, knives, sisors, lawn mores,[5] Fixed." Two rows of articles, and the triumphantly definitive "Fixed" below.[6] The black paint had run down in little sharp points beneath each letter.

Elisa, squatting on the ground, watched[7] to see the crazy, loose-jointed wagon pass by. But it didn't pass. It turned into the farm road in front of her house, crooked old wheels skirling and squeaking. The rangy dog darted from between the wheels and ran ahead. Instantly the two ranch shepherds[8] flew out at him. Then all three stopped, and with stiff and quivering tails, with taut straight legs, with ambassadorial dignity, they slowly circled, sniffing daintily. The caravan[9] pulled up to Elisa's wire fence and stopped. Now the newcomer dog, feeling outnumbered, lowered his tail and retired under the wagon with raised hackles[10] and bared teeth.

The man on the wagon seat called out, "That's a bad dog in a fight when he gets started."

Elisa laughed. "I see he is. How soon does he generally get started?"

The man caught up her laughter and echoed it heartily. "Sometimes not for weeks and weeks," he said. He climbed stiffly down, over the wheel. The horse and the donkey drooped like unwatered flowers.

Elisa saw that he was a very big man. Although his hair and beard were graying, he did not look old. His worn black suit was wrinkled and spotted with grease. The laughter had disappeared from his face and eyes the moment his laughing voice ceased. His eyes were dark, and they were full of the brooding that gets in the eyes of teamsters[11] and of sailors. The calloused hands he rested on the wire fence were cracked, and every crack

---

[1] cottonwoods: 三角叶杨树。
[2] prairie schooner: (美国早期移民过大草原时用的)有篷大车, 也称作 prairie wagon。
[3] burro: 小毛驴。
[4] a lean and rangy mongrel dog: 一只身体瘦削、四肢细长的杂种狗。
[5] sisors, lawn mores = scissors, lawn mowers; 作者在这里故意用拼写错误来表明人物的身份。
[6] Two rows of article, … "Fixed" below = Two rows of articles were printed above and the triumphantly definitive "Fixed" was written below. Two rows of articles pots… lawn mores 这类东西的名称分别写成了两行。
[7] watched: 等待的。
[8] the two ranch shepherds: 农场里的两只牧羊犬。
[9] caravan: 这里指有篷马车。
[10] hackles: (狗等动物)因恼怒而颈背部竖起的毛。
[11] teamsters: 联畜运输车驾驭者。

was a black line. He took off his battered hat.

"I'm off my general road, ma'am," he said. "Does this dirt road cut over across the river to the Los Angeles highway?"

Elisa stood up and shoved the thick scissors in her apron pocket. "Well, yes, it does, but it winds around and then fords the river.[1] I don't think your team could pull through the sand."

He replied with some asperity[2], "It might surprise you what them beasts can pull through."

"When they get started?" she asked.

He smiled for a second. "Yes. When they get started."

"Well," said Elisa, "I think you'll save time if you go back to the Salinas road and pick up the highway there."

He drew a big finger down the chicken wire and made it sing.[3] "I ain't in any hurry, ma'am. I go from Seattle to San Diego and back every year. Takes all my time. About six months each way. I aim to follow nice weather."

Elisa took off her gloves and stuffed them in the apron pocket with the scissors. She touched the under edge of her man's hat, searching for fugitive hairs. "That sounds like a nice kind of a way to live," she said.

He leaned confidentially over the fence. "Maybe you noticed the writing on my wagon. I mend pots and sharpen knives and scissors. You got any of them things to do?"

"Oh, no," she said quickly. "Nothing like that." Her eyes hardened with resistance.

"Scissors is the worst thing," he explained. "Most people just ruin scissors trying to sharpen'em, but I know how. I got a special tool. It's a little bobbit kind of thing, and patented. But it sure does the trick."

"No. My scissors are all sharp."

"All right, then. Take a pot," he continued earnestly, "a bent pot, or a pot with a hole. I can make it like new so you don't have to buy no new ones.[4] That's a saving for you."

"No," she said shortly. "I tell you I have nothing like that for you to do."

His face fell to an exaggerated sadness. His voice took on a whining undertone. "I ain't had a thing to do today. Maybe I won't have no supper tonight. You see I'm off my regular road. I know folks on the highway clear from Seattle to San Diego. They save

---

[1] fords the river: 跨过河流。
[2] asperity: (声音)刺耳。
[3] He drew a big... and make it sing: 他用粗壮的手指拨了一下栅栏上细软的铁丝, 使它发出嗡嗡的声响。chicken wire: 铁丝织网, 用来做鸡栏。
[4] you don't have to buy no new ones = you don't have to buy any new ones。注意这句话是不规范的英语表达。这篇小说中类似的不规范用法还有: 用 them 代表 these 或 those, 用 ain't 代替 haven't, isn't。作者用不规范英语来表明人物的身份。

their things for me to sharpen up because they know I do it so good and save them money."

"I'm sorry," Elisa said irritably. "I haven't anything for you to do."

His eyes left her face and fell to searching the ground. They roamed about until they came to the chrysanthemum bed where she had been working. "What's them plants, ma'am?"

The irritation and resistance melted from Elisa's face. "Oh, those are chrysanthemums, giant whites and yellows. I raise them every year, bigger than anybody around here."

"Kind of a long-stemmed flower? Looks like a quick puff of colored smoke?" he asked.

"That's it. What a nice way to describe them."

"They smell kind of nasty till you get used to them," he said.

"It's a good bitter smell," she retorted, "not nasty at all."

He changed his tone quickly. "I like the smell myself."

"I had ten-inch blooms this year," she said.

The man leaned farther over the fence. "Look. I know a lady down the road a piece, has got the nicest garden you ever seen. Got nearly every kind of flower but no chrysanthemums. Last time I was mending a copper-bottom washtub for her (that was a hard job but I do it good), she said to me, 'If you ever run acrost some nice chrysanthemums I wish you'd try to get me a few seeds.' That's what she told me."

Elisa's eyes grew alert and eager. "She couldn't have known much about chrysanthemums. You can raise them from seed, but it's much easier to root the little sprouts you see there."

"Oh," he said. "I s'pose[1] I can't take none to her, then."

"Why yes you can," Elisa cried. "I can put some in damp sand, and you can carry them right along with you. They'll take root in the pot if you keep them damp. And then she can transplant them."

"She'd sure like to have some, ma'am. You say they're nice ones?"

"Beautiful," she said. "Oh, beautiful." Her eyes shone. She tore off the battered hat and shook out her dark pretty hair. "I'll put them in a flower pot, and you can take them right with you. Come into the yard."

While the man came through the picket gate[2] Elisa ran excitedly along the geranium-bordered path to the back of the house. And she returned carrying a big red flower pot. The gloves were forgotten now. She kneeled on the ground by the starting bed and dug up the sandy soil with her fingers and scooped it into the bright new flower pot. Then she picked up the little pile of shoots she had prepared. With her strong

---

[1] s'pose = suppose.
[2] the picket gate: 用木桩钉成的大门。

fingers she pressed them into the sand and tamped around them with her knuckles. The man stood over her. "I'll tell you what to do," she said. "You remember so you can tell the lady."

"Yes, I'll try to remember."

"Well, look. These will take root in about a month. Then she must set them out, about a foot apart in good rich earth like this, see?" She lifted a handful of dark soil for him to look at. "They'll grow fast and tall. Now remember this. In July tell her to cut them down, about eight inches from the ground."

"Before they bloom?" he asked.

"Yes, before they bloom." Her face was tight with eagerness. "They'll grow right up again. About the last of September the buds will start."

She stopped and seemed perplexed. "It's the budding that takes the most care," she said hesitantly. "I don't know how to tell you." She looked deep into his eyes, searchingly. His mouth opened a little, and he seemed to be listening. "I'll try to tell you," she said. "Did you ever hear of planting hands?"

"Can't say I have, ma'am."

"Well, I can only tell you what it feels like. It's when you're picking off the buds you don't want. Everything goes right down into your fingertips. You watch your fingers work. They do it themselves. You can feel how it is. They pick and pick the buds. They never make a mistake. They're with the plant. Do you see? Your fingers and the plant. You can feel that, right up your arm. They know. They never make a mistake. You can feel it. When you're like that you can't do anything wrong. Do you see that? Can you understand that?"

She was kneeling on the ground looking up at him. Her breast swelled passionately.

The man's eyes narrowed. He looked away self-consciously. "Maybe I know," he said. "Sometimes in the night in the wagon there—"

Elisa's voice grew husky. She broke in on him. "I've never lived as you do, but I know what you mean. When the night is dark—why, the stars are sharp-pointed, and there's quiet. Why, you rise up and up! Every pointed star gets driven into your body. It's like that. Hot and sharp and—lovely."

Kneeling there, her hand went out toward his legs in the greasy black trousers. Her hesitant fingers almost touched the cloth. Then her hand dropped to the ground. She crouched low like a fawning dog.[1]

He said, "It's nice, just like you say. Only when you don't have no dinner, it ain't."

She stood up then, very straight, and her face was ashamed. She held the flower pot out to him and placed it gently in his arms. "Here. Put it in your wagon, on the seat, where you can watch it. Maybe I can find something for you to do."

---

[1] a fawning dog: 一只摇尾乞怜的狗。

At the back of the house she dug in the can pile and found two old and battered aluminum saucepans. She carried them back and gave them to him. "Here, maybe you can fix these."

His manner changed. He became professional. "Good as new I can fix them." At the back of his wagon he set a little anvil[1], and out of an oily tool box dug a small machine hammer. Elisa came through the gate to watch him while he pounded out the dents in the kettles.[2] His mouth grew sure and knowing. At a difficult part of the work he sucked his under-lip.

"You sleep right in the wagon?" Elisa asked.

"Right in the wagon, ma'am. Rain or shine I'm dry as a cow in there."

"It must be nice," she said. "It must be very nice. I wish women could do such things."

"It ain't the right kind of a life for a woman."

Her upper lip raised a little, showing her teeth. "How do you know? How can you tell?" she said.

"I don't know, ma'am," he protested. "Of course I don't know. Now here's your kettles, done. You don't have to buy no new ones."

"How much?"

"Oh, fifty cents'll do. I keep my prices down and my work good. That's why I have all them satisfied customers up and down the highway."

Elisa brought him a fifty-cent piece from the house and dropped it in his hand. "You might be surprised to have a rival some time. I can sharpen scissors, too. And I can beat the dents out of little pots. I could show you what a woman might do."

He put his hammer back in the oily box and shoved the little anvil out of sight. "It would be a lonely life for a woman, ma'am, and a scarey life, too, with animals creeping under the wagon all night." He climbed over the singletree[3], steadying himself with a hand on the burro's white rump[4]. He settled himself in the seat, picked up the lines. "Thank you kindly, ma'am," he said. "I'll do like you told me; I'll go back and catch the Salinas road."

"Mind," she called, "if you're long in getting there, keep the sand damp."

"Sand, ma'am? ... Sand? Oh, sure. You mean around the chrysanthemums. Sure I will." He clucked his tongue. The beasts leaned luxuriously into their collars[5]. The mongrel dog took his place between the back wheels. The wagon turned and crawled out the entrance road and back the way it had come, along the river.

Elisa stood in front of her wire fence watching the slow progress of the caravan.

---

[1] anvil：铁砧。
[2] he pounded out... in the kettles：他将锅上的凹痕敲平。the kettles 即前面提到的 the saucepans。
[3] singletree：车前横木。
[4] rump：(兽的)臀部。
[5] collars：马颈上的轭具。

Her shoulders were straight, her head thrown back, her eyes half-closed, so that the scene came vaguely into them. Her lips moved silently, forming the words "Good-bye—good-bye." Then she whispered, "That's a bright direction. There's a glowing there." The sound of her whisper startled her. She shook herself free and looked about to see whether anyone had been listening. Only the dogs had heard. They lifted their heads toward her from their sleeping in the dust, and then stretched out their chins and settled asleep again. Elisa turned and ran hurriedly into the house.

In the kitchen she reached behind the stove and felt the water tank. It was full of hot water from the noonday cooking. In the bathroom she tore off her soiled clothes and flung them into the corner. And then she scrubbed herself with a little block of pumice[1], legs and thighs, loins and chest and arms, until her skin was scratched and red. When she had dried herself she stood in front of a mirror in her bedroom and looked at her body. She tightened her stomach and threw out her chest. She turned and looked over her shoulder at her back.

After a while she began to dress, slowly. She put on her newest underclothing and her nicest stockings and the dress which was the symbol of her prettiness. She worked carefully on her hair, pencilled her eyebrows and rouged her lips.

Before she was finished she heard the little thunder of hoofs and the shouts of Henry and his helper as they drove the red steers into the corral[2]. She heard the gate bang shut and set herself for Henry's arrival.

His step sounded on the porch. He entered the house calling, "Elisa, where are you?"

"In my room, dressing. I'm not ready. There's hot water for your bath. Hurry up. It's getting late."

When she heard him splashing in the tub, Elisa laid his dark suit on the bed, and shirt and socks and tie beside it. She stood his polished shoes on the floor beside the bed. Then she went to the porch and sat primly and stiffly down. She looked toward the river road where the willow-line was still yellow with frosted leaves so that under the high grey fog they seemed a thin band of sunshine. This was the only color in the grey afternoon. She sat unmoving for a long time. Her eyes blinked rarely.

Henry came banging out of the door, shoving his tie inside his vest as he came. Elisa stiffened and her face grew tight. Henry stopped short and looked at her. "Why—why, Elisa. You look so nice!"

"Nice? You think I look nice? What do you mean by 'nice'?"

Henry blundered on. "I don't know. I mean you look different, strong and happy."

"I am strong? Yes, strong. What do you mean 'strong'?"

He looked bewildered. "You're playing some kind of a game," he said helplessly. "It's a kind of a play. You look strong enough to break a calf over your knee, happy

---

[1] pumice:浮石块。
[2] corral:牲畜栅。

enough to eat it like a watermelon."

For a second she lost her rigidity. "Henry! Don't talk like that. You didn't know what you said." She grew complete again. "I'm strong," she boasted. "I never knew before how strong."

Henry looked down toward the tractor shed, and when he brought his eyes back to her, they were his own again. "I'll get out the car. You can put on your coat while I'm starting."

Elisa went into the house. She heard him drive to the gate and idle down his motor,[1] and then she took a long time to put on her hat. She pulled it here and pressed it there. When Henry turned the motor off she slipped into her coat and went out.

The little roadster[2] bounced along on the dirt road by the river, raising the birds and driving the rabbits into the brush. Two cranes flapped heavily over the willow-line and dropped into the river-bed.

Far ahead on the road Elisa saw a dark speck. She knew.

She tried not to look as they passed it, but her eyes would not obey. She whispered to herself sadly, "He might have thrown them off the road. That wouldn't have been much trouble, not very much. But he kept the pot," she explained. "He had to keep the pot. That's why he couldn't get them off the road."

The roadster turned a bend and she saw the caravan ahead. She swung full around toward her husband so she could not see the little covered wagon and the mismatched team as the car passed them.

In a moment it was over. The thing was done. She did not look back. She said loudly, to be heard above the motor, "It will be good, tonight, a good dinner."

"Now you're changed again," Henry complained. He took one hand from the wheel and patted her knee. "I ought to take you in to dinner oftener. It would be good for both of us. We get so heavy out on the ranch."

"Henry," she asked, "could we have wine at dinner?"

"Sure we could. Say! That will be fine."

She was silent for a while; then she said, "Henry, at those prize fights, do the men hurt each other very much?"

"Sometimes a little, not often. Why?"

"Well, I've read how they break noses, and blood runs down their chests. I've read how the fighting gloves get heavy and soggy with blood."

He looked around at her. "What's the matter, Elisa? I didn't know you read things like that." He brought the car to a stop, then turned to the right over the Salinas River bridge.

"Do any women ever go to the fights?" she asked.

---

[1] idle down his motor: 让马达空转。

[2] roadster: 双人座敞篷汽车。

"Oh, sure, some. What's the matter, Elisa? Do you want to go? I don't think you'd like it, but I'll take you if you really want to go."

She relaxed limply in the seat. "Oh, no. No. I don't want to go. I'm sure I don't." Her face was turned away from him. "It will be enough if we can have wine. It will be plenty." She turned up her coat collar so he could not see that she was crying weakly—like an old woman.

1938

赏 析

《菊花》最初发表于 1937 年,收入斯坦贝克的第一部短篇小说集《长长的山谷》(*The Long Valley*, 1938)。从一开始,它就被公认为斯坦贝克的名篇之一。作品包含了几个斯坦贝克小说创作的典型因素,如作为故事背景的"长长的山谷"萨利纳斯谷、不幸的婚姻,以及作为象征的自然因素,如季节、气候、动植物等。《菊花》是斯坦贝克被收录入集最多、讨论最多的短篇作品,争论较多的问题是主人公伊丽莎是值得同情的还是冷漠的,她是坚强的还是软弱的。

故事里最常见的手法是象征,如灰色法兰绒一般的冬雾像盖子一样罩住山谷、没有阳光的山谷、沟壑纵横的黑色田野,这些都暗示了伊丽莎生活的氛围和心境。小说最核心的象征物是菊花。鲜亮硕大的菊花代表伊丽莎作为一个女人的特性和欲望。她丈夫是个农民,很少关心妻子作为一个女性的内心世界。他很实在,在表扬妻子是个种花能手后,又改口道,"我希望你到果园里干点活,种出这么大的苹果。"两人交谈所用的正式口吻暗示夫妻俩缺乏情投意合的亲密感。花园和栅栏是禁锢艾莉莎的象征。缺少丈夫关爱使伊丽莎在外貌上变成一个"非女人":"她的脸瘦而结实……园艺工作服把她紧紧裹住,显得体态臃肿,一顶男人戴的黑帽低低压在头上……给一件大大的灯芯绒围裙罩得严严实实……"本来她对絮叨的补锅佬没什么好声色,可一旦他提到她精心养育的菊花,提到有一位老太太想要花苗,她立刻变得热情欢快起来,不但让他补锅,还送上一盆花种。补锅匠的几句话令伊丽莎精神焕发,她重拾自信,精心打扮,然而在进城的路上,她看到自己送给补锅匠的花苗被扔在了路边,这给了她很大的打击。她最终没能从男性那里得到需要的关注。

有人认为这个故事折射了作者在文学创作中所感到的沮丧、孤独和挫败,也有人认为女主人公的原型是斯坦贝克的第一任妻子,她充满活力,头脑聪明,却为了丈夫放弃自己的事业。无论伊丽莎这一形象源自何处,斯坦贝克作为一个男性作家,能如此深刻地洞察一个聪慧女性备受压抑的生活和渴望,并用富含喻义的象征和情节表现出来,这难能可贵。

相关评论

Symbolism in John Steinbeck's "The Chrysanthemums"
Anonymous

John Steinbeck's "The Chrysanthemums" had taken a look at the symbolism that he conveyed in his short story. Critics have been both positive and negative in their critiques on this fine work. Elisa is the center of this story. She is a complex woman, unloved, and unappreciated. She desires above all else to be wanted and loved as well as being recognized as a sexual being, instead of a workforce that her husband sees her as. The reader must forgive her for her insecurity and loneliness. Elisa is reacting to things as only she knows how. All these things and more are vividly symbolized in "The Chrysanthemums", and the reader can almost feel her desperation that her life has bred in her.

Steinbeck obviously writes with nature in mind. Not just the idiosyncrasies of human nature, but the subtle beauty and chaotic whims[1] of Mother Nature. Elisa was written with this same template[2]. Since she sees the chrysanthemums as a replacement for not only children, but also her very womanhood, she is playing the part of both human and raw primeval nature. Her desire to grow and nurture the plants is both beautiful and horrifying to see. The attachment she has made is almost unholy in nature, and makes one think she might be more than a little not right in her mind. Sadly, her unstable nature has much to do with her husband's lack of understanding his wife's inner being. How else can one look at what she perceives as true? As the Chrysanthemums express her feminine side when her husband inhibits her, she must care for them as if they were her. The existence of the flowers mirrors her own. If Elisa were to let them die, either by her own hand, or through neglect of others, she herself would experience death—a death of what she needs, but cannot have in any other way and maintain her marriage. This would create a collapse of her sense of self, and make her into an empty shell of a woman. Sullivan, on the other hand, says that Elisa is like a mongrel dog, always slinking and scrambling around seeking love and acceptance; even when there is truly none to be found. Her actions are compared to the tinker's dog and one can see how such a comparison can be accurately made, demeaning[3] though as it is. "The Dog imagery related to Elisa is uncomplimentary. In her garden she always destroys unpleasant creatures such as 'aphids,' 'bugs,' 'snails,' 'cutworms,' and similar pests with her 'terrier fingers'". How is it that a woman, someone who is by very nature to be loving and caring, can be compared to a beast? A small, dirty animal that must rely solely on desperate measures to survive. Elisa does not deserve such a demeaning comparison, to be sure. In fact, she even tries to move beyond this stigma, "Elisa, in the course of the story, moves out of her accustomed role to challenge Henry and the tinker on their home ground, their occupations and sexuality". Unfortunately, both her husband and the tinker deprive her of even this small victory over the empty life she has so far led for herself. This is not truly her fault. Elisa must move however, or she will soon have no escape from her pain.

David Leon Higdon writes a critique on Steinbeck's view of the 1930's America, and of his insights into the character of a woman like Elisa during those times. Though

---

[1] whims:反复无常；一时的兴致。
[2] template:模板。
[3] demeaning:贬低的，有损身份的。

Steinbeck is a man, he shows surprising depth of character when he writes of Elisa. "With astonishing deftness and economy, Steinbeck quickly establishes the complexities and depths of the 35 year old Elisa in this study of the repression of her feminine, sexual, and creative impulses." This is all too true, as her husband and the tinker both inhibit her femininity by dismissing her obvious attempts at expressing it. When she speaks of her flowers as something other than material things, her husband asks her why she does not serve her abilities in a more practical venue; asking her why she does not grow apples in the orchard as large as the Chrysanthemums. One cannot truly blame him for his more practical sense of things, after all, he is just a farmer. Although his ways of doing things might sound like a better way, his wife's needs as a woman are being smothered and her spirit would die without the flowers. Henry's lack of seeing his wife as a sexual being is also fatally damaging to her spirit and he sees her dressing up at the end of the day as an affront to his own masculinity.

"When Henry returns from rounding up the steers, he is startled by her transformation, telling her that she looks "nice... different, strong and happy." Her appearance so discomposes him that he breaks into metaphor, telling her "you look strong enough to break a calf over your knee, happy enough to eat it like a watermelon." This must be utterly devastating to her, as she has just been denied her sensuality not only by the tinker, but also by the very person who should see and appreciate the sexuality within her. The reader is moved to must pity Elisa, as she is just being put more and more into a realm of pain and loneliness that no one in her life is willing to see or attempt to rectify. How can anyone see this as being controversial? Simple, during those times women were still seen as objects, not fit for anything else but sex and motherhood. Elisa is living the life that no one should ever lead; a life of emptiness, solitude, and deep turmoil that will surely plunge her into a nightmare she will have no chance of waking from.

Sadly, Elisa can never wake up from her nightmarish hell. Elisa is in a place where only she can make her life as she wishes. No one can rescue her. The Chrysanthemums that provide her a source of stability is killing her as well. When one places such a bond on anything other than what it is supposed to be to, one risks annihilation in doing so. Elisa can blame no one for her hell. Her husband is not the villain, neither is the tinker. The fence did not ask her to think of it as a prison. The Chrysanthemums did not ask her to see them as her children. A source of love and worth that she should not put in anything other than herself. As long as Elisa keeps on linking her womanhood (thus her sense of self) with those flowers, then she will surely fall. Withered, decayed, and as dead as a Chrysanthemum in a hot Texas summer.

Source: http://www.associatedcontent.com/article/31379/symbolism_in_john_steinbecks_the_chrysanthemums.html?cat=38. (May 10, 2006)

问题与思考

1. What kind of woman is Elisa? What is awakened or exposed in Elisa during her meeting with the tinker? What do we know about her inner world which is unknown to her husband and probably unknown to herself before she meets the tinker?
2. What effect does the discovery of the fate of her young plants have upon her? Why does Elisa ask her husband if fighters hurt each other very much? What is the significance of the ending "she was crying weakly—like an old woman"?
3. Sum up your impression of the tinker. What peculiarity does Steinbeck give him? What elements of his character lead Elisa to believing him?
4. As a character,is Henry,Elisa's husband,"round" or "flat"? What is his most outstanding feature? What is revealed through his dialogue with Elisa?
5. The chrysanthemum is an important thing in the story. It also is an important symbol. What does it symbolize? Study other symbols you can find in the story and discuss how they are effectively used in the story.

阅读链接

1. http：//images. search. yahoo. com/search/images？＿adv＿prop＝image&fr＝yfp-t-701&va＝John＋Ernest＋Steinbeck：斯坦贝克个人和作品的图片。
2. http：//www. enotes. com/twentieth-century-criticism/grapes-wrath-john-steinbeck：对《愤怒的葡萄》的介绍和评论。
3. http：//www. freeessays. cc/db/18/evj265. shtml：对《人与鼠》的介绍和评论。

Bernard Malamud (1914 —1986)

作者简介

伯纳德·马拉默德(Bernard Malamud，1914—1986)出生于纽约市布鲁克林一俄国犹太移民家庭，1928 到 1932 年在当地求学。年轻时他看过很多电影，特别喜欢卓别林的喜剧片，喜剧色彩因而成为其作品的一个特点。马拉默德靠政府贷款上了纽约市城市学院，1936 年本科毕业。1942 获得哥伦比亚大学英文硕士学位后他想当英语教师，但因就业市场不佳，迫使他在华盛顿特区的人口普查局找了一份工作，但不久就回到纽约市布鲁克林的成人夜校教书。从 1949 年起，他在俄勒冈州立大学教写作课，每周坚持挤出三天进行文学创作，50 年代逐渐成为美国知名作家。1961 年他离开俄勒冈州立大学到佛蒙特州的本宁顿学院任教，一年当中有一半时间住在佛蒙特，一半时间住在纽约。马拉默德于 1967 年从学院退休，1986 年在纽约逝世，享年 71 岁。

文学创作

马拉默德是美国第二代犹太移民作家的代表人物，一生创作了八部长篇小说和 54 篇短篇小说，长篇小说代表作有《店员》(*The Assistant*，又译《伙计》，1957)，讲的是一位意大利裔青年在种种磨难中获得道德的重生，最终皈依犹太教。《基辅怨》(*The Fixer*，1967)将具体的历史背景巧妙融入虚幻的情节中，是关于沙俄时代犹太人遭受残酷迫害的一部力作，同时获普利策奖和国家图书奖。《上帝的福佑》(*God's Grace*，1982)糅合了寓言和魔幻现实主义，反映了马拉默德在创作手法上的革新。马拉默德的创作生涯跨越 20 世纪下半叶，其作品大多描写城市贫民区中犹太下层人民的灰暗生活。在这样的生活中，受难是中心主题，但不失对希望的追求。他笔下的主人公多为犹太人,受难是他们生活的组成部分,也是获得再生的途径。作为一名道德作家,马拉默德用充满人道主义意味的眼光观照世界,力图证明小说人物的坎坷命运是现代人所共同具有的。他的小说深深扎根于现实,对现代生活做了最真实、最细腻的描写。

马拉默德的短篇小说收在《魔桶》(*The Magic Barrel*,1958)、《白痴优先》(*Idiots First*,1963)、《伦勃朗的帽子》(*Rembrandt's Hat*,1973)等集子中。《魔桶》获 1959 年国家图书奖。他的优秀短篇小说有《我的儿子:杀人犯》("My Son the Murderer")、《天使莱文》("The Angel Levine")、《犹太鸟》("The Jew Bird")等。马拉默德既是个严肃的作家,又能用幽默来强调荒谬,突现悲伤,教育读者。

作　　品

The Magic Barrel

Not long ago there lived in uptown New York, in a small, almost meager room, though crowded with books, Leo Finkle, a rabbinical student[1] in the Yeshivah University. Finkle, after six years of study, was to be ordained[2] in June and had been advised by an acquaintance that he might find it easier to win himself a congregation[3] if he were married. Since he had no present prospects of marriage, after two tormented days of turning it over in his mind, he called in Pinye Salzman, a marriage broker whose two-line advertisement he had read in the *Forward*.[4]

The matchmaker appeared one night out of the dark fourth-floor hallway of the graystone rooming house where Finkle lived, grasping a black, strapped portfolio that had been worn thin with use. Salzman, who had been long in the business, was of slight but dignified build, wearing an old hat, and an overcoat too short and tight for him. He smelled frankly of fish,[5] which he loved to eat, and although he was missing a few teeth, his presence was not displeasing, because of an amiable manner curiously contrasted with mournful eyes. His voice, his lips, his wisp of beard, his bony fingers were animated, but give him a moment of repose[6] and his mild blue eyes revealed a depth of sadness, a characteristic that put Leo a little at ease although the situation, for him, was inherently tense.

He at once informed Salzman why he had asked him to come, explaining that his home was in Cleveland[7], and that but for his parents, who had married comparatively late in life, he was alone in the world. He had for six years devoted himself almost entirely to his studies, as a result of which, understandably, he had found himself

---

[1] rabbinical student:攻读犹太法典的学生。
[2] to be ordained:指要被任命为拉比。
[3] a congregation:(某地区的)全体教徒。
[4] the *Forward*:全称是 the Jewish Daily Forward,意第绪语(Yiddish)报纸。
[5] He smelled frankly of fish:他浑身散发着鱼腥味。
[6] but give him a moment of repose:但一让他安静下来。
[7] Cleveland:克利夫兰,俄亥俄州(Ohio)东北部城市。

without time for a social life and the company of young women. Therefore he thought it the better part of trial and error—of embarrassing fumbling—to call in an experienced person to advise him on these matters.[1] He remarked in passing that the function of the marriage broker was ancient and honorable, highly approved in the Jewish community, because it made practical the necessary without hindering joy. Moreover, his own parents had been brought together by a matchmaker. They had made, if not a financially profitable marriage—since neither had possessed any worldly goods to speak of—at least a successful one in the sense of their everlasting devotion to each other. Salzman listened in embarrassed surprise, sensing a sort of apology. Later, however, he experienced a glow of pride in his work, an emotion that had left him years ago, and he heartily approved of Finkle.

The two went to their business. Leo had led Salzman to the only clear place in the room, a table near a window that overlooked the lamp-lit city. He seated himself at the matchmaker's side but facing him, attempting by an act of will[2] to suppress the unpleasant tickle in his throat. Salzman eagerly unstrapped his portfolio and removed a loose rubber band from a thin packet of much-handled cards. As he flipped through them, a gesture and sound that physically hurt Leo, the student pretended not to see and gazed steadfastly out the window. Although it was still February, winter was on its last legs,[3] signs of which he had for the first time in years begun to notice. He now observed the round white moon, moving high in the sky through a cloud menagerie,[4] and watched with half-open mouth as it[5] penetrated a huge hen, and dropped out of her like an egg laying itself. Salzman, though pretending through eye-glasses he had just slipped on, to be engaged in scanning the writing on the cards, stole occasional glances at the young man's distinguished face, noting with pleasure the long, severe scholar's nose, brown eyes heavy with learning, sensitive yet ascetic[6] lips, and a certain, almost hollow quality of the dark cheeks.[7] He gazed around at shelves upon shelves of books and let out a soft, contented sigh.

When Leo's eyes fell upon the cards, he counted six spread out in Salzman's hand.

"So few?" he asked in disappointment.

"You wouldn't believe me how much cards I got in my office," Salzman replied. "The drawers are already filled to the top, so I keep them now in a barrel, but is every girl good for a new rabbi?"

---

[1] He thought it... on these matters: 他想与其讨苦吃，弄出差错——瞎闯、丢丑，还不如请一位经验丰富的人在这方面给他出出主意。
[2] attempting by an act of will: 企图用意志的力量。
[3] winter was on its last legs: 冬天快要过去了。on one's last legs: (口)奄奄一息, 垂死。
[4] through a cloud menagerie: 穿过各种动物形状的云层。menagerie: 动物园。
[5] it: 指月亮。
[6] ascetic: 禁欲的。
[7] a certain almost... the dark cheeks: 黑黝黝的腮帮子几乎凹陷下去。

Leo blushed at this, regretting all he had revealed of himself in a curriculum vitae[1] he had sent to Salzman. He had thought it best to acquaint him with his strict standards and specifications, but in having done so, felt he had told the marriage broker more than was absolutely necessary.

He hesitantly inquired, "Do you keep photographs of your clients on file?"

"First comes family, amount of dowry, also what kind of promises," Salzman replied, unbuttoning his tight coat and settling himself in the chair. "After comes pictures, rabbi."

"Call me Mr. Finkle. I'm not yet a rabbi."

Salzman said he would, but instead called him doctor, which he changed to rabbi when Leo was not listening too attentively.

Salzman adjusted his horn-rimmed spectacles[2], gently cleared his throat and read in an eager voice the contents of the top card:

"Sophie P. Twenty-four years. Widow one year. No children. Educated high school and two years college. Father promises eight thousand dollars. Has wonderful wholesale business. Also real estate. On the mother's side comes teachers, also one actor. Well known on Second Avenue."

Leo gazed up in surprise. "Did you say a widow?"

"A widow don't mean spoiled, rabbi. She lived with her husband maybe four months. He was a sick boy she made a mistake to marry him."

"Marrying a widow has never entered my mind."

"This is because you have no experience. A widow, especially if she is young and healthy like this girl, is a wonderful person to marry. She will be thankful to you the rest of her life. Believe me, if I was looking now for a bride, I would marry a widow."

Leo reflected, then shook his head.

Salzman hunched his shoulders in an almost imperceptible gesture of disappointment. He placed the card down on the wooden table and began to read another:

"Lily H. High school teacher. Regular. Not a substitute[3]. Has savings and new Dodge car. Lived in Paris one year. Father is successful dentist thirty-five years. Interested in professional man. Well Americanized family. Wonderful opportunity."

"I knew her personally," said Salzman. "I wish you could see this girl. She is a doll. Also very intelligent. All day you could talk to her about books and theyater[4] and what not. She also knows current events."

"I don't believe you mentioned her age?"

---

[1] curriculum vitae:简历。
[2] horn-rimmed spectacles:角质架的眼镜。
[3] substitute:代课教师。
[4] theyater = theater.

"Her age?" Salzman said, raising his brows. "Her age is thirty-two years."

Leo said after a while, "I'm afraid that seems a little too old."

Salzman let out a laugh. "So how old are you, rabbi?"

"Twenty-seven."

"So what is the difference, tell me, between twenty-seven and thirty-two? My own wife is seven years older than me. So what did I suffer? —Nothing. If Rothschild[1]'s daughter wants to marry you, would you say on account her age, no?"

"Yes," Leo said dryly.

Salzman shook off the no in the eyes.[2] "Five years don't mean a thing. I give you my word that when you will live with her for one week you will forget her age. What does it mean five years—that she lived more and knows more than somebody who is younger? On this girl, God bless her, years are not wasted. Each one that it comes makes better the bargain."

"What subject does she teach in high school?"

"Languages. If you heard the way she speaks French, you will think it is music. I am in the business twenty-five years, and I recommend her with my whole heart. Believe me, I know what I'm talking, rabbi."

"What's on the next card?" Leo said abruptly.

Salzman reluctantly turned up the third card:

"Ruth K. Nineteen years. Honor student. Father offers thirteen thousand cash to the right bridegroom. He is a medical doctor. Stomach specialist with marvelous practice. Brother in law owns garment business. Particular people."

Salzman looked as if he had read his trump card[3].

"Did you say nineteen?" Leo asked with interest.

"On the dot."

"Is she attractive?" He blushed. "Pretty?"

Salzman kissed his finger tips. "A little doll. On this I give you my word. Let me call the father tonight and you will see what means pretty."

But Leo was troubled. "You're sure she's that young?"

"This I am positive. The father will show you the birth certificate."

"Are you positive there isn't something wrong with her?" Leo insisted.

"Who says there is wrong?"

"I don't understand why an American girl her age should go to a marriage broker."

A smile spread over Salzman's face.

"So for the same reason you went, she comes."

Leo flushed. "I am passed for time."

---

[1] Rothschild: 罗斯柴尔德家族,欧洲最著名的犹太金融财阀。

[2] shook off the no in the yes: 不理会"是"里面"不"的意思。这里指 Salzman 认为 Finkle 心口不一。

[3] trump card: 王牌。

Salzman, realizing he had been tactless, quickly explained. "The father came, not her. He wants she should have the best, so he looks around himself. When we will locate the right boy he will introduce him and encourage. This makes a better marriage than if a young girl without experience takes for herself. I don't have to tell you this."

"But don't you think this young girl believes in love?" Leo spoke uneasily.

Salzman was about to guffaw[1] but caught himself and said soberly, "Love comes with the right person, not before."

Leo parted dry lips but did not speak. Noticing that Salzman had snatched a glance at the next card, he cleverly asked, "How is her health?"

"Perfect," Salzman said, breathing with difficulty. "Of course, she is a little lame on her right foot from an auto accident that it happened to her when she was twelve years, but nobody notices on account she is so brilliant and also beautiful."

Leo got up heavily and went to the window. He felt curiously bitter and upbraided[2] himself for having called in the marriage broker. Finally, he shook his head.

"Why not?" Salzman persisted, the pitch of his voice rising.

"Because I detest stomach specialists."

"So what do you care what is his business? After you marry her do you need him? Who says he must come every Friday night in your house?"

Ashamed of the way the talk was going, Leo dismissed Salzman, who went home with heavy, melancholy eyes.

Though he had felt only relief at the marriage broker's departure, Leo was in low spirits the next day. He explained it[3] as rising from Salzman's failure to produce a suitable bride for him. He did not care for his type of clientele[4]. But when Leo found himself hesitating whether to seek out another matchmaker, one more polished than Pinye, he wondered if it could be—protestations to the contrary, and although he honored his father and mother—that he did not, in essence, care for the matchmaking institution? This thought he quickly put out of mind yet found himself still upset. All day he ran around the woods—missed an important appointment, forgot to give out his laundry, walked out of a Broadway cafeteria without paying and had to run back with the ticket[5] in his hand; had even not recognized his landlady in the street when she passed with a friend and courteously called out, "A good evening to you, Doctor Finkle." By nightfall, however, he had regained sufficient calm to sink his nose into a book[6] and there found peace from his thoughts.

---

[1] guffaw:大笑,狂笑。
[2] upbraided:责备。
[3] it:指情绪低落。
[4] clientele:顾客。
[5] ticket:钞票。
[6] to sink his nose into a book:埋头读书。

Almost at once there came a knock on the door. Before Leo could say enter, Salzman, commercial cupid,[1] was standing in the room. His face was gray and meager, his expression hungry, and he looked as if he would expire on his feet. Yet the marriage broker managed, by some trick of the muscles to display a broad smile.

"So good evening. I am invited?"

Leo nodded, disturbed to see him again, yet unwilling to ask the man to leave.

Beaming still, Salzman laid his portfolio on the table. "Rabbi, I got for you tonight good news."

"I've asked you not to call me rabbi. I'm still a student."

"Your worries are finished. I have for you a first-class bride."

"Leave me in peace concerning this subject." Leo pretended lack of interest.

"The world will dance at your wedding."

"Please, Mr. Salzman, no more."

"But first must come back my strength," Salzman said weakly. He fumbled with the portfolio straps and took out of the leather case an oily paper bag, from which he extracted a hard, seeded roll[2] and a small, smoked white fish. With a quick emotion of his hand he stripped the fish out of its skin and began ravenously to chew. "All day in a rush," he muttered.

Leo watched him eat.

"A sliced tomato you have maybe?" Salzman hesitantly inquired.

"No."

The marriage broker shut his eyes and ate. When he had finished he carefully cleaned up the crumbs and rolled up the remains of the fish, in the paper bag. His spectacled eyes roamed the room until he discovered, amid some piles of books, a one-burner gas stove. Lifting his hat he humbly asked, "A glass of tea you got, rabbi?"

Conscience-stricken, Leo rose and brewed the tea. He served it with a chunk of lemon and two cubes of lump sugar, delighting Salzman.

After he had drunk his tea, Salzman's strength and good spirits were restored.

"So tell me rabbi," he said amiably, "you considered some more the three clients I mentioned yesterday?"

"There was no need to consider."

"Why not?"

"None of them suits me."

"What then suits you?"

Leo let it pass because he could give only a confused answer.

Without waiting for a reply, Salzman asked, "You remember this girl I talked to

---

[1] commercial cupid: 爱情商人。Cupid: 丘比特,罗马神话中的小爱神,他长有翅膀,手持弓箭,射中谁,谁就会坠入爱河。

[2] seeded roll: 果仁面包圈。

you—the high school teacher?"

"Age thirty-two?"

But surprisingly, Salzman's face lit in a smile. "Age twenty-nine."

Leo shot him a look. "Reduced from thirty-two?"

"A mistake," Salzman avowed. "I talked today with the dentist. He took me to his safety deposit box and showed me the birth certificate. She was twenty-nine years last August. They made her a party in the mountains where she went for her vacation. When her father spoke to me the first time I forgot to write the age and I told you thirty-two, but now I remember this was a different client, a widow."

"The same one you told me about? I thought she was twenty-four?"

"A different. Am I responsible that the world is filled with widows?"

"No, but I'm not interested in them, nor for that matter, in school teachers."

Salzman pulled his clasped hand to his breast. Looking at the ceiling he devoutly exclaimed, "Yiddishe kinder,[1] what can I say to somebody that he is not interested in high school teachers? So what then you are interested?"

Leo flushed but controlled himself.

"In what else will you be interested," Salzman went on, "if you not interested in this fine girl that she speaks four languages and has personally in the bank ten thousand dollars? Also her father guarantees further twelve thousand. Also she has a new car, wonderful clothes, talks on all subjects, and she will give you a first-class home and children. How near do we come in our life to paradise?"

"If she's so wonderful, why wasn't she married ten years ago?"

"Why?" said Salzman with a heavy laugh—"Why? Because she is *partikiler*[2]. This is why. She wants the best."

Leo was silent, amused at how he had entangled himself. But Salzman had aroused his interest in Lily H., and he began seriously to consider calling on her. When the marriage broker observed how intently Leo's mind was at work on the facts he had supplied, he felt certain they would soon come to an agreement.

Late Saturday afternoon, conscious of Salzman,[3]. Leo Finkle walked with Lily Hirschorn along Riverside Drive[4]. He walked briskly and erectly, wearing with distinction the black fedora[5] he had that morning taken with trepidation out of the dusty hat box on his closet shelf, and the heavy black Saturday coat[6] he had thoroughly whisked clean. Leo also owned a walking stick, a present from a distant relative, but quickly put temptation aside and did not use it. Lily, petite and not unpretty, had on

---

[1] Yiddishe kinder:(意第绪语)犹太小孩。
[2] partikilar = particular,挑剔的。
[3] conscious of Salzman:总觉得 Salzman 在尾随自己。
[4] Riverside Drive:纽约市街名。
[5] fedora:浅顶软呢帽。
[6] Saturday coat:星期六出客时穿的、庄重的外套。

something signifying the approach of spring. She was au courant[1], animatedly, with all sorts of subjects, and he weighed her words and found her surprisingly sound[2]—score another for Salzman, whom he uneasily sensed to be somewhere around, hiding perhaps high in a tree along the street, flashing the lady signals with a pocket mirror; or perhaps a cloven-hoofed Pan[3], piping nuptial ditties[4] as he danced his invisible way before them, strewing wild buds on the walk and purple grapes in their path, symbolizing fruit of a union, though there was of course still none.

Lily startled Leo by remarking, "I was thinking of Mr. Salzman, a curious figure, wouldn't you say?"

Not certain what to answer, he nodded.

She bravely went on, blushing, "I for one am grateful for his introducing us. Aren't you?"

He courteously replied, "I am."

"I mean," she said with a little laugh—and it was all in good taste, to at least gave the effect of being not in bad—"do you mind that we came together so?"

He was not displeased with her honesty, recognizing that she meant to set the relationship aright, and understanding that it took a certain amount of experience in life, and courage, to want to do it quite that way. One had to have some sort of past to make that kind of beginning.

He said that he did not mind. Salzman's function was traditional and honorable—valuable for what it might achieve, which, he pointed out, was frequently nothing.

Lily agreed with a sigh. They walked on for a while and she said after a long silence, again with a nervous laugh, "Would you mind if I asked you something a little bit personal? Frankly, I find the subject fascinating." Although Leo shrugged, she went on half embarrassedly, "How was it that you came to your calling[5]? I mean was it a sudden passionate inspiration?"

Leo, after a time, slowly replied, "I was always interested in the Law."

"You saw revealed in it the presence of the Highest?"

He nodded and changed the subject. "I understand that you spent a little time in Paris, Miss Hirschorn?"

"Oh, did Mr. Salzman tell you, Rabbi Finkle?" Leo winced but she went on, "It was ages ago and almost forgotten. I remember I had to return for my sister's wedding."

And Lily would not be put off. "When," she asked in a trembly voice, "did you become enamored of God?"

He stared at her. Then it came to him that she was talking not about Leo Finkle,

---

[1] au courant: 时髦的；流行的。
[2] sound: 有头脑的。
[3] a cloven-hoofed Pan: 羊腿潘神。Pan: 希腊神话中的牧畜神，羊身人足。cloven-hoof: （动物）偶蹄。
[4] nuptial ditties: 结婚的小曲儿。
[5] calling: 职业，行当。

but of a total stranger, some mystical figure, perhaps even passionate prophet that Salzman had dreamed up for her—no relation to the living or dead. Leo trembled with rage and weakness. The trickster had obviously sold her a bill of goods,[1] just as he had him, who'd expected to become acquainted with a young lady of twenty-nine, only to behold, the moment he laid eyes upon her strained and anxious face, a woman past thirty-five and aging rapidly. Only his self control had kept him this long in her presence.

"I am not," he said gravely, "a talented religious person," and in seeking words to go on, found himself possessed by shame and fear. "I think," he said in a strained manner, "that I came to God not because I love Him, but because I did not."

This confession he spoke harshly because its unexpectedness shook him.

Lily wilted. Leo saw a profusion of loaves of bread go flying like ducks high over his head, not unlike the winged loaves by which he had counted himself to sleep last night. Mercifully, then, it snowed, which he would not put past Salzman's machinations.[2]

He was infuriated with the marriage broker and swore he would throw him out of the room the minute he reappeared. But Salzman did not come that night, and when Leo's anger had subsided, an unaccountable despair grew in its place. At first he thought this was caused by his disappointment in Lily, but before long it became evident that he had involved himself with Salzman without a true knowledge of his own intent. He gradually realized—with an emptiness that seized him with six hands—that he had called in the broker to find him a bride because he was incapable of doing it himself. This terrifying insight he had derived as a result of his meeting and conversation with Lily Hirschorn. Her probing questions had somehow irritated him into revealing—to himself more than her—the true nature of his relationship to God, and from that it had come upon him, with shocking force, that apart from his parents, he had never loved anyone. Or perhaps it went the other way, that he did not love God so well as he might, because he had not loved man. It seemed to Leo that his whole life stood starkly revealed and he saw himself for the first time as he truly was—unloved and loveless. This bitter but somehow not fully unexpected revelation brought him to a point to panic, controlled only by extraordinary effort. He covered his face with his hands and cried.

The week that followed was the worst of his life. He did not eat and lost weight. His beard darkened and grew ragged. He stopped attending seminars and almost never opened a book. He seriously considered leaving the Yeshiva, although he was deeply troubled at the thought of the loss of all his years of study—saw them like pages torn from a book, strewn over the city—and at the devastating effect of this decision upon his parents. But he had lived without knowledge of himself, and never in the Five Books

---

[1] The trickster had... bill of goods: 这骗子显然耍了花招哄了她。
[2] which he would... Salzman's machinations: 他相信这是 Salzman 的又一计谋。

and all the Commentaries[1]—mea culpa[2]—had the truth been revealed to him. He did not know where to turn, and in all this desolating loneliness there was no *to whom*, although he often thought of Lily but not once could bring himself to go downstairs and make the call. He became touchy and irritable, especially with his landlady, who asked him all manner of personal questions; on the other hand sensing his own disagreeableness, he waylaid her on the stairs and apologized abjectly, until mortified, she ran from him. Out of this, however, he drew the consolation that he was a Jew and that a Jew suffered. But generally, as the long and terrible week drew to a close, he regained his composure and some idea of purpose in life to go on as planned. Although he was imperfect, the ideal was not. As for his quest of a bride, the thought of continuing afflicted him with anxiety and heartburn, yet perhaps with this new knowledge of himself he would be more successful than in the past. Perhaps love would now come to him and a bride to that love. And for this sanctified seeking who needed a Salzman?

The marriage broker, a skeleton with haunted eyes, returned that very night. He looked, withal, the picture of frustrated expectancy—as if he had steadfastly waited the week at Miss Lily Hirschorn's side for a telephone call that never came.

Casually coughing, Salzman came immediately to the point: "So how did you like her?"

Leo's anger rose and he could not refrain from chiding the matchmaker: "Why did you lie to me, Salzman?"

Salzman's pale face went dead white, the world had snowed on him.

"Did you not state that she was twenty-nine?" Leo insisted.

"I give you my word—"

"She was thirty-five, if a day.[3] At least thirty-five."

"Of this don't be too sure. Her father told me—"

"Never mind. The worst of it was that you lied to her."

"How did I lie to her, tell me?"

"You told her things about me that weren't true. You made out to be more, consequently less than I am. She had in mind a totally different person, a sort of semi-mystical Wonder Rabbi."

"All I said, you was a religious man."

"I can imagine."

Salzman sighed. "This is my weakness that I have," he confessed. "My wife says to me I shouldn't be a salesman, but when I have two fine people that they would be

---

[1] the Five Books and all the Commentaries:指《圣经·旧约》中的摩西五书——《创世纪》、《出埃及记》、《利未记》、《民数记》、《申命记》和对五书的评论。

[2] mea culpa:(意第绪语)我犯下了罪过。

[3] if a day:(岁月等)十足。

wonderful to be married, I am so happy that I talk too much." He smiled wanly. "This is why Salzman is a poor man."

Leo's anger left him. "Well, Salzman, I'm afraid that's all."

The marriage broker fastened hungry eyes on him.

"You don't want any more a bride?"

"I do," said Leo, "but I have decided to seek her in a different way. I am no longer interested in an arranged marriage. To be frank, I now admit the necessity of premarital love. That is, I want to be in love with the one I marry."

"Love?" said Salzman, astounded. After a moment he remarked, "For us, our love is our life, not for the ladies. In the ghetto they—"

"I know, I know," said Leo. "I've thought of it often. Love, I have said to myself, should be a by-product of living and worship rather than its own end. Yet for myself I find it necessary to establish the level of my need and fulfill it."

Salzman shrugged but answered, "Listen, rabbi, if you want love, this I can find for you also. I have such beautiful clients that you will love them the minute your eyes will see them."

Leo smiled unhappily. "I'm afraid you don't understand."

But Salzman hastily unstrapped his portfolio and withdrew a manila[1] packet from it.

"Pictures," he said, quickly laying the envelope on the table.

Leo called after him to take the pictures away, but as if on the wings of the wind, Salzman had disappeared.

March came. Leo had returned to his regular routine. Although he felt not quite himself yet—lacked energy—he was making plans for a more active social life. Of course it would cost something, but he was an expert in cutting corners; and when there were no corners left he would make circles rounder.[2] All the while Salzman's pictures had lain on the table, gathering dust. Occasionally as Leo sat studying, or enjoying a cup of tea, his eyes fell on the manila envelope, but he never opened it.

The days went by and no social life to speak of developed with a member of the opposite sex—it was difficult, given the circumstances of his situation. One morning Leo toiled up the stairs to his room and stared out the window at the city. Although the day was bright his view of it was dark. For some time he watched the people in the street below hurrying along and then turned with a heavy heart to his little room. On the table was the packet. With a sudden relentless gesture he tore it open. For a half-hour he stood by the table in a state of excitement, examining the photographs of the ladies Salzman had included. Finally, with a deep sigh he put them down. There were six, of

---

[1] manila: 吕宋纸。
[2] he was an expert... make circles rounder: 他善于精打细算, 临到细无可细之时, 还能精益求精。cut corners: 以最简捷、经济的方式做事。

varying degree of attractiveness, but look at them along enough and they all became Lily Hirschorn: all past their prime, all starved behind bright smiles, not a true personality in the lot. Life, despite their frantic yoohooings,[1] had passed them by; they were pictures in a brief case that stank of fish. After a while, however, as Leo attempted to return the photographs into the envelope, he found in it another, a snapshot of the type taken by a machine for a quarter.[2] He gazed at it a moment and let out a cry.

Her face deeply moved him. Why, he could at first not say. It gave him the impression of youth—spring flowers, yet age—a sense of having been used to the bone, wasted;[3] this came from the eyes, which were hauntingly familiar, yet absolutely strange. He had a vivid impression that he had met her before, but try as he might he could not place her although he could almost recall her name, as he had read it in her own handwriting. No, this couldn't be; he would have remembered her. It was not, he affirmed, that she had an extraordinary beauty—no, though her face was attractive enough; it was that something about her moved him. Feature for feature, even some of the ladies of the photographs could do better; but she lapsed forth to this heart—had lived, or wanted to—more than just wanted, perhaps regretted how she had lived—had somehow deeply suffered: it could be seen in the depths of those reluctant eyes, and from the way the light enclosed and shone from her, and within her, opening realms of possibility: this was her own. Her he desired. His head ached and eyes narrowed with the intensity of his gazing, then as if an obscure fog had blown up in the mind, he experienced fear of her and was aware that he had received an impression, somehow, of evil. He shuddered, saying softly, it is thus with us all. Leo brewed some tea in a small pot and sat sipping it without sugar, to calm himself. But before he had finished drinking, again with excitement he examined the face and found it good: good for Leo Finkle. Only such a one could understand him and help him seek whatever he was seeking. She might, perhaps, love him. How she had happened to be among the discards in Salzman's barrel he could never guess, but he knew he must urgently go find her.

Leo rushed downstairs, grabbed up the Bronx[4] telephone book, and searched for Salzman's home address. He was not listed, nor was his office. Neither was he in the Manhattan book. But Leo remembered having written down the address on a slip of paper after he had read Salzman's advertisement in the "personals" column of the Forward. He ran up to his room and tore through his papers, without luck. It was exasperating. Just when he needed the matchmaker he was nowhere to be found. Fortunately Leo remembered to look in his wallet. There on a card he found his name written and a Bronx address. No phone number was listed, the reason—Leo now

---

[1] frantic yoohooings: 拼命叫喊。
[2] a quarter: 二毛五分钱。
[3] yet age—a sense of... to the bone, wasted: 岁月销蚀,又留下了风尘的浪迹。
[4] Bronx: 布朗克斯,纽约市行政区。

recalled—he had originally communicated with Salzman by letter. He got on his coat, put a hat on over his skull cap[1] and hurried to the subway station. All the way to the far end of the Bronx he sat on the edge of his seat. He was more than once tempted to take out the picture and see if the girl's face was as he remembered it, but he refrained, allowing the snapshot to remain in his inside coat pocket, content to have her so close. When the train pulled into the station he was waiting at the door and bolted out. He quickly located the street Salzman had advertised.

The building he sought was less than a block from the subway, but it was not an office building, nor even a loft[2], nor a store in which one could rent office space. It was a very old tenement house. Leo found Salzman's name in pencil on a soiled tag under the bell and climbed three dark flights to his apartment. When he knocked, the door was opened by a think, asthmatic[3], gray-haired woman in felt slippers.

"Yes?" she said, expecting nothing. She listened without listening. He could have sworn he had seen her, too, before but knew it was an illusion.

"Salzman—does he live here? Pinye Salzman," he said, "the matchmaker?"

She stared at him a long minute. "Of course."

He felt embarrassed. "Is he in?"

"No." Her mouth, though left open, offered nothing more.

"The matter is urgent. Can you tell me where his office is?"

"In the air." She pointed upward.

"You mean he has no office?" Leo asked.

"In his socks."

He peered into the apartment. It was sunless and dingy, one large room divided by a half-open curtain, beyond which he could see a sagging metal bed. The near side of the room was crowded with rickety chairs, old bureaus, a three-legged table, racks of cooking utensils, and all the apparatus of a kitchen. But there was no sign of Salzman or his magic barrel, probably also a figment of the imagination. An odor of frying fish made weak to the knees.

"Where is he?" he insisted. "I've got to see your husband."

At length she answered, "So who knows where he is? Every time he thinks a new thought he runs to a different place. Go home, he will find you."

"Tell him Leo Finkle."

She gave no sign she had heard.

He walked downstairs, depressed.

But Salzman, breathless, stood waiting at his door.

Leo was astounded and overjoyed. "How did you get here before me?"

---

[1] skull cap: 睡帽。
[2] loft: (仓库、工厂的) 不分隔的统楼。
[3] asthmatic: 患气喘病的。

"I rushed."

"Come inside."

They entered. Leo fixed tea, and a sardine sandwich for Salzman. As they were drinking he reached behind him for the packet of pictures and handed them to the marriage broker.

Salzman put down his glass and said expectantly, "You found somebody you like?"

"Not among these."

The marriage broker turned away.

"Here is the one I want." Leo held forth the snapshot.

Salzman slipped on his glasses and took the picture into his trembling hand. He turned ghastly and let out a groan.

"What's the matter?" cried Leo.

"Excuse me. Was an accident this picture. She isn't for you."

Salzman frantically shoved the manila packet into his portfolio. He thrust the snapshot into his pocket and fled down the stairs.

Leo, after momentary paralysis, gave chase and cornered the marriage broker in the vestibule[1]. The landlady made hysterical out cries but neither of them listened.

"Give me back the picture, Salzman."

"No." The pain in his eyes was terrible.

"Tell me who she is then."

"This I can't tell you. Excuse me."

He made to depart, but Leo, forgetting himself, seized the matchmaker by his tight coat and shook him frenziedly.

"Please," sighed Salzman. "*Please.*"

Leo ashamedly let him go. "Tell me who she is," he begged. "It's very important to me to know."

"She is not for you. She is a wild one—wild, without shame. This is not a bride for a rabbi."

"What do you mean wild?"

"Like an animal. Like a dog. For her to be poor was a sin. This is why to me she is dead now."

"In God's name, what do you mean?"

"Her I can't introduce to you," Salzman cried.

"Why are you so excited?"

"Why, he asks," Salzman said, bursting into tear. "This is my baby, my Stella, she should burn in hell."

Leo hurried up to bed and hid under the covers. Under the covers he thought his life through. Although he soon fell asleep he could not sleep her out of his mind. He woke,

---

[1] vestibule:门厅。

beating his breast. Though he prayed to be rid of her, his prayers went unanswered. Through days of torment he endlessly struggled not to love her; fearing success, he escaped it. He then concluded to convert her to goodness, himself to God. The idea alternately nauseated and exalted him.

He perhaps did not know that he had come to a final decision until he encountered Salzman in a Broadway cafeteria. He was sitting alone at a rear table, sucking the bony remains of a fish. The marriage broker appeared haggard, and transparent to the point of vanishing.

Salzman looked up at first without recognizing him. Leo had grown a pointed beard and his eyes were weighted with wisdom.

"Salzman," he said, "love has at last come to my heart."

"Who can love from a picture?" mocked the marriage broker.

"It is not impossible."

"If you can love her, then you can love anybody. Let me show you some new clients that they just sent me their photographs. One is a little doll."

"Just her I want," Leo murmured.

"Don't be a fool, doctor. Don't bother with her."

"Put me in touch with her, Salzman," Leo said humbly. "Perhaps I can be of service."

Salzman had stopped eating and Leo understood with emotion that it was now arranged.

Leaving the cafeteria, he was, however, afflicted by a tormenting suspicion that Salzman had planned it all to happen this way.

Leo was informed by letter that she would meet him on a certain corner, and she was there one spring night, waiting under a street lamp. He appeared carrying a small bouquet of violets and rosebuds. Stella stood by the lamp post, smoking. She wore white with red shoes, which fitted his expectations, although in a troubled moment he had imagined the dress red, and only the shoes white. She waited uneasily and shyly. From afar he saw that her eyes—clearly her father's—were filled with desperate innocence. He pictured, in her, his own redemption. Violins and lit candles revolved in the sky. Leo ran forward with flowers outthrust.

Around the corner, Salzman, leaning against a wall, chanted prayers for the dead.

1954

赏　析

短篇小说《魔桶》通过相亲的事件、幽默的语调和突变的情节讲述了一个犹太青年的成长故事。主人公候任拉比列奥开始只是为了自己的事业才想到要找个妻子。他对爱情的理解也是理想化的，而媒人沙兹曼代表了在犹太社区过着艰苦生活的老一辈人，对他们来说，生存是头等大事，浪漫爱情是一种可望不可及的奢侈。沙兹曼和列奥不同的择偶观促成了列奥在精神上的成长。列奥和莉莉的第一次见面使他发现自己"除了父母,没爱过任何人",这个将要成为上帝使者的人连上帝也不爱,"这令他大为震惊"。列奥发现自己没有爱的能力,痛苦不已,这是他成长的第一步。第二步就是他决定通过追求沙兹曼"堕落的女儿"史黛拉来拯救自己。这位未来的拉比希望"通过使她向善而使自己心向上帝"。但这种爱情终究会拯救列奥还是会毁灭他,小说没有给出明确的答案,但提出了一个发人深省的问题:要爱上帝,是不是先得爱人?

故事的结尾引起诸多争论。读者不知道史黛拉到底做了什么,使她父亲对她如此绝望;沙兹曼吟唱为死者祈祷的赞美诗究竟是在为谁祈祷呢?为女儿,为自己,还是为列奥?如果说死亡是新生的开始,而且是沙兹曼设计让列奥爱上自己的女儿,那么这位媒人的吟唱可能既是庆祝心中无爱的旧列奥的死去,又在庆祝努力去爱的新列奥的新生。另一种解释是,为死者祈祷的赞美诗并非总是指死亡或哀悼,相反,它在赞美上帝和纪念死者的同时,也肯定生活将继续。如此,沙兹曼就是在肯定列奥获得了拯救。他没有把列奥爱上史黛拉看作令人绝望的死亡,而是祝福他们走到一起。这也是沙兹曼作为媒人一直努力做到的。

在塑造人物方面,作品笔墨俭省,只凭简短的对话和心理活动便使列奥和沙兹曼这两个主要人物活跃于纸上,在幽默与诙谐中给人以亲切之感。

相关评论

Pinye Salzman, Pan, and "The Magic Barrel"
Michael L. Storey

Pinye Salzman, the marriage broker in Bernard Malamud's "The Magic Barrel," presents a paradox to the reader. He is seen as both earthy and magical: at times "sucking the bony remains of a fish" and at other times moving about "as if on the wings of the wind." Furthermore, his intentions are unclear in assisting the protagonist, sixth-year rabbinical student Leo Finkle, who has hired Salzman to find him a bride. A question is whether or not Salzman secretly intends for Leo to marry Stella, the marriage broker's daughter. When Leo asks to meet Stella, after finding her snapshot in a packet of photographs of clientele Salzman has left with Leo, Salzman claims that it was accidental that the snapshot was among the photographs, and he refuses to introduce Leo to the profligate[1] Stella. The vehemence of his refusal and his respect for rabbis convince the reader that Salzman has no intentions of bringing the two together. But just when they seem clear, Salzman's intentions are made ambiguous by the fact that Leo, after forcing Salzman to arrange the meeting with Stella, is "afflicted by a tormenting suspicion that Salzman had planned it all to happen this way." It just might be, the reader feels, that Salzman has artfully arranged the salvation of his daughter through love and marriage with a rabbi.

I believe that Salzman has intended all along to unite Leo and Stella and that Malamud makes this clear through a virtually unnoticed analogy of Salzman and Pan, the goat-god. This analogy also resolves the seemingly contradictory elements—the earthy

---

[1] profligate:放荡的,不检点的。

and the magical—in Salzman's character because, as a god, Pan possesses the magical characteristics assigned to Salzman, and his half-goat, half-man form gives him that earthiness which Salzman displays.

A direct allusion to Pan is made only once in the story. When Leo is out walking one afternoon with Lily Hirschorn, one of Salzman's clients, he senses that Salzman is around, "perhaps a cloven-hoofed Pan, piping nuptial ditties as he danced his invisible way before them, strewing wild buds on the walk and purple grapes in their path, symbolizing fruit of a union." That Malamud intends this to be a key allusion in the conception of Salzman's character is suggested by several other[s], less explicit parallels he draws between Salzman and Pan.

Salzman's physical characteristics—"his wisp of beard, his bony fingers", his "skeleton with haunted eyes"—resemble at least one artistic depiction of Pan: the fourth-century, B. C., engraved bronze mirror "Aphrodite and Pan Playing Five-Stones." His ravenous appetite, gluttonous[1] habits, and fishy smell also give Salzman the suggestion of a goat. In addition, Salzman imitates Pan's habit of suddenly appearing and disappearing. Salzman first appears to Leo "one night out of the dark fourth-floor hallway." Later, he disappears "as if on the wings of the wind." When Leo goes to Salzman's apartment to question him about the picture of Stella, Salzman's wife tells Leo that Salzman's office is "In the air" and that it is difficult to keep track of the marriage broker: "Every time he thinks a new thought he runs to a different place." Near the end of the story, Malamud describes Salzman as "transparent to the point of vanishing." Salzman's occupation of marriage broker gives him still another likeness to Pan, who is traditionally associated with amorousness[2] and fertility.

Another important parallel between Salzman and Pan is created through the depiction of Stella, Salzman's daughter. Pan's daughter is Iynx, who was transformed into a bird by Heré for attempting to charm Zeus sexually. She is considered symbolic of "restless, passionate love." Stella is also depicted as restless, passionate love. Salzman describes her as "a wild one—wild, without shame," and when we see her in the final scene she is standing "by the lamp post, smoking", dressed all in white, except for red shoes, colors traditionally associated with love and passion. Stella's name, Latin for star, also hints at her nature, for stars are popularly associated with love, passion, and restlessness (as in "wandering star"). When Leo first sees Stella's picture, it both moves and frightens him because he recognizes that Stella has experienced passion, perhaps of an evil kind, and is capable of love.

The most significant parallel between Salzman and Pan in terms of ascertaining Salzman's intentions is revealed in the effect that Salzman has on Leo. Pan is traditionally credited with bringing both nightmares and panic (to which he lends his

---

[1] gluttonous:暴食的,贪吃的。
[2] amorousness:多情;爱情。

name) to humans. Also, in much twentieth-century literature, such as the stories of Foster and Lawrence, Pan-figures have the power of bringing characters into contact with reality. Throughout "The Magic Barrel" Salzman produces these same effects on Leo.

The day after his initial meeting with Salzman, which ends with Leo dismissing the marriage broker, Leo finds himself figuratively in Pan's woods and literally in a state of confusion bordering on panic: "All day he ran around in the woods—missed an important appointment, forgot to give out his laundry, walked out of a Broadway cafeteria without paying and had to run back with the ticket in his hand."

That evening just as Leo is able to regain "sufficient calm" and "peace," Salzman unexpectedly arrives to convince him to meet Lily Hirschorn. It is this meeting, during which Leo envisions[1] Salzman as Pan, which has the effect of bringing Leo into contact with reality and to the state of panic. When Lily presses upon Leo questions about his relationship to God ("'When,' she asked in a trembly voice, 'did you become enamored of God?'") he realizes what Salzman has done:

> Then it came to him that she was talking not about Leo Finkle, but of a total stranger, some mystical figure, perhaps even passionate prophet that Salzman had dreamed up for her—no relation to the living or dead. Leo trembled with rage and weakness.

It is the traditional method of the Jewish marriage broker to exaggerate the qualities of both parties in order to increase the chances of a match, but here Salzman's exaggerations have the effect, not of bringing Leo and Lily together, but of bringing Leo to a sense of reality and a state of panic. Shortly after this walk with Lily, Leo realizes that

> Her probing questions had somehow irritated him into revealing—to himself more than her—the true nature of his relationship to God, and from that it had come upon him, with shocking force, that apart from his parents, he had never loved anyone. Or perhaps it went the other way, that he did not love God so well as he might, because he had not loved man. It seemed to Leo that his whole life stood starkly revealed and he saw himself for the first time as he truly was—unloved and loveless. This bitter but somehow not fully unexpected revelation brought him to a point of panic (my underline).

While Lily's questions are the immediate cause of Leo's new sense of reality and state of panic, it is Salzman who is responsible for Lily's questions and is therefore the real cause of Leo's present state.

Later, Leo experiences nightmares, also traditionally credited to Pan. These occur when Leo attempts to forget Stella after Salzman has refused to arrange a meeting: "Leo

---

[1] envisions: 想象。

hurried up to bed and hid under the covers. Under the covers he thought his life through. Although he soon fell asleep he could not sleep her out of his mind. He woke, beating his breast."

Panic, nightmares, "days of torment," and the realization of what his life is really like convince Leo "to convert [Stella] to goodness, himself to God." It is significant that this conviction is accompanied by physical changes in Leo which give him a resemblance to Pan-Salzman: "Leo had grown a pointed beard and his eyes were weighted with wisdom."

This transformation in Leo seems to indicate that Salzman's plan has not been designed entirely for the benefit of Stella, that he is concerned with Leo's salvation as well. Salzman has thrust Leo into a meeting with Lily in order to expose to Leo his own specious life. Until Leo is aware that he has pursued the spiritual at the expense of the earthly and that the spiritual will come only through the earthly, he is unable to choose the right bride. Hence Salzman cannot lead him directly to Stella but must first take him to a new sense of reality made vivid in a state of panic. Once Leo has faced the stark facts of his life, he is ready for marriage with the right woman—not Lily, the ascetic, of whom the goat-god would hardly approve, but Stella, daughter of the goat-god, whose passionate nature is the perfect complement to Leo's ascetic nature.

Source: *Studies in Short Fiction* 18.2 (Spring 1981): 180—183. Rpt. in *Contemporary Literary Criticism Selection*.

问题与思考

1. What does Leo Finkle come to learn about himself and about his capacity to love?
2. How do you evaluate Salzman? Does Malamud only make him a marriage salesman who manipulates the whole affair for his own benefit? Discuss.
3. What role do Lily Hirschorn and Stella play in the process of Finkle's self-discovery? What is there in Stella's picture that so attracts Finkle?
4. Malamud uses strange images in the story, such as the changing appearance of Salzman, the Moon going through a cloud which looks like a hen laying egg. Note the other images in the story and discuss their effect upon the story.
5. What is the significance of the conclusion of the story? Why does Salzman lean "against a wall and chant prayers for the dead"?

阅读链接

1. http://www.joi.org/books/reading/TheCompleteStories_print.htm：对《马拉默德短篇小说全集》的介绍和作品目录。
2. http://en.wikipedia.org/wiki/The_Assistant_(novel)：对《店员》的介绍和评论。
3. http://www.enotes.com/fixer：《基辅怨》导读。

6. 实验小说(Experimental Fiction)

现实主义作家关注小说与现实的关系,讲述生活中可能发生的故事,将真实奉为圭臬。20世纪60年代以来,一批前卫作家力图突破传统小说的人物、情节、线性叙述的程式,对小说形式进行实验,创作了一批新颖独特的作品,批评家把他们称为"后现代"作家。约翰·巴斯、威廉·加斯、唐纳德·巴塞尔姆、罗伯特·库弗、唐·德里罗、基思·福特等人创作的后现代小说摒弃现实主义的"真实"观念,并不追求反映客观现实生活,其实验性主要表现为以"元小说"(metafiction)展示小说虚构的本质,以"反形式"(anti-form)反映西方当代生活的状态。后现代作家执意与现实主义分道扬镳,有时过分陶醉于语言游戏之中,但是他们的革新促使当时文坛发生变化,对当代小说发展产生了深刻影响。

传统的作家经常会摆出自己是在讲述真实故事的样子,尽量使自己的作品看上去自如流畅、天工巧成,而后现代作家喜欢凸显作品的虚构性,希望读者意识到他们正在使用的创作技巧。这种关注虚构技巧的元小说讲述作品自身的故事,把叙述行为直接作为小说的内容。基思·福特的《铲煤者》很好地说明了作者如何有意识地审视小说虚构的过程,而这种审视和对形式的展示成了故事的一部分。这篇实验小说以"钟在滴答地走"开头,紧接着作者马上对此进行自我分析:"对我这个短篇故事来讲,这个开头不好。"中间他数次直接插入自己对小说创作的看法,而且将这些看法置于段首,意在引起读者的注意,如:"这个情节是不是听起来很熟?像是乔伊斯的《死者》。我不是有意要模仿这个故事,但它就像陷阱一样等在那里,我没法不模仿。""如果我使用象征,那么我在很大程度上也要看读者是否愿意接受我的象征主义想表达的意思。"

"反形式"表现在作家采用戏仿、拼贴、碎片化、文字游戏等手法来打破传统小说的线性叙述和人为的逻辑性,如《铲煤者》由五个片断组成,彼此没有明确的关联性。巴塞尔姆将广告、新闻、电影的语言用在小说创作中,以描绘都市生活的复杂和混乱。他的《白雪公主》(1967)是对同名童话故事的戏仿,里面的王子变得平常、庸俗,令白雪公主大失所望。巴思的《喀迈拉》(1971)以《天方夜谭》和希腊神话为素材,讨论如何讲故事的问题。后现代作家还喜欢在作品中混用书面语和口头语,科技语言也频频出现在文学作品中,有时还会将符号或图案插入文本中。

实验小说有别于传统小说还有更深层次的原因,那就是认识世界的方式。传统小说家遵循摹仿观,试图使自己构筑的想象世界看起来像真实的世界一样,而实验作家持相反的看法,他们认为虚构的世界不能混同于真实的世界,小说只是观照世界的一种方式。要使这种观照尽量准确,我们就必须意识到自己的所见所闻是被观看的镜头扭曲了的。如果说语言就是这一镜头,那么我们必须认清它是人在具体的历史语境中创造出来的,具有夸大、缩小、加强和掩盖的力量,有着内在的局限性。

对习惯于传统小说的读者来说,后现代小说的创新技巧给阅读带来了很大的困难,因为这样的文本往往不是封闭性的。巴塞尔姆的《学校》就是一个例子。这篇短小的故事的叙述语调十分正常,可事件却变得越来越离奇,除了"死亡",它们之间没有清晰可见的逻辑性和连贯性,其实连死亡本身也是莫名其妙的,故事结局不但不明确,而且更加令人莫明其妙。这种与传统的现实主义小说大相径庭的文本没有把意义强加给读者,它利用许多"空白"激励读者自己去填补这些"空白",去生产文本意义。这样读者不再被禁锢在"本文"中,不再等待作者向他灌输思想。对小说进行实验的后现代作家把小说的力量转向小说本身。如果我们在阅读当代小说时抛弃阅读传统小说的期待,就会发现后现代小说和传统小说一样令人愉悦。

Donald Barthelme (1931—1989)

作者简介

唐纳德·巴塞尔姆(Donald Barthelme, 1931—1989)出生在美国费城,父亲是休斯敦大学建筑学教授,他对现代建筑的理解在很大程度上影响了巴塞尔姆的文学创作。巴塞尔姆10岁那年就决心要当一名作家,高中毕业后在休斯敦大学学习新闻。1953年他参军,刚到朝鲜战场两国便宣布停火。巴塞尔姆一度在军中做报纸编辑,回国后继续在休斯敦大学学习哲学。虽然他一直上课上到1957年,但没拿到学位。30岁时巴塞尔姆担任休斯敦当代艺术博物馆馆长,介绍了许多前卫的艺术家及其作品。1962年他迁居纽约市,当过报社记者和文学杂志的编辑。他用大部分时间从事写作,同时在波士顿大学、布法罗大学、纽约市立学院等几所高校任教,1974到1975年间他成为纽约市立学院的杰出教授。1989年7月23日,巴塞尔姆因喉癌去世,终年58岁。

文学创作

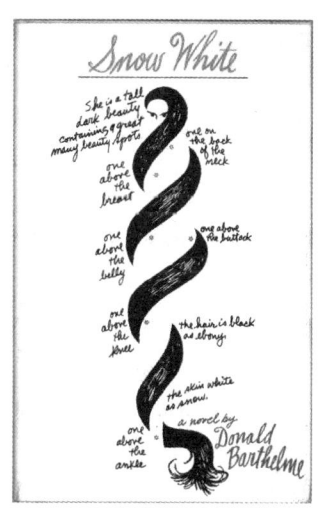

巴塞尔姆是美国后现代文坛上著名的小说家,其创作以短篇小说为主,共出版了八部短篇小说集,主要有《回来,卡利加里博士》(*Come Back, Dr. Caligari*, 1964)、《难以启齿的行为,不自然的行动》(*Unspeakable Practices, Unnatural Acts*, 1968)、《城市生活》(*City Life*, 1970)、《愁苦》(*Sadness*, 1972)、《业余爱好者》(*Amateurs*, 1976)和《一夜间去很多遥远的城市》(*Overnight to Many Distant Cities*, 1983)等。他最优秀的作品汇集在《故事60篇》(*Sixty Stories*, 1981)和《故事40篇》(*Forty Stories*, 1987)中。除了短篇小说,巴塞尔姆还有五部中长篇小说,其中代表作《白雪公主》(*Snow White*, 1967)获国家图书奖,被称为后现代小说的经典之作。

巴塞尔姆一反传统的写作手法,以碎片、戏仿和反讽作为自己创作的标志。他认为,"碎片比整体更显真实。"他在一些作品中插入图片、符号或单调的色块,把它们与文章拼贴在一起,因为他认为这种方式最能反映这个荒诞的、破碎的、混乱的世界。

巴塞尔姆从主题到形式都展现了戏仿传统的才能。《白雪公主》中的现代白雪公主不再清纯善良,而是一个妓女,而她的白马王子则是个失业的笨蛋。长篇小说《国王》(*The King*,1990)是对中世纪传奇《亚瑟王之死》的戏仿。《欧也妮·葛朗台》("Eugenie Grandet",1968)以短篇戏仿巴尔扎克同名的著名小说,作品中有女主人公欧也妮的手的插图。《辛伯达》("Sindbad",1984)则是对《一千零一夜》中的水手辛伯达的滑稽模仿。戏仿是为了讽刺,巴塞尔姆常常用冷嘲热讽的口气对丑恶的现实竭尽揶揄、挞伐之能事,甚至因为对现实的不信任使他对人类的交际工具——语言也产生了怀疑。他的人物对话恍如梦呓、语无伦次却深含意味。

作　　品

The School

Well, we had all these children out planting trees, see, because we figured that... that was part of their education, to see how, you know, the root systems... and also the sense of responsibility, taking care of things, being individually responsible. You know what I mean. And the trees all died. They were orange trees. I don't know why they died, they just died. Something wrong with the soil possibly or maybe the stuff we got from the nursery wasn't the best. We complained about it. So we've got thirty kids there, each kid had his or her own little tree to plant and we've got these thirty dead trees. All these kids looking at these little brown sticks, it was depressing.

It wouldn't have been so bad except that just a couple of weeks before the thing with the trees, the snakes all died. But I think that the snakes—well, the reason that the snakes kicked off [1] was that... you remember, the boiler was shut off for four days because of the strike, and that was explicable. It was something you could explain to the kids because of the strike. I mean, none of their parents would let them cross the picket line and they knew there was a strike going on and what it meant. So when things got started up again and we found the snakes they weren't too disturbed.

With the herb gardens it was probably a case of overwatering, and at least now they know not to overwater. The children were very conscientious with the herb gardens and some of them probably... you know, slipped them a little extra water when we weren't looking. Or maybe... well, I don't like to think about sabotage[2], although it did occur to us. I mean, it was something that crossed our minds. We were thinking that way probably because before that the gerbils[3] had died, and the white mice had died, and

---

[1] kicked off:(俚)死了。
[2] sabotage:破坏活动。
[3] gerbils:沙鼠。

the salamander[1] ... well, now they know not to carry them around in plastic bags.

Of course we expected the tropical fish to die, that was no surprise. Those numbers, you look at them crooked and they're belly-up on the surface. But the lesson plan called for a tropical fish input at that point, there was nothing we could do, it happens every year, you just have to hurry past it.

We weren't even supposed to have a puppy.

We weren't even supposed to have one, it was just a puppy the Murdoch girl found under a Gristede's truck one day and she was afraid the truck would run over it when the driver had finished making his delivery, so she stuck it in her knapsack[2] and brought it to the school with her. So we had this puppy. As soon as I saw the puppy I thought, Oh Christ, I bet it will live for about two weeks and then... And that's what it did. It wasn't supposed to be in the classroom at all, there's some kind of regulation about it, but you can't tell them they can't have a puppy when the puppy is already there, right in front of them, running around on the floor and yap yap yapping. They named it Edgar—that is, they named it after me. They had a lot of fun running after it and yelling, "Here, Edgar! Nice Edgar!" Then they'd laugh like hell. They enjoyed the ambiguity. I enjoyed it myself. I don't mind being kidded[3]. They made a little house for it in the supply closet and all that. I don't know what it died of. Distemper[4], I guess. It probably hadn't had any shots[5]. I got it out of there before the kids got to school. I checked the supply closet each morning, routinely, because I knew what was going to happen. I gave it to the custodian.

And then there was this Korean orphan that the class adopted through the *Help the Children* program, all the kids brought in a quarter a month, that was the idea. It was an unfortunate thing, the kid's name was Kim and maybe we adopted him too late or something. The cause of death was not stated in the letter we got, they suggested we adopt another child instead and sent us some interesting case histories, but we didn't have the heart.[6] The class took it pretty hard,[7] they began (I think, nobody ever said anything to me directly) to feel that maybe there was something wrong with the school. But I don't think there's anything wrong with the school, particularly, I've seen better and I've seen worse. It was just a run of bad luck. We had an extraordinary number of parents passing away, for instance. There were I think two heart attacks and two suicides, one drowning, and four killed together in a car accident. One stroke. And we had the usual heavy mortality rate among the grandparents, or maybe it was heavier

---

[1] salamander:蝾螈。
[2] knapsack:(帆布)背包。
[3] kidded:开玩笑,戏弄。
[4] distemper:犬瘟热。
[5] shots:注射疫苗。
[6] we didn't have the heart:我们不忍心接收;have the heart:(常用于否定句中)有勇气(做某事);忍心(做某事)。
[7] the class took it pretty hard:整个班级对此感到十分不快。

this year, it seemed so. And finally the tragedy.

The tragedy occurred when Matthew Wein and Tony Mavrogordo were playing over where they're excavating for the new federal office building. There were all these big wooden beams stacked, you know, at the edge of the excavation. There's a court case coming out of that, the parents are claiming that the beams were poorly stacked. I don't know what's true and what's not. It's been a strange year.

I forgot to mention Billy Brandt's father who was knifed fatally when he grappled with a masked intruder in his home.

One day, we had a discussion in class. They asked me, where did they go? The trees, the salamander, the tropical fish, Edgar, the poppas and mommas, Matthew and Tony, where did they go? And I said, I don't know, I don't know. And they said, who knows? and I said, nobody knows. And they said, is death that which gives meaning to life? And I said no, life is that which gives meaning to life. Then they said, but isn't death, considered as a fundamental datum, the means by which the taken-for-granted mundanity[1] of the everyday may be transcended in the direction of—

I said, yes, maybe.

They said, we don't like it.

I said, that's sound.

They said, it's a bloody shame!

I said, it is.

They said, will you make love now with Helen (our teaching assistant) so that we can see how it is done? We know you like Helen.

I do like Helen but I said that I would not.

We've heard so much about it, they said, but we've never seen it.

I said I would be fired and that it was never, or almost never, done as a demonstration. Helen looked out the window.

They said, please, please make love with Helen, we require an assertion of value, we are frightened.

I said that they shouldn't be frightened (although I am often frightened) and that there was value everywhere. Helen came and embraced me. I kissed her a few times on the brow. We held each other. The children were excited. Then there was a knock on the door, I opened the door, and the new gerbil walked in. The children cheered wildly.

1974

赏 析

作为一篇后现代短篇小说,巴塞尔姆的《学校》的实验性主要表现在故事情节的安排上,后现代小说反对传统小说按时间顺序发展,讲究前因后果的线性叙事。《学校》放弃传统小说的开

---

[1] mundanity:尘俗。

头—发展—高潮—结局的框架,以随和的聊天口吻叙述,没有明确的时间和地点转换,接二连三的死亡事件之间也缺乏明晰的逻辑关系。尤其是结尾,学生提出荒唐的要求。比这个要求更荒诞的是,有人敲门,老师开门,进来的竟是一只沙鼠。

然而,故事看似荒诞、简单,却是对死亡这一人生大问题的思考。叙述者是一位小学老师,他为培养学生的责任心而让他们去种树养蛇养鱼,甚至养小狗,养孤儿,但它们一一死掉。从树、蛇、到狗、人,故事变得越来越怪异,死亡的节奏越来越快,学生和老师越来越困惑,孩子们问老师,是不是死亡使得生活有意义?老师回答,不,是生命赋予生活意义。但孩子们不太相信他的话,老师的一番苦心教育以失败而告终,因为连他自己也无法解释死亡为什么会接踵而至。死亡是如此平常,又如此无常。但最后,一只沙鼠走进门来,它也许代表新的生命。生命最终战胜死亡,所以孩子们欢呼雀跃,因为他们多少了解到了生命的意义。

《学校》说明了后现代小说的荒诞性带来开放性思考,读者必须深入到文本中,积极思考,对缺乏逻辑的情节找出尽量合理的解释。这是后现代作品与传统的现实主义小说的重要区别:前者要求读者参与到文本意义的建构中,后者则是读者被动地接受作者通过文本施予的教化。

相关评论

Social Institutions in "The School" and "A & P"
Anonymous

The short story "The School" by Donald Barthelme and "A & P" by John Updike take place primarily in two conventional social institutions, a school and a place of employment respectively. Within these two social institutions, we see how quite often such institutions are responsible for shaping identity and behavior in the individuals that are impacted[1] by them. In Barthelme's "The School", the students have their identity and behavior shaped by a series of projects that are meant to help develop nurturing skills in them but result in the untimely deaths of snakes, trees, a puppy, and even an adopted Korean orphan. In "A & P", a teenage cashier named Sammy learns that to maintain one's own identity in opposition to conventional norms and values exacts a heavy sacrifice upon the individual. In both stories, the impact of social institutions demonstrates how identity and behavior are shaped in society.

In "The School", the story is narrated by the teacher of a group of students who tries to develop a sense of responsibility and nurturing in them through a series of projects aimed at watching life unfold. As the narrator explains about a tree-plating project at the opening of the story, "that was part of their education, to see how, you know, the root systems... also the sense of responsibility, taking care of things, being individually responsible". In "The School", a number of parents also die in the story, and two sets of parents are suing a contractor because of "poorly stacked" logs that kill two students playing among them. After every animal or plant the students attempt to

---

[1] impacted:受影响,产生……效果。

nurture dies, they begin to believe "there [is] something wrong with the school". In "A & P", when one of the girls explains she is just picking up snacks, Sammy imagines himself in her home watching a scene that is as conventional as the routine he encounters daily at the "A & P", "Her father and the other men were standing around in ice-cream coats and bow ties and the women were in sandals picking up herring snacks on toothpicks off a big plate and they were all holding drinks the color of water with olives and sprigs of mint in them". Lengel has embarrassed the girls, the only sign of life in the story. Despite the premature death of all of the different flora and fauna of the student projects, such an ending teaches them lessons if not the ones originally intended. This is because just like the bad luck and disappointments the school students will encounter as they develop, Sammy knows to retain his identity he will have to face an overwhelming number of Mr. Sammy likens the patrons to sheep and the married women as "house-slaves". Lengel, censures the girls for being "inappropriate", Sammy takes offense to his comments. However, from mice and salamanders to puppies and trees, all of these projects end in premature death. As such, we can see that social institutions like school, the workplace, and the home have an impact on our development, identity, and behavior. In "A & P", Updike provides us with the limiting impact of the social institution of the workplace. When Sammy finally walks out of the "A & P", he knows "how hard the world [is] going to be [for him] hereafter". Lengel's conventional mindset cannot understand Sammy's act of independence.

Source: http://www.lotsofessays.com/viewpaper/1710037.html(2010-11-3)

The Failed Education in "The School"

Anonymous

"The School" by David Barthelme represents more than a series of unfortunate events that befalls a group of students; in actuality, the text serves as an active criticism of the educational system. Through its incompetent instructor, failed curriculum, and ironic ending, "The School" demonstrates that the educational system adheres to cut-and-dried[1] methods, even after no reward is gained.

When examining the archetypes associated with a school one thinks of an institution to gain and achieve a higher understanding; however, that is not the case Barthelme represents in his short story. Rather than encountering a teacher who educates properly, the reader stumbles upon[2] an incompetent instructor. For instance, when the narrator mentions the orange trees' death, his only commentary is "I don't know why they died, they just died". The fact that the instructor does not provide an answer, symbolizes that students are not learning as they should in schools.

However, Barthelme not only critiques the competency of the teacher, he also

---

[1] cut-and-dried:惯常的,俗套的。
[2] stumbles upon:偶然发现。

scrutinizes the curriculum the instructor must follow. Throughout the text Barthelme cites various projects the students are required to complete, no matter how nonsensical[1]. The incoherency in the curriculum is especially highlighted when the instructor lists the order of the projects, from "gerbils ... [to] white mice ... [to] salamanders"; there is no apparent bridge or transitions from each to the next. The disjointed curriculum needs to be scrapped and rebuilt; nonetheless, that does not occur because the instructor states that "it happens every year". This blatant[2] lack of change demonstrates that the educational system clings to the old, ineffective ways.

The layout of the story follows the same pattern project after project, a teacher blindly following the flawed curriculum; until, the students asked "where did [the trees] go?", the teacher then responds that he does not know. The meaning is clear: the students are not satisfied with the current educational standard and are striving for a higher understanding. The story then continues with the educationally unsatisfied students deterring from the curriculum completely by requesting for their instructor to "make love with Helen, so that [they] can see how it is done". The reader must look beyond the literal sex and realize that it represents a rudimentary[3] act that even the most incompetent person can demonstrate. In response to this, Barthelme depicts an ideal educational system because when the instructor is able to pry himself from the flawed curriculum and proves competent in a subject the students react by getting excited.

However, this attempt to deviate from the ineffective curriculum is not meant to last, just as the students were watching with eager anticipation "the new gerbil walked in", resulting in the children cheering wildly. The gerbil and the enthusiasm displayed upon its arrival symbolize the adherence to the flawed educational system. Although the students were at the verge of achieving a higher understanding they rush to the gerbil, and the teacher does nothing to deter this. Barthelme's ending serves to prove that education will always fall back onto the ineffective regardless of its inefficiency.

Barthelme's choice of vernacular[4] throughout "The School" provides evidence as to who is the target audience. Throughout a large part of the text the language is not affluent or confusing to follow; in actuality, it is laid-back[5] and casual displaying that Barthelme is targeting the average citizen. During an interview with J. D. O'Hara, Barthelme states that he is not an "esoteric[6] writer addressing a coterie[7] audience" and this choice of delivery allows the reader to understand what social class is heavily

---

[1] nonsensical:无意义的,荒谬的。
[2] blatant:非常明显的,公然的。
[3] rudimentary:基本的。
[4] vernacular:日常用语;本地话。
[5] laid-back:松弛的,随便的。
[6] esoteric:深奥的。
[7] coterie:同行,圈内人。

affected by the by a poor educational structure.

"The School" serves more than an entertaining read; it attacks the educational system by pointing out several flaws. Barthelme's choice of delivery also highlights what social class is most impacted by this poor system. Through its incompetent instructor, failed curriculum, and ironic ending "The School" demonstrates that the educational system adheres to cut-and-dried methods, even after no reward is gained.

Source: http://iudiciumundus.wordpress.com/2011/05/19/short-story-the-school-by-donald-barthelme.

问题与思考

1. What is the significance of the title of the story? What does the school represent?
2. In the story the teacher tries to explain things to children. Does he succeed in doing this? What does he stand for?
3. The story ends with the arrival of the new gerbils. What does this seemingly absurd incident signify?
4. In what way the story is different from a realistic story?

阅读链接

1. http://www.todayinliterature.com/biography/donald.barthelme.asp: 巴塞尔姆的生平介绍和相关链接。
2. http://www.npr.org/programs/death/readings/stories/bart.html: 巴塞尔姆作品节选。
3. http://books.google.com.hk/books?id＝vY89AAAAIAAJ&printsec＝frontcover&dq＝Donald＋Barthelme&source＝bl&ots＝0Id7xXMcVs&sig＝rE7jZ9sMsilIpOCTA8ra_KPotpNk&hl＝en&ei＝U4HkTMuNE5CYvAO1tbSn_Dg&sa＝X&oi＝book_result&ct＝result&resnum＝8&ved＝0CCgQ6AEwBw♯v＝onepage&q&f＝false: 巴塞尔姆长篇小说《死亡的父亲》节选。

Keith Fort (1933—2004)

作者简介

基思·福特(Keith Fort,1933—2004)生于美国田纳西州东南部城市查塔努加,在田纳西希瓦尼的南方大学以优异成绩获学士学位,1961年获硕士学位,三年后在明尼苏达大学获比较文学博士学位,并获富布莱特奖学金到法国的蒙彼利埃大学进修。福特曾在空军服兵役18个月,还当过记者。从1962年起他在乔治敦大学任教,时间长达37年,教授过讽刺文学理论及发展、写作入门等多门课程。福特对教学法、教学管理、宗教都有研究,发表了不少有见地的文章。1969年,他因教学出色而受到乔治敦大学的褒奖。1999年,福特因为对退休教工机构作出重要贡献再次获得乔治敦大学的奖励。20世纪60年代到70年代,他成为学校一项奖学金的发起人之一,此项奖学金为华盛顿特区非白人青年上大学提供了机会。2004年福特因患慢性阻塞性肺病去世,享年71岁。

文学创作

基思·福特是美国后现代主义作家,其文学创作以短篇小说为主,仅创作了一部长篇小说。他发表了不少文学评论和评论写作文章,出版了两部学术著作:一部是基于其博士论文(1964)的专著《超越绝望:比较四部小说》(*Beyond Despair: A Comparative Study of Four Novels*,1969),所研究的四部小说——卡夫卡的《审判》(1925)、萨特的《恶心》(1938)、加谬的《陌生人》(1942)和塞林格的《麦田里的守望者》(1951)——分别为欧美20世纪20年代到50年代的代表作;另一部是《自1900年以来的伯恩利》(*Burnley Since 1900*,1988),介绍英国西北部煤矿和纺织中心伯恩利的历史变迁。福特的短篇小说多具后现代小说的实验特点,其中以《铲煤者》最为知名,被收入《反故事:实验小说选集》(1971)和《短篇小说名作概要大全》(2004)中。

作为一位典型的后现代小说家和评论者,福特喜欢研究故事的虚构过程,以及虚构形式和理解之间的关系。后现代小说注重形式的革新,在这方面福特与其他后现代作家有共识,即形式不是模仿的对象,而是思辨的工具;形式不是饼干模型切割刀,现实不是现成铺好等待成形的面团,要用形式来加以模式化。福特指出,"对形式的实验就是指我们如何认知和整理经验"。福特的小说展示了作家对形式的把握,以及对情节、主题、人物塑造和视角的认识和理解。

除了对形式的极大关注,福特对文学评论这一工作也有自己的见解。他在《职业化文学研究一般用语的精神病理学》一文中将文学评论的写作比作让孩子离开温暖的家,去面对老师和编辑的评判;把文学评论的发表比作送孩子上学后父母怀有的焦虑感。这一观点说明了文本(评论文章)、作者和读者(编辑和市场)三者的关系。文学评论反映作者思想的独立性,同时在一定程度上也受到读者的影响,好的文论其形式(这里指语言和思想的结合)是完善的,经得起任何权威的挑剔。

作　　品

The Coal Shoveller

"The clock is ticking."

That's a poor beginning for my short story. The trouble with "clock" is that it symbolizes time, and I don't want to introduce any big ideas into my story. Besides, I actually have an electric clock which whirrs.

It is a snowy day in midwinter. Out of my second-story window I see the street. The snow is so deep that all traffic has stopped. The last vehicle to come by was a truck which dumped five or six tons of coal on the sidewalk beside the red brick Victorian building[1] across the street. It was once a fine mansion, or so my mother told me during her visit. She had lived in Washington in the early 1900's when her father was a senator. She said that a school for young ladies was there, and the "best people"[2] sent their daughters to it. Now the building is divided into small, cheap apartments for government workers. When I walk by, I sometimes see rats in the yard. The land is quite valuable, and in time[3] the grey cupolas, the bay windows,[4] and the portico will come down to be replaced by a new glass and steel office building in the style of the Holiday Inn which is just behind it. On top of the inn is a lattice fence which, I assume, shields some kind of sun porch.[5] At night they turn pink flood-lights on the lattice.

A Negro man is shovelling the coal into the basement. I am separated from him by Massachusetts Avenue. The task I have set myself is not a very difficult one. The scene

---

[1] Victorian building:维多利亚女王时代建筑风格的楼房。
[2] the "best people":上等人家。
[3] in time:eventually,总有一天。
[4] the bay windows:windows jutting out from the wall of a building and forming an alcove within, esp. one rising from ground level,凸出墙外的窗户。
[5] sun porch:日光室(供日光浴用),也可称作 sun-room。

is visually appealing to me. I would like to write a simple short story describing the scene and, perhaps, giving some idea of the rather interesting neighborhood in which I live. I have no theme to draw out of the scene. The thing itself is enough. So it seems that the best style for me would be something on the order of the new novels.[1]

  The northeast wind blows the snow almost horizontally down Seventeenth Street. It slaps against the coal shoveller's face, sticks to him briefly, melts and falls. He is wearing a faded green army jacket. A black strip over his left breast has the words "U. S. Army" printed on it in gold letters. The Negro's face is partially muffled by a grey hat with ear flaps and a red scarf wrapped high around his neck. His eyes are turned onto the coal pile in front of him. The lumps are of various sizes, the smaller pieces on the bottom. The head of the coal scoop runs along the snow and enters the coal. The handle is brown with a faded red stripe where it meets the scoop. The shovel comes out. He swings around to the south. The blue flag on the Australian embassy. The white house next to it. The tops of parked cars. The whiteness of Seventeenth Street. The elaborate concrete curves of the B'nai Brith[2] building. The blue fence around the Holiday Inn swimming pool. The red brick building. The black hole into the cellar.[3] The coal clatters down into the chute.[4] Black dust flecks the snow. He continues his movement, turning north into the wind. The apartment building across Massachusetts Avenue. The window on the second floor. Up Seventeenth Street. The flashing red sign "The Bacchus."[5] The coal pile. The shovel goes in. The wood is brown, surrounded by a red stripe where the handle meets the black scoop. A grey glove with a hole in it. The skin beneath the hole is black.

  I can't go on like that. Words have a powerful integrity of their own which no amount of authorial intention can eliminate. I could write a hundred essays on how objective I am going to be, but the connotations of "white," "snow," and "black" would still be there. All that I wanted was to describe the scene, but who could fail to see in my story a comment on the white noose[6] that is strangling our black inner-city?

  You might argue that my objections to continuing my story as I stared it are based solely on the assumption of a faulty reader reaction, and that I should be skillful enough to remake the consciousness of my audience as I write. Can someone like Robbe-Grillet[7] actually believe that he is reshaping the mind of man as he writes? I don't have

---

[1] the new novels:新小说。这个词源于法语 nouveau roman。新小说是始于20世纪50年代法国的新文学流派,代表人物是法国作家 Alain Robbe-Grillet。他在创作中摈弃了传统小说的情节、叙述、主题思想、人物等要素。他认为小说应该只写事物(things),对物体(objects)作系统而有分析的记录。
[2] B'nai Brith:大楼名。
[3] The black hole into the cellar:黑洞洞的大门通往地窖。
[4] clatters down into the chute:哗啦啦地落在斜槽里。
[5] The Bacchus:酒吧名。Bacchus:巴克斯,希腊神话中酒神狄俄尼索斯(Dionysus)的别名。
[6] noose:套索。
[7] Robbe-Grillet:阿兰•罗伯-格里耶(Alain Robbe-Grillet,1922—2008),法国"新小说"的倡导者,强调存在于事物、姿态及情景间的关系,避免对心理动机作"评述"。他著有小说《窥视者》(Le Voyeur,1955)、《在迷宫》(Dans le Labyrinthe,1959)等。

the arrogance to deny reality in the name of an idea of reality.

Nor am I convinced that fiction should try to approximate painting (or the films). Prose has been headed in this direction for some time, but like most movements in art this one was begun on ill-defined premises and succeeding writers merely spun out a potential. We have come to a point now where the weaknesses inherent in the original assumptions prevent us from going further. To ask words to make fiction into photographic realism is to demand a performance which they are totally incapable of giving.

Since I cannot escape words and since words are necessarily symbols, I might as well write a more traditional story in which I admit that every time I use a word I am interpreting reality. The only ideas I can draw out of the scene are my own because they are obviously the only ones I know. I have no concept of the way in which the coal shoveller sees the world.

Amelia, who was six, had exhausted every possibility for entertainment she could find in the house. She had played with her dolls, colored the book she had been given at the school Christmas party the day before, and had made two entirely different houses out of the sofa pillows. An unusual inclination to help her mother had resulted in her being ushered out of the kitchen when she had spilled a cup of milk that was to be used for the Christmas cookies. On most holidays she would have gone to visit one of her friends, but the private school she went to was in the suburbs where most of the pupils lived, and her mother wasn't willing to risk driving through the snow. If she were at someone else's house they could at least watch television, but her father allowed only two programs a week and she had squandered her time for two solid hours on Sunday. Amelia had finally settled by the window where she watched the snow and the old colored man across the street who was shovelling the coal. She wanted to go outside and play, but it wasn't allowed because of the traffic.

In desperation she went back to the kitchen and asked her mother to take her out, but "There is too much to be done, darling," was all she got.

"There's not any cars in the street."

"It's still dangerous. Maybe your father will take you out when he's through working."

Amelia went back into the living room and tried to color another picture, but the tiger she was working on didn't interest her. She closed the book and looked at the door which led into her father's study. The rule that "Daddy is not to be bothered when he's working" was, she knew, an absolute one.

Under most circumstances this suited her well enough because she was actually frightened by the room. The study had been built on the side of the house the summer before when her father had published a book and had been given a big raise. To help him in his work the room had no windows and a special control which kept the room at the same temperature all the time. The darkness and the quietness bothered her, but she had reached her limit.

She walked to the door as quietly as she could, turned the knob, and had started in when her mother heard her.

"Don't bother daddy."

Her mother came running from the kitchen and pulled her away. The door was open a crack. She saw her father in the dark room with the bright light over his typewriter making his face look all black and white.

"I'm sorry, Michael," her mother said as she closed the door. "It's snowin and she wanted to go out."

"That's all right," Michael said through the closed door. "I'll take her out in a few minutes. My train of thought[1] is broken now anyway." He had been married for ten years and the way his wife said "snowin" still bothered him. It was embarrassing for a sociologist, active in the Civil Rights movement, to have a Southern wife.

Michael turned back to his desk. Actually he was pleased with the interruption. He was almost through with the article he had been working on about the problems of urban Negroes in Washington. He had attacked the question from various angles, poking at it first with the intellect then with the emotions. The piece now had about the right amount of feeling and thought to make it acceptable to one of the slick[2] magazines. It would be good to let the manuscript sit overnight. One more polishing tomorrow, and it would be finished. He took the last page out of the typewriter, laid it neatly with the others, leaned back in his chair, and surveyed with satisfaction the day's production.

The bright lights in the living room hurt his eyes. His wife was making more than the usual amount of noise in the kitchen. Out of the window he saw the curtain of snow that was falling over the street. In the distance the old Negro man was shovelling coal.

"Let's go, daddy," Amelia said. "There's lots of snow."

She was dressed in a bright red snow suit.

"Where are your galoshes?" he asked.

"Margaret," he called into the kitchen, "are you trying to make the child sick by letting her go out without her galoshes?"

His wife came out of the kitchen. "Amelia, I told you to put them on."

"I don't want to go out," Amelia said sullenly.

"Now that I've stopped work," he father said, "we are going out into the snow."

Amelia went to the closet, and with her mother's help laboriously pulled on the galoshes. Michael got on his own overshoes and coat.

"I wish I could go with you," his wife said. "The snow is beautiful."

"When I was a boy in Wisconsin, we wouldn't have called this anything but a

---

[1] train of thought: 我的思路。
[2] slick: (俚)第一流的。

flurry[1]," he said with a smile.

"I've never seen so much," Amelia said.

From there on the story writes itself. Michael goes into the snow. He gradually discovers the reality of his wife's life and that he has never understood the Negroes at all. Finally, he arrives at some understanding of the emotional sterility of his owe life, which is sentimentally compared to his childhood back in Wisconsin.

Sound familiar? Joyce's "The Dead."[2] I didn't deliberately set out to imitate the story, but it was there waiting for me like a trap. I couldn't avoid imitation.

In addition to my feeling that this has been done already better than I could do it, there are other reasons why I don't like my story. The focus is on the main character's movement towards self-under-standing. It posits that intellectual and emotional development is all that accounts. The reality of the Negro coal shoveller, even the realness of the snow and the house, is not considered important beside the ideas which I have extracted (or perhaps created) from them. My story would end by suggesting the subordination of thing to idea. I am inclined to agree with those who say that literature (no matter how negative the themes) which reinforced the habit of extracting ideas from reality panders to[3] the self-interest of the middle class. You can be sure that both you and I would prefer a few hours of anguish trying to understand the validity of various attitudes that one could take toward the Negro shovelling coal to five minutes of real or fictional exposure to the reality of that man's life and his work.

Not only am I blocked philosophically from writing a Joycean[4] story—I am also incompatible with its style. I lack the necessary innocence. When the symbolic technique was devised, writers must have been able to allow their symbols to emerge "naturally." I have studied fiction too long. Take the "study" in my story. Is that too heavy-handed? How subtle should a symbol be? I honestly don't know. I rather imagine that a good symbol is one that takes an English teacher about two minutes to decipher and one of his students ten. Talk of "organic symbols" that grow out of reality is absolute garbage at this point in the evolution of fictional techniques.

If I use symbols I also depend heavily on my readers' being willing to accept my symbolism for what I intend. For example, I said in my story that Michael laid the last page "neatly" on the others. "Neatly" is a symbol for certain aspects of his character. But what is actually wrong with being neat? If there weren't a general, if ill-defined, prejudice of modern readers in favor of emotional spontaneity, that word might be honorific[5]. If you say that *in the context* the symbol is made meaningful, I reply that

---

[1] flurry:小雪。
[2] Joyce's "The Dead":指乔伊斯(James Joyce)的短篇小说《死者》("The Dead")。这篇小说以下雪作故事背景。
[3] panders to:迎合。
[4] Joycean:of James Joyce.
[5] honorific:敬语。

my story is nothing but a pastiche[1] of such symbols.

Underlying all of them is a series of romantic values epitomized by the noble Negro coal shoveller, the goodness of nature (represented by the snow), and the joys of childhood. When I draw these values out of my story, as I am doing now, they are subject to attack. But one of the advantages that comes to the fictionalist is that he doesn't have to defend his assumptions. The critics tell us that he doesn't have to defend his assumptions. The critics tell us that we should examine literature from within. This idea has been forced on them by the "creative" writers. Who can blame an author like Henry James[2] for wanting his value assumptions considered "out of bounds"?

Then there is the rather obvious point that I have completely distorted reality in my story. I live in a small apartment. A house on Massachusetts Avenue would cost a fortune. I am the one from the south, not my wife.

Since I am aware of the ideas behind my symbols, why not write an essay instead of a short story? I reject that at once. My first inclination is to explain this rejection by saying something about the "mystery of art." Many writers talk of this mystery, and it seems to me that they do so primarily to convince themselves that they are somehow "special" and belong to a cult of super souls who have powers (and, more importantly, privileges) that ordinary mortals can't understand. The real reason that I prefer fiction is that it gives me a feeling of righteousness which is denied to me in essays. In fiction I redefine reality by style. When I survey the new world I have created in my story I can say, "Yes, by God, since the world is like that I am completely justified in feeling what I feel." I am quick to admit that I need this kind of self-justification and that I want to use the devices of fiction to make others second[3] my righteousness.

In the fragment of my story on Michael, I disguised, under the illusion of objectivity, my own need to use fiction to justify myself and gain approval of readers. But now that I admit this need, I might as well try an autobiographical story in which I reveal myself more directly and, consequently, make a more overt appeal for approval. I will use the time (mentioned earlier) when my mother came to visit me here.

The woman stands in the small, cramped apartment. She looks down on the oblivious snow in the avenue—not knowing that she or he existed. The woman in front of him—a mother, but not a mother because mothers are associated with home, and here is not home. She, vaguely ashamed to be here—not of him because it is not his fault that he lives here with Yankee wife, but of herself, of her dead husband, and her dead father and the long line of failures that have reduced the family to the point of living in a small apartment.

---

[1] pastiche：现代派"大拼盘"手法。
[2] Henry James：亨利·詹姆斯(1843—1916)，美国小说家、散文家和文学评论家。其作品对人物刻画惟妙惟肖，笔法多样，文体独特。代表作品有《鸽翼》(*The Wings of the Dove*, 1902)、《大使们》(*The Ambassadors*, 1903)和《金碗》(*The Golden Bowl*, 1904)。
[3] second：支持，赞成。

He puts her bag on the floor and waits awkwardly for her to do something. She asks for a glass of sherry. It is almost twilight. The snow is falling harder outside—the blanket is making all men equal in cold and misery and accentuating the memory of warm Southern summers with the smell of purple wisteria[1] twisting through honeysuckle when the bright colors differentiated people: blacks from whites and whites from poor whites. And it is all over for her now because there is no more home to live in and no more wooded yards lined with flowers, and she and the son and the Negro servants have all fled north to Washington, where they are equal under the snow but hating that equality—the Negro because the equalness is not real, the son because he is poor, and the Mother because she knows that she is better. She sips sherry in the twilight and the son straight whiskey[2]—waiting.

He has put out on the table a book of family history because it will please her to know that he cares. She looks at it, and the book, like a trigger, explodes the blocks against history, and between sips of sherry there pours out the talk that he has heard so often, but that still can make him desire again to be a child in a world where he could maintain the illusion of a baronial grandeur bequeathed to him by the past—but for him so long away that the memory he had received is like the deformed last of the litter: a tiny final effort from the exhausted womb of the old South. Too twisted and confused to do more than make him wish he had been closer to the source of the myth.

"Do you see that house?" she says as she walks to the window.

"Yes."

"I went to school there when your grandfather was a senator. He was a great man. I drove up every morning to that building in a carriage. All the great people sent their children there. At least I think that's the building. So much has changed."

As she talks, he thinks:

He was a child. It was summer at his grandmother's. The large rambling house with its rows of bedrooms and the porch that ran all around the house high up in the foothills of the Georgia Blue Ridge. "On a clear day," his grandmother said, "you can see to the sea." But even then he knew that was not true. It had been a summer place, but now a few of the downstairs rooms had been insulated so that she could live there—not in isolation but still fighting with the ferocious anger that her mother before her had used to hold the family together after the War[3], but which had not been able to cope with Yankee businessmen, boll weevils,[4] and resentful Negro workers in South Georgia. Now she lived on the hill surrounded by thick underbrush which kept from her the knowledge of the encroaching townspeople whose squat, white houses lapped at the hill. All that was

---

[1] wisteria:紫藤。
[2] straight whiskey:纯威士忌酒。
[3] the war:指美国内战。
[4] boll weevils:棉铃象虫。

left outside of the underbrush of what had once been a great estate was the Episcopal church at the foot of the hill which his great-grand-father had built just after the War for the use of the family and the other summer people.

Then the summer when he was seven he came and his grandmother told him that he could no longer play in the church because it had been sold. She said "sold" with an icy pride which made him afraid. On the first Sunday when he was there his grandmother was sitting on the porch reading Sir Walter Scott[1] to him—he not understanding, but made peaceful by the words which flowed in and out of the mimosa[2] trees and the humming of bees. She stopped. "Did you understand that?"

"What, ma'am?"

"What I read to you."

"Not exactly."

"Listen. 'My foot is on my native heath,[3] and my name is MacGregor!' Does that mean anything to you?"

"Yes, ma'am," he lied. But it did. A thousand times since he had said it. When he came home from college and the heath was a quarter-acre yard with an old Ford in it. And even now when he walked into the little apartment on Massachusetts Avenue he said it with bitterness.

Before she started reading again, the church bell sounded from outside of the underbrush. He heard singing coming out of a loudspeaker—cracked twangy accents of country people. He felt his grandmother stiffen.

"Angela," she said.

"Yes'm." The fat old Negro woman came out onto the porch drying her hands on her apron. The enormous kindness of the woman became a natural part of the warm summer morning.

"What is that noise?"

"There's more folks want to go to the church than it'll hold. They put up speakers for those who's outside."

"Thank you, Angela."

Angela went back to fix Sunday dinner.

"I want you to remember," his grandmother said to him, "that Sunday morning is God's of Peace. For one as old as I, Peace is sacred."

"Yes, ma'am," he said.

That night as he lay in his bed and watched the moon lie on the state of Georgia he saw a frail woman carrying a big can move like a black shadow away from the house and

---

[1] Sir Walter Scott: 沃尔特·司各特(1771—1832),英国的民谣家和小说家,他发展了历史小说这一流派。主要作品包括长篇小说《威弗利》(*Waverley*,1814)和《艾凡赫》(*Ivanhoe*,1819)。

[2] mimosa:含羞草属植物。

[3] my native heath:我的出生地;我幼年生活过的地方。

into the underbrush. He was afraid, too afraid to think, and he waited until the orange light had taken away the silver moonlight, and he slept.

When the vacation was over and he was home he asked his mother and father why it happened. They pretended not to understand but answered anyway. "Your grandmother is a fine, strong woman," his father said with pride. But he could not understand this because when his father's boss would call on Sunday morning his father would grumble but go to work. "We have to eat," he would say. And his father worked for a Baptist although the boss became an Episcopalian like him later on.

And he could not understand how Sunday mornings could both be sacred and not sacred and he saw that his father loved the strength of his grandmother but also wanted to get a raise from the Baptist[1]. Being a child he could not stand uncertainty and found a third way which he believed could eventually fuse the opposition into oneness—intelligence, which he now knew was the weakest weapon he could have chosen because it compounded, not resolved, the opposition. The more clearly his mind failed to understand why Sundays were sacred the more he longed to share in his grandmother's pride. But unlike his father for whom the beliefs were closer and more real and who lost his life trying to work for the Baptist and live by his grandmother's sureness, the dream of the peace of Sunday mornings was so far removed from him that he was almost denied the pleasure of having it as a dream; and yet at times like this, when his mother was talking, he could almost reach out to the voice of his grandmother ("MY foot is on my native heath") that created in him, for however short a time, the innocence of dreaming, when he could free himself of knowing the inconsistencies, the injustices, the contradictions that were housed in his grandmother's impoverished Eden. Perhaps, he thought, if there is another generation the dream will be taken away and we can function in the Baptists' world (although he did not understand the legitimacy of the Baptist as symbol any more) and the sins of the fathers will be gone. But in the small apartment with its books and its typewriter the disease was all the peace and beauty which he had ever known and the cure seemed worse than the illness. And he watched the coal shoveller—a man without hope, for whom jail and the welfare line are the legacies of a belief in the sanctity of Sunday morning, and the mother's voice, now crumbled into mumbling quests after the ability of words to rebuild a belief in the present reality of the dream, is also the legacy. And he knows that the dream has produced evil, but knowing is, as it always had been for him, a false god.

His mother says: "That old colored man—I suppose you say 'Negro' now—reminds me of old Dick the footman who used to open the carriage door for us when we came to school. Your grandfather sent him money every year. ..."

---

[1] the Baptist: 指前面提到的 Boss。

I wish that I could honestly see the fall of the Old South as tragic in the way that Faulkner[1] did. Only occasionally do I even care about the fact that I don't care. The story gives a completely false impression of what I actually feel on the subject. I blame the misrepresentation on the style which was so intoxicating that it carried me where I didn't want to go.

And where was I going? Deeper and deeper into my mind or at least into the pseudo-mind which the words were creating as they went along. By the time thinking has become words it has ceased to be self.

Style dominates the piece and focuses the reader's attention on my way of seeing the world. Like most middle-class writers I have a decided anti-middle-class bias, and I don't believe the "I" is worth a sustained story. (Someday I would like to study the strong streak of masochism[2] which runs through or even dominates modern fiction. Middle-class writers take great pleasure in writing about the "emotional bankruptcy" of middle-class writers. And certainly there is no better way to be popular with the general public than to tell them how horrible they are. The way in which this masochism works is obvious in my own story of Michael the sociologist. I have some of my hero's characteristics, and in the story I objectified my own sins and controlled things in such a way that Michael is punished. Having paid for my errors by sticking pins in my image, I can continue to muddle along as usual without feeling the need to take any real action.) I am also interested in the extent to which certain kinds of beliefs control ideas. Does my Faulknerian story depend on my putting myself into a frame of mind where I can believe in the reality of the myth of the Old South? And did the symbolic technique in my first story depend on the romantic values which formed the assumptions on which the story was based? I think the answer to both questions is yes.

At this point I accuse myself of not being able to finish any of these stories because I am a nihilist[3]. But I immediately recognize that nothing is further from the truth. I believe in a great many things—so many in fact that the beliefs tend to cancel each other out. Good writers are successful because they can eliminate (at least in a given work) all but one possible way of seeing the world. They develop styles and structures because they are following through with this single vision. Robbe-Grillet's novels, for example, are the product of one particular way of looking at the world. As he was writing, he was able to block from his mind the knowledge that during most of his life he sees the world in many different ways. If he looked at reality in his daily life as he does in his novels, he would never be able to do a single practical thing like catching a train or showing up for a speaking engagement on time. Is arrogant, spiritual narrowmindedness the essence of

---

[1] Faulkner：威廉·福克纳(1897—1962)美国作家，他的许多作品都以虚构的约克纳帕塔法县为背景，揭示了南方传统价值观的衰败，如小说《喧嚣与骚动》(The Sound and the Fury, 1929)和《不可战胜》(The Unvanquished, 1938)。1949年他获诺贝尔文学奖。

[2] masochism：受虐狂。

[3] nihilist：虚无主义者。

the writer?

The scene is still there. The janitor[1] is still shovelling coal. Because the street is quiet, I can hear the shovel as it scrapes into the coal. Do you believe that? You might. But it is cold and the window is closed. Massachusetts Avenue is a big street. I hear nothing. Why did I add the sound to my description? Writers are supposed to "render" and not "report." Writing classes do more harm than good.

That's neither here nor there. Since I am beginning to understand the extent to which masochism is a dominant motivation in all of my stories, perhaps I should try to be more honest and objectify my "antiself" into an active romantic. I must have bottled up[2] in myself an enormous amount of anti-intellectual, anti-establishment hostility. As I have said before, I know nothing of what the coal shoveller actually thinks, but I can easily make him into whatever I want. I'll make him the rogue hero that I might like to be.

My anti-hero's name is to be Reginald Cowpersmith. He is twenty-eight, married, and unemployed. He finds himself on this particular snowy day walking by the pile of coal, where he sees an angry building superintendent starting to shovel the coal. Reginald, who is broke[3], asks for the job.

"The boy who is supposed to look after this sort of thing didn't show up," the superintendent said. He was winded from the one or two shovelfuls he had tossed down the chute.

"It's hard to know who to trust these days." Reginald said.

"That's very true. I'm lucky you happened to be passing by."

"I could certainly use the work." Reginald said in his most serious tone.

"I'm surprised a nice-looking young man like yourself has to go around looking for odd jobs."

"I'm at the University, sir," Reginald said. "It's very expensive. I also have a family to support. I try to supplement my income in whatever way I can."

"I wish other people in this city had your ambition."

"*They* need our sympathy, sir."

"Quite right. I know I can trust you. Here's five dollars. Shovel the coal into the cellar. I want to get home while I can." The superintendent shuffled toward Rhode Island Avenue and the bus home.

"Cheerio[4]." Reginald called after him as he waved good-bye. "And," he added, when he saw the superintendent was out of earshot. "do me the pleasure of applying thy rosy lips to the gentle curvature of my buttocks."

---

[1] janitor: 大楼管理员,照看或打扫筑物的人。
[2] bottled up: 抑制。
[3] broke: (口)一个钱也没有。
[4] Cheerio: (俚)再会。

Reginald imagined the superintendent at home in some place like Hyattsville[1] sitting in front of a fire telling his wife, children, and sadeyed cocker spaniel[2] how lucky he was to fin "this white boy" to shovel his coal instead of "that no-good nigger."

"Cowpersmith,"Reginald asked himself,"what would you like for Christmas out of this five dollars?"

"Perhaps, a gift for a needy family," Reginald replied.

"Not likely."

"A bottle of whiskey?"

"It's on the list," Cowpersmith said.

"A fuck in a neighborhood brothel?"

"Agreed."

Reginald stuck the shovel into the pile of coal and retired into the apartment house to contemplate the laws of economics which prevented a five-dollar bill from buying both presents.

He lit a cigarette and leaned against the radiator. Beside him was a row of old mailboxes. He reached into the nearest one and came up with a handful of letters. A hand-addressed one from Des Moines[3]. The writing suggested aged parents. A circular from Catholic Charities, Inc.[4] A request for funds from CORE[5]. An announcement of the January offerings of the Apollo film club and a letter from the Civil Service Commission advertising "New Benefits for Government Employees."

"The poor creature must be lonely." Reginald said.

"It's hard to be away from home at Christmas time." Cowpersmith agreed.

"We might as well give ourselves one of our presents free."

"In what apartment does the lonely young lady live?" Cowpersmith asked.

"In NO. three. After you, Mr. Cowpersmith."

"Thank you, Reggie."

Reginald walked up the stairs.

The hall smelled of rotten gentility. Reginald pictured the time when liveried Uncle Toms[6] served great ladies in these halls. He had a fleeting image of himself as a Southern Senator walking down these stairs before the big rooms had been divided up into apartments. "Good evening, Senator Cowpersmith, the ladies are waiting in the drawing room."

He knocked on apartment number three.

---

[1] Hyattsville:海厄茨维尔,在马里兰州。
[2] cocker spaniel:西班牙长耳狗。
[3] Des Moines:得梅因,依阿华州首府。
[4] A circular from Catholic Charities, Inc.:天主教慈善公司的通函。
[5] CORE:Congress of Racial Equality 的缩写。
[6] Uncle Toms:泛指黑人。Uncle Tom 是美国女作家斯托尔(Harriet E. Stowe,1811—1896)的小说《汤姆叔叔的小屋》(*Uncle Tom's Cabin*,1852)中的主人公。

The girl who opened the door had four immediately observable characteristics. Two large tits and two wide, frightened eyes.

"Excuse me, ma-am," he said. "I'm the substitute janitor and the superintendent asked me to look at your radiator."

"I didn't know anything was wrong with it."

"It'll only take a second."

"All right."

He went in. The apartment was warm and homey. The living room—bedroom was neat. The convertible couch in the corner, for which he had future plans, seemed adequate to support the two of them, and he was sure that the sheets would be clean, a detail which he had come to insist on since he had been married and had come to appreciate some of the refinements that go with domestic bliss. On the desk in one corner were three pictures. Two were of "mom" and "dad". A third tinted photograph showed an insipid-looking young man in a uniform.

As he fiddled with the radiator he talked to her. "It is certainly a cold day. But then Christmas without snow is like a day without wine, as the French say."

She nodded suspiciously. The use of "French" and "wine" had been a mistake.

"Christmas brings out the best in us," he said, taking a new approach. "Love, charity, the simple virtues that seem SO far removed from city life."

"You're an educated man," she said. "It's funny but I've lived in Washington now for almost a year and I haven't really talked to anybody during that time."

"I guess the city isn't what you expected," he said. "It must be very lonely for you."

"Yes."

Any "yes" is a good sign, Reginald thought. Affirm one idea and you will tend to affirm everything.

"How does it happen that you are working as a janitor?" she asked.

"I'm a writer."

"Really?"

"Yes. I have a novel I'm working on. I need the money from odd jobs, but I also want to find out the kind of life the poor people live here, particularly the Negroes."

"I've thought of the same thing," she said excitedly.

"They have a hard time." He stopped fiddling with the radiator and stood up.

"I'll bet you do too." she said.

"Adversity is the trifling burden which man must bear if he is to fulfill the kingdom of God on earth. I do what I can." He was a little anxious about the last statement. It might have been too extreme, but he recognized as he watched her that by adopting the "writer" tag he had adequately prepared her for exaggerated language.

"Would you like some coffee?"

"Thank you, but I have to get back outside to finish shovelling the coal. I think your radiator will be all right now."

"You have time for just a cup."

"I guess so."

She went into the tiny kitchen. Her ass, a fifth characteristic which he had not previously had the opportunity to observe, waved in a friendly way. He followed her. As she put the pot on the stove he moved in on her. ...

God, but I hate bastards who write stories like that. They think that cruelty is cute and justified in the name of their own super souls. Kerouac, Donleavy, Miller,[1] the whole lot of them. Dividing up the world into two parts—themselves and the squares. They condemn with a thoughtless pride grounded in a morality of immorality which is more rigid than the Calvinist code[2] which they profess to hate. Being "right", they are justified in doing anything to the enemy. How many people could Reginald Cowpersmith hurt in the course of one short story? Four or five probably. Maybe two dozen in a novel. When I read *The Catcher in the Rye* my sympathies are with Mr. and Mrs. Caulfield and "old Spencer".[3] I care more about Miss Frost in *The Gingerman* than about the Gingerman.

Does that sound too moral? I would personally be happy with a situation where writers had no effect at all on the immediate existence of readers. But fictionalists have for so long thought of themselves as prophets that they have talked a gullible, freedom-escaping world into believing that they are. Given the function of art in our time, I agree with Bellow[4] when he says that we must have writers who think.

What would happen if the neo-romantics did think? They would find among other things that they are paranoid. They write fiction in which Society tries to destroy them, a theme which serves no other purpose than to inflate their egos. Actually Society cares very little about them. The role of the rebel is a self-serving one.

And, furthermore, the rebellion of these anti-heroes is usually much tamer than it seems on the surface because they don't challenge the basic value systems of society. I also feel that my own story (like most of those in the genre) would have ended sentimentally with Reginald showing that at heart he was a swell fellow and that my readers should love him. Behind every romantic hero is a maudlin[5] child.

---

[1] Kerouac, Donleavy, Miller: Kerouac: 凯鲁亚克(Jack Kerouac, 1922—1969), 美国诗人, 小说家, "跨掉的一代"运动的领袖, 宣扬发狂地追求新体验。代表作有《在路上》(*On the Road*, 1957)、《达摩流浪记》(*The Dharma Bums*, 1958)。Donleavy: 唐利维(James Patrick Donleavy, 1926—), 美国小说家, 作品用第一人称传达思想, 用第三人称表现行为, 集观察者和参与者于一身。主要作品有《姜人》(*The Gingerman*, 1955)、《一个怪人》(*A Singular Man*, 1963)。Miller: 米勒(Arthur Miller, 1915—2005), 美国剧作家, 《推销员之死》(*Death of A Salesman*, 1949)是其代表作。

[2] Calvinist code: 加尔文教派教义。

[3] Mr. and Mrs. Caulfield and "old Spencer": Mr. and Mrs. Caulfield 是《麦田里的守望者》中的主人公 Holden Caulfield 的父母亲; old Spencer 是 Holden 的老师。

[4] Bellow: 美国犹太小说家贝娄(Saul Bellow, 1915—2005), 代表作有《赛勒姆先生的行星》(*Mr. Sammler's Planet*, 1970)、《洪堡的礼物》(*Humboldt's Gift*, 1975), 1976 年获诺贝尔奖。

[5] maudlin: 感情脆弱的。

What is left to me? I seem to lack the necessary emotional commitment to follow through with any of the styles I have tried. Of all writers, the satirist is the closest to being beyond innocence. He accepts, as a given, the futility of self-assertion. Ultimately, of course, no one who bothers to write can be completely un-innocent, but by writing satire I can approach this condition.

I have a perfect scene for my story. There is a little bar around the corner called "The Bacchus." I go there occasionally. It is the place for Washington hipsters[1], so I can ridicule my romantic enemies who hang out there. These habitués are also vaguely associated with the arts, and there is nothing more delightful to one in my position than to attack those who still are committed to the muses[2].

I need a norm by which the objects of my satire are to be measured. The coal shoveller will do. He is a man who has a job to do and a family to support—a practical, realistic person.

The man was sitting alone in a booth near the bar, drinking beer and watching the scene in front of him. The young hipsters and their older gurus[3] milled around. The door opened. The man turned around. An old Negro was shuffling through the room toward the bar. He wore a "surplus"[4] green jacket. Over his left pocket was a black strip with "U. S. Army" stitched on it in gold. The man in the booth felt suddenly excited. He tried to call to the coal shoveller, but he had already taken a seat at the bar. The man watched and listened.

The coal shoveller spoke to the bartender. "I'll have a beer," he said. The bartender gave him a large draft. "I been shovelling coal so long," the coal shoveller said. "I was mighty cold. The boss gone home."

"A cold day." the bartender agreed.

"I wasn't sure about coming in here. Some places still don't like the colored customers."

"It's okay in here." the bartender laughed.

"I knew it'd be okay. I seen that sign over the door. About Bacchus and all. He's the place licker[5] for the Cardinals[6], ain't he? Man he sure is a fat fellow. Can you think of gettin' all the money he does without having to stay in shape."

The bartender, who was waiting on another customer, nodded automatically.

"I knew it was okay to come in a place where football fans come. I know a good bit

---

[1] hipsters: 嬉皮士。
[2] the muses: 文学艺术。The Muses: 缪斯, 希腊神话中宙斯和记忆女神的九位女儿, 掌管文艺、音乐、天文等。这里代指文学艺术。
[3] gurus: 古鲁, 印度教中传经授道的宗教大师; 此处指头头。
[4] surplus: 指多余的军需物资。
[5] place licker: 踢定位球者。
[6] the Cardinals: 圣路易(St. Louis)的橄榄球队。

about football. I seen Bacchus kick four field goals[1] on TV against the Browns[2] just last Sunday."

He drank some of his beer. "Lots of Redskin[3] fans in here. But you can carry that football business too far. Letting your hair grow long just for a football team."

The bartender wasn't listening to him, so he spoke to the man beside him.

"I think Jerry Smith's a good tight end."

"Really?" said the man. "I don't know him, but I'd like to."

A pretty white girl sat down on the other side of him. "Do you use consciousness expansion drugs?"[4] she asked.

"No, ma'am. I'm a janitor."

"You're cute." she said.

The coal shoveller was embarrassed. Several others were now standing around him. "Do you play an instrument?" one of them asked.

He pulled a harmonica[5] out of his pocket.

"Give us a tune," they said. A crowd had gathered. He began to play "Ole Black Joe."[6]

The man in the booth looked on with disgust at the hipsters.

God, but I hate bastards like that, the man thought. In their arrogant moral sureness. Dividing the world up into two parts—themselves and the squares—and condemning with a thoughtless pride grounded in a morality of immorality which is more rigid than the Calvinist code which they profess to hate. They know nothing of the coal shoveller and they don't care. Poor bastard caught in that stupid conversation.

The coal shoveller had finished his tune.

The crowd standing around him joined in a chorus of praise.

—It's *it*.

—The real thing.

—No Joan Baez crap[7] here.

—Authentic.

—Close to Leadbelly[8].

—Real Delta Blues.[9]

---

[1] field goals: (橄榄球)越过球门横木的3分球。
[2] the Browns: 克利夫兰(Cleveland)的橄榄球队。
[3] Redskin: 华盛顿的橄榄球队。
[4] consciousness expansion drugs: 刺激人产生幻想的一种毒品,20世纪60年代流行于美国。
[5] harmonica: 口琴。
[6] Ole Black Joe: 一首流传较广的黑人歌曲。
[7] Joan Baez: 贝茨(1941—),美国民歌女歌唱家,以纯正的女高音演唱民歌、乡村歌曲而驰名歌坛,曾积极参与非暴力民权运动及反越战运动;crap:废话。
[8] Leadbelly: 利德贝利,原名为 Huddie Ledbetter (1888—1949),美国布鲁斯歌曲演唱家,吉它演奏家。
[9] Real Delta Blues: 真正的密西西比三角洲地区的布鲁斯音乐。Blues: 美国民间音乐,源于19世纪初美国黑人民歌,通常忧郁低沉,长于表达情绪,其富于表情的变音极大地影响了现代流行音乐。

"Thank you." the shoveller said.

"You must come and give US a concert." the blonde girl said.

"I'll try to." the coal shoveller said. "Right now, I've got to get back to my shoveling."

He got up from the bar stool and shuffled toward the door.

The man in the booth impulsively grabbed his arm as he passed. "Have a beer with me," he said.

"Thank you," the coal shoveller replied, "but I got to get back to my shoveling."

"Please."

The urgency of the request startled the coal shoveller. He sat down. The man ordered two beers. "Those people are all phony," he said. "They don't understand you. They are using you as a symbol."

"I was glad to have a chance to play my harmonica," the coal shoveller said. "My wife don't let me play at home."

"I've been watching you shovel the coal. I live on the second floor of the building across the street."

"Is that a fact?"

"I don't come in here often."

"What kind of business you in?"

"I'm a writer," the man said, "but I try to avoid attributing an essence to myself in view of the cultist[1] associations with the Artist in our time. I prefer to say, 'I write.'"

"What you write? I like stories on sports."

"That's why it's so important that I talk to you. Right now I'm trying to write a story about you shovelling coal."

"Is that a fact?" the coal shoveller said. He smiled broadly. "Where can I read it?"

"I don't know who'll take it. It's an experimental story."

"Oh." He looked disappointed. "What you experimenting about?"

"With the problems of language." the man said, growing excited. "I am trying to show that literary language is a shifting kaleidoscope of lights and shadows, full at once of absences and replenishments. A word is a door that opens onto the hypocritical and inexact world of idea. The very fact that I must attempt such a story shows that Western tradition has run its course. Art has been dehumanized so that no man can honestly write on anything but the problem of writing. The word as means has become the word as end. But I say to myself, so what? Let's not avoid the reality of this problem, but face it as I am in my story. We can reduce the long history of ideological and bourgeois domination of the arts in which reality has been subordinated by idea ..." He punctuated his last statement with a violent wave of his arm. He knocked over the bowl of pretzels[2] on the

---

[1] cultist:狂热的崇拜者。

[2] pretzels:椒盐卷饼。

table. The coal shoveller began carefully to replace them.

"You see," the man continued, looking urgently at the shoveller, "words are symbols. Perceiving is not done with words. So when I try to describe you shovelling coal, my story takes on connotations and implications which I don't want and which inevitably reflect my own mind. But if I can help to make both readers and writers question the assumptions on which they work. we will begin to level[1] Western society. The hunger for the word, the nutritive value of idea will be burned out of the literate middle class. And from the courage to criticize the assumptions which have thus far guided our civilization we will reach the zero degree of culture. Of course, I am no fool. I know that the absolute is an abstraction which will never be reached, because you cannot use language to destroy language..."

"You're right," the shoveller interrupted. "Zero is a little low. I was listening to WOOK[2] a while back and they said it'd be about 15 tonight. Could I have a Cigarette?"

"Sure," the man said. He gave a cigarette to the coal shoveller and took one for himself.

"Got a light?"

The coal shoveller lit the cigarettes.

"Nor do I think," the man continued, "that destruction of this cultural edifice we have raised would be any great loss. Art has become only another profession. Words are used by people to get ahead in their jobs, to gain prestige. It is not like it must have been with the grand amateurism of my grandfather. But all of these minds working on art with the tools of science eventually will see the emptiness as the center of art. Now literature is a worthless commodity in the market place where it is bartered for money..."

"Having money troubles?" the coal shoveller asked sympathetically. "Christmas is a hard time."

"It's not a question of money," the man said irritably. "You see in my business it's publish or ..." He checked himself. "After all my short story has enormous social overtones as well. You and the other poor people of the world have been hoodwinked[3] by ideas for so long. You will be the ones ultimately benefited by writers' willingness to examine their assumptions."

The man clapped the coal shoveller on the back with such force that he bumped against the table and spilled the pretzels again. "It is for you that I am writing this story."

"I certainly appreciate that," the coal shoveller said as he started replacing the pretzels. "Not many white people think about us colored people. Have a pretzel."

But, good Lord, what has any of this got to do with the original aim of my short

---

[1] level:夷平,毁坏。
[2] WOOK:地方电台的呼号。
[3] hoodwinked:欺骗。

story?

Little has changed. It is darker now. The snow is still falling heavily. The streets are still empty. The streetlights are on. The coal shoveller is slowly and steadily shoveling. I don't want to turn on the light because it would prevent me from seeing clearly out the window, but it is too dark for me to continue writing.

1969

赏 析

《铲煤者》是一篇典型的后现代小说。后现代小说统指第二次世界大战后出现的各种小说流派,是现代主义文学的延续和发展,其思想基础是反语言中心主义和反基础主义,主要流派有新小说派、黑色幽默、垮掉的一代、魔幻现实主义,主要特点有碎片化、戏仿、不可靠的叙述者、拼贴、元小说、黑色幽默等。美国后现代小说出现在 20 世纪 60 年代,以反战小说《第二十二条军规》(*Catch-22*, 1961)为标志。

《铲煤者》是讨论小说创作的小说,属元小说。作者以四个故事片断说明,对同一个题材(铲煤者和铲煤这一事件),作家可以随心所欲地虚构出不同的文学文本。同时,从一开始,每个故事片断的叙述经常被作者自己打断,进而对由这一片断引出的小说创作进行评论,这种"夹叙夹议"有两个作用,一是作者意在表明,所有的故事是"编"出来的,而不像现实主义小说家那样努力掩盖这种虚构性,竭力让读者相信他"编"出来的故事是真的;二是颠覆了传统的线性叙事,使整个作品变成"碎片"的组合。

除了强调小说的虚构性,小说从头到尾还穿插了大量作者对小说创作过程的评述,如思想和语言的关系("By the time thinking has become words it has ceased to be self."),象征的作用,风格决定一切("Style dominates the piece")。他也表明了自己的文学观点,如反对对现实的逼真临摹,人物的独立性("I know nothing of what the coal shoveller actually thinks"),文学创作是一种文字游戏("The word as means has become the word as end.")等等。

到了结尾,作者似乎还没有厘清作者与文本之间的关系,他陷入了两难的境地:开灯,他看不到窗外之景,也就无法进行描写;不开灯,他又无法在黑暗中进行创作。这似乎暗示,文学创作离不开现实,但仅仅临摹现实又是远远不够的。

相关评论

A Comprehensive Reading of "The Coal Shoveller"
Bill Delaney

Themes and Meanings

"The Coal Shoveller" is an important work in which Keith Fort has found the ideal form for expressing the problems of many aspiring writers. Although dissatisfied with the old styles—especially realism and naturalism—they cannot find new styles that will liberate them to express themselves. The main theme throughout this story concerns the difficulty of being honest. Its narrator admires many great writers of the past and appreciates that they were great because they wrote what they passionately believed. He wishes to emulate[1] them, but without imitating them. As a modern man, however, he finds it difficult to know in what he should believe.

The narrator's abortive attempts to concoct[2] a story based on a man shoveling coal are efforts to discover what he himself truly believes. His mind is full of ideas, but he does not know whether he really believes any of them. His indictment[3] of certain anti-intellectual writers suggests that he would agree with William Butler Yeats'[4] assessment of the modern condition in "The Second Coming" (1921): "The best lack all conviction while the worst are full of passionate intensity."

It might be argued that the theme of "The Coal Shoveller" is the difficulty of finding a theme, because a theme represents what a writer believes. It is appropriate to such an experimental story that its theme and meaning should be the search for theme and meaning. One thing in which the author does believe is the truth. He cannot force himself to regard the coal shoveller as either a victim or a hero. Such attitudes can lead into stylistic dead ends and ideological traps. He rejects one style after another because he feels that although they might have been appropriate for authors such as Alain Robbe-Grillet, James Joyce, Henry James, William Faulkner, Jack Kerouac, J. P. Donleavy, and Henry Miller,[5] they are false for him. He does not mention Ernest Hemingway, who was one of the most influential writers of the twentieth century, but he would certainly subscribe to Hemingway's dictum that a good writer's most essential gift is a built-in, shockproof bunk[6] detector, the "writer's radar" that all great writers have. The author does not know what he believes in, but he knows what he does not believe in, and that knowledge serves as his radar.

It may be more difficult to be creative in modern times because people have become too educated, too intellectual, and too sophisticated. The problem that many aspiring writers have in creating fiction is related to problems that others have in trying to read fiction. Many readers, because of the glut[7] of media information that they absorb, have become too intellectual and too jaded to believe in fiction. People are increasingly asking why they should be concerned about the problems of people who do not even exist.

It is understandable that short story writers should wonder whether they have anything meaningful to communicate when their labor is largely a labor of love. Short fiction might become obsolete without the patronage of literary journals subsidized by

---

[1] emulate: 效仿;(通过效仿)努力赶上或超过。
[2] concoct: 虚构,杜撰。
[3] indictment: 原意为控告,这里指批评。
[4] William Butler Yeats: 威廉·巴特勒·叶芝(1865—1939),爱尔兰诗人,被认为是20世纪最伟大的诗人之一,1923年获诺贝尔文学奖。
[5] Henry Miller: 亨利·米勒(1891—1980),美国作家,主要作品有小说《北回归线》(*Tropic of Cancer*, 1934)和《南回归线》(*Tropic of Capricorn*, 1939)。
[6] bunk: 空话,胡言乱语。
[7] glut: 原意为暴食,这里指吸收过多。

academic institutions. It is not unusual for writers—like the narrator of "The Coal Shoveller"—to be professors, and for them to wonder whether they are writers who teach, or teachers who write. If writers persist despite guilt, frustration, and self-doubt—as the author and his alter egos do in "The Coal Shoveller"—they may create new forms of fiction more suited to alienated, agnostic modern times. Writers such as Fort are creating forms that often seem like bizarre amalgamations[1] of fact and fantasy. The problem of the writer—like many other problems—may prove to be an opportunity in disguise.

Style and Technique

Although an experimental work classified as an antistory, "The Coal Shoveller" has important elements in common with conventional stories. In order to interest the reader, any story must be dramatic. Drama is provided by conflicting motives, which have been categorized as "man against man," "man against nature," and "man against himself." "The Coal Shoveller" falls into the last category. Its narrator is strongly motivated to write a story but finds, after a number of false starts, that he cannot do so. His strong motivation to persevere is what keeps the reader wanting to learn whether he ever succeeds.

William Shakespeare's *Hamlet* (1600—1601) is a classic example of "man against himself." Fort's protagonist resembles Prince Hamlet in being intelligent: He has too much education, he has read too many books, he has too much imagination, and he thinks too much. He is his own worst enemy. If dramatic conflict usually involves a protagonist pitted against an antagonist, then the narrator of "The Coal Shoveller" can be seen as both protagonist and antagonist.

"The Coal Shoveller" is a combination story, essay, and journal entry. The reader forms the impression that the narrator is in the habit of writing in this manner. He writes about his thoughts, observations, and problems, including problems in trying to find something worth writing about. Occasionally he comes across the germ of an idea that he can develop into a full-fledged story.

On the occasion that is chronicled in "The Coal Shoveller," the narrator is not necessarily defeated in his attempt to write a short story. What he is going through is his own personal method of working, his way of jump-starting his creativity. He may not be able to expect a successful outcome every time that he uses this technique, but he is better off writing about writing—or writing about writing about writing—than he would be simply staring at a blank sheet of paper. It would be a mistake to regard him as a failure because he has not succeeded in writing a story about a man shoveling coal. He has produced germs of several stories that might one day blossom into finished works.

---

[1] amalgamation:混杂,合成一体。

Source: unknown.

问题与思考

1. Fort tries out a passage "on the order of the new novels". He is referring primarily to the fiction of a group of French novelists of the 1960s whose chief theoretician is Alain Robbe-Grillet. Trying to give us back the world as-it-is, without trappings of "humanism," Robbe-Grillet rejects any description by which the author imposes human interpretation on a scene: a desolate hillside, a gay party. What is Fort's objection to Robbe-Grillet's way of getting at reality?
2. Who is the narrator of "The Coal Shoveller"? From what point of view is the narration presented?
3. In the narrator's second "try", why does he place the father in a sealed room? What does Fort mean by, "I couldn't avoid imitation"? What is wrong with this version? It is dramatic and thematically unified. Why is the narrator dissatisfied?
4. The narrator tells us that the beautiful passage on his mother and grandmother was emotionally false: he doesn't feel the tragedy of the fall of the Old South. Why then did he write as he did? Imagine writing a piece about a relative you weren't close to who has died. What false voices might you find yourself employing?
5. In the satire toward the end of the story, Fort gives us a character, a writer, who says to the coal shoveller much of what Fort's narrator has been saying throughout the story. What is the effect of this talk? Is Fort making fun of his own ideas? What's wrong with his speech to the coal shoveller?
6. What does Fort imply by the choices in the final sentence?

阅读链接

1. http://www.enotes.com/coal-shoveller-salem/coal-shoveller：对《铲煤者》的情节介绍。
2. http://ayjw.org/articles.php?id=757434：论文"The Qualities of Post-Modern Fiction"，包含对《铲煤者》的评论。

Joseph Conrad (1857—1924)

作者简介

约瑟夫·康拉德(Joseph Conrad,1857—1924)出生于波兰一个地主家庭,原姓克尔泽尼奥夫斯基。父亲是个有文学才华的爱国贵族,1862年因参加波兰民族独立运动被沙俄政府流放。康拉德11岁时双亲去世,由亲戚抚养长大。17岁当上水手,后升为大副、船长,其航海生涯达20余年,到过非洲、南美、澳洲和远东等地。1878年他第一次随船来到英国,几乎不会说一句英语,八年后加入英国国籍,并正式使用英语化的约瑟夫·康拉德这个名字。直到1889年康拉德才开始用英语从事文学创作,第一部作品于1895年出版。此后他定居英国,开始了职业作家的生活,直到去世前一天还在勤奋创作。1924年8月康拉德因心力衰竭,在英国的坎特伯雷突然去世,享年67岁。

文学创作

康拉德是20世纪初英国最杰出的小说家之一,西方现代主义小说的先驱之一,共出版14部长篇小说、7部短篇小说、3出戏剧和2卷回忆录及政论、书信等。评论界一般把他的小说分为航海小说、丛林小说和社会政治小说三类。海洋小说的代表作有长篇小说《水仙号上的黑家伙》(*The Nigger of the Narcissus*,1897)、中短篇小说《台风》(*Typhoon*,1899—1902)、《青春》(*Youth*,1898)和《秘密的分享者》(*The Secret Sharer*,1912)。丛林小说以《吉姆爷》(*Lord Jim*,1900)和《黑暗之心》(*Heart of Darkness*,1902)最为知名。社会政治小说主要有《诺斯特罗莫》(*Nostromo*,1904)和《间谍》(*The Secret Agent*,1907)。

康拉德的作品广泛探讨了人与自然的各种关系,反映了帝国主义和殖民主义的暴行,挖掘了人性的各个层面。在他的航海小说里,海洋和船只是人类社会的缩影,一次穿越暴风骤雨、克服人之恐惧和敌视的航程带来的是人在精神上的成长。相比带有英雄色彩的航海小说来说,他的丛林小说充满了悲剧和忧愤的意味,表现了人性的分裂与冲突,人与自然的冷漠与敌视,人与人之间的疏离与对抗。社会政治小说常以欧洲或南美某个国家的都市为背景,或揭示"物质利益"对个人的腐蚀力,或抨击都市道德虚无主义,反映出康拉德反对极端、憎恶暴力的保守主义倾向。总之,康拉德对所处时代的历史、社会和人性的洞察使他的艺术创作成功地"给予事物、事件和人的'理想'价值以全部的关注"。

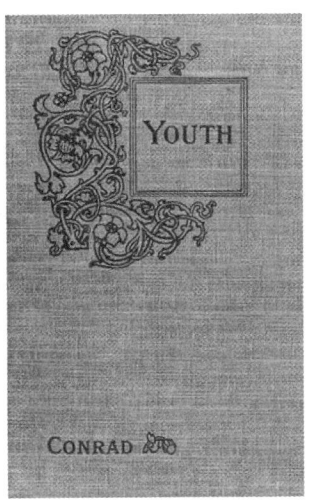

在艺术手法上，康拉德认为，一切艺术都仰赖感觉。为此，他特别强调感官的作用，大量运用光与影、黑与白的明暗对比，着力刻画细致的行为动作，突出错落有致的叙述节奏。色彩、大海、船只、丛林、飞鸟等，由于反复出现而具有丰富的象征意义。康拉德的现代主义意识还表现在他的印象主义手法中，即"以人物在某一时刻的经历给人留下的强烈印象开始"，前后穿插进行叙述，他的框架故事叙事模式颠覆了传统的现实主义小说的平铺直叙。

作　品

Youth

  This could have occurred nowhere but in England, where men and sea interpenetrate, so to speak—the sea entering into the life of most men, and the men knowing something or everything about the sea, in the way of amusement, of travel, or of bread-winning.

  We were sitting round a mahogany table that reflected the bottle, the claret[1]-glasses, and our faces as we leaned on our elbows. There was a director of companies, an accountant, a lawyer, Marlow[2], and myself. The director had been a *Conway* boy[3], the accountant had served four years at sea, the lawyer—a fine crusted Tory, High Churchman,[4] the best of old fellows, the soul of honor—had been chief officer in the P.& O.[5] service in the good old days when mail-boats were square-rigged[6] at

---

[1] claret：红葡萄酒。
[2] Marlow：康拉德的其他小说中也出现过此人物，如 *Heart of the Darkness*。
[3] a *Conway* boy：一个 Conway 舰上的练习生。Conway 是英国的一艘护航舰，在很长一段时间内曾是训练水手的练习船。
[4] a crusted Tory, High Churchman：一个老牌的保守派，偏激的英国国教教徒。Tory：托利党，现在的英国保守党（Conservative）的前身，1830 年正式改名为保守党。这里指 the lawyer 在政治和宗教方面都非常保守。
[5] P.& O.：Peninsular and Oriental Company 的缩写。
[6] square-rigged：横帆的。

least on two masts, and used to come down the China Sea before a fair monsoon[1] with stun'-sails[2] set alow and aloft. We all began life in the merchant service. Between the five of us there was the strong bond of the sea, and also the fellowship of the craft, which no amount of enthusiasm for yachting, cruising, and so on can give, since one is only the amusement of life and the other is life itself.

Marlow (at least I think that is how he spelt his name) told the story, or rather the chronicle, of a voyage:

"Yes, I have seen a little of the Eastern seas; but what I remember best is my first voyage there. You fellows know there are those voyages that seem ordered for the illustration of life, that might stand for a symbol of existence. You fight, work, sweat, nearly kill yourself, sometimes do kill yourself, trying to accomplish something—and you can't. Not from any fault of yours. You simply can do nothing, neither great nor little—not a thing in the world—not even marry an old maid, or get a wretched 600-ton cargo of coal to its port of destination.

"It was altogether a memorable affair. It was my first voyage to the East, and my first voyage as second mate; it was also my skipper's[3] first command. You'll admit it was time. He was sixty if a day; a little man, with a broad, not very straight back, with bowed shoulders and one leg more bandy[4] than the other, he had that queer twisted-about appearance you see so often in men who work in the fields. He had a nut-cracker face[5]—chin and nose trying to come together over a sunken mouth—and it was framed in iron-gray fluffy[6] hair, that looked like a chinstrap[7] of cotton-wool sprinkled with coal-dust. And he had blue eyes in that old face of his, which were amazingly like a boy's, with that candid expression some quite common men preserve to the end of their days by a rare internal gift of simplicity of heart and rectitude of soul. What induced him to accept me was a wonder. I had come out of a crack Australian clipper,[8] where I had been third officer, and he seemed to have a prejudice against crack clippers as aristocratic and high-toned. He said to me, 'You know, in this ship you will have to work'. I said I had to work in every ship I had ever been in. 'Ah, but this is different, and you gentlemen out of them big ships; ... but there! I dare say you will do. Join tomorrow.'

"I joined to-morrow. It was twenty-two years ago; and I was just twenty. How time passes! It was one of the happiest days of my life. Fancy! Second mate for the first

---

[1] monsoon:印度洋北部的季风。fair:顺风的。
[2] stun'-sails:翼帆(=studding sail)。
[3] skipper:(商船)船长。
[4] bandy:弯曲的。
[5] a nut-cracker face:瘪嘴。
[6] fluffy:蓬松的。
[7] chinstrap:从下巴过的帽绳。
[8] a crack Australian clipper:第一流的澳大利亚快速帆船。

time—a really responsible officer! I wouldn't have thrown up my new billet[1] for a fortune. The mate looked me over carefully. He was also an old chap, but of another stamp.[2] He had a Roman nose, a snow-white, long beard, and his name was Mahon, but he insisted that it should be pronounced Mann. He was well connected; yet there was something wrong with his luck, and he had never got on.

"As to the captain, he had been for years in coasters[3], then in the Mediterranean, and last in the West Indian trade. He had never been round the Capes[4]. He could just write a kind of sketchy hand[5], and didn't care for writing at all. Both were thorough good seamen of course, and between those two old chaps I felt like a small boy between two grandfathers.

"The ship also was old. Her name was the *Judea*[6]. Queer name, isn't it? She belonged to a man Wilmer, Wilcox—some name like that; but he has been bankrupt and dead these twenty years or more, and his name don't matter. She had been laid up in Shadwell basin[7] for ever so long. You can imagine her state. She was all rust, dust, grime—soot aloft, dirt on deck. To me it was like coming out of a palace into a ruined cottage. She was about 400 tons, had a primitive windlass[8], wooden latches to the doors, not a bit of brass about her, and a big square stern[9]. There was on it, below her name in big letters, a lot of scrollwork[10], with the gilt off, and some sort of a coat of arms[11], with the motto 'Do or Die'[12] underneath. I remember it took my fancy immensely. There was a touch of romance in it, something that made me love the old thing—something that appealed to my youth!

"We left London in ballast[13]—sand ballast—to load a cargo of coal in a northern port for Bankok. Bankok! I thrilled. I had been six years at sea, but had only seen Melbourne and Sydney, very good places, charming places in their way—but Bankok!

"We worked out of the Thames under canvas[14], with a North Sea pilot on board. His name was Jermyn, and he dodged all day long about the galley[15] drying his handkerchief before the stove. Apparently he never slept. He was a dismal man, with a

---

[1]　billet:职位,工作。
[2]　of another stamp:另一种类型的。
[3]　coasters:近海贸易货船。
[4]　the Capes:这里指非洲南端的好望角与南美洲的合恩角。
[5]　hand:书法。
[6]　Judea：古巴勒斯坦国的南部曾叫Judea。
[7]　Shadwell basin:伦敦泰晤士河上的一处码头。basin:水坞,内湾。
[8]　windlass:起锚机。
[9]　stern:船尾。
[10]　scrollwork:涡形装饰。
[11]　a coat of arms:盾形纹章。
[12]　Do or Die:决一死战。
[13]　ballast:(保持平衡用的)压舱物。
[14]　under canvas:扯着风帆的。
[15]　dodged all day long about the galley:成天躲在船上的厨房里。

perpetual tear sparkling at the end of his nose, who either had been in trouble, or was in trouble, or expected to be in trouble—couldn't be happy unless something went wrong. He mistrusted my youth, my common-sense, and my seamanship, and made a point of showing it in a hundred little ways. I dare say he was right. It seems to me I knew very little then, and I know not much more now; but I cherish a hate for that Jermyn to this day.

"We were a week working up as far as Yarmouth Roads[1], and then we got into a gale[2]—the famous October gale of twenty-two years ago. It was wind, lightning, sleet, snow, and a terrific sea. We were flying light, and you may imagine how bad it was when I tell you we had smashed bulwarks[3] and a flooded deck. On the second night she shifted her ballast into the lee bow[4], and by that time we had been blown off somewhere on the Dogger Bank.[5] There was nothing for it but go below with shovels and try to right her[6], and there we were in that vast hold, gloomy like a cavern, the tallow dips[7] stuck and flickering on the beams, the gale howling above, the ship tossing about like mad on her side; there we all were, Jermyn, the captain, everyone, hardly able to keep our feet, engaged on that gravedigger's work, and trying to toss shovelfuls of wet sand up to windward. At every tumble of the ship you could see vaguely in the dim light men falling down with a great flourish of shovels. One of the ship's boys (we had two), impressed by the weirdness of the scene, wept as if his heart would break. We could hear him blubbering somewhere in the shadows.

"On the third day the gale died out, and by-and-by a north-country tug[8] picked us up. We took sixteen days in all to get from London to the Tyne![9] When we got into dock we had lost our turn for loading, and they hauled us off to a tier where we remained for a month. Mrs. Beard (the captain's name was Beard) came from Colchester[10] to see the old man. She lived on board. The crew of runners[11] had left, and there remained only the officers, one boy, and the steward, a mulatto[12] who answered to the name of Abraham. Mrs. Beard was an old woman, with a face all wrinkled and ruddy like a winter apple, and the figure of a young girl. She caught sight of me once, sewing on a button, and insisted on having my shirts to repair. This was

[1] Yarmouth Roads: 英格兰东部港口城市亚茅斯(Yarmouth)附近的停泊地。
[2] gale: 大风(尤指八级大风)。
[3] bulwarks: 舷墙(比上中板还高的船侧的一部分)。
[4] lee bow: 下船首。
[5] the Dogger Bank: 多格滩，北海中部一大沙洲，距英格兰东北岸约100公里。
[6] right her: 给船调整方向。Her 和 she 用来指船。
[7] the tallow dips: (蜡)烛火。
[8] tug: 拖船。
[9] the Tyne: 泰茵河，在英格兰东北部，流入北海。
[10] Colchester: 科尔切斯特，英格兰东南部城市。
[11] The crew of runners: 机组操作人员。
[12] mulatto: (白人与黑人的)混血儿。

something different from the captains' wives I had known on board crack clippers. When I brought her the shirts, she said: 'And the socks? They want mending, I am sure, and John's—Captain Beard's—things are all in order now. I would be glad of something to do'. Bless the old woman. She overhauled my outfit for me,[1] and meantime I read for the first time *Sartor Resartus*[2] and Burnaby's *Ride to Khiva*.[3] I didn't understand much of the first then; but I remember I preferred the soldier to the philosopher at the time; a preference which life has only confirmed. One was a man, and the other was either more—or less. However, they are both dead, and Mrs. Beard is dead, and youth, strength, genius, thoughts, achievements, simple hearts—all die... No matter.

"They loaded us at last. We shipped a crew. Eight able seamen and two boys. We hauled off one evening to the buoys at the dock-gates,[4] ready to go out, and with a fair prospect of beginning the voyage next day. Mrs. Beard was to start for home by a late train. When the ship was fast we went to tea. We sat rather silent through the meal—Mahon, the old couple, and I. I finished first, and slipped away for a smoke, my cabin being in a deck-house just against the poop.[5] It was high water, blowing fresh with a drizzle; the double dock-gates were opened, and the steam colliers[6] were going in and out in the darkness with their lights burning bright, a great plashing of propellers, rattling of winches[7], and a lot of hailing on the pier-heads.[8] I watched the procession of head-lights gliding high and of green lights gliding low in the night, when suddenly a red gleam flashed at me, vanished, came into view again, and remained. The fore-end of a steamer loomed up close. I shouted down the cabin, 'Come up, quick!' and then heard a startled voice saying afar in the dark, 'Stop her, sir.' A bell jingled. Another voice cried warningly, 'We are going right into that barque[9], sir.' The answer to this was a gruff 'All right,' and the next thing was a heavy crash as the steamer struck a glancing blow with the bluff[10] of her bow about our fore-rigging.[11] There was a moment of confusion, yelling, and running about. Steam roared. Then somebody was heard saying, 'All clear, sir.' ... 'Are you all right?' asked the gruff

---

[1] She overhauled my outfit for me:她把我的衣服通通补了一遍。overhaul:仔细检查,彻底修理。

[2] *Sartor Resartus*:《旧衣新裁》,英国历史学家卡莱尔(Thomas Carlyle, 1795—1881)的哲学著作。

[3] Burnaby's *Ride to Khiva*:伯纳比的《希瓦游记》。伯纳比(Frederick Gustavus Burnaby, 1842—1885),英国士兵、旅行家;《希瓦游记》为他所作,记录他在1874—1876年间骑马穿越中亚的经历。19世纪70年代这本书曾风靡一时。

[4] We hauled off one... at the dock gates:一天晚上我们掉转船头向船坞大门的浮标驶去。haul off:使(船)改变航向。

[5] the poop:后甲板。

[6] steam colliers:蒸汽机驱动的运煤船。

[7] winches:起吊机。

[8] pier-heads:码头外端。

[9] barque:三桅帆船,即 bark。

[10] bluff:(船头)前面垂直而平阔的部分。

[11] fore-rigging:前帆缆。

voice. I had jumped forward to see the damage, and hailed back, 'I think so.' 'Easy astern,'[1] said the gruff voice. A bell jingled. 'What steamer is that?' screamed Mahon. By that time she was no more to us than a bulky shadow maneuvering a little way off. They shouted at us some name—a woman's name, Miranda or Melissa—or some such thing. 'This means another month in this beastly hole,' said Mahon to me, as we peered with lamps about the splintered bulwarks and broken braces.[2] 'But where's the captain?'

"We had not heard or seen anything of him all that time. We went aft[3] to look. A doleful voice arose hailing somewhere in the middle of the dock, '*Judea* ahoy[4]!' ... How the devil did he get there? ... 'Hallo!' we shouted. 'I am adrift in our boat without oars,' he cried. A belated waterman[5] offered his services, and Mahon struck a bargain with him for half-a-crown to tow our skipper alongside; but it was Mrs. Beard that came up the ladder first. They had been floating about the dock in that mizzly[6] cold rain for nearly an hour. I was never so surprised in my life.

"It appears that when he heard my shout 'Come up,' he understood at once what was the matter, caught up his wife, ran on deck, and across, and down into our boat, which was fast to the ladder. Not bad for a sixty-year-old. Just imagine that old fellow saving heroically in his arms that old woman—the woman of his life. He set her down on a thwart[7], and was ready to climb back on board when the painter[8] came adrift somehow, and away they went together. Of course in the confusion we did not hear him shouting. He looked abashed. She said cheerfully, 'I suppose it does not matter my losing the train now?' 'No, Jenny—you go below and get warm,' he growled. Then to us: 'A sailor has no business with a wife—I say. There I was, out of the ship. Well, no harm done this time. Let's go and look at what that fool of a steamer smashed.'

"It wasn't much, but it delayed us three weeks. At the end of that time, the captain being engaged with his agents, I carried Mrs. Beard's bag to the railway-station and put her all comfy[9] into a third-class carriage. She lowered the window to say, 'You are a good young man. If you see John—Captain Beard—without his muffler at night, just remind him from me to keep his throat well wrapped up.' 'Certainly, Mrs. Beard,' I said. 'You are a good young man; I noticed how attentive you are to John—to Captain—' The train pulled out suddenly; I took my cap off to the old woman: I never

---

[1] Easy astern:低速后退。
[2] braces:转帆索。
[3] aft:在船尾。
[4] ahoy:喂！呵喵！（船夫招呼船只和人的喊声）。
[5] waterman:水手,船夫。
[6] mizzly:下着蒙蒙雨的,即 drizzling。
[7] thwart:（划艇上横贯船体的）座板。
[8] painter:（小船）船口缆索。
[9] comfy:(口)comfortable。

saw her again... Pass the bottle.[1]

"We went to sea next day. When we made that start for Bankok we had been already three months out of London. We had expected to be a fortnight or so—at the outside.

"It was January, and the weather was beautiful—the beautiful sunny winter weather that has more charm than in the summer-time, because it is unexpected, and crisp, and you know it won't, it can't, last long. It's like a windfall, like a Godsend[2], like an unexpected piece of luck.

"It lasted all down the North Sea, all down Channel[3]; and it lasted till we were three hundred miles or so to the westward of the Lizards[4]; then the wind went round to the sou'west and began to pipe up. In two days it blew a gale. The *Judea*, hove[5] to, wallowed[6] on the Atlantic like an old candle-box. It blew day after day; it blew with spite, without interval, without mercy, without rest. The world was nothing but an immensity of great foaming waves rushing at us, under a sky low enough to touch with the hand and dirty like a smoked ceiling. In the stormy space surrounding us there was as much flying spray as air. Day after day and night after night there was nothing round the ship but the howl of the wind, the tumult of the sea, the noise of water pouring over her deck. There was no rest for her and no rest for us. She tossed, she pitched, she stood on her head, she sat on her tail, she rolled, she groaned, and we had to hold on while on deck and cling to our bunks[7] when below, in a constant effort of body and worry of mind.

"One night Mahon spoke through the small window of my berth[8]. It opened right into my very bed, and I was lying there sleepless, in my boots, feeling as though I had not slept for years, and could not if I tried. He said excitedly—

"You got the sounding-rod[9] in here, Marlow? I can't get the pumps to suck.[10] By God! it's no child's play."

"I gave him the sounding-rod and lay down again, trying to think of various things—but I thought only of the pumps. When I came on deck they were still at it, and my watch relieved at the pumps. By the light of the lantern brought on deck to examine the sounding-rod I caught a glimpse of their weary, serious faces. We pumped all the

---

[1] Pass the bottle:把酒瓶递过来。这一句是对坐在讲故事的 Marlow 身边的人说的。
[2] Godsend:天赐之物。
[3] Channel:英吉利海峡(English Channel),位于欧洲西北部英法之间的海湾,伸入大西洋。
[4] the Lizards:指利泽德岬(Lizard Point),位于不列颠岛最南端。
[5] hove:(船体在水里上下)升沉。
[6] wallow:颠簸。
[7] bunks:(船上依壁而设的)床铺。
[8] berth:(船口)住舱。
[9] sounding-rod:量水尺。
[10] get the pumps to suck:开动水泵排水。

four hours. We pumped all night, all day, all the week,—watch[1] and watch. She was working herself loose, and leaked badly—not enough to drown us at once, but enough to kill us with the work at the pumps. And while we pumped the ship was going from us piecemeal[2]: the bulwarks went, the stanchions[3] were torn out, the ventilators smashed, the cabin-door burst in. There was not a dry spot in the ship. She was being gutted bit by bit. The long-boat[4] changed, as if by magic, into matchwood where she stood in her gripes[5]. I had lashed her myself, and was rather proud of my handiwork, which had withstood so long the malice of the sea. And we pumped. And there was no break in the weather. The sea was white like a sheet of foam, like a caldron[6] of boiling milk; there was not a break in the clouds, no—not the size of a man's hand—no, not for so much as ten seconds. There was for us no sky, there were for us no stars, no sun, no universe—nothing but angry clouds and an infuriated sea. We pumped watch and watch, for dear life; and it seemed to last for months, for years, for all eternity, as though we had been dead and gone to a hell for sailors. We forgot the day of the week, the name of the month, what year it was, and whether we had ever been ashore. The sails blew away, she lay broadside on under a weather-cloth, the ocean poured over her, and we did not care. We turned those handles, and had the eyes of idiots. As soon as we had crawled on deck I used to take a round turn with a rope about the men, the pumps, and the mainmast, and we turned, we turned incessantly, with the water to our waists, to our necks, over our heads. It was all one. We had forgotten how it felt to be dry.

"And there was somewhere in me the thought: By Jove![7] this is the deuce of an adventure[8]—something you read about; and it is my first voyage as second mate—and I am only twenty—and here I am lasting it out as well as any of these men, and keeping my chaps up to the mark. I was pleased. I would not have given up the experience for worlds. I had moments of exultation. Whenever the old dismantled craft pitched heavily with her counter high in the air, she seemed to me to throw up, like an appeal, like a defiance, like a cry to the clouds without mercy, the words written on her stern: '*Judea*, London. Do or Die.'

"O youth! The strength of it, the faith of it, the imagination of it! To me she was not an old rattle-trap carting about the world a lot of coal for a freight—to me she was the endeavor, the test, the trial of life. I think of her with pleasure, with affection, with regret—as you would think of someone dead you have loved. I shall never forget

---

[1] watch: (海员的)值班时间。
[2] piecemeal: 成碎片地，分开地。
[3] stanchions: 支柱。
[4] long-boat: 轮船上携带的较大的救生艇。
[5] gripes: (把救生艇系于支架上的)绊带。
[6] caldron: 大锅。
[7] By Jove: 啊！(表示惊讶等)，即 By Jupiter!
[8] this is the deuce of an adventure: 这真是场倒霉的冒险。

her... Pass the bottle.

"One night when tied to the mast, as I explained, we were pumping on, deafened with the wind, and without spirit enough in us to wish ourselves dead, a heavy sea [1] crashed aboard and swept clean over us. As soon as I got my breath I shouted, as in duty bound, 'Keep on, boys!' when suddenly I felt something hard floating on deck strike the calf of my leg. I made a grab at it and missed. It was so dark we could not see each other's faces within a foot—you understand.

"After that thump the ship kept quiet for a while, and the thing, whatever it was, struck my leg again. This time I caught it—and it was a sauce-pan. At first, being stupid with fatigue and thinking of nothing but the pumps, I did not understand what I had in my hand. Suddenly it dawned upon me, and I shouted, 'Boys, the house on deck is gone. Leave this, and let's look for the cook.'

"There was a deck-house forward, which contained the galley, the cook's berth, and the quarters of the crew. As we had expected for days to see it swept away, the hands[2] had been ordered to sleep in the cabin—the only safe place in the ship. The steward, Abraham, however, persisted in clinging to his berth, stupidly, like a mule—from sheer fright I believe, like an animal that won't leave a stable falling in an earthquake. So we went to look for him. It was chancing death, since once out of our lashings we were as exposed as if on a raft. But we went. The house was shattered as if a shell had exploded inside. Most of it had gone overboard—stove, men's quarters, and their property, all was gone; but two posts, holding a portion of the bulkhead[3] to which Abraham's bunk was attached, remained as if by a miracle. We groped in the ruins and came upon this, and there he was, sitting in his bunk, surrounded by foam and wreckage, jabbering[4] cheerfully to himself. He was out of his mind; completely and for ever mad, with this sudden shock coming upon the fag-end[5] of his endurance. We snatched him up, lugged him aft, and pitched him head-first down the cabin companion. You understand there was no time to carry him down with infinite precautions and wait to see how he got on. Those below would pick him up at the bottom of the stairs all right. We were in a hurry to go back to the pumps. That business could not wait. A bad leak is an inhuman thing.

"One would think that the sole purpose of that fiendish gale had been to make a lunatic of that poor devil of a mulatto. It eased before morning, and next day the sky cleared, and as the sea went down the leak took up. When it came to bending a fresh set of sails the crew demanded to put back—and really there was nothing else to do. Boats

---

[1] sea:海浪。
[2] hands:全体船员。
[3] bulkhead:(船)舱壁。
[4] jabbering:急促、含混不清或无意义地讲话。
[5] fag-end:最后的部分。

gone, decks swept clean, cabin gutted, men without a stitch[1] but what they stood in, stores spoiled, ship strained. We put her head for home, and—would you believe it? The wind came east right in our teeth. It blew fresh, it blew continuously. We had to beat up every inch of the way, but she did not leak so badly, the water keeping comparatively smooth. Two hours' pumping in every four is no joke—but it kept her afloat as far as Falmouth.[2]

"The good people there live on casualties of the sea, and no doubt were glad to see us. A hungry crowd of shipwrights[3] sharpened their chisels at the sight of that carcass of a ship. And, by Jove! they had pretty pickings off us before they were done. I fancy the owner was already in a tight place. There were delays. Then it was decided to take part of the cargo out and calk[4] her topsides. This was done, the repairs finished, cargo reshipped; a new crew came on board, and we went out—for Bankok. At the end of a week we were back again. The crew said they weren't going to Bankok—a hundred and fifty days' passage—in a something hooker[5] that wanted pumping eight hours out of the twenty-four; and the nautical papers[6] inserted again the little paragraph: '*Judea*. Bark. Tyne to Bankok; coals; put back to Falmouth leaky and with crew refusing duty.'

"There were more delays—more tinkering. The owner came down for a day, and said she was as right as a little fiddle. Poor old Captain Beard looked like the ghost of a Geordie[7] skipper—through the worry and humiliation of it. Remember he was sixty, and it was his first command. Mahon said it was a foolish business, and would end badly. I loved the ship more than ever, and wanted awfully to get to Bankok. To Bankok! Magic name, blessed name. Mesopotamia[8] wasn't a patch on it. Remember I was twenty, and it was my first second mate's billet, and the East was waiting for me.

"We went out and anchored in the outer roads with a fresh crew—the third. She leaked worse than ever. It was as if those confounded shipwrights had actually made a hole in her. This time we did not even go outside. The crew simply refused to man the windlass.

"They towed us back to the inner harbor, and we became a fixture, a feature, an institution of the place. People pointed us out to visitors as 'That'ere bark that's going to Bankok—has been here six months—put back three times.' On holidays the small boys pulling about in boats would hail, '*Judea*, ahoy!' and if a head showed above the rail shouted, 'Where you bound to?—Bankok?' and jeered. We were only three on board.

---

[1] without a stitch: 光着身子。
[2] Falmouth: 法尔茅斯, 英格兰西南部康沃尔郡城镇, 英吉利海峡主要港口。
[3] shipwrights: 修理、制造船只的木匠。
[4] calk: 堵……的缝。
[5] hooker: 一只用旧的或笨重的船。
[6] nautical papers: 航海报纸。
[7] Geordie: 运煤船。
[8] Mesopotamia: 美索不达米亚, 位于底格里斯河 (The Tigris) 与幼发拉底河 (The Euphrates) 之间的平原, 古文明发祥地。

The poor old skipper mooned in the cabin. Mahon undertook the cooking, and unexpectedly developed all a Frenchman's genius for preparing nice little messes[1]. I looked languidly after the rigging. We became citizens of Falmouth. Every shopkeeper knew us. At the barber's or tobacconist's they asked familiarly, 'Do you think you will ever get to Bankok?' Meantime the owner, the underwriters, and the charterers squabbled[2] amongst themselves in London, and our pay went on... Pass the bottle.

"It was horrid. Morally it was worse than pumping for life. It seemed as though we had been forgotten by the world, belonged to nobody, would get nowhere; it seemed that, as if bewitched, we would have to live for ever and ever in that inner harbor, a derision and a byword to generations of long-shore loafers and dishonest boatmen. I obtained three months' pay and a five days' leave, and made a rush for London. It took me a day to get there and pretty well another to come back—but three months' pay went all the same. I don't know what I did with it. I went to a music-hall, I believe, lunched, dined, and supped in a swell place in Regent Street,[3] and was back to time, with nothing but a complete set of Byron's works and a new railway rug[4] to show for three months' work. The boatman who pulled me off to the ship said: 'Hallo! I thought you had left the old thing. *She* will never get to Bankok.' 'That's all *you* know about it,' I said scornfully—but I didn't like that prophecy at all.

"Suddenly a man, some kind of agent to somebody, appeared with full powers. He had grog blossoms[5] all over his face, an indomitable energy, and was a jolly soul. We leaped into life again. A hulk came alongside, took our cargo, and then we went into dry dock to get our copper stripped. No wonder she leaked. The poor thing, strained beyond endurance by the gale, had, as if in disgust, spat out all the oakum[6] of her lower seams. She was recalked, new coppered, and made as tight as a bottle. We went back to the hulk and re-shipped our cargo.

"Then on a fine moonlight night, all the rats left the ship.

"We had been infested with them. They had destroyed our sails, consumed more stores than the crew, affably shared our beds and our dangers, and now, when the ship was made seaworthy, concluded to clear out. I called Mahon to enjoy the spectacle. Rat after rat appeared on our rail, took a last look over his shoulder, and leaped with a hollow thud into the empty hulk. We tried to count them, but soon lost the tale. Mahon said: 'Well, well! don't talk to me about the intelligence of rats. They ought to have left before, when we had that narrow squeak from foundering[7]. There you have the

---

[1] messes：集体膳食。
[2] charterers：租用人；squabbled：吵架，口角。
[3] Regent Street：摄政王大街，伦敦市中心繁华大街。
[4] railway rug：旅行时用于保暖的厚毯子。
[5] grog blossoms：(因饮酒过多而引起的)丘疹。
[6] oakum：填絮(用于填塞船缝)。
[7] foundering：沉没。

proof how silly is the superstition about them. They leave a good ship for an old rotten hulk, where there is nothing to eat, too, the fools!... I don't believe they know what is safe or what is good for them, any more than you or I.'

"And after some more talk we agreed that the wisdom of rats had been grossly overrated, being in fact no greater than that of men.

"The story of the ship was known, by this, all up the Channel from Land's End[1] to the Forelands[2], and we could get no crew on the south coast. They sent us one all complete from Liverpool, and we left once more—for Bankok.

"We had fair breezes, smooth water right into the tropics, and the old *Judea* lumbered along in the sunshine. When she went eight knots[3] everything cracked aloft, and we tied our caps to our heads; but mostly she strolled on at the rate of three miles an hour. What could you expect? She was tired—that old ship. Her youth was where mine is—where yours is—you fellows who listen to this yarn; and what friend would throw your years and your weariness in your face? We didn't grumble at her. To us aft, at least, it seemed as though we had been born in her, reared in her, had lived in her for ages, had never known any other ship. I would just as soon have abused the old village church at home for not being a cathedral.

"And for me there was also my youth to make me patient. There was all the East before me, and all life, and the thought that I had been tried in that ship and had come out pretty well. And I thought of men of old who, centuries ago, went that road in ships that sailed no better, to the land of palms, and spices, and yellow sands, and of brown nations ruled by kings more cruel than Nero the Roman[4] and more splendid than Solomon the Jew.[5] The old bark lumbered on, heavy with her age and the burden of her cargo, while I lived the life of youth in ignorance and hope. She lumbered on through an interminable procession of days; and the fresh gilding flashed back at the setting sun, seemed to cry out over the darkening sea the words painted on her stern, '*Judea*, London. Do or Die.'

"Then we entered the Indian Ocean and steered northerly for Java Head.[6] The winds were light. Weeks slipped by. She crawled on, do or die, and people at home began to think of posting us as overdue.

"One Saturday evening, I being off duty, the men asked me to give them an extra bucket of water or so—for washing clothes. As I did not wish to screw on the fresh-water pump so late, I went forward whistling, and with a key in my hand to unlock the

---

[1] Land's End:兰慈角,英格兰康沃尔群西南端的半岛。
[2] Forelands:南、北海角,英格兰东南部肯特郡的两个白垩海角,临多佛海峡。
[3] eight knots:每小时行驶八海里。
[4] Nero the Roman:尼禄(公元37—68年),古罗马皇帝,以残暴闻名于世。
[5] Solomon the Jew:所罗门(?—公元前922年),古代以色列国第三个国王,以财富和智慧著名。
[6] Java Head:爪哇岛的西端。爪哇岛是印度尼西亚第四大岛,位于苏门答腊岛与巴厘岛之间,北临爪哇海,南滨印度洋。

forepeak scuttle,[1] intending to serve the water out of a spare tank we kept there.

"The smell down below was as unexpected as it was frightful. One would have thought hundreds of paraffin-lamps[2] had been flaring and smoking in that hole for days. I was glad to get out. The man with me coughed and said, 'Funny smell, sir.' I answered negligently, 'It's good for the health, they say,' and walked aft.

"The first thing I did was to put my head down the square of the midship ventilator. As I lifted the lid a visible breath, something like a thin fog, a puff of faint haze, rose from the opening. The ascending air was hot, and had a heavy, sooty, paraffiny smell. I gave one sniff, and put down the lid gently. It was no use choking myself. The cargo was on fire.

"Next day she began to smoke in earnest. You see it was to be expected, for though the coal was of a safe kind, that cargo had been so handled, so broken up with handling, that it looked more like smithy coal[3] than anything else. Then it had been wetted—more than once. It rained all the time we were taking it back from the hulk, and now with this long passage it got heated, and there was another case of spontaneous combustion.

"The captain called us into the cabin. He had a chart spread on the table, and looked unhappy. He said, 'The coast of West Australia is near, but I mean to proceed to our destination. It is the hurricane month too; but we will just keep her head for Bankok, and fight the fire. No more putting back anywhere, if we all get roasted. We will try first to stifle this'ere damned combustion by want of air.'

"We tried. We battened down everything, and still she smoked. The smoke kept coming out through imperceptible crevices; it forced itself through bulkheads and covers; it oozed here and there and everywhere in slender threads, in an invisible film, in an incomprehensible manner. It made its way into the cabin, into the forecastle; it poisoned the sheltered places on the deck, it could be sniffed as high as the mainyard[4]. It was clear that if the smoke came out the air came in. This was disheartening. This combustion refused to be stifled.

"We resolved to try water, and took the hatches off. Enormous volumes of smoke, whitish, yellowish, thick, greasy, misty, choking, ascended as high as the trucks[5]. All hands cleared out aft. Then the poisonous cloud blew away, and we went back to work in a smoke that was no thicker now than that of an ordinary factory chimney.

"We rigged the force pump, got the hose along, and by-and-by it burst. Well, it was as old as the ship—a prehistoric hose, and past repair. Then we pumped with the

---

[1] forepeak scuttle: 前舱口。
[2] paraffin-lamps: 煤油灯。
[3] smithy coal: 锻冶煤。
[4] mainyard: 主桅的桅横杆。
[5] trucks: (桅杆顶端有孔穿绳索的)桅冠。

feeble head-pump[1], drew water with buckets, and in this way managed in time to pour lots of Indian Ocean into the main hatch. The bright stream flashed in sunshine, fell into a layer of white crawling smoke, and vanished on the black surface of coal. Steam ascended mingling with the smoke. We poured salt water as into a barrel without a bottom. It was our fate to pump in that ship, to pump out of her, to pump into her; and after keeping water out of her to save ourselves from being drowned, we frantically poured water into her to save ourselves from being burnt.

"And she crawled on, do or die, in the serene weather. The sky was a miracle of purity, a miracle of azure. The sea was polished, was blue, was pellucid[2], was sparkling like a precious stone, extending on all sides, all round to the horizon—as if the whole terrestrial globe had been one jewel, one colossal sapphire[3], a single gem fashioned into a planet. And on the luster of the great calm waters the *Judea* glided imperceptibly, enveloped in languid and unclean vapors, in a lazy cloud that drifted to leeward[4], light and slow: a pestiferous cloud defiling the splendor of sea and sky.

"All this time of course we saw no fire. The cargo smoldered at the bottom somewhere. Once Mahon, as we were working side by side, said to me with a queer smile: 'Now, if she only would spring a tidy leak—like that time when we first left the Channel—it would put a stopper on this fire. Wouldn't it?' I remarked irrelevantly, 'Do you remember the rats?'

"We fought the fire and sailed the ship too as carefully as though nothing had been the matter. The steward cooked and attended on us. Of the other twelve men, eight worked while four rested. Everyone took his turn, captain included. There was equality, and if not exactly fraternity, then a deal of good feeling. Sometimes a man, as he dashed a bucketful of water down the hatchway, would yell out, 'Hurrah for Bankok!' and the rest laughed. But generally we were taciturn and serious—and thirsty. Oh! how thirsty! And we had to be careful with the water. Strict allowance. The ship smoked, the sun blazed... Pass the bottle.

"We tried everything. We even made an attempt to dig down to the fire. No good, of course. No man could remain more than a minute below. Mahon, who went first, fainted there, and the man who went to fetch him out did likewise. We lugged them out on deck. Then I leaped down to show how easily it could be done. They had learned wisdom by that time, and contented themselves by fishing for me with a chain-hook tied to a broom-handle, I believe. I did not offer to go and fetch up my shovel, which was left down below.

"Things began to look bad. We put the long-boat into the water. The second boat

---

[1] head-pump: 甲板冲洗泵。
[2] pellucid: 透明的，清澈的。
[3] sapphire: 蓝宝石。
[4] leeward: 在下风处的，背风的。

was ready to swing out. We had also another, a fourteen-foot thing, on davits[1] aft, where it was quite safe.

"Then behold, the smoke suddenly decreased. We redoubled our efforts to flood the bottom of the ship. In two days there was no smoke at all. Everybody was on the broad grin. This was on a Friday. On Saturday no work, but sailing the ship of course was done. The men washed their clothes and their faces for the first time in a fortnight, and had a special dinner given them. They spoke of spontaneous combustion with contempt, and implied *they* were the boys to put out combustions. Somehow we all felt as though we each had inherited a large fortune. But a beastly smell of burning hung about the ship. Captain Beard had hollow eyes and sunken cheeks. I had never noticed so much before how twisted and bowed he was. He and Mahon prowled soberly about hatches and ventilators, sniffing. It struck me suddenly poor Mahon was a very, very old chap. As to me, I was as pleased and proud as though I had helped to win a great naval battle. O! Youth!

"The night was fine. In the morning a homeward-bound ship passed us hull down,—the first we had seen for months; but we were nearing the land at last, Java Head being about 190 miles off, and nearly due north.

"Next day it was my watch on deck from eight to twelve. At breakfast the captain observed, 'It's wonderful how that smell hangs about the cabin.' About ten, the mate being on the poop, I stepped down on the main-deck for a moment. The carpenter's bench stood abaft[2] the mainmast: I leaned against it sucking at my pipe, and the carpenter, a young chap, came to talk to me. He remarked, 'I think we have done very well, haven't we?' and then I perceived with annoyance the fool was trying to tilt the bench. I said curtly, 'Don't, Chips,' and immediately became aware of a queer sensation, of an absurd delusion,—I seemed somehow to be in the air. I heard all round me like a pent-up breath released—as if a thousand giants simultaneously had said Phoo! —and felt a dull concussion[3] which made my ribs ache suddenly. No doubt about it—I was in the air, and my body was describing a short parabola[4]. But short as it was, I had the time to think several thoughts in, as far as I can remember, the following order: 'This can't be the carpenter—What is it? —Some accident—Submarine volcano? —Coals, gas! —By Jove! we are being blown up—Everybody's dead—I am falling into the after-hatch—I see fire in it.'

"The coal-dust suspended in the air of the hold had glowed dull-red at the moment of the explosion. In the twinkling of an eye, in an infinitesimal[5] fraction of a second since the first tilt of the bench, I was sprawling full length on the cargo. I picked myself

---

[1] davits: 用吊柱吊住。
[2] abaft: 在船尾。
[3] concussion: 冲击, 震荡。
[4] parabola: 抛物线。
[5] infinitesimal: 无穷小的。

up and scrambled out. It was quick like a rebound. The deck was a wilderness of smashed timber, lying crosswise like trees in a wood after a hurricane; an immense curtain of soiled rags waved gently before me—it was the mainsail blown to strips. I thought: The masts will be toppling over directly; and to get out of the way bolted on all-fours towards the poop-ladder. The first person I saw was Mahon, with eyes like saucers, his mouth open, and the long white hair standing straight on end round his head like a silver halo. He was just about to go down when the sight of the main-deck stirring, heaving up, and changing into splinters before his eyes, petrified him on the top step. I stared at him in unbelief, and he stared at me with a queer kind of shocked curiosity. I did not know that I had no hair, no eyebrows, no eyelashes, that my young mustache was burnt off, that my face was black, one cheek laid open, my nose cut, and my chin bleeding. I had lost my cap, one of my slippers, and my shirt was torn to rags. Of all this I was not aware. I was amazed to see the ship still afloat, the poop-deck whole—and, most of all, to see anybody alive. Also the peace of the sky and the serenity of the sea were distinctly surprising. I suppose I expected to see them convulsed with horror... Pass the bottle.

"There was a voice hailing the ship from somewhere—in the air, in the sky—I couldn't tell. Presently I saw the captain—and he was mad. He asked me eagerly, 'Where's the cabin-table?' and to hear such a question was a frightful shock. I had just been blown up, you understand, and vibrated with that experience,—I wasn't quite sure whether I was alive. Mahon began to stamp with both feet and yelled at him, 'Good God! don't you see the deck's blown out of her?' I found my voice, and stammered out as if conscious of some gross neglect of duty, 'I don't know where the cabin-table is.' It was like an absurd dream.

"Do you know what he wanted next? Well, he wanted to trim the yards. Very placidly, and as if lost in thought, he insisted on having the foreyard squared.[1] 'I don't know if there's anybody alive,' said Mahon, almost tearfully. 'Surely,' he said gently, 'there will be enough left to square the foreyard.'

"The old chap, it seems, was in his own berth, winding up the chronometers[2], when the shock sent him spinning. Immediately it occurred to him—as he said afterwards—that the ship had struck something, and he ran out into the cabin. There, he saw, the cabin-table had vanished somewhere. The deck being blown up, it had fallen down into the lazarette[3] of course. Where we had our breakfast that morning he saw only a great hole in the floor. This appeared to him so awfully mysterious, and impressed him so immensely, that what he saw and heard after he got on deck were mere trifles in comparison. And, mark, he noticed directly the wheel deserted and his bark

---

[1] having the foreyard squared:将底桁放正了。
[2] chronometers:钟。
[3] lazarette:近船尾贮藏室。

off her course—and his only thought was to get that miserable, stripped, undecked, smoldering shell of a ship back again with her head pointing at her port of destination. Bankok! That's what he was after. I tell you this quiet, bowed, bandy-legged, almost deformed little man was immense in the singleness of his idea and in his placid ignorance of our agitation. He motioned us forward with a commanding gesture, and went to take the wheel himself.

"Yes; that was the first thing we did—trim the yards of that wreck! No one was killed, or even disabled, but everyone was more or less hurt. You should have seen them! Some were in rags, with black faces, like coal-heavers, like sweeps[1], and had bullet heads that seemed closely cropped, but were in fact singed to the skin. Others, of the watch below, awakened by being shot out from their collapsing bunks, shivered incessantly, and kept on groaning even as we went about our work. But they all worked. That crew of Liverpool hard cases had in them the right stuff. It's my experience they always have. It is the sea that gives it—the vastness, the loneliness surrounding their dark stolid souls. Ah! Well! we stumbled, we crept, we fell, we barked[2] our shins on the wreckage, we hauled. The masts stood, but we did not know how much they might be charred down below. It was nearly calm, but a long swell ran from the west and made her roll. They might go at any moment. We looked at them with apprehension. One could not foresee which way they would fall.

"Then we retreated aft and looked about us. The deck was a tangle of planks on edge, of planks on end, of splinters, of ruined woodwork. The masts rose from that chaos like big trees above a matted undergrowth. The interstices[3] of that mass of wreckage were full of something whitish, sluggish, stirring—of something that was like a greasy fog. The smoke of the invisible fire was coming up again, was trailing, like a poisonous thick mist in some valley choked with dead wood. Already lazy wisps were beginning to curl upwards amongst the mass of splinters. Here and there a piece of timber, stuck upright, resembled a post. Half of a fiferail[4] had been shot through the foresail, and the sky made a patch of glorious blue in the ignobly soiled canvas. A portion of several boards holding together had fallen across the rail, and one end protruded overboard, like a gangway[5] leading upon nothing, like a gangway leading over the deep sea, leading to death—as if inviting us to walk the plank at once and be done with our ridiculous troubles. And still the air, the sky—a ghost, something invisible was hailing the ship.

"Someone had the sense to look over, and there was the helmsman[6], who had

---

[1] sweeps:扫烟囱工人。
[2] barked:擦破,擦伤。
[3] interstices:空隙,裂缝。
[4] fiferail:桅杆栅栏。
[5] gangway:跳板,即 gangplank。
[6] helmsman:舵手。

impulsively jumped overboard, anxious to come back. He yelled and swam lustily like a merman[1], keeping up with the ship. We threw him a rope, and presently he stood amongst us streaming with water and very crest-fallen. The captain had surrendered the wheel, and apart, elbow on rail and chin in hand, gazed at the sea wistfully. We asked ourselves, What next? I thought. Now, this is something like. This is great. I wonder what will happen. O youth!

"Suddenly Mahon sighted a steamer far astern. Captain Beard said, 'We may do something with her yet.' We hoisted two flags, which said in the international language of the sea, 'On fire. Want immediate assistance.' The steamer grew bigger rapidly, and by-and-by spoke with two flags on her foremast, 'I am coming to your assistance.'

"In half an hour she was abreast, to windward, within hail, and rolling slightly, with her engines stopped. We lost our composure, and yelled all together with excitement, 'We've been blown up.' A man in a white helmet, on the bridge, cried, 'Yes! All right! all right!' and he nodded his head, and smiled, and made soothing motions with his hand as though at a lot of frightened children. One of the boats dropped in the water, and walked towards us upon the sea with her long oars. Four Calashes[2] pulled a swinging stroke. This was my first sight of Malay seamen.[3] I've known them since, but what struck me then was their unconcern: they came alongside, and even the bowman standing up and holding to our main-chains with the boat-hook did not deign to lift his head for a glance. I thought people who had been blown up deserved more attention.

"A little man, dry like a chip and agile like a monkey, clambered up. It was the mate of the steamer. He gave one look, and cried, 'O boys—you had better quit.'

"We were silent. He talked apart with the captain for a time,—seemed to argue with him. Then they went away together to the steamer.

"When our skipper came back we learned that the steamer was the *Sommerville*, Captain Nash, from West Australia to Singapore *viâ* Batavia[4] with mails, and that the agreement was she should tow us to Anjer[5] or Batavia, if possible, where we could extinguish the fire by scuttling, and then proceed on our voyage—to Bankok! The old man seemed excited. 'We will do it yet,' he said to Mahon, fiercely. He shook his fist at the sky. Nobody else said a word.

"At noon the steamer began to tow. She went ahead slim and high, and what was left of the *Judea* followed at the end of seventy fathom[6] of tow-rope,—followed her swiftly like a cloud of smoke with mastheads protruding above. We went aloft to furl the

---

[1] merman: 童话里半人半神的怪物。
[2] Calashes: 一种轻型马车。
[3] Malay seamen: 马来族水手。
[4] Batavia: 爪哇岛西南海岸港口城市，即现在的雅加达。
[5] Anjer: 爪哇岛西海岸一小城市。
[6] fathom: 呼，等于6英尺。

sails. We coughed on the yards, and were careful about the bunts. Do you see the lot of us there, putting a neat furl on the sails of that ship doomed to arrive nowhere? There was not a man who didn't think that at any moment the masts would topple over. From aloft we could not see the ship for smoke, and they worked carefully, passing the gaskets[1] with even turns. 'Harbor furl—aloft there!' cried Mahon from below.

"You understand this? I don't think one of those chaps expected to get down in the usual way. When we did I heard them saying to each other, 'Well, I thought we would come down overboard, in a lump—sticks and all—blame me if I didn't.' 'That's what I was thinking to myself,' would answer wearily another battered and bandaged scarecrow. And, mind, these were men without the drilled-in habit of obedience. To an onlooker they would be a lot of profane scallywags[2] without a redeeming point. What made them do it—what made them obey me when I, thinking consciously how fine it was, made them drop the bunt of the foresail twice to try and do it better? What? They had no professional reputation—no examples, no praise. It wasn't a sense of duty; they all knew well enough how to shirk, and laze, and dodge—when they had a mind to it—and mostly they had. Was it the two pounds ten a-month[3] that sent them there? They didn't think their pay half good enough. No; it was something in them, something inborn and subtle and everlasting. I don't say positively that the crew of a French or German merchant-man wouldn't have done it, but I doubt whether it would have been done in the same way. There was a completeness in it, something solid like a principle, and masterful like an instinct—a disclosure of something secret—of that hidden something, that gift, of good or evil that makes racial difference, that shapes the fate of nations.

"It was that night at ten that, for the first time since we had been fighting it, we saw the fire. The speed of the towing had fanned the smoldering destruction. A blue gleam appeared forward, shining below the wreck of the deck. It wavered in patches, it seemed to stir and creep like the light of a glowworm[4]. I saw it first, and told Mahon. 'Then the game's up,' he said. 'We had better stop this towing, or she will burst out suddenly fore and aft before we can clear out.' We set up a yell; rang bells to attract their attention; they towed on. At last Mahon and I had to crawl forward and cut the rope with an ax. There was no time to cast off the lashings. Red tongues could be seen licking the wilderness of splinters under our feet as we made our way back to the poop.

"Of course they very soon found out in the steamer that the rope was gone. She gave a loud blast of her whistle, her lights were seen sweeping in a wide circle, she came up ranging close alongside, and stopped. We were all in a tight group on the poop looking

---

[1] gaskets:束帆索。
[2] scallywags:饭桶,无赖汉。
[3] two pounds ten a-month:指船员的工资,一月2镑10先令。
[4] glowworm:萤火虫。

at her. Every man had saved a little bundle or a bag. Suddenly a conical flame with a twisted top shot up forward and threw upon the black sea a circle of light, with the two vessels side by side and heaving gently in its center. Captain Beard had been sitting on the gratings still and mute for hours, but now he rose slowly and advanced in front of us, to the mizzen-shrouds[1]. Captain Nash hailed: 'Come along! Look sharp. I have mail-bags on board. I will take you and your boats to Singapore.'

"'Thank you! No!' said our skipper. 'We must see the last of the ship.'

"'I can't stand by any longer,' shouted the other. 'Mails—you know.'

"'Ay! ay! We are all right.'

"'Very well! I'll report you in Singapore…. Good-by!'

"He waved his hand. Our men dropped their bundles quietly. The steamer moved ahead, and passing out of the circle of light, vanished at once from our sight, dazzled by the fire which burned fiercely. And then I knew that I would see the East first as commander of a small boat. I thought it fine; and the fidelity to the old ship was fine. We should see the last of her. Oh the glamour of youth! Oh the fire of it, more dazzling than the flames of the burning ship, throwing a magic light on the wide earth, leaping audaciously to the sky, presently to be quenched by time, more cruel, more pitiless, more bitter than the sea—and like the flames of the burning ship surrounded by an impenetrable night.

* * * * *

"The old man warned us in his gentle and inflexible way that it was part of our duty to save for the under-writers as much as we could of the ship's gear. Accordingly we went to work aft, while she blazed forward to give us plenty of light. We lugged out a lot of rubbish. What didn't we save? An old barometer fixed with an absurd quantity of screws nearly cost me my life: a sudden rush of smoke came upon me, and I just got away in time. There were various stores, bolts of canvas, coils of rope; the poop looked like a marine bazaar, and the boats were lumbered to the gunwales[2]. One would have thought the old man wanted to take as much as he could of his first command with him. He was very very quiet, but off his balance evidently. Would you believe it? He wanted to take a length of old stream-cable[3] and a kedge-anchor[4] with him in the long-boat. We said, 'Ay, ay, sir,' deferentially, and on the quiet let the thing slip overboard. The heavy medicine-chest went that way, two bags of green coffee, tins of paint—fancy, paint! —a whole lot of things. Then I was ordered with two hands into the boats to make a stowage and get them ready against the time it would be proper for us to leave

---

〔1〕 mizzen-shrouds:后樯支索。
〔2〕 gunwales:船舷的上缘。
〔3〕 stream-cable:锚链。
〔4〕 kedge-anchor:小锚。

the ship.

"We put everything straight, stepped the long-boat's mast for our skipper, who was in charge of her, and I was not sorry to sit down for a moment. My face felt raw, every limb ached as if broken, I was aware of all my ribs, and would have sworn to a twist in the back-bone. The boats, fast astern, lay in a deep shadow, and all around I could see the circle of the sea lighted by the fire. A gigantic flame arose forward straight and clear. It flared there, with noises like the whir of wings, with rumbles as of thunder. There were cracks, detonations, and from the cone of flame the sparks flew upwards, as man is born to trouble, to leaky ships, and to ships that burn.

"What bothered me was that the ship, lying broadside to the swell and to such wind as there was—a mere breath—the boats would not keep astern where they were safe, but persisted, in a pig-headed way boats have, in getting under the counter and then swinging alongside. They were knocking about dangerously and coming near the flame, while the ship rolled on them, and, of course, there was always the danger of the masts going over the side at any moment. I and my two boat-keepers kept them off as best we could with oars and boat-hooks; but to be constantly at it became exasperating, since there was no reason why we should not leave at once. We could not see those on board, nor could we imagine what caused the delay. The boat-keepers were swearing feebly, and I had not only my share of the work, but also had to keep at it two men who showed a constant inclination to lay themselves down and let things slide.

"At last I hailed 'On deck there,' and someone looked over. 'We're ready here,' I said. The head disappeared, and very soon popped up again. 'The captain says, All right, sir, and to keep the boats well clear of the ship.'

"Half an hour passed. Suddenly there was a frightful racket, rattle, clanking of chain, hiss of water, and millions of sparks flew up into the shivering column of smoke that stood leaning slightly above the ship. The cat-heads[1] had burned away, and the two red-hot anchors had gone to the bottom, tearing out after them two hundred fathom of red-hot chain. The ship trembled, the mass of flame swayed as if ready to collapse, and the fore top-gallant-mast[2] fell. It darted down like an arrow of fire, shot under, and instantly leaping up within an oar's-length of the boats, floated quietly, very black on the luminous sea. I hailed the deck again. After some time a man in an unexpectedly cheerful but also muffled tone, as though he had been trying to speak with his mouth shut, informed me, 'Coming directly, sir,' and vanished. For a long time I heard nothing but the whir and roar of the fire. There were also whistling sounds. The boats jumped, tugged at the painters, ran at each other play-fully, knocked their sides together, or, do what we would, swung in a bunch against the ship's side. I couldn't stand it any longer, and swarming up a rope, clambered aboard over the stern.

---

[1] cat-heads:锚架。
[2] top-gallant-mast:顶桅。

"It was as bright as day. Coming up like this, the sheet of fire facing me, was a terrifying sight, and the heat seemed hardly bearable at first. On a settee cushion dragged out of the cabin, Captain Beard, with his legs drawn up and one arm under his head, slept with the light playing on him. Do you know what the rest were busy about? They were sitting on deck right aft, round an open case, eating bread and cheese and drinking bottled stout[1].

"On the background of flames twisting in fierce tongues above their heads they seemed at home like salamanders[2], and looked like a band of desperate pirates. The fire sparkled in the whites of their eyes, gleamed on patches of white skin seen through the torn shirts. Each had the marks as of a battle about him—bandaged heads, tied-up arms, a strip of dirty rag round a knee—and each man had a bottle between his legs and a chunk of cheese in his hand. Mahon got up. With his handsome and disreputable head, his hooked profile, his long white beard, and with an uncorked bottle in his hand, he resembled one of those reckless sea-robbers of old making merry amidst violence and disaster. 'The last meal on board,' he explained solemnly. 'We had nothing to eat all day, and it was no use leaving all this.' He flourished the bottle and indicated the sleeping skipper. 'He said he couldn't swallow anything, so I got him to lie down,' he went on; and as I stared, 'I don't know whether you are aware, young fellow, the man had no sleep to speak of for days—and there will be dam'little sleep in the boats.' 'There will be no boats by-and-by if you fool about much longer,' I said, indignantly. I walked up to the skipper and shook him by the shoulder. At last he opened his eyes, but did not move. 'Time to leave her, sir,' I said, quietly.

"He got up painfully, looked at the flames, at the sea sparkling round the ship, and black, black as ink farther away; he looked at the stars shining dim through a thin veil of smoke in a sky black, black as Erebus[3].

"'Youngest first,' he said.

"And the ordinary seaman, wiping his mouth with the back of his hand, got up, clambered over the taffrail[4], and vanished. Others followed. One, on the point of going over, stopped short to drain his bottle, and with a great swing of his arm flung it at the fire. 'Take this!' he cried.

"The skipper lingered disconsolately, and we left him to commune alone for awhile with his first command. Then I went up again and brought him away at last. It was time. The ironwork on the poop was hot to the touch.

"Then the painter of the long-boat was cut, and the three boats, tied together, drifted clear of the ship. It was just sixteen hours after the explosion when we

---

[1] stout:烈性黑啤酒。
[2] salamanders:传说中的火怪。
[3] Erebus:厄瑞波斯,希腊神话人物,是永久黑暗的化身,代表着冥国周围的黑暗区域。
[4] taffrail:船尾部的栏杆。

abandoned her. Mahon had charge of the second boat, and I had the smallest—the 14-foot thing. The long-boat would have taken the lot of us; but the skipper said we must save as much property as we could—for the under-writers—and so I got my first command. I had two men with me, a bag of biscuits, a few tins of meat, and a breaker[1] of water. I was ordered to keep close to the long-boat, that in case of bad weather we might be taken into her.

"And do you know what I thought? I thought I would part company as soon as I could. I wanted to have my first command all to myself. I wasn't going to sail in a squadron[2] if there were a chance for independent cruising. I would make land by myself. I would beat the other boats. Youth! All youth! The silly, charming, beautiful youth.

"But we did not make a start at once. We must see the last of the ship. And so the boats drifted about that night, heaving and setting on the swell[3]. The men dozed, waked, sighed, groaned. I looked at the burning ship.

"Between the darkness of earth and heaven she was burning fiercely upon a disc of purple sea shot by the blood-red play of gleams; upon a disc of water glittering and sinister. A high, clear flame, an immense and lonely flame, ascended from the ocean, and from its summit the black smoke poured continuously at the sky. She burned furiously, mournful and imposing like a funeral pile kindled in the night, surrounded by the sea, watched over by the stars. A magnificent death had come like a grace, like a gift, like a reward to that old ship at the end of her laborious days. The surrender of her weary ghost to the keeping of stars and sea was stirring like the sight of a glorious triumph. The masts fell just before daybreak, and for a moment there was a burst and turmoil of sparks that seemed to fill with flying fire the night patient and watchful, the vast night lying silent upon the sea. At daylight she was only a charred shell, floating still under a cloud of smoke and bearing a glowing mass of coal within.

"Then the oars were got out, and the boats forming in a line moved round her remains as if in procession—the long-boat leading. As we pulled across her stern a slim dart of fire shot out viciously at us, and suddenly she went down, head first, in a great hiss of steam. The unconsumed stern was the last to sink; but the paint had gone, had cracked, had peeled off, and there were no letters, there was no word, no stubborn device that was like her soul, to flash at the rising sun her creed and her name.

"We made our way north. A breeze sprang up, and about noon all the boats came together for the last time. I had no mast or sail in mine, but I made a mast out of a spare oar and hoisted a boat-awning for a sail, with a boat-hook for a yard. She was certainly over-masted, but I had the satisfaction of knowing that with the wind aft I could beat

---

[1] breaker: 救生艇上装淡水的小木桶。
[2] squadron: 船队。
[3] swell: 连续起伏的波浪。

the other two. I had to wait for them. Then we all had a look at the captain's chart, and, after a sociable meal of hard bread and water, got our last instructions. These were simple: steer north, and keep together as much as possible. 'Be careful with that jury rig,[1] Marlow,' said the captain; and Mahon, as I sailed proudly past his boat, wrinkled his curved nose and hailed, 'You will sail that ship of yours under water, if you don't look out, young fellow.' He was a malicious old man—and may the deep sea where he sleeps now rock him gently, rock him tenderly to the end of time!

"Before sunset a thick rain-squall passed over the two boats, which were far astern, and that was the last I saw of them for a time. Next day I sat steering my cockle-shell[2]—my first command—with nothing but water and sky around me. I did sight in the afternoon the upper sails of a ship far away, but said nothing, and my men did not notice her. You see I was afraid she might be homeward bound, and I had no mind to turn back from the portals of the East. I was steering for Java—another blessed name—like Bankok, you know. I steered many days.

"I need not tell you what it is to be knocking about in an open boat. I remember nights and days of calm when we pulled, we pulled, and the boat seemed to stand still, as if bewitched within the circle of the sea horizon. I remember the heat, the deluge of rain-squalls that kept us baling for dear life (but filled our water-cask), and I remember sixteen hours on end with a mouth dry as a cinder and a steering-oar over the stern to keep my first command head on to a breaking sea. I did not know how good a man I was till then. I remember the drawn faces, the dejected figures of my two men, and I remember my youth and the feeling that will never come back any more—the feeling that I could last for ever, outlast the sea, the earth, and all men; the deceitful feeling that lures us on to joys, to perils, to love, to vain effort—to death; the triumphant conviction of strength, the heat of life in the handful of dust, the glow in the heart that with every year grows dim, grows cold, grows small, and expires—and expires, too soon—before life itself.

"And this is how I see the East. I have seen its secret places and have looked into its very soul; but now I see it always from a small boat, a high outline of mountains, blue and afar in the morning; like faint mist at noon; a jagged wall of purple at sunset. I have the feel of the oar in my hand, the vision of a scorching blue sea in my eyes. And I see a bay, a wide bay, smooth as glass and polished like ice, shimmering in the dark. A red light burns far off upon the gloom of the land, and the night is soft and warm. We drag at the oars with aching arms, and suddenly a puff of wind, a puff faint and tepid and laden with strange odors of blossoms, of aromatic[3] wood, comes out of the still night—the first sigh of the East on my face. That I can never forget. It was impalpable

---

[1] jury rig: 临时配备的帆。
[2] cockle-shell: 轻舟。
[3] aromatic: 芳香的。

and enslaving, like a charm, like a whispered promise of mysterious delight.

"We had been pulling this finishing spell for eleven hours. Two pulled, and he whose turn it was to rest sat at the tiller[1]. We had made out the red light in that bay and steered for it, guessing it must mark some small coasting port. We passed two vessels, outlandish and high-sterned, sleeping at anchor, and, approaching the light, now very dim, ran the boat's nose against the end of a jutting wharf. We were blind with fatigue. My men dropped the oars and fell off the thwarts as if dead. I made fast to a pile. A current rippled softly. The scented obscurity of the shore was grouped into vast masses, a density of colossal clumps of vegetation, probably—mute and fantastic shapes. And at their foot the semicircle of a beach gleamed faintly, like an illusion. There was not a light, not a stir, not a sound. The mysterious East faced me, perfumed like a flower, silent like death, dark like a grave.

"And I sat weary beyond expression, exulting like a conqueror, sleepless and entranced as if before a profound, a fateful enigma.

"A splashing of oars, a measured dip reverberating on the level of water, intensified by the silence of the shore into loud claps, made me jump up. A boat, a European boat, was coming in. I invoked the name of the dead; I hailed: *Judea* ahoy! A thin shout answered."It was the captain. I had beaten the flagship by three hours, and I was glad to hear the old man's voice, tremulous and tired. 'Is it you, Marlow?' 'Mind the end of that jetty, sir,' I cried.

"He approached cautiously, and brought up with the deep-sea lead-line[2] which we had saved—for the underwriters. I eased my painter and fell alongside. He sat, a broken figure at the stern, wet with dew, his hands clasped in his lap. His men were asleep already. 'I had a terrible time of it,' he murmured. 'Mahon is behind—not very far.' We conversed in whispers, in low whispers, as if afraid to wake up the land. Guns, thunder, earthquakes would not have awakened the men just then.

"Looking around as we talked, I saw away at sea a bright light traveling in the night. 'There's a steamer passing the bay,' I said. She was not passing, she was entering, and she even came close and anchored. 'I wish,' said the old man, 'you would find out whether she is English. Perhaps they could give us a passage somewhere.' He seemed nervously anxious. So by dint of punching and kicking I started one of my men into a state of somnambulism[3], and giving him an oar, took another and pulled towards the lights of the steamer.

"There was a murmur of voices in her, metallic hollow clangs of the engine-room, footsteps on the deck. Her ports shone, round like dilated eyes. Shapes moved about, and there was a shadowy man high up on the bridge. He heard my oars.

---

[1] tiller:舵柄。
[2] lead-line:测深绳。
[3] somnambulism:梦游。

"And then, before I could open my lips, the East spoke to me, but it was in a Western voice. A torrent of words was poured into the enigmatical, the fateful silence; outlandish, angry words, mixed with words and even whole sentences of good English, less strange but even more surprising. The voice swore and cursed violently; it riddled the solemn peace of the bay by a volley of[1] abuse. It began by calling me Pig, and from that went crescendo[2] into unmentionable adjectives—in English. The man up there raged aloud in two languages, and with a sincerity in his fury that almost convinced me I had, in some way, sinned against the harmony of the universe. I could hardly see him, but began to think he would work himself into a fit.

"Suddenly he ceased, and I could hear him snorting and blowing like a porpoise. I said—

"'What steamer is this, pray?'

"'Eh? What's this? And who are you?'

"'Castaway crew of an English bark burnt at sea. We came here tonight. I am the second mate. The captain is in the long-boat, and wishes to know if you would give us a passage somewhere.'

"'Oh, my goodness! I say... This is the *Celestial* from Singapore on her return trip. I'll arrange with your captain in the morning... and, ... I say... did you hear me just now?'

"'I should think the whole bay heard you.'

"'I thought you were a shore-boat[3]. Now, look here—this infernal lazy scoundrel of a caretaker has gone to sleep again—curse him. The light is out, and I nearly ran foul of the end of this damned jetty[4]. This is the third time he plays me this trick. Now, I ask you, can anybody stand this kind of thing? It's enough to drive a man out of his mind. I'll report him.... I'll get the Assistant Resident to give him the sack, by... See—there's no light. It's out, isn't it? I take you to witness the light's out. There should be a light, you know. A red light on the—'

"'There was a light,' I said, mildly.

"'But it's out, man! What's the use of talking like this? You can see for yourself it's out—don't you? If you had to take a valuable steamer along this God-forsaken coast you would want a light too. I'll kick him from end to end of his miserable wharf. You'll see if I don't. I will—'

"'So I may tell my captain you'll take us?' I broke in.

"'Yes, I'll take you. Good night,' he said, brusquely.

"I pulled back, made fast again to the jetty, and then went to sleep at last. I had faced the silence of the East. I had heard some of its languages. But when I opened my

---

[1] a volley of:一阵(咒骂等)。
[2] crescendo:逐渐增强。
[3] shore-boat:沿岸小艇。
[4] jetty:码头。

eyes again the silence was as complete as though it had never been broken. I was lying in a flood of light, and the sky had never looked so far, so high, before. I opened my eyes and lay without moving.

"And then I saw the men of the East—they were looking at me. The whole length of the jetty was full of people. I saw brown, bronze, yellow faces, the black eyes, the glitter, the color of an Eastern crowd. And all these beings stared without a murmur, without a sigh, without a movement. They stared down at the boats, at the sleeping men who at night had come to them from the sea. Nothing moved. The fronds[1] of palms stood still against the sky. Not a branch stirred along the shore, and the brown roofs of hidden houses peeped through the green foliage, through the big leaves that hung shining and still like leaves forged of heavy metal. This was the East of the ancient navigators, so old, so mysterious, resplendent and somber, living and unchanged, full of danger and promise. And these were the men. I sat up suddenly. A wave of movement passed through the crowd from end to end, passed along the heads, swayed the bodies, ran along the jetty like a ripple on the water, like a breath of wind on a field—and all was still again. I see it now—the wide sweep of the bay, the glittering sands, the wealth of green infinite and varied, the sea blue like the sea of a dream, the crowd of attentive faces, the blaze of vivid color—the water reflecting it all, the curve of the shore, the jetty, the high-sterned outlandish craft floating still, and the three boats with tired men from the West sleeping unconscious of the land and the people and of the violence of sunshine. They slept thrown across the thwarts, curled on bottom-boards, in the careless attitudes of death. The head of the old skipper, leaning back in the stern of the long-boat, had fallen on his breast, and he looked as though he would never wake. Farther out old Mahon's face was upturned to the sky, with the long white beard spread out on his breast, as though he had been shot where he sat at the tiller; and a man, all in a heap in the bows of the boat, slept with both arms embracing the stem-head and with his cheek laid on the gunwale. The East looked at them without a sound.

"I have known its fascinations since: I have seen the mysterious shores, the still water, the lands of brown nations, where a stealthy Nemesis[2] lies in wait, pursues, overtakes so many of the conquering race, who are proud of their wisdom, of their knowledge, of their strength. But for me all the East is contained in that vision of my youth. It is all in that moment when I opened my young eyes on it. I came upon it from a tussle with the sea—and I was young—and I saw it looking at me. And this is all that is left of it! Only a moment; a moment of strength, of romance, of glamour—of youth!... A flick of sunshine upon a strange shore, the time to remember, the time for a sigh, and—good-by! —Night—Good-by...!"

He drank.

---

[1] fronds:(棕榈)叶。
[2] Nemesis:涅墨西斯,希腊神话里的复仇女神。

"Ah! The good old time—the good old time. Youth and the sea. Glamour and the sea! The good, strong sea, the salt, bitter sea, that could whisper to you and roar at you and knock your breath out of you."

He drank again.

"By all that's wonderful, it is the sea, I believe, the sea itself—or is it youth alone? Who can tell? But you here—you all had something out of life: money, love—whatever one gets on shore—and, tell me, wasn't that the best time, that time when we were young at sea; young and had nothing, on the sea that gives nothing, except hard knocks—and sometimes a chance to feel your strength—that only—what you all regret?"

And we all nodded at him: the man of finance, the man of accounts, the man of law, we all nodded at him over the polished table that like a still sheet of brown water reflected our faces, lined, wrinkled; our faces marked by toil, by deceptions, by success, by love; our weary eyes looking still, looking always, looking anxiously for something out of life, that while it is expected is already gone—has passed unseen, in a sigh, in a flash—together with the youth, with the strength, with the romance of illusions.

1898

赏 析

《青春》是康拉德的短篇名作,曾被他同时代的评论家称为"现代英国的海洋史诗"。作品源于作者第一次远航东方的经历,是一篇"小说化了的自传"。而且,在康拉德不少重要作品中出现的叙述者兼故事人物马洛在这里第一次出现。

这是一个框架故事,即故事套故事。第一叙述者是无名氏,他写下了马洛讲述的另一个故事。已是42岁的马洛回忆自己20岁时第一次以二副的身份随船运送六百吨煤去曼谷,航程一波三折,最后破旧的"朱迪亚"号运煤船发生自燃,沉入海中,但马洛与其他水手经过艰苦努力,最终到达终点。故事的主题是青春,而青春的活力是通过对比来强化的,如年轻的马洛觉得自己和六十岁的船长和当了祖父的大副在一起,如同"一个小男孩站在两位爷爷中间",他对东方充满向往,对冒险充满兴奋,对生命充满自信。然而,《青春》又不是一个简单的年轻人冒险的故事,它是一个成长故事。回忆者是一个历经风霜的中年人,从他的眼光来审察事件,"可以保留和重现作者年轻时的意气而又避免过多从感情上卷入作品",这样的回顾使得青春的涵义超越了纯粹的浪漫和幻想。大风大浪和艰难救船使马洛认识到工作的艰苦和生存的不易,当他看到东方时,他已经失去了青春的单纯和幼稚,而成功地战胜大自然的挑战,又使他真正成为一个男子汉。

作品采用有限视角,这种主观色彩能避免全知视角的无所不知,从而增强故事的真实感和感染力。对烟、火、海浪的搏斗进行了详细描绘,诉诸声、光、色、形的感官冲击,使读者有身临其境之感。从成长主题看,大海、航行、旧船都具有象征意义。

相关评论

Conrad's Frame Story[1]: a Constructivist Reading of "Youth"
Joep. à Campo

As the title *Youth*: *A Narrative* explicitly indicates: it is a story about the narrative Marlow delivers to his companions, and also that is it *a* narrative, just one alternative out of many possible versions. Therefore it is proper to pay attention to some narratological features, and to Conrad's use of the anonymous frame narrator and the narrator Marlow. Their methods of narration have to be distinguished.

As is evident from the summary of the story, it is presented as "narrative", told in the setting of yarning[2] sea stories. The frame narrator relates how the narrator performs from memory. This framing of the narrative, because of the metalepsis[3] between the two levels, has two important functions. First, it draws as it were the reader into the scene. Although Marlow's narration is largely diegetic[4], by the device of framing, the storytelling is mimetically[5] rendered as a performance. Secondly, it creates a distance between the author and the narrator, as the frame narrator observes and comments on the narration.

How does Marlow relate to his own story? On the one hand, as a sailor he is "one of us". On the other, he quite often delivers judgments on the nautical and other qualities of his fellows. Moreover, he distinguishes himself from the crew as a literate man. He tells that he read books (by Thomas Carlyle, Frederick Burnaby, George Byron) implicating that others did not, and mentions that even captain Beard was semiliterate:

He could just write a kind of sketchy hand, and didn't care for writing at all.

By presenting himself as literary minded, Marlow tried to dissociate from his fellows and identify more closely with his educated audience.

As Marlow is telling from memory, he is able to reflect and comment on his experience. At these moments he jumps from the events of the fateful voyage to the present and back again. The act of memorizing is testified in the story in several ways. Marlow forgets, or blurs several names, or must put effort in remembering. This creates a distance between Marlow the former sailor and Marlow the present narrator. The duration of memorizing is inversely[6] commensurate to[7] the experiential[8] duration

---

[1] frame story: 框架故事(将故事嵌入在另一个故事内的叙事)。
[2] yarning: 漫谈的,有趣的。
[3] metalepsis: 指把已作比喻用的词进一步用于另一比喻意义的一种修辞法。这里指两个层次互为比喻。
[4] diegetic: 故事叙述的。
[5] mimetically: 模仿地。
[6] inversely: 相反地,逆向地。
[7] commensurate to: 相称的,成比例的。
[8] experiential: 经验的,凭经验的。

and proportional to its intensity. Thus, the story focuses on the short, but intensely experienced episodes, and passes over the boring and uneventful stretches of time. The voyage is also presented as a "first experience", which counts in psychology as having the strongest impact, especially on youngsters on the verge of adulthood. Later voyages and travels in the East simply have been skipped. Thus the indulging in his youth at his later age may also be an instance of the memory bulb. Most importantly, this memory bulb displays the tendency of rose-colouring memories. Indeed, the high expectations in England and the exulting feelings at the arrival in the East are fore grounded, whereas the boredom of the seemingly endless delays and the disappointments of the East are downplayed or ironised.

The frame narrator, however sparse his interventions may have been, critically comments on the story in two ways. First, he notes how Marlow interspersed his narrating, with increasing frequency as the narrating goes on, by asking: "Pass the bottle". The drinking and talking of Marlow mirror the toil of putting water in and out of the ship. The drinking quells the thirst and at the same time fuels the memorizing and the narrating spirit. The considerable amount of drinking, however, must have detracted from the credibility of the eulogies[1] on youth and romance. Secondly, at the end of the story the audience reacts in a rather sober way, by nodding numbedly. The story learns how youth is being constructed in older age, interpreting the formative years and its key experiences from the hindsight of one's life story. This conforms to recent insights in the functioning of memory at older age. It also illustrates how history is constructed, if not fabricated, retrospectively. We realize what happened after it has passed. Thus we may apply the term "delayed decoding" not only to a feature of Conrad's innovative narrative technique to passages where the impact of sensory impressions is unfolded only gradually. It applies to his sense of history as well.

Whereas Marlow delivers his oral testimony, and tries to bring the distant time and place back home, the frame narrator acts not unlike an oral historian. In the tradition of positivist[2] historiography academic history used to be seen as an antidote to the subjectively coloured individual and social memory. The romanticist tradition held the other way around, and considered "counter" memory as a valuable corrective to official history, and held that even "false memory" should be studied seriously.

Source: the *Erasmus School of History, Culture and Communication*, on Tuesday 18 January 2011.

问题与思考

1. What is the purpose of having Marlow tell his story to a group of middle-aged men,

---

[1] eulogies:称颂,赞美。
[2] positivist:实证主义的。

some twenty years after the events have taken place, rather than having him tell it directly to the reader?
2. What is the purpose or function of his internal audience? What kind of audience do they in fact represent?
3. What traits and attitudes characterize the older Marlow? How does the old, more experienced Marlow view his twenty-year-old self? How are such differences reflected in the story's language and tone?
4. How do the young Marlow, Captain Beard, and Mahon, differ in their responses to events? What does young Marlow apparently learn from his experience?
5. What do you think is the story's theme?

阅读链接

1. http://www.josephconradsociety.org：康拉德官方网站,包括新闻、评论、学习和研究资源等。
2. http://www.literaturepage.com/authors/Joseph-Conrad.html：在线阅读《黑暗之心》和《诺斯特罗莫》。
3. http://en.wikipedia.org/wiki/Heart_of_Darkness：对《黑暗之心》的介绍、评论和相关链接。

Glossary of Critical Terms

allegory A story with a double meaning: a primary or surface meaning and a secondary or under-the-surface meaning. It is a story, therefore, that can be read, understood and interpreted at two or more levels. In allegory narrative details are chosen and arranged mainly to illustrate moral, religious, or political truth without attempting to create a perfect illusion of reality.

antagonist A character who blocks the efforts of the hero or protagonist to attain his goal.

anti-hero A "non-hero", or the antithesis of a hero/heroine of the old-fashioned kind who was capable of heroic deeds, who was dashing, strong, brave and resourceful. The anti-hero is not a villain or a satiric figure; rather he suggests that in the 20th century the older heroic virtues have become meaningless to some writers.

chronological structure The use of time references to organize the episodes of a story. Chronological structure is important in stories in which action is significantly related to the passing of time.

climax The most intense or highest point of action where a crisis is reached and resolution achieved.

conflict The struggle between opposing forces in a story. Conflict may be external, either between two characters or between a character and some nonhuman force (e.g. a hurricane) or condition (e.g. time, fate). It may also be internal. Often both types of conflict occur simultaneously, the outer struggle reflecting the inner.

connotation The suggestion or implication evoked by a word as distinguished from what it explicitly names (or denotes), as "cobra" denotes a particular kind of snake but connotes "danger", "deadliness", and so on. Some critics employ connotation to include also the emotional force of a word as well as all the feeling which the image of "cobra" might arouse.

denotation The most literal and limited meaning of a word, regardless of what one may feel about it or the suggestions and ideas it connotes.

denouement The event or events following the major climax of a plot, or the unraveling of a plot's complication at the end of a story.

description A passage that sets forth the details of setting or scene, details which often are thematically important. Description also signifies a means of creating character.

design The shape of a story when it is considered as a completed object rather than an ongoing process.

dialogue The parts of a story in which the words of characters are directly reported. Writers usually attempt to give the illusion of real speech. But literary dialogue, however convincing, is always different from everyday speech. It is functional, characterizing the speaker, advancing the plot, and unfolding the theme.

epiphany Generally the term denotes a manifestation of God's presence in the world. James Joyce gave this word a particular literary connotation: "a sudden spiritual manifestation, whether in the vulgarity of speech or of gesture or in a memorable phase of the mind itself." An epiphany is a sudden revelation of an essential truth about a character or about the human condition.

episode An incident or scene that forms part of a narrative. Some stories consist of only a single episode; more commonly they have several, which are linked to form the plot. When a story consists of a series of such incidents which are only loosely and superficially tied together, its structure is described as episodic.

exposition At the beginning of his story the writer is often committed to giving a certain amount of information about the plot and the events which are to come. He may also have to give information about what has "already happened". All this comes under the heading of exposition.

fable A tale, usually brief, illustrative of a moral truth, which is often explicitly stated at the end. In many fables, though not in all, the characters are animals representing human behavior.

fantasy A story of events that violate our sense of natural possibilities in this world; the more extreme the violation, the more fantastic the story.

flashback A term which probably derives from the cinema, and which is now frequently used in fiction to describe any scene or episode which is inserted to show events that happened at an earlier time.

foreshadowing The technique of arranging events and information in a narrative in such a way that later events are prepared for or shadowed forth beforehand.

hero A term equivalent to protagonist, denoting the central character of a story, who may or may not be heroic in a moral sense.

image A word or expression that refers to something which can be perceived. Most images are directed toward vision, but they may also appeal to hearing, smell, touch, taste, or even our sense of movement and balance. Collectively images are referred to as imagery. A reader should pay close attention to patterns of imagery which are clues to meaning.

irony The reader's awareness of a reality that differs from or is opposite to the reality the characters perceive (i.e. dramatic irony) or the literal meaning of the author's words (i.e. verbal irony).

juxtaposition The way episodes or elements of a plot are located next to one another to contribute to the design of a story.

metaphor A figure of speech in which one thing is described in terms of another. A comparison is usually implicit in the remark "He is a lion in battle".

metonymy A figure of speech in which a word stands for a closely related idea. In the expression 'The pen is mightier than the sword', pen and sword are metonymies for written ideas and military force respectively.

myth In general a myth is a story which is not 'true' and which involves gods or other super-human figures. Many myths explain something about the cosmos, man's condition or human society.

narrative A category of literature including all stories which are told (whether orally or in writing) as distinguished from stories which are enacted. Thus the novel, the short story, and even the epic poem may be spoken of as varieties of narrative.

narrator The person who tells a story.

parable A story that takes the form of a simple allegory, using humble characters and situations to illustrate a moral.

pathos A feeling of deep pity for those who suffer; also used of a story or passage which evokes feelings of tenderness, pity or sorrow. In criticism the pathetic and the tragic are regarded as different. The pathetic sufferer is an innocent victim and lacks the strong will and purpose of the tragic figure.

persona A word used to designate the author in his role of storyteller. In some cases the persona is an unseen voice; in others he appears as a nameless "I", the pronoun referring not to a character, but to the writer himself. When the narrator of a story is an actual character, the term does not apply.

picaresque A kind of story that blends comedy and satire. It tells the adventures of a knave or picaroon who is the servant of several masters. Through his experience this picaroon satirizes the society in which he lives.

plot The plan, order or pattern of events in a story as an ongoing process.

protagonist A term borrowed from Greek drama, where it designated the first actor, or lead. In fiction it refers to the principal character, or hero.

pun A figure of speech which involves a play upon words. It designates a type of verbal wit in which a word is used to mean both itself and another word of identical or similar sound.

realism A mode of fiction that depicts life with fidelity. The realist tells of a story in a manner that is faithful to the reader's experience of real life, limiting events in the plot to things that might actually happen and characters to people who might actually exist.

romance A story that is neither wildly fantastic nor bound by the conventions of realism, but offers a heightened version of reality.

satire A story that ridicules human foibles and faults. Unlike preaching, satire relied upon witty and often amusing verbal devices such as irony, exaggeration, and fantasy. Unlike comedy, in which laughter is the end in itself, satire provokes laughter as a means to the end of ridiculing what is silly or vicious.

setting The place where the story occurs, whether indoors or out, and the atmosphere associated with that place.

simile A figurative speech in which one thing is likened to another, in such a way as to clarify and enhance an image. It is an explicit comparison (as opposed to the metaphor where the comparison is implicit) recognizable by the use of the words "like" or "as". For example, "He had a face like a hatchet."

stream of consciousness A fictional in which the thoughts of a character are entirely opened to the reader, usually being presented as a flow of ideas and feelings, apparently without logical organization.

style The manner in which a writer says things. The analysis and assessment of style involves examination of a writer's choice of words, his figures of speech, the shape of his sentences (whether they be loose or periodic), the shape of his paragraphs—indeed, of every conceivable aspect of his language and the way in which he uses it.

suspense A state of uncertainty, anticipation and curiosity as to the outcome of a story.

tale A narrative, written or spoken. When in prose, barely distinguishable from a short story. If there is a difference, then a tale suggests something written in the tone or voice of someone speaking. Usually the theme of a tale is fairly simple but the method of relating it may be complex and skilled.

tone A writer's attitude toward his reader and subject which are conveyed through language without being presented directly as statements.

type A character representing people who belong to a particular class. Type characters are usually two-dimensional and predictable.

understatement A device of emphasis which works paradoxically by playing down what is important.

verisimilitude The use of certain lifelike details to give an imaginative narrative work the semblance of reality or actuality.

villain An evil character who opposes the hero. He is cast in the role of antagonist, but not all antagonists are villains.

后　记

《英美短篇小说》的前身是 1991 年出版的《英美小说》，当时我们没有因袭国内英美文学教材通行的"选读本"模式，而是精选英美著名作家完整的作品，按小说要素进行编排，以培养学生对文本整体的分析和感悟能力。《英美小说》为全国多所高等学校所选用，受到广大师生的欢迎，曾多次重印，1995 年获全国高校外国文学教学研究会首届优秀教材奖。

《英美短篇小说》这一书名更加符合本教材的内容，即以短篇小说为学习、讨论的文本，语言难度适合英语专业本科生，注重培养学生对英语文学的兴趣，掌握文学研究的基本方法。在选文方面，本书增加了美国作家凯特·肖邦（Kate Chopin）的名篇《一个小时的故事》（"Story of an Hour"）。该作品语言简练，意蕴深刻，结尾的突变设计巧妙，充分体现了短篇小说以小见大的特点。

在单元内容上，《英美短篇小说》较原教材有不少补充和变动：一是提供作家的照片以及作品的图片，意在使学生对这些文学大师及其创作有一种直观感受。二是将原书中小说要素的英文介绍、作者生平及文学创作的英文简介改为中文。小说要素是作品赏析的有效方法手段，"作者简介"勾勒作家的人生轨迹，"文学创作"主要介绍作家的文学成就、创作主题和艺术特点，以帮助学生对所学作品的作者有一个基本的认识。三是增加中文的"赏析"和英文的"相关评论"。"赏析"对文本进行分析点评，必要时对一些文学流派进行简要引入，以便教师引导学生进行文本细读，启发他们进行独立思考，扩大知识面。"相关评论"提供一到两篇原文评论，长短适宜，语言适中，配以适当的中文注解，作为中文赏析的补充和拓展，使学习者在了解更多读解文本的视角的同时，也了解如何写小说评论；四是增加"阅读链接"，每个单元附上三个与作家及其作品相关的英文网址，供学习者课后查找参考资料。

学习文学宜采用"读、写、议"相结合的方法，而阅读是基础。实践证明，大量阅读优秀的文学作品，有助于提高文学文化的批评鉴赏能力，并能培养语感，有效提高英语水平。《英美短篇小说》以小说要素的形式介绍了学习、赏析短篇小说的基本方法，这些方法同样可以应用到长篇小说上。因此，教师在教学过程中可以根据实际情况，鼓励学生课外阅读所学作家的长篇小说，以作为课堂教学的补充。

本书在修订过程中，广西师范大学外国语学院在美国进修的梁志健老师和在剑桥大学进修的谢世坚博士、美国北卡罗来纳大学的 Steven Rosefielde 教授和他的学生 April Lee 在查找资料方面给予了很多帮助，在此深表谢忱。

王守仁

2011 年 12 月于南京大学